RENEWALS 458-4...

Global Games

SPORT AND SOCIETY

Series Editors
Benjamin G. Rader
Randy Roberts

*A list of books in the series appears at
the end of this book.*

Global Games

MAARTEN VAN BOTTENBURG

Translated from the Dutch by Beverley Jackson

WITHDRAWN
UTSA Libraries

University of Illinois Press

URBANA AND CHICAGO

English-language translation © 2001 by the Board of Trustees of
the University of Illinois
All rights reserved
Manufactured in the United States of America
C 5 4 3 2 1
∞ This book is printed on acid-free paper.

Previously published in Dutch as *Verborgen competitie: Over de uiteenlopende populariteit van sporten* (Amsterdam: Bert Bakker, 1994). The
translation of this book was supported financially by the Netherlands
Organization for Scientific Research (NWO).

Library of Congress Cataloging-in-Publication Data
Van Bottenburg, Maarten, 1962–
[Verborgen competitie. English]
Global games / Maarten Van Bottenburg ; translated from the Dutch
by Beverley Jackson.
p.   cm. — (Sport and society)
Includes bibliographical references and index.
ISBN 0-252-02654-3 (alk. paper)
1. Sports—Social aspects. I. Title. II. Series.
GV706.5.B67   2001
796—dc21   00-012587

Library
University of Texas
at San Antonio

Contents

Preface

WHY ARE THE PEOPLE of the United States devoted to American football and barely interested in soccer, while the reverse applies on the other side of the Atlantic? Why is China a stronghold of table tennis, the Netherlands a speed skating country, and New Zealand a rugby nation? My experience is that people all over the world ponder questions of this kind, in contexts ranging from cocktail parties to academic papers. Satisfying answers, however, are in short supply.

In the late 1980s I was given the opportunity to research these questions for four years at the University of Amsterdam in the Netherlands, which led to the dissertation I produced in 1994. Besides exploring the reasons for the differences of popularity between sports, I wanted to use the subject to develop a more general grasp of cultural differences between countries as well as the connections between social developments at the global level and the shaping of individual preferences. I profited from the scholarship and commitment of Johan Goudsblom and Ruud Stokvis, who supervised my work.

During my research, the University of Münster and the Netherlands Organization for Scientific Research (NWO) provided funds enabling me to undertake a study trip through Europe and the United States. One of the highlights of that trip was my visit to Allen Guttmann at Amherst College in 1991. He was doing sociohistorical research on the same subject, culminating in 1994 in his much praised book *Games and Empires: Modern Sports and Cultural Imperialism*. I was very grateful to Guttmann for taking the time and trouble to exchange views with me on the differential diffusion and popularization of sports.

This meeting fired my enthusiasm still further, and I invited Guttmann to

address a conference I was organizing in Amsterdam entitled "Diffusion of Sports: Americanization or Globalization?" Another expert speaker on that occasion, Joseph Maguire of Loughborough University, England, was also studying this subject in the 1990s, and like myself he was inspired by the "figurational sociology" of Norbert Elias. With his *Global Sport: Identities, Societies, Civilizations* (1999), Maguire also made his mark on the debate on the globalization of sport.

I was unfortunately unable to profit from either of these books while working on my dissertation; when my work on the differential populariza-tion of sports earned me a doctorate in February 1994, neither *Games and Empire* nor *Global Sport* had yet appeared. So while I was updating my dis-sertation for this English edition, it was all the more gratifying to see the many ways in which these books supplement and reinforce my own work.

It was the NWO, once again, that made this English translation possible. That it has become a readable translation is to the credit of Beverley Jack-son, with whom I also have enjoyed an excellent working relationship. I am very grateful both to her and to the NWO.

Global Games

1. A Global Panorama of Sports

The Rise of the Global Sporting System

Friday, June 8, 1990. As dusk falls on a summer evening in Milan and a winter's day dawns in Sydney, people all over the world have their eyes glued to TV screens, waiting for a French referee to blow his whistle. This is the signal for twenty-two players from Argentina and Cameroon to kick off the opening match of the world soccer championships in Milan's Giuseppe Meazza Stadium. The players on the Argentine side earn their living in Spain, Italy, France, Germany, Mexico, and Colombia—and some in Argentina. Their opponents have a Russian coach, and most of them play for African clubs, though some work in France, Switzerland, or Spain. The Argentine and Cameroon sides are among the survivors from a large number of qualifying matches involving more than a hundred countries. Egypt eliminated Malawi and Kenya, South Korea defeated Nepal and China, and Belgium defeated Czechoslovakia and Portugal. At the opening match in Milan, the crowd represents countless nations, although the majority of the eighty thousand spectators are Italian. Television cameras and satellite beams make it possible for 2.65 billion people in 118 countries to follow the finals as a live event. Almost all of them understand the significance of positions and tactics, the toss before the game starts, the kick-off, fouls, penalties, goals, corners, what it means for a player to be offside, and yellow and red cards. All over the planet people excitedly debate questionable decisions, brilliant maneuvers, and dirty fouls.

Sports exist worldwide in a standardized form. Someone who is familiar with a sport can practice it anywhere. The rules, sanctions, number of players, size of the playing field and goal, prescribed clothing, rituals, and sym-

bols of each sport are the same in every country. From Stockholm to Sydney, tennis players know all about volleys, smashes, and double faults, and they count from love, through fifteen, thirty, and forty to game; from Sao Paulo to Kiev, basketball players make personal fouls and fight for the rebound; from Delhi to Bermuda, white-clad cricket players have lunch or tea in the interval. The meanings of such actions and the responses they elicit are the same wherever the venue may be. A global sporting system now connects people throughout the world.[1]

This universality is now taken for granted—so much so that no one sees anything remarkable about it. And yet the development from local variation to international standardization has fundamentally transformed sport.[2] This metamorphosis from sportlike pastimes into standardized and internationally recognized sports will be referred to in this book as the "sportization" of recreational activities.[3] It could not have been achieved without people organizing and regulating these activities, but it was fostered by other developments too. The sports historian Allen Guttmann singles out seven of these for special emphasis: secularization, egalitarianism, bureaucratization, specialization, rationalization, quantification, and the desire to break records.[4] Without wishing to underplay the importance of these factors, I shall be focusing on international standardization. I shall therefore limit the scope this study, taking as my point of departure for each sport the period in which the first standardized rules were laid down that would later achieve international recognition.

Sportlike pastimes are common to all times and places. Many originally had to do with essential skills needed for hunting, transportation, or war—archery, running, horse riding, swimming, skating, swordfighting, and wrestling, for instance. But ball games, which have a stronger element of play, were also prevalent everywhere. Some, like the North African *om el mahag* and the Indian *gulli danda,* resembled baseball. Others were more like present-day soccer or handball; these included the *tlaxtli* played in Central America. *Chueco* and *linao,* ball games played by Native Americans in the southernmost parts of the American continent, contained elements of today's hockey and rugby. An early form of polo was a popular diversion in various Asian countries.

All these sportlike activities were tied to a specific place; their rules differed from one country to the next. This was true in Europe as elsewhere; many historical pastimes can be recognized as precursors of today's sports. There was no cohesive system of competition, and matches were played incidentally or as part of traditional festivities. Rules were local and variable; only the most basic information, if any, was recorded on paper. Games would be played for a different length of time and with a different number of participants on each occasion, and there was no referee to settle disputes. A referee

might indeed have been a useful attribute in many popular recreational activities, where things were fairly chaotic and violent from our early-twenty-first-century vantage point.

We can gain an impression of these games from the football-like activities played in England between 1300 and 1900, such as *knappan* and the folk game of hurling. They were played by a changeable number of players, often dozens or even hundreds at a time, on some occasions stretching to more than a thousand. Players would sometimes change sides, or spectators would join in. The purpose was to get the ball to a certain place or into a particular area, for instance the opponents' village. The unwritten rules of these games varied from one village or region to the next. There were no clear distinctions between kicking, throwing, carrying, or hitting the ball, such as those we apply in today's soccer, handball, rugby, and hockey. While there was some recognition of the difference between handling and kicking, this was no more than a rough rule of thumb. The ball was sometimes carried in a "kicking" game and kicked or hit in a "throwing" game. Ways of gaining possession were scarcely restricted, and rules were generally lax. Compared to what many view as the overly rough play of present-day soccer, these activities were a good deal more violent: "heads and legs were broken and deaths were not unusual as the sides pushed, hacked, and kicked their way through streets of shuttered shops, through streams and mud, waste land and fallow."[5] Competitions often led to chaotic mass gatherings. For this reason they were regularly forbidden.[6]

In European societies everyday life was conducted at the local or regional level well into the nineteenth century. Hours of the day, coins, units of measurement, and costumes all varied according to local regulations. Most people from lower social classes spoke only in dialect and were scarcely aware of events outside their own region. They had little opportunity to travel or to learn of different types of cultural behavior. The lowest layers of society, especially the rural poor, were almost exclusively oriented toward their own community. In the highest circles of society international connections flourished and foreign journeys were not unusual, although this internationalism was confined to Europe. These differences in power and lifestyle between the highest and lowest classes were reflected in their recreational activities. Before the nineteenth century it was only in a few aristocratic circles that there was any degree of regulation or organization above the regional level.

In the latter half of the nineteenth century geographical and social relations were quickly transformed, partly through the advent of new transportation and communications networks. Trains, trams, and bicycles took the place of slower means of transportation. Mail, telegraph, and telephone services expanded the scope and range of social contacts, and magazines and

newspapers informed more people about a greater variety of behavior. All this had the effect of bridging cultural differences. Variations between regional costumes became blurred, standard languages came to predominate over dialects, national feast days demoted local festivities to the status of folklore, and nationally standardized sports became more important than local recreational activities.[7] Without these processes of integration and increases in scale it would have been impossible for sportsmen and sportswomen from different regions (let alone countries) to compete with any regularity or for competitions to be organized and coordinated with set rules at the national and eventually international level. Countries that modernized later were also relatively late in setting up national sports organizations. In the wake of these wider processes sport spread domestically as well. As Allen Guttmann remarks with reference to Antonio Pap, the map of soccer retraces the map of foreign capital in Italy. Likewise, the proliferation of soccer associations in the Netherlands roughly followed the expansion of the railway network.[8]

In England and Scotland, where the pace of change in society accelerated before most other countries, various domestic forms of recreation evolved into modern sports even before the mid-nineteenth century. A crucial factor here was the increasing trend for the upper classes to found exclusive associations throughout the country, which enabled them to regulate and standardize local and variable activities (such as hunting, cricket, fencing, boxing, and golf) under their patronage and to follow their own physical and moral ideals in doing so. Here they took over from individual entrepreneurs such as innkeepers, who had previously been the main organizers and promoters of local competitions.

Boxing and horse racing already exhibited many features of their present-day equivalents, aside from the international dimension, in the eighteenth century.[9] Most other sports did not acquire such characteristics until after the mid-nineteenth century (see table 1). The regulation, organization, and

Table 1. Periods in Which the First Standardized Rules Were Developed for Different Sports, Clubs Were Set Up, and Regulated Competitions Were Held

Pre-1800	horse racing, golf, cricket, boxing, rowing, fencing
1800–1840	shooting, yachting
1840–1860	baseball, soccer, rugby, swimming
1860–1870	track and field, skiing, polo, cycling, canoeing
1870–1880	football, tennis, badminton, field hockey, bandy
1880–1900	ice hockey, gymnastics, basketball, volleyball, judo, table tennis, bowling, weightlifting, skating
Post-1900	e.g., squash, netball, handball, korfball, orienteering, karate, aikido, tae kwon do

Sources: Various, especially Arlott, *Oxford Companion to Sports and Games.*

standardization of present-day sports are Western innovations. Today, however, sports in this form have supplanted similar pastimes—which may now be looked on as variants or as their precursors—throughout the world.

Dynamics of Globalization

The development from local variation to international standardization was rapid. After 1870 virtually all Western countries emulated England in setting up sports clubs and national organizations. Within less than a generation thousands of organizations had sprung up, and major regional and national competitions were held.[10] International organizations had been established for sixteen sports before the outbreak of World War I. One was the International Skating Union. When this was founded in 1892, the oldest national skating unions had only existed for about ten years. Before this there had been no standardized skating competitions above the regional level. The Dutch Soccer Association was founded by six regional associations in 1889, ten years after the establishment of the country's first soccer club. While soccer had been unknown to the Dutch a mere fifty years before, in 1904 the Netherlands was one of six countries to found the Fédération Internationale de Football Association, heralding the international standardization of the world's most popular sport.

This rapid change resulted from an accelerated expansion of all kinds of transnational contacts. A chain reaction developed, as the major Western powers competed fiercely for territorial expansion and greater influence outside Europe. At the same time there was greater interdependency between nations than ever before. In the latter half of the nineteenth century increasing pressure to harmonize efforts led to international standardization in various fields—mail services and health care as well as sport.[11]

Another reason for the swift internationalization of numerous sports was the fact that they were primarily played by young men from the kind of families that regularly mixed with foreigners, whether because of their schooling or through trade and travel. In the lower classes, certainly outside the major cities, social horizons were purely regional for much longer. While in 1886 one French teacher described travelling the fifty-six kilometers from his home town to Toulouse as a journey "that stands out in one's life," Pierre de Coubertin saw nothing remarkable about spending his summer vacation in England that same year. As a member of a cosmopolitan, aristocratic family, he was fairly blasé about foreign travel. In 1883 he visited England, a country he much admired and returned to on several occasions. He also journeyed to many other European countries, the United States, and Canada.[12]

Because of England's international allure in the nineteenth century, people in key positions of power in other modernizing countries were often fascinated by the lifestyle of the British upper classes. This lifestyle included certain sports that outsiders viewed as new and distinguished forms of recreation, superior to the local forms of recreation in their own countries. British sports were less violent, more strictly regulated and organized, and fairly easy to practice in exclusive associations by setting up clubs. By adopting these sports, or by "sportizing" the pastimes of their own country in line with English models, they distinguished themselves from the "rabble." In their eyes, the common people were still indulging in backward, old-fashioned, and often violent forms of popular recreation—the Netherlands, for instance, had its *kolven, beugelen, katknuppelen,* and *palingtrekken.*[13] International contacts enabled them to make sporting connections with the elite in other countries, boosting their image still further. In contrast to popular recreation, sports acquired an international cachet.

Several different lines of influence may be distinguished in the globalization of sports. In the first place, migration had a significant impact. Rapid population growth set in motion vast flows of European emigrants, and one side effect of their individual efforts to better themselves was to foster the globalization of European culture.

Economic and political expansion also played a part. Competitiveness between European states and companies stimulated colonization and international trade. English and later other Western sailors, merchants, employees, and administrative officials took sports to all parts of the world. Infrastructural improvements made with the aid of Western companies opened up a great many areas and incorporated them into the dynamics of the world economy, world politics, and world culture.

Other, related lines of influence had to do with the army, school, and church. Mobilization and international troop movements during the two world wars brought thousands of young men into contact with sports. Colonial army units were stationed abroad for long periods of time and introduced many local inhabitants to Western sports, as did missionaries and other church groups through the Western-style educational systems they set up. The Young Men's Christian Association (YMCA) in particular combined religious propaganda with education and sports.

The media also contributed to the globalization of sports. In higher social circles, newspapers and magazines were already playing a significant role in the late nineteenth and early twentieth centuries. The rise of electronic media in the latter half of the twentieth century unleashed a true revolution in the dissemination of culture. Television and other media informed a grow-

ing number of people in a growing number of countries faster and in increasing detail about events in other parts of the world.[14]

To sum up, groups with international links—through their involvement in migration, colonization, or trade or in the activities of the armed forces, schools, churches, or the media—acted as catalysts, whether intentionally or not, in the diffusion and popularization of sports.

The global sporting system was also based in part on the internal dynamic energy that was inherent to modern sports. Trials of strength between players were a central feature of sport from the outset. Stricter standardization of rules and games being played throughout the world meant that players soon had an almost unlimited number of potential opponents. By the latter half of the nineteenth century a new phenomenon had arisen—the "world champion." Initially those who claimed this title were probably the winners of international competitions featuring British champions. Britain enjoyed such a lead over other countries that the winners of the country's national championships (which were generally also open to competitors from other countries) proclaimed themselves "world champions." The rivalry between Britain and the United States also probably fostered the rise of the "world champion." The competitions they organized pitted superb players from two continents against one another, and the winners were acclaimed as "world champions." Commercial as well as sporting motives underlay these claims. Title-holders soon achieved international renown and challenged all who dared to compete against them for large sums of money. The sculler Edward Hanlan, regarded as world champion from 1880 to 1884, rowed himself to a fortune in this way within a few years.[15]

Claims of this kind aroused indignation among competitors in other countries,[16] centering on issues such as who was entitled to call himself "world champion," who was his legitimate challenger, and how the championship should be decided. The world title controversy was one of the factors behind the drive to introduce international sports events and organizations. Pim Mulier (who introduced most English sports in the Netherlands) wrote of the Norwegian Axel Paulsen, who had proclaimed himself World Champion Speed and Figure Skater, that "in view of the fame he had won for himself in the Netherlands, America, and elsewhere," there was a great desire "to see how this man would fare against the champions of this country." Thus Paulsen "unwittingly became the major reason for different nationalities to seek to compete with one another."[17] Another thorny issue was whether anyone who defeated Paulsen would be entitled to call himself "world champion," and if so, on what basis. The new international organizations were created partly to bring order to the chaos of records and championships. The

leaders of national sports organizations set out to forge international agreement on the registration and recognition of records and champions, the holding of championships, and international competition rules.[18]

What made sports "modern" was that play was no longer haphazard. Each had special clubs with official statutes, membership fees, and, where possible, their own premises. This new structure made it easier to agree on rules and their enforcement and to introduce regularity into contests between individuals or teams. This in turn made it possible to plan competitions and training on a long-term basis and provided an incentive to quantify and specialize aspects of sport. Competition became the key word and "*citius, altius, fortius*" the motto. Champions developed into potential idols and attracted increasing attention from commerce and organizers.

There are currently more than seventy international sports organizations, and the international reach of the sports they represent is enormous. Thirty-five sports have national umbrella organizations in more than a hundred countries. Thus an international network connects players in the smallest villages to international organizations and local contests to world championships and the Olympic Games.[19] There is a measure of cohesion on a global scale—a global sporting system. The seven-year-old boys who chase soccer balls over small patches of land in remote villages play in clubs that teach them the international rules, and they are watched by trainers along the sidelines. They may be selected to play for a more senior team, and eventually they might find themselves on the regional and possibly even the national team. Occasionally some youngster is "discovered" by a scout for a professional club who scours the country looking for talent. If he is good enough, he may be asked to represent his country in the long qualifying series leading to the world soccer championships.

The Olympic Games, held every four years, are the preeminent symbol of the global character of sport. Although the lack of the best soccer players, boxers, cyclists, and—until recently—tennis and basketball players is seen as a slur on the reputation of the Olympics, for most competitors in most sports an Olympic gold medal is the supreme prize, and in some cases it means a substantial source of income as well. Leading competitors gear their training completely toward this goal and see lesser competitions as practice rather than as goals in themselves. Media and industry too are keen to be involved: they profit from the global diffusion of sport and contribute to it themselves.

The prestige of the Olympics also impacts organization. As inclusion in the Olympic movement is seen as the most coveted sign of recognition, players and managers of all kinds of sports endeavor to comply with the criteria set by the International Olympic Committee. These official criteria include

global participation. Rule 43 of the Olympic Charter (specifically on sports practiced by male competitors) states: "Only sports widely practiced by men in at least fifty countries and three continents may be included in the programme of the Games of the Olympiad."[20] Representatives of lesser-known sports often do their best to encourage more people to participate. They are sent off to tour the world as "missionaries" or ambassadors.

"Voilà vraiment un emblème international," said Pierre de Coubertin at the 1914 conference in Paris, where he first presented the Olympic emblem. Five rings, each a different color (blue, yellow, black, green, and red) symbolize the union of the five continents and the meeting of athletes from all countries of the world. In spite of its global aspirations, the first Olympic Games in 1896 included participants from only thirteen countries. By 1912 the number had risen to twenty-eight, in 1948 it was fifty-eight, and 113 countries participated in 1968. By the Atlanta Olympic Games in 1996, a century after the first Olympics, the number of participating countries had grown to 197, allowing the IOC to claim with justification that virtually all the countries of the world were represented. International organizations promoting the interests of individual branches of sport also have members all over the planet. Those for basketball, track and field, soccer, and volleyball actually have more national members than there are countries represented at the United Nations.

The Differential Popularization of Sports

All this means that the dissemination of standardized sports is approaching its absolute geographical limit. This is not to say, however, that a uniform world of sport has evolved whose history is nearing completion. The global sporting system is marked by internal differentiation and is subject to constant change. One sport exercises far more appeal than another. Some grow in popularity, while others lose ground. New sports are constantly being created, as the model of established sport is applied to old and new activities alike. While in the early 1980s frisbee was still a more or less unregulated beach activity, with numerous local variations, it is now practiced internationally according to standardized rules.[21] Other new sports include triathlon, speed skiing, snowboarding, professional wrestling, and rollerblade racing. Some older sports or events are vanishing or becoming marginalized, such as one-arm weightlifting, rope climbing, tandem cycling, lacrosse, croquet, and racquets, all of which were included in the Olympic program in 1900.

The ranking of the most widely diffused competitive sports worldwide can be determined fairly accurately by ascertaining for each sport how many

countries have a national umbrella organization that is affiliated with an international sports federation and the International Olympic Committee. Based on these figures, soccer, track and field, basketball, and volleyball emerge as the most widely diffused sports in the world (see table 2). Determining which sports have the most participants worldwide, however, is far more difficult. On the basis of the (incomplete) data of international sports federations it may be inferred that soccer is the sport practiced in some or-

Table 2. Most Widely Diffused Sports Worldwide and the Number of Countries with a National Organization in the Relevant Branch of the Sport (as of 1998)

Rank	Sport	Number of Countries	Rank	Sport	Number of Countries
1	volleyball	217	34	baseball	105
2	track and field	210	35	bridge	103
3	soccer	203	36	skiing	100
4	basketball	201	37	fencing	99
5	tennis	190	38	billiards	97
6	boxing	190	39	air sports	95
7	table tennis	185	40	underwater sports	94
8	judo	182	41	pentathlon	94
9	swimming	171	42	rugby	91
10	cycling	169	43	racquets	90
11	bodybuilding	169	44	mountaineering	82
12	weightlifting	167	45	sumo	81
13	tae kwon do	157	46	motorcycling	80
14	chess	156	47	water skiing	80
15	shooting	151	48	golf	77
16	karate	150	49	boules	73
17	handball	142	50	skating	72
18	badminton	140	51	dance sport	71
19	wrestling	136	52	power boating	60
20	lifesaving	131	53	biathlon	59
21	equestrian sports	125	54	sports acrobatics	57
22	archery	124	55	orienteering	55
23	triathlon	123	56	bobsledding/tobogganing	59
24	gymnastics	122	57	ice hockey	55
25	yachting	121	58	polo	48
26	field hockey	120	59	trampoline	46
27	bowling	120	60	surfing	43
28	motor sports	117	61	luge	41
29	squash	115	62	netball	40
30	softball	115	63	curling	35
31	canoeing	108	64	korfball	34
32	roller skating	107	65	tug-of-war	28
33	rowing	106	66	pelota	25

Sources: Official Web site of the International Olympic Committee <http://www.olympic.org> and related links to international sports federations.

ganized form by the largest number of players. In 1990 the national soccer federations affiliated with the Fédération Internationale de Football Association (FIFA) had a total of about 114 million registered members. Basketball, volleyball, and track and field probably come next, with between 50 and 100 million organized competitors. Tennis is played by an estimated 45 million people in an organized framework. Gymnastics and table tennis, with 29 and 17 million club players respectively, also rank among the world's biggest sports. For most other sports, however, it is scarcely possible to arrive at reliable estimates.[22]

Global popularity is quite different, of course, from national preferences. Soccer is the most popular sport worldwide, but it is not the leading sport everywhere. In New Zealand rugby has more players than soccer; the same applies to baseball in Japan and to American football in the United States, while in Austria the most popular sport is skiing, and in Switzerland it is shooting. For other sports the contrasts are even more marked. Cricket is a national sport in India, Pakistan, Australia, Barbados, and England; the number of people who play it in most other countries is negligible. The Netherlands has almost a hundred thousand korfball players,[23] while other countries have at most a few thousand. As table 3 and the appendix make clear, preferences vary greatly both geographically and over time.

This book sets out to identify the reasons for these variations in the global sporting system. Why is one sport favored in a particular period? Why does one sport fall from grace while another flourishes? How do we explain the differences between countries? In more general terms, what are the causes of the differential popularization of sport?

These are wide-ranging questions. I shall be looking at the diffusion and popularization of about thirty sports worldwide over a period of about a hundred years. The breadth of the subject makes it impossible to describe the development of each sport in every country,[24] nor is this my aim. The panoramic perspective I envisage is the major strength of this study. To systematize the huge quantity of data on the many sports that are discussed, I take a strictly limited number of points of departure. Whether I am discussing the spread of cricket or football or the popularization of tennis or baseball, I shall attempt to explain these developments using a fairly simple, cohesive theoretical model, based on a number of theoretical traditions. Central to this model is the idea that the current popularity of sports can only be understood by taking historical trends in popularity into account and by seeking the explanation not in the inherent features of the sports but in the shifting makeup of society that forms the backdrop for their growth and practice. I shall discuss this model at length at the end of the second

Table 3. Shifts in Popularity Rankings of Organized Sports in the Netherlands, 1910–98

	1910		1930		1954		1976		1998	
1	skating	17,000	soccer	98,000	soccer	328,900	soccer	924,388	soccer	1,022,288
2	fives	10,000	skating	30,000	gymnastics	207,800	tennis	354,155	tennis	724,021
3	soccer	7,500	gymnastics	25,000	skating	146,000	gymnastics	249,300	gymnastics	246,788
4	gymnastics	6,000	tennis	22,500	swimming	38,300	skating	160,000	skating	162,418
5	swimming	6,000	korfball	15,000	tennis	34,100	swimming	145,000	swimming	152,927
6	korfball	5,500	swimming	13,000	korfball	28,600	korfball	84,150	volleyball	144,792
7	field hockey	3,000	fives	10,000	yachting	21,600	volleyball	82,000	skiing	140,769
8	track & field	2,000	track & field	5,000	handball	20,100	handball	81,450	equestrian sports	137,864
9	rowing	2,000	rowing	5,000	hiking	17,900	field hockey	76,000	field hockey	129,054
10	tennis	1,000	field hockey	4,000	field hockey	17,800	judo	66,706	golf	119,994
11	bowling	500	handball	3,000	table tennis	13,800	yachting	56,000	bridge	108,231
12			bowling	2,500	volleyball	13,700	badminton	39,000	yachting	100,823
13			billiards	2,000	billiards	12,200	track & field	33,749	korfball	96,217
14					track & field	11,900	table tennis	31,311	track & field	84,755
15					fives	10,300	bridge	29,500	badminton	82,383

Source: Miermans, Voetbal in Nederland; Nederlandse Sport Federatie, Cijfers van het georganiseerde sportleven; Venekamp and Wolters, Sporters in cijfers; NOC*NSF, Ledentallen, 1998.

chapter, after first subjecting several rather unsatisfactory explanations to critical analysis.

The data used in this study do not generally come from what Henning Eichberg calls the "fan literature"—results, rankings, troublesome transfers, gossip, myths, and legends. Most of my information comes from another type of literature, in which sports are viewed as cultural products that develop within sociohistorical contexts. One disadvantage of this literature is that it is mainly limited to developments in the Western world. Information on other continents is at best fragmentary, often collected in wide-ranging surveys. In consequence, this study will accord less attention to the differential popularization of sports outside Europe and the United States than might be expected on the basis of population size or surface area.

The Structure of This Book

Before analyzing the differential spread and popularization of sports, I shall devote part of the next chapter to ways of measuring and explaining the popularity of sports. First I shall explain why I have chosen to confine myself almost exclusively to active, organized sporting activity. I discuss two distinctions: between numbers of participants and spectators and between numbers of club members and informal players. This discussion should clarify what I mean in this book by sports and their popularity. I then look at alternative explanations that have been given for the differential popularization of sports. This includes influences as various as landscape and climate, national character, individualization, specific champions, the media, and sporting facilities. The discussion of these explanations leads to an elaboration of a different approach.

The sports practiced by most people worldwide originate from four centers of diffusion: Britain, Germany, the United States, and Japan. Chapter 3 focuses on the development of sport in these countries and asks how and why each of these countries evolved its own sports. Chapters 4 and 5 discuss the international spread and popularization of these sports. Chapter 4 deals with Europe, chapter 5 with the "White Dominions" (Britain's name for Canada, Australia, and New Zealand), Asia, Latin America, and Africa. Chapter 4 discusses the differential popularity of sport largely from the vantage point of trends in the Netherlands, while in chapter 5 I shall discuss specific national developments only where they are illustrative of a wider pattern or deviate from this pattern in some way.

In analyzing the diffusion of sports, I follow the same scheme in each section. First I define the relationship between the international position and

sphere of influence of the centers from which these sports spread and their relationship to the countries where they were adopted. In explaining differences in the way sports spread, it is crucial to examine whether or not there were close ties or colonial or trade relations between the centers of diffusion and the "adoptive" countries. Second, I discuss the institutions and groups that acted as propagandists for specific sports, including what I refer to as catalysts of diffusion. The question arises of who they were targeting and why they should have promoted certain sports and not others. In answering this question, I link the diffusion of sports to the structure of society. To lay bare this relationship I examine which sports became popular among which groups, whether they acquired an open or exclusive character, the organizational frameworks that were set up, and the kind of images that became associated with different sports.

The Netherlands is a small country with a small population. From a global perspective, this country receives a disproportionate amount of attention in chapters 2 and 4. Detailed information about trends in the Netherlands was simply closest to hand. But the primary purpose served by this information is to help expose the dynamic forces underlying the differential popularization of sports and to furnish more precise data for a discussion of the effects of macrosociological processes on the development of individual preferences.

2. The Popularity of Sports: Measurement and Interpretation

Active versus Passive Popularity

Explanations of the popularity of sports often fail to indicate whether they are focusing on the number of people who practice a particular sport or on the number of spectators. This is a source of confusion. Cycling is more popular than badminton in the Netherlands, in the sense that it attracts a wider public. But from a different perspective one would be justified in calling badminton the more popular of the two, as it has more club members. How you define "popularity" makes all the difference. In this book I shall be measuring it solely in terms of the number of active participants.

How close is the correlation between numbers of participants and spectators? Table 4 compares these figures by ranking participants, spectators, and viewers. (In this book, the term "participants" will refer to people who practice a sport in an organized form, such as a club; I shall justify this focus at length below.)

The figures in the first column are based on club membership. In most European countries, including the Netherlands, club members are automatically registered as members of the appropriate national federation.

The second column gives numbers of spectators, based on the answers that the agency Inter/View obtained in a 1986 survey, the question being "What sports have you attended as a spectator in the past twelve months?" Spectators are primarily interested in big-time sports. Intermediate levels also command interest, but few figures are available for these. Even finding comparable statistics for spectators at different top-class sporting events is a problem. In most countries, large crowds attend weekly major-league soccer matches. But most other sports do not have weekly events; their big

Table 4. Sports in the Netherlands Ranked by the Number of Players
(in Clubs), Spectators, and Viewers

Rank	By Players (1986)	By Spectators (1986)	By Viewers (1989)
1	soccer	soccer	speed skating
2	tennis	volleyball	ski-jumping
3	gymnastics	tennis	skiing
4	volleyball	cycling	soccer
5	swimming	handball	track and field
6	skating	basketball	gymnastics
7	field hockey	motor sports	tennis
8	skiing	equestrian sports	cycling
9	korfball	korfball	figure skating
10	badminton	field hockey	bobsledding

Sources: For players, Nederlandse Sport Federatie, *Ledentallen;* for spectators, Inter/View,
Sport Scanner; for viewers, Nederlandse Omroepprogramma Stichting, *Kÿk en
Luisteronderzoek.*

matches are often organized within international circuits, and crowds only
congregate for these major events. Because the number of major events in a
country differs from one sport to the next, basing any comparison on the total
number of spectators for each sport produces a highly distorted picture.
Furthermore, totals of this kind tell us nothing about how many different
people are involved, as the same person may attend any number of matches.
The figures in table 4—which relate solely to the Netherlands—do not contain any such overlaps and do not focus exclusively on major events.

The instrument of measurement used in the third column is television ratings, based on responses to a questionnaire conducted by the Netherlands
Broadcasting Authority (NOS) in 1989. Respondents were given a list of
thirty-seven sports and asked which they enjoyed watching on television;
based on their replies, the NOS drew up the ranking reproduced here. The
figures obtained in December 1989 could be compared with those from three
previous surveys, from February 1984, October 1978, and June 1972. One of
the conclusions was that the timing of the questionnaire (at the beginning
of the winter season) was scarcely, if at all, responsible for the high scores of
winter sports. Other methods can be used to measure this kind of interest,
but all are more problematic. For instance, the amount of broadcasting time
allocated to each branch of sport partly reflects the interests of the program-
mers. Furthermore, many countries also receive foreign broadcasts containing a large proportion of sports. Another problem is that broadcasters have
to tailor their policies to the supply of matches that have been recorded and
are available for international distribution, which means that some sports are
televised far more than others.

Table 4 shows that the ranking of sports depends on the instrument of measurement. In the case of soccer and tennis, large numbers of players coincide with substantial public interest. Swimming, field hockey, and badminton, however, are far higher up the scale of active participants than that of spectators, while the reverse is true of cycling, basketball, and ski-jumping.

The public's interest is influenced by a variety of factors. Within one sport, high-level matches attract more spectators, especially when national or international champions are involved. Some sports intrinsically have more excitement to offer, however. In rowing races, for instance, the advantage does not swing back and forth as it does in tennis matches, and there is less diversity of approach than in ice hockey.[1] Such factors influence spectators far more than participants.

In some respects there is a definite correlation between active and passive interest in sport. For instance, there is an inverse correlation in the case of violent and dangerous sports. Speed skiing, ski-jumping, auto racing, full-contact karate, and kickboxing are all real spectator sports. The more violence and danger involved, the wider the gap between active and passive involvement. The excitement comes from the public's fascination with people driving themselves to the limits of human endurance; spectators watch in a mixture of admiration and dread. The appeal of such sports is not unlike that of circuses, gladiator combat, and public executions.

We can often trace a positive correlation (as might seem more logical at first sight) between active and passive involvement. This has been confirmed by numerous researchers and is reflected by the similar social background of players and spectators in each branch of sport. Golfers and tennis players generally come from higher income categories than people who play soccer or ice hockey.[2] Differences in social position grow from variations in socialization—largely a derivative of origins and education. Expressed in patterns of behavior and ways of establishing social relationships, they determine the kinds of company in which people feel at home. Social surroundings not only differentiate between people, they mold them.[3] Whether or not someone decides to play or watch a sport partly depends on the kind of people he or she expects to meet, patterns of expected behavior, and other social characteristics associated with the sport.[4]

Organized versus Nonorganized Sports

Failure to distinguish between club sports and casual activities is another source of confusion in studies of the differential popularization of sports. Although the dividing line between these categories is fairly fluid, the two

can and should be distinguished as social phenomena that make different demands and have different things to offer. The statistics for these two categories may diverge considerably (see table 5). In the Netherlands soccer and ice skating are widely practiced both casually and in an organized framework. Walking, cycling, and running are far more popular as informal activities, whereas hockey and judo are usually practiced in clubs. This book will focus exclusively on organized sports. In this regard it differs from several other studies of participation based on the results of large-scale questionnaires.[5]

My decision to focus on organized sports is motivated by practical and theoretical considerations. On the practical side, data amenable to comparison is available for more countries and more years when the focus is limited to clubs. Every branch of sport has umbrella organizations that keep records of club memberships. In virtually all European countries, these figures are collected by national sports federations, sometimes broken down by age, sex, and region. Studies of nonorganized sporting activities tend to be based on mammoth surveys. The information they generate is less easy to interpret and compare, for three reasons.

First, respondents are left to interpret "sports" as they please. A questionnaire that asks "What sports do you participate in?" will usually conclude that swimming and walking are the most popular sports; whether the reference is to anything more strenuous than a dip in the sea or a daily walk to the corner store often remains unclear. This makes it particularly difficult to compare figures relating to long periods of time. Especially in the years following the Second World War, the boundaries of sports were very vague: definitions became rather diffuse. Many activities classed as sports today were not regarded as such in the past.[6]

Table 5. Sports with the Most Club and Informal Players in the Netherlands and Germany

	The Netherlands (1987)		Germany (1985)	
Rank	Clubs	Informal	Clubs	Informal
1	soccer	swimming	soccer	swimming
2	tennis	cycling	gymnastics	walking
3	gymnastics	walking	tennis	bowling
4	volleyball	skating	shooting	gymnastics
5	swimming	soccer	track and field	running
6	skating	tennis	handball	cycling
7	skiing	running	table tennis	cross-country skiing
8	field hockey	gymnastics	skiing	alpine skiing
9	korfball	water sports	swimming	miniature golf
10	badminton	badminton	equestrian sports	table tennis

Sources: Nederlandse Sport Federatie, *Ledentallen;* Centraal Bureau voor de Statistiek, *Sportbeoefening;* Deutsche Sportbund, *Bestandserhebung;* Deutsche Gesellschaft für Freizeit, *Freizeit, Sport, Bewegung.*

Another problem is that surveys only indicate what people say they do or have done; there is no check on the truth of their assertions.[7] Respondents tend to give socially desirable answers, and since participating in sports is generally thought to be a good thing, people are more likely to classify what they do as sports. The preferences of club members, however, are more un-equivocal; they have made a definite choice that involves paying membership dues and observing a club's rules and etiquette.[8]

Third, each survey asks different questions, which makes it difficult to compare the answers, especially between countries. Only a few standardized surveys of the active pursuit of sports have been conducted at the European level.[9] Up to now, even these few have focused on different periods of time. Some have questioned respondents about their activities over the past twelve months, while others have asked about the previous week or month. Long reference periods have the disadvantage of yielding more memory-related distortion, while short periods have the disadvantage of seasonal bias.[10]

Besides these practical objections, there are two theoretical arguments in favor of the focus on organized sports. As explained in the first chapter, the main difference between modern sports and similar pastimes from previous centuries is today's worldwide standardization. The rise of the global sports system is a remarkable development, as people in all corners of the world have adopted the same rules and customs for different branches of a sport. This would not have been possible without the formation of organizations to set rules and standardize practices. Their decisions affect even informal games. Whether we are talking about a Wimbledon final or a friendly tennis match between two middle-aged Australian workers, an Olympic volleyball final or an informal students' match in Korea, all participants tend to abide by the international rules and customs. The second theoretical argument is the key role of competitions in organized sport. Although activities without this el-ement are also defined as sports, the emphasis on competition is one of the most constant characteristics of sports in the past hundred years. Here, too, organizations are crucial. Staging a major international competition would be impossible without coordinating bodies.[11]

Organized, regulated, and internationally standardized competition is one of the foremost characteristics of present-day sport, and I shall restrict my study to activities that fall under this definition. This deliberate limitation is not an attempt to define the "essence" of sport. No definition could do jus-tice to such a highly differentiated phenomenon that has evolved over time and is still evolving today. As Nietzsche said, "Definierbar ist nur das, was keine Geschichte hat" (Only that which has no history can be defined).[12]

Despite all the advantages of using club membership figures to indicate popularity, it also has its drawbacks. The institutional nature of organized

sports makes them "conservative" by nature; many trends, fads, and fashions develop outside of institutions and are not inscribed within any framework until later, if at all. Then there are other, more serious objections. In the first place, most clubs include "nonactive" members—people who do not actually take part. Some are former players, while others are donors whose affection for a particular club stems from some other reason. Most statistics fail to differentiate between participants and nonparticipants, which may distort our interpretation of them. Even where some attempt at differentiation is made, there will probably be a tendency to overestimate the number of active members, partly because it is in the interests of clubs and federations to do so.[13] Such distortion can be considerable. For instance, 20 percent of the total membership of the Danish soccer federation are merely supporters, whereas the comparable figure for the Danish swimming federation is only 3 percent. It is not possible to overcome this problem altogether. However, this study is not about absolute numbers of players but about the differences between the ranking of sports. Combining participants and supporters in the statistics produces less of a distortion when it comes to these rankings. Even if we disregard the nonactive membership figures, the Danish soccer federation remains the largest in Denmark, and the swimming federation is still in fourth place. Whether or not we count nonactive members does not alter the ranking of the eleven most popular sports in Denmark (except for handball and badminton, which change places). In minor sports, the number of nonactive members has more influence on their ranking, as membership numbers are small and all lie within the same small range.

Another problem is that "membership" can be interpreted in many ways. In the Netherlands, the number of boxers is determined by counting the number of licensed competitors, whereas few of the members of the Dutch Skiing Association, for instance, ever take part in a competition. Setting a standard criterion is simply not feasible. I shall therefore use "membership," for the purposes of this study, to indicate all those who, according to the statutes, regulations, or competition rules, belong to the relevant federation either directly or through a club. This means that the total membership includes members who do not compete and those who do not, or no longer, pursue the sport actively. But these members, by joining a club or federation, have demonstrated their interest in the active pursuit of a specific sport.

In most European countries sports are organized through clubs. Outside Europe, however, this is far less common. In the United States and various countries that have once been within the American sphere of influence, the framework is provided by schools, colleges, and universities. This means that different kinds of statistics have to be used for these countries.

Another problem is the low club membership in relatively poor countries. Although sports clubs do exist in many such countries, counting membership figures would be a wildly inaccurate measure of popularity. First, it is quite common for these figures not to be counted, and second, club membership figures reflect only a small proportion of the people who actually play a particular sport. The lower the degree of organization, the more groups will be poorly represented, which may give rise to distortions between sports. In order to gain a picture of the relative popularity of sports in these countries, I have therefore used supplementary information. The work of historians, social scientists, and sports officials who have written about the development of sport in various countries provides information on the relative popularity of sports that is not based on membership statistics but on sound knowledge gained from long-term residence and research in the countries concerned.

One sociologically interesting problem is the poor representation in clubs of groups such as the unemployed and ethnic minorities, who are not fully integrated into society.[14] This problem is linked to the development of club life and the requirements imposed by membership. Although club membership has come within the reach of more and more people over the course of the twentieth century, certain groups remain poorly represented. Aside from membership fees, joining a club calls for skills that should not be underestimated. You bind yourself to people, most of whom you do not know, you assume that you will be able to adapt to the more or less unfamiliar customs of the club, and you expect to find enough people you can relate to, that you will be accepted as a full member of the club. For some people considerations of this kind create insurmountable barriers. Hence the decision to join a club does not depend solely on whether a person can afford the membership fees but also on his or her self-confidence, sense of affinity with the other members, previous experiences with club life, and the help of others. People who are fully integrated into the life of society will therefore find it easier to join clubs than those who live a marginal existence.[15]

Explanations for the Popularity of Sports

The national popularity ranking in terms of club membership figures, as listed in the appendix, provide a fascinating picture of the differences in popularity within and between countries and trends over time. Many explanations have been suggested for these differences, the most important of which will be discussed in the following section. It will soon become clear that each is wholly inadequate. This is a problem for sports federations, governments, and commercial companies, who would all like to have a sound analysis of this issue

in order to evaluate policies pursued and/or to be able to anticipate future trends. For instance, in the early 1980s the Royal Netherlands Rowing Federation commissioned a study to discover why it was benefitting less than other federations from the general growth in club membership. In the same period, the Coca-Cola Company commissioned a worldwide study of the popularity of sports by its branch managers in order to allocate marketing budgets.[16] Sports journalists and social scientists have frequently urged the importance of more research, the former to discover more about different sporting cultures, the latter to acquire a more general knowledge of the backgrounds underlying cultural developments and differences.[17]

In my discussion of the explanations that have been suggested in the past, I follow the tried and tested strategy of the French sociologist Emile Durkheim, whose book *Le suicide* starts with a critique of existing explanations of suicide before proceeding to advance his own sociological interpretation.[18] My analysis, like Durkheim's, begins with explanations definable as nonsocial or "extrasocial" before going on to assess those in which the causes are defined in terms of social factors.

The Influence of Climate and the Land

Natural surroundings create better conditions for the practice of certain sports in some countries than others. That ice skating and ice hockey are more common in countries with ice-covered canals, rivers, and lakes, that mountain climbing and most types of skiing are practiced predominantly in mountain regions, and that lakes or seas are required for yachting is more than obvious. But for almost all other sports climatological and geographical conditions alone are inadequate explanations. Authors who believe that the worldwide popularity of soccer is partly attributable to the fact that it can be played in any climate,[19] that soccer did not take on in the Caribbean because of the baking hot climate,[20] that cricket does better in former British colonies because of the heat,[21] or that volleyball and basketball rather than baseball rose to popularity in the Philippines because they can be played inside when it rains[22] go too far. There is no reason to assume that soccer is suited to a wider range of climates than tennis, rowing, or boxing. While cricket is the national sport in sweltering India, it is scarcely practiced at all in Algeria or Cuba—other countries on the tropic of Cancer—and is extremely popular in England and Australia. Indoor sports are not more popular in Scandinavia than in southern Europe. Furthermore, they can also be played outside. The opposite does not apply to specific field sports such as soccer, rugby, hockey, baseball, or cricket, but these too are extremely popular in widely differing climates.

Even in the case of sports that depend upon natural conditions, geograph-

ical and climatological explanations are of only limited value. First, the popularity of these sports differs in countries with roughly similar natural conditions. Long-distance skating is more popular in the Netherlands than in other countries with fairly harsh winters. Figure skating and ice hockey, however, are relatively uncommon in the Netherlands. Second, organized sports increase or decrease in popularity independently of natural conditions. There is no connection between average winter temperatures and the membership of the Royal Netherlands Skating Federation. The number of skiers has increased in many countries, while natural conditions have scarcely changed; people have more opportunities to go skiing, but that is a different matter altogether. Geographical and climatological conditions were once necessary conditions for skiing and skating, but they certainly do not provide a sufficient explanation for the development and popularization of these activities as sports (see chapter 4).

Sports Preferences and Physical Build

The worldwide popularity of soccer has sometimes been attributed to its suitability for all types of physique. The advantage of soccer compared to other sports, according to this theory, is that anyone can play it, regardless of height, weight, or strength.[23] Certain sports will never become popular, the story goes, because they can only be practiced or enjoyed by a limited number of people with certain physical qualities. Some attract strong, well-built people, while others call for supple, athletic types, and still others are only for the extremely tall. The fallacy in explanations of this kind is that they compare soccer as played worldwide at all levels of proficiency with a few other sports as practiced at the highest level.

No sport was ever especially developed for people with a certain build. The idea that you need certain physical characteristics to play specific sports is only relevant to major international competitions. At that level, the players' height becomes a crucial factor in basketball or volleyball. That does not mean that such sports are unsuitable for shorter people, but that they would find it far more difficult to reach the absolute top.

International comparisons confirm this criticism. According to the physique theory, soccer is more popular than rugby because the latter requires specific physical qualities. But this difference in popularity is not universal. Whereas rugby is far less popular than soccer in the Netherlands, played by only about sixty-four hundred men, in New Zealand it has become the leading sport, with more than two hundred thousand players. Yet the men of New Zealand do not differ greatly from those of the Netherlands in terms of average weight, height, or strength.

Differences in Facilities

The growth or decline of club membership in a particular sport has sometimes been associated with the presence or absence of facilities.[24] The presence of facilities, the theory goes, creates an incentive for people to choose a
particular sport, while the absence of facilities has a discouraging effect.

Two objections may be raised to this line of argument. First, people rarely
refer to the presence of facilities as a reason for choosing a particular sport.[25]
Second, the poor use of swimming pools and numerous sports fields in the
Netherlands in the 1980s proves that the presence of facilities does not in itself encourage people to take part in a particular activity. In general the causal
relationship is the other way around: the level of facilities depends on the
demand for them. In the Netherlands, the government sees it as its responsibility to make sports accessible to everyone. It allocates funds for new
facilities according to demand, based on club membership figures.[26] Commercial establishments also assess demand before developing new sports
complexes. Most new complexes in the Netherlands were built between 1970
and 1985 for tennis, the fastest growing sport in absolute numbers.[27]

A lack of facilities can of course retard a potential growth in the number
of people taking part in some activity. The increase in the membership of
the Netherlands Golf Federation, from 10,735 in 1980 to 48,685 in 1990 and
119,994 in 1998, is in itself spectacular, but the increase would have been even
larger had there been enough golf courses. Market research performed in the
late 1980s revealed that hundreds of thousands of people wanted to try their
hand at golf. Because golf players have good incomes and are a commercial-
ly attractive set of consumers, entrepreneurs responded eagerly by building
golf courses. However, the growth in supply was still inadequate to meet the
demand, so the real increase in the number of golf players in the Netherlands
lagged behind the potential growth. There are still long waiting lists of people who cannot find a golf club to join. This is a common situation when there
is a sudden surge of enthusiasm for a sport. The question remains, what lies
behind this enthusiasm and these waiting lists in the Netherlands? There is
no similar pressure on clubs in Portugal, for instance, where excellent facilities are combined with a relatively small number of golf players.[28]

Unequal Costs

Yet another explanation sometimes given for the worldwide popularization
of soccer is that it is cheaper to play than other sports.[29] Assertions of this kind
are seldom accompanied by a comparative cost analysis but tend to be the result of a process of free association: in most countries soccer is played by the

lower classes, so it must be one of the cheaper sports. The same explanation has been advanced for the enormous popularity of baseball in the United States (see chapter 3 on the social class of baseball players).[30] One exception to this dearth of analysis is the excellent study by Marijke Taks. She has charted the consumer price of sports and investigated the correlation between this price and the hierarchy of social status that exists between sports. In determining the consumer price she includes both direct costs (membership dues, facilities, lessons, and equipment) and indirect costs (travel expenses, costs of social participation, food, and additional insurance). Her study reveals that golf is the most expensive sport, followed by windsurfing, bowling, bodybuilding, and hang gliding. Moderately expensive are cycle touring, fishing, and track and field. Relatively cheap sports include volleyball, tennis, and judo, while table tennis, running, soccer, and swimming are cheaper still.[31]

The differences in costs between sports were greater in the past than they are today, which had little to do with the necessary primary costs but was mainly related to social allure. There are very few sports, like yachting and auto racing, that are inherently expensive. Informal cricket matches played in the streets and open fields of England and Sri Lanka show how relative are the costs involved with such activities. The equipment necessary for cricket scarcely costs any more than that for soccer. For cricket you need a bat, a ball, and a wicket, while for soccer you need a ball and a goal. Even so, cricket was long regarded as an expensive sport compared to soccer. This was caused by factors that could theoretically have been developed for soccer, such as a field in perfect condition, a high annual contribution, and a system of fines for leaving the field prematurely or failure to wear the prescribed clothes. The question that must always be asked is why certain sports are so expensive for those who take part. Is it a matter of necessary costs that are inherent to a particular sport, or are the economic barriers the result of attempts to distinguish participants in terms of social status?

The gap between rich and poor in Western societies has narrowed, and consequently the contrast between "exclusive" and "popular" sports is less sharply defined today. The sports that emerge from Marijke Taks's study as "expensive" cost an average of between eighteen hundred and twenty-four hundred dollars annually. The moderately expensive sports cost an average of twelve hundred to eighteen hundred dollars, while the relatively inexpensive ones cost between six hundred and twelve hundred dollars annually. These differences have little or no effect on the sport chosen by people from higher or lower social groups. Taks concludes that there is no discernible correspondence between the economic and social/professional status of sports. True, golf is the most expensive and also enjoys the highest status in

social and professional terms, and soccer is both fairly cheap and a working-class sport, but that is where the correspondence between economic and social status ends. Typical low-status sports such as bodybuilding, fishing, and cycle tourism are among the most expensive. Sports with a higher social status such as tennis, volleyball, table tennis, and running are among the cheapest. Money, or the ticket price of a particular sport, Taks concludes, does not account for the social and professional connotations of a specific sport.

Taks agrees that people may well be motivated by financial considerations when they decide what sport to take up, but money plays a secondary role. Choosing a sport is in all cases a question of habitus, she maintains, while in some cases it is a question of habitus combined with money. For golf, money (for reasons only partly related to its intrinsic features) is a *sine qua non.* Windsurfing, bowling, bodybuilding, hang gliding, cycle touring, fishing, and track and field are also expensive, yet they tend to attract the less affluent members of society.[32]

Following from this, it may be noted in general that there is scarcely any correlation between the costs of a sport and the number of participants. In the Netherlands, more people participate in skiing and golf than table tennis, rowing, or badminton. The degree of popularity of sports with similar costs may vary enormously. Clearly, it is futile to seek to explain differences in popularity in financial terms.[33]

Developments in the popularity of sports point in the same direction. The costs of sports such as tennis and golf developed in inverse proportion to their popularity. Both were initially expensive but nonetheless (or precisely for this reason?) became increasingly popular. As a result, facilities and products proliferated to meet this demand, and costs declined.

Intrinsic Features of Sports: General Human Preferences

Perhaps the differential popularity of sports is simply a derivative of ordinary human preferences. After all, are not some sports inherently more fun to play than others? Is tennis more popular than fives because hitting a ball with a racket is more enjoyable and more satisfying than hitting it with your hand? Does soccer have a natural advantage over rugby because kicking a ball is more fun than throwing it? In the 1950s, the psychologist F. J. J. Buytendijk used arguments of this kind to explain the popularity of soccer, which was then played in the Netherlands by about one in three of those who were active in sport. According to Buytendijk, there were reasons to assume that ball sports have more appeal than other sports. "The ball is . . . one of the most natural and perfect objects for play." He went on to discuss the difference in

popularity between the various ball sports among men. Why was soccer more popular than handball? He suggested that kicking was more daring and aggressive and hence a manifestation of masculinity. Besides, the repetitive ceremony involved in the lineup and the dramatic nature of play added to soccer's attractions. But, as other sports shared these characteristics, Buytendijk concluded that the only possible explanation had to do with "the special and hence specific nature of soccer, namely . . . the foot itself. It is the foot and nothing else that explains the secret of soccer's appeal as opposed to other ball sports."[34]

Buytendijk's conclusion—that soccer's popularity ultimately derives from the pleasure that men in particular take in kicking a ball—invokes a historical and universal psychological constant. But since the rules are the same everywhere and have undergone few changes, this implies that soccer ought to be equally popular among men everywhere and that this popularity ought to remain fairly constant over time. This is not the case, however. There are many countries—including Japan, the United States, New Zealand, and Cuba—in which soccer has never been the most popular sport. In the United States baseball reigned supreme for a long time, until it was overtaken in the 1950s by American football, "in which the foot plays almost no role at all."[35] In Buytendijk's sports landscape, therefore, American football cannot be seen as an equivalent for soccer.

In countries where soccer is the most popular sport, participation varies according to social class. The upper echelons of society are not keen soccer players in today's world. How different from a hundred years ago! In the Netherlands, soccer was basically an elite sport until the First World War.[36] In those days, ice skating, fives, and possibly for a while even gymnastics attracted larger numbers of enthusiasts. Between the wars, soccer grew to become by far the most popular Dutch sport. But since the 1960s the competition of other sports has increased again. In the 1950s there was only one tennis player for every ten soccer players; by 1998 there were seven. General human preferences for constant properties of sports cannot be invoked to explain trends like these.

Buytendijk's explanation was still more specific than that of the American psychologist Patrick, whose work he quoted and who had referred to soccer in 1903 as the most primitive game of all. Patrick is not alone in this opinion. One hundred years later, many still believe that soccer ranks highest in popularity because it is the simplest of all sports to learn and play.[37] According to this same explanation, cricket has fewer adherents because it is more complicated, more difficult, and stricter in terms of formal regulations.[38] This theory is predicated on two assumptions: first, that people pre-

fer easy sports to more difficult ones; and second, that soccer is easier to play than other sports, such as cricket. Both are uncorroborated. There is little ground for believing that soccer is easier to learn than, say, tennis, volleyball, track and field, or rowing. One sport may be a little more complicated than another, but the basic rules of any sport can be learnt in a single day.[39] Little-known sports are generally perceived as difficult. Many people in the Netherlands know virtually nothing about American football or cricket and therefore think them more complex and difficult than other sports, while in the United States and India, respectively, these are among the most popular sports. Going simply by the number of rules, there is probably no sport simpler than running. But this says little about the popularity of running.

Sports Preferences and National Temperament

Buytendijk's explanation took no account of differences in popularity between countries. Other theories, however, take national temperament to be the lynchpin of the argument. The sociologist Lieuwe Pietersen, for instance, maintains that "Underlying a people's preference for a particular sport is the influence of national temperament."[40] Cricket, he explains with reference to Rijsdorp, holds the key to the British soul.[41] Handball is typically German, because it requires discipline and leaves little room for individualism. The Frisians gravitate toward fives because it encapsulates their fundamental character traits: individualism and persistence.[42] Likewise, rugby's popularity in France is an expression of "the fundamental French character, which is temperamental yet geared toward self-control."[43] Allen Guttmann, in his analysis of why baseball was the national sport in the United States for many decades, quotes from numerous authors who espoused such theories, most of them from the late nineteenth and early twentieth centuries: "'Baseball is a game which is particularly suited to the American temperament and disposition . . . , has all the attributes of American origin, American character, and unbounded public favor in America . . . , fits Americans; it pleases, satisfies, represents us.'"[44] The reasons underlying the divergent popularity of baseball and cricket, Henry Chadwick explained, have to do with their differing appeal to the British and American national temperaments: "'Each game . . . suits the people of the two nations.'"[45] Such explanations have nationalist overtones. They were aired just after the Civil War, when many Americans were eager to emphasize their nation's social, political, and cultural unity and identity. Underlying these theories are the implicit arguments that baseball games are shorter, faster-moving, and more exciting than cricket matches and that Americans find these qualities more appealing than do the

British. However, baseball games were initially much slower than they are today, not much shorter than a game of cricket. Games lasting four hours or more were not exceptional.[46]

Guttmann rightly dismisses all such theories as obsolete. Attributing psychological characteristics to nations, certainly in this rigid way, is untenable and is scarcely found in today's social science. Yet similar explanations are still being suggested, if more obliquely, in our own times. For instance, in 1989 the following comments appeared in a Dutch newspaper: "Rugby appeals to the Afrikaner imagination because the struggle for the oval ball corresponds to their mentality of 'battling their way through.' . . . Soccer is incredibly popular among the black majority. . . . The pace of football and the skill with which the ball is played rouses the supporters of a leading club such as the Kaiser Chiefs of Soweto to ecstasy."[47] And the following passage appeared in the 1990s: "In spite of the raw mentality of the Australian, who adapted to the numerous European immigrants, first boxing and rugby, and later swimming and tennis came to rank among the most popular sports."[48]

Pronouncements of this kind are full of tacit judgments. They appeal to prejudices about character traits of ethnic groups and corresponding preferences for certain characteristics of sport. None of the information they convey—on the sport itself, the people, or the relationship between them—can be backed up empirically. They also overlook changes in the popularity of sports and different preferences among the groups covered by their sweeping generalizations.

Sports Preferences and Individualization

According to the Netherlands Olympic Committee * Netherlands Sports Federation (NOC*NSF), over the past few decades team sports have lost ground in relation to individual sports. In 1975 people participating in team sports made up 49 percent of the total membership of sports clubs. In 1987 this percentage was 42 percent, and by 1998 it had fallen to 36 percent (see fig. 1).[49]

Some authors see this development as one of the consequences of the individualization of society.[50] Their interpretation corresponds to that of sociologists who refer to modern times as an egocentric era of hedonism, narcissism, and consumerism.[51] Individualization, it is claimed, promotes self-absorption and diminishes solidarity. Ties between people are weakening, and the very fabric of society is crumbling. Team sports, according to this theory, call for loyalty and cooperation, which no longer interest modern men and women. Individual sports profit from this, as they can be pursued relatively independently of others. But careful analysis of the development of the

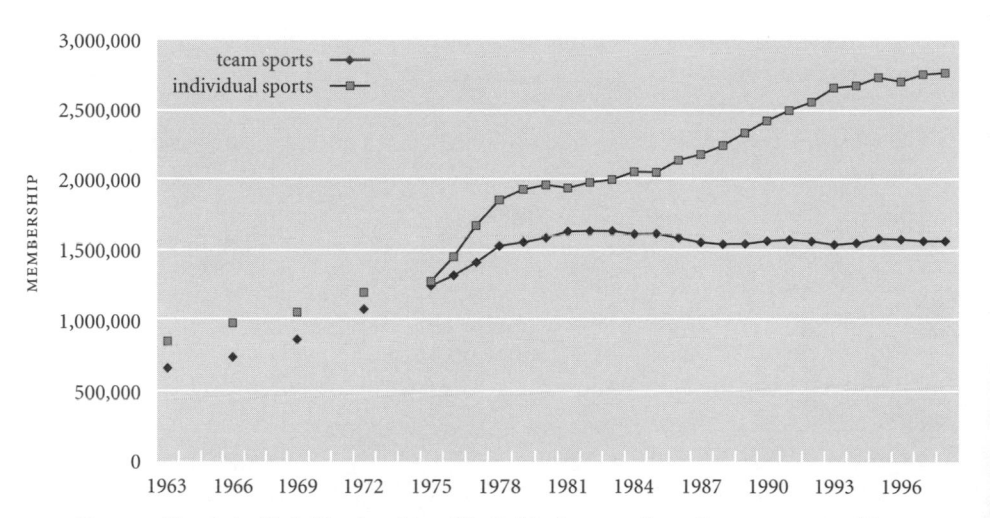

Figure 1. Trends in Club Membership of Individual versus Team Sports, 1963–98. (Data processed by the author from Nederlandse Sport Federatie, *Ledentallen,* 1963–92; NOC*NSF, *Ledentallen,* 1989–93.)

two types of sports reveals that this theory too is untenable. Five objections may be raised to it.

In the first place, the definition of team sports is not as clear-cut as it may seem. The NOC*NSF defines them as sports in which participation in competitions is impossible without other people and includes under this heading American football, baseball, softball, cricket, handball, field hockey, fives, korfball, rugby, tug-of-war, soccer, volleyball, and ice hockey.[52] This definition suggests that individual sports *could* be played without others, although these too are obviously pursued in a social context. All those who take part in individual sports at a club need officials, people to provide facilities, and, above all, opponents! Even the number of strokes that someone needs to complete a golf course is meaningless unless compared with the achievements of others. Furthermore, the NOC*NSF includes under the heading of "individual sports" several that often call for teams, including bridge, cycling, rowing, and tennis.

In the second place, the total number of sports club members in the Netherlands grew by 77 percent between 1975 and 1998, while the population rose by 16 percent. The individualization of society has apparently not made inroads into formal collective participation in sports. People taking up a sport increasingly seek out kindred spirits by joining a club. This is scarcely consistent with the above explanation for the decline of team sports. Becoming

a club member is a social act par excellence. It binds people not only to other members but also to the club's customs and regulations.

The third objection is that team sports still dominate the scene. In the Netherlands, soccer is the most popular sport, while volleyball stands in sixth and hockey in ninth place. In 1975, five team sports were among the top fifteen; in 1998 there were four. Some have risen a little in popularity while others have declined, but there has not been a fundamental shift in the pattern of team versus individual sports.

The fourth objection is that international comparisons fail to reveal any link between individualization and a decline in popularity of team sports. Although to my knowledge no one has ever drawn up national index figures for individualization on the basis of sound criteria, in general it is fair to say that the United States is a far more individualized society than Japan. The ranking of sports with the most participants is known for 1967 for Japan and for 1987 for the United States. Since the individualization theory assumes that the degree of individualization has greatly increased over time, one would expect to find—certainly given the twenty-year gap—that individual sports are far more popular in the United States than in Japan. Yet the opposite is true. In Japan, team sports occupy first (baseball), second (volleyball), fifth (basketball), and ninth (softball) place, while in the United States they stand at first (American football), second (basketball), fourth (baseball), fifth (soccer), sixth (volleyball), and ninth (softball) place.

The fifth and most important argument against the individualization theory concerns the way in which comparisons are drawn. The NOC*NSF bases its comparison on all team sports as compared to all individual sports. Once the trend is looked at within each sport, however, a far more heterogeneous picture emerges. Several sports of both types display a development that runs counter to the expected trend. Only three of the thirteen team sports (handball, korfball, and soccer) display a decline in membership corresponding to the pattern shown in figure 1. Others display a different pattern. The cricket, fives, and ice hockey federations' figures are capricious and do not correspond to the trend for team sports as a whole. (These four sports are played by so few people that they have little effect on the statistics.) Baseball, softball, basketball, rugby, and tug-of-war also diverge from the general trend. Their growth has more or less kept pace with the general expansion of sports. Finally, hockey and volleyball have actually witnessed a steady relative increase in membership exceeding the average growth of sports. In short, the pattern is extremely varied and does not present a consistent picture. The supposed general decline in team sports is entirely at-

tributable to developments in three team sports: soccer, handball, and korfball (see fig. 2).

An equally diverse picture emerges when we look at individual sports.
Developments in sports with fewer than ten thousand members are varied
and diverge from the overall trend in individual sports. Three of the larger
individual sports (badminton, billiards, and shooting) display a pattern
roughly equal to the overall increase in sports club membership and almost
identical to the pattern seen in the team sports baseball, softball, basketball,
rugby, and tug-of-war. The trend in many other individual sports (bowling,
gymnastics, judo, skittles, miniature golf, auto racing, chess, ice skating, table tennis, walking, cycling, and swimming) is closer to the overall trend in
team sports than to that of individual sports. That the individual sports as a
whole nevertheless display a rising trend is due to ten specific sports: mountaineering, track and field, bridge, golf, tennis, rowing, skiing, yachting,
squash, and equestrian sports (see fig. 3).

Individualization in society is an implausible explanation for the above-
average growth in these ten sports. After all, the number of volleyball and
hockey devotees also increased at an above-average rate over the same period. Moreover, the growth in the vast majority of individual sports lagged
behind the trend in sports as a whole, while many others displayed a pattern
similar to the average trend in team sports.[53] In chapter 4 I posit a relation-

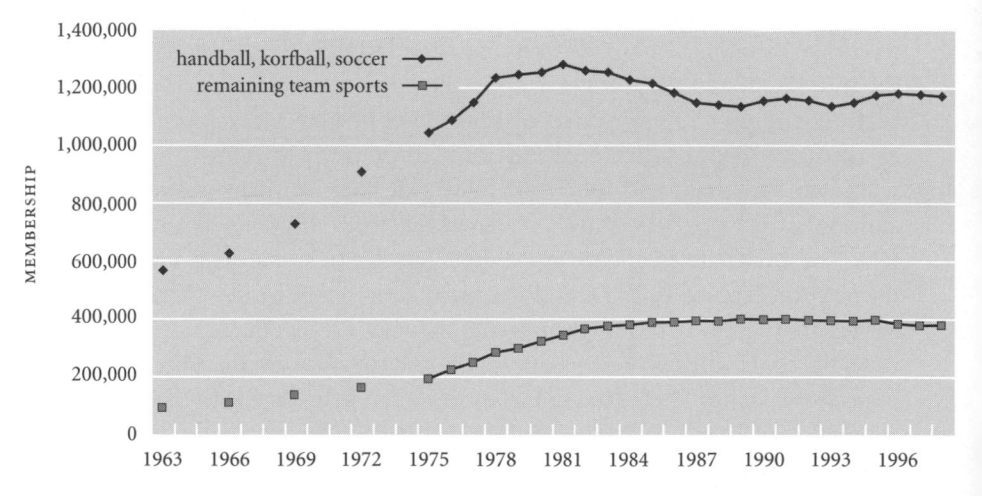

Figure 2. Comparison of Membership Figures of Handball, Soccer, and Korfball Federations with the Rest of Team Sports. (Data processed by the author from Nederlandse Sport
Federatie, *Ledentallen*, 1963–92; NOC*NSF, *Ledentallen*, 1993–99.)

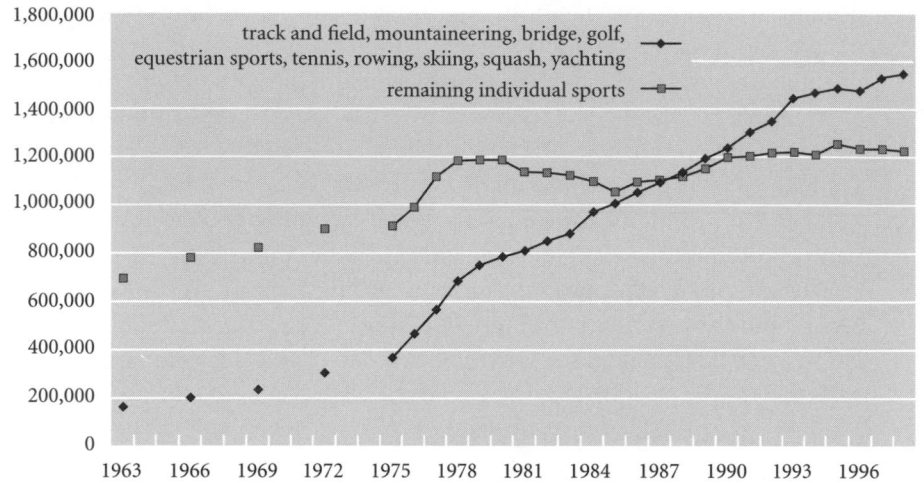

Figure 3. Trends in Club Membership of Two Groups of Individual Sports. (Data processed by the author from Nederlandse Sport Federatie, *Ledentallen,* 1963–92; NOC*NSF, *Ledentallen,* 1993–99.)

ship with a social trend that I believe provides a better explanation for the pronounced growth in popularity of the ten sports listed above.

Sports Preferences and the Protestant Ethic

Building on Max Weber's classic proposition of the link between the Protestant ethic and the rise of capitalism, the German sports sociologist Günther Lüschen has posited a connection between a Protestant—as opposed to Catholic—background and a preference for individual sports. Because of the greater emphasis on the struggle for success and a personal, ascetic way of life, Protestants are supposedly more inclined to participate in sports in general, more inclined to favor individual sports, and more likely to excel.[54] Only the second of these assertions, of course, is of relevance here. He bases it on the notion that Catholics value collectivities more highly and hence gravitate toward team sports. Partly in view of the analysis given in the previous section, this proposition can be challenged on several fronts. As Lüschen himself notes, more Protestants than Catholics tend to join sports clubs in general. Even if they are more likely to choose an individual sport, their very membership means opting for a collective mode of activity. Besides, the relationship between the growth of team sports and that of individual sports is primarily determined, as already noted, by the trends in a few relatively large sports. Participation in these appears to be closely linked to social back-

ground.[55] It may be inferred from this that even if it can be shown that Catholics prefer team sports and Protestants individual sports, this may come down to class differences between the two denominations.

In support of his thesis, Lüschen cites a survey conducted among young German sports enthusiasts. The national popularity rankings given in chapter 1 enable us to examine this connection from a different vantage point. If Lüschen were right, individual sports would be more popular in predominantly Protestant than in predominantly Catholic countries.

Table 6 ranks ten European countries according to the proportion of Protestants and the preference for individual sports. The Spearman rank correlation coefficient enables the two to be compared, and this comparison reveals that the proposition that there is no correlation between the two factors cannot be refuted (Rs = 0.25, df = 8, alpha = 0.05, testing in one direction).

The Boris Becker Effect

One of the best-known explanations for the rise in a sport's popularity is that participation is boosted in response to wins by champions who capture the public's imagination. In the Netherlands this is sometimes called the "Ard and Keesie effect," after the world titles and Olympic medals won by the speed skaters Ard Schenk and Kees Verkerk in the 1960s and 1970s. Their achievements, so the tale goes, stimulated skating in the Netherlands. This "Ard and Keesie effect" also applied, it was said, to judo after Anton Geesink's titles in the 1960s, to soccer after Ajax and Feyenoord triumphed in the European

Table 6. Countries with Protestants in the National Population and Players in Individual Sports by Country

Country	Rank Based on the Percentage of:	
	Protestants in the National Population	Players in Individual Sports
Sweden	1	9
Finland	2	7
Denmark	3	3
Switzerland	4	1
Germany	5	2
The Netherlands	6	4
France	7	5
Luxembourg	8	6
Italy	9	10
Spain	10	8

Sources: Encarta Winkler Prins (for Protestants in the national population); popularity rankings in the appendix (for players in individual sports).

Champions' League in the early 1970s, to cycling after the Tour de France victories of the Dutchmen Jan Janssen and Joop Zoetemelk, and to rowing when Rienks and Florijn won gold in Seoul and the national eight triumphed in Atlanta. Likewise, in Germany Boris Becker and Steffi Graf are said to have encouraged numerous young people to take up tennis, in England field hockey's upsurge is attributed to the Olympic gold medal won in Seoul, and the huge rise in popularity of table tennis in China is often attributed to Rong Guotuan, the country's first world champion in this sport.[56]

Major wins by countrymen and countrywomen certainly generate enormous enthusiasm. They receive huge media coverage, are incorporated into advertisements, and are standard lunchtime topics at work. But whether they actually encourage people to take up the sport concerned and boost club membership is another matter altogether.

According to Rob Minee and Ruud Stokvis, the facts do not confirm this correlation. Having studied twenty-seven international championships since the Second World War, they concluded that in twenty-four cases there was no discernible effect on membership figures. Even in the remaining three cases it was unlikely that the growth was the result of champions' achievements.[57] Their research reveals that people are far too ready to speak of a "champions' effect."

If the existence of such an effect is to be convincingly demonstrated, the rise in sports federation membership figures must fulfill three criteria:

1. The federation's growth in membership must be more marked than that of other sports federations, in which no major championship win has been achieved. Otherwise the rise in membership could simply reflect a general trend. In other words, it is important to look at relative, not absolute, growth.
2. The federation's growth in membership must be more marked than before the championship success. It is therefore essential to look at the figures over a long period of time.
3. The federation's growth in membership must be more marked than in other countries, in the same sport, where no major win has been achieved. So international comparison must be part of the analysis.

Using these criteria, I analyzed more than thirty championships (most in the Netherlands and Germany), and in almost all cases I found no demonstrable effect on membership growth. I shall illustrate my findings by citing two case studies: one relating to trends in Germany in the wake of wins by the tennis champions Boris Becker and Steffi Graf and the other relating to trends in the Netherlands following the success of the Dutch national volleyball team.

THE EFFECT OF GERMAN TENNIS TRIUMPHS ON TENNIS IN GERMANY
Many European countries have witnessed a boom in tennis in the past few
decades. In Germany this growth was accompanied in the 1980s and 1990s by
major wins in men's and women's tennis. Boris Becker won Wimbledon in
1985, 1986, and 1989, Steffi Graf won in 1988, 1989, and 1992, and Michael Stich
won in 1991. In addition to several other Grand Slam wins, the German Davis
Cup team also triumphed in 1988, 1989, and 1993. Yet figure 4 makes it clear
that the number of tennis club members in Germany did not really increase
in relative terms. In fact, by the end of the 1980s relative growth had become
relative decline. Tennis grew faster in the Netherlands than in Germany, even
though when Richard Krajicek won Wimbledon in 1996 he was the first Dutchman to win a Grand Slam title. Even without champions, the Dutch tennis
federation prospered slightly better than its German equivalent.

THE EFFECT OF DUTCH VOLLEYBALL TRIUMPHS ON VOLLEYBALL IN THE
NETHERLANDS In the 1960s and 1970s there was an enormous increase in the
number of volleyball players in the Netherlands. It was many years, however,
before any appreciable international success ensued. The arrival of Arie Sel-
inger, previously the successful coach of the United States women's team,
wrought a dramatic change. He brought about a revolution in volleyball in
the Netherlands by taking the best players away from their clubs and appoint-

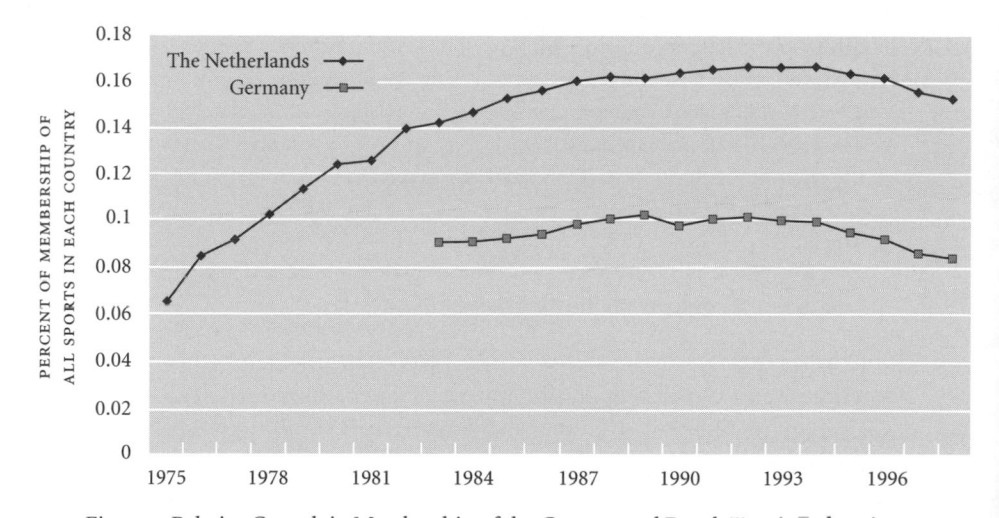

Figure 4. Relative Growth in Membership of the German and Dutch Tennis Federations,
1975–98. (Data from Nederlandse Sport Federatie, *Ledentallen*, 1975–92; NOC*NSF, *Ledentallen*, 1993–98; Deutsche Sportbund, *Bestandserhebung*, 1971–91; Deutsche Sportbund,
Mitgliederzahl, 1992–98.)

ing them as full professionals, so that they could devote themselves entirely to training and playing for the national selection. The Dutch men's volleyball teams were soon among the world's best, and several players were signed up by wealthy Italian clubs. This trend also boosted performance. In 1992 the Dutch men's team won a silver medal at the Barcelona Olympic Games, and in 1996 they won gold. Figure 5 shows that these wins did not lead to a growth in membership. On the contrary, from 1985 onwards the membership of the Dutch volleyball federation actually declined in relative terms. Meanwhile, the membership of the German volleyball federation increased more rapidly than the total membership of sport confederations in Germany, even though German volleyball was not doing particularly well in the international arena.

* * *

In most of the cases I analyzed, I found that championship wins had no significant impact on membership figures. However, there were two notable exceptions: namely, the successes of the Dutch judoist Anton Geesink in the early 1960s and Raymond van Barnevelt's capture of the world darts title in the late 1990s. In both cases, however, the growth was largely explicable as a consequence of the sport's wider diffusion. When a top-class player reaches the final of a major international event, increased media coverage brings many people into contact with the sport for the first time. This may prompt

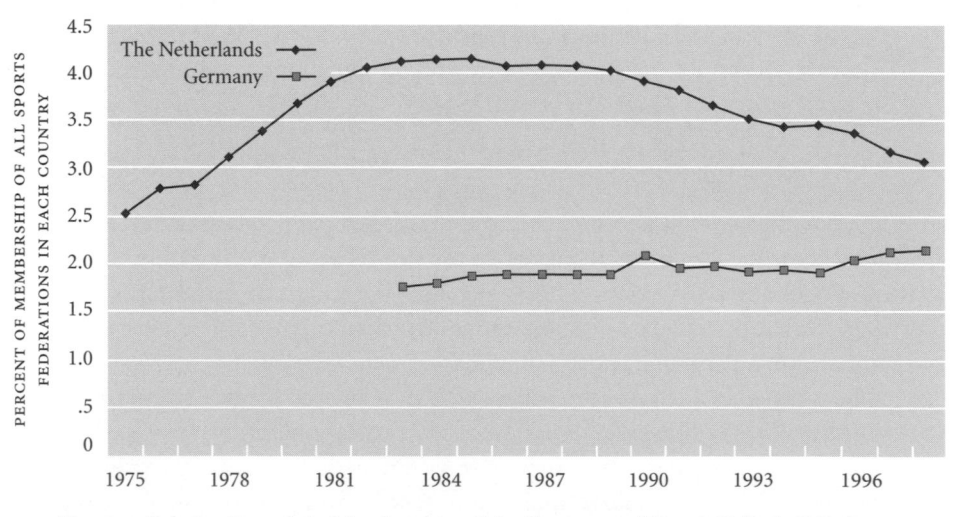

Figure 5. Relative Growth in Membership of the German and Dutch Volleyball Federations, 1975–98. (Data from Nederlandse Sport Federatie, *Ledentallen*, 1975–92; NOC*NSF, *Ledentallen*, 1993–98; Deutsche Sportbund, *Bestandserhebung*, 1971–91; Deutsche Sportbund, Mitgliederzahl, 1992–98.)

them to try it out, certainly amid such success and the enthusiasm emanating from newspapers and television. Once a sport is established, however, international titles seldom lead to a sport's further popularization, certainly not in the long term.

That the growth of membership figures in the long term cannot be attributed to champions' achievements is hardly surprising. Sports stars know better than anyone that the euphoria of success is short-lived; the thrill of a superb win at one event is soon followed by disappointment at another. Moreover, neither the public nor the media tend to concentrate on a single sport for very long.

Rather than any "Boris Becker effect," the relationship would appear to work the other way around: after or during a period of rapid expansion in a particular sport there is a greater likelihood of someone winning a major title. This recalls Pierre de Coubertin's remark that for every thousand participants one hundred will excel, one of whom will be star material.[58]

That people are less likely than some have claimed to run off and join a club because a countryman has won the world title does not detract from the champion's achievement, nor from its social significance. Club membership may not grow, but public interest may certainly undergo a tremendous boost, albeit only for a short time.[59] Major sporting events attract vast audiences, and the comings and goings of national sports figures are constant topics of conversation. Big matches and events are followed by millions of people live on radio and television in living rooms, in bars, and at work. This shared interest and identification binds people who may have little else in common. It can also have a positive impact on sports organizations' income from sponsorship, which can be reinvested to diffuse the sport more widely.

The Lure of Big Money

It is possible to make a fortune out of sports, but the rewards for comparable achievements vary from one sport to the next. This is an inevitable consequence of differing degrees of professionalization and commercialization. Do these differences make one sport more attractive than another? Do people embark on a particular sport with dollar signs in their eyes?

It is implausible that many people would be swayed by such factors. Certainly not in the Netherlands, where many professionalized sports, such as boxing, cycling, and to a lesser extent track and field, have fewer participants than far less professionalized sports such as swimming, hockey, korfball, and handball. Moreover, professionalization does not necessarily lead to expansion. Professional soccer was legalized in the Netherlands in 1956, when al-

most one-third of all sports club members played soccer. The salaries of the first professional soccer players were extremely low; this did not change until the major successes in the early 1970s. Since then pay has soared, yet the proportion of active sports participants opting for soccer has declined. And, as we saw in the previous section, the professionalization and commercialization of Dutch volleyball also failed to trigger an influx of new players.

Notwithstanding this evidence, there may be what Van Tijn has called a "lottery effect," meaning that though blanks far outnumber prizes, many will play in the hope of a lucky draw.[60] But the new arrival will soon discover whether he is star material. If not, as applies to the vast majority, struggling against the odds could be discouraging. So the number of people who carry on playing a sport with a view to making big money will never be much more than the top ranks will accommodate.

It is not inconceivable that a sport's commercialization and professionalization may discourage some potential new members. Many years ago, mass recreation and commercialization undermined the status of sports such as cycling and soccer. Increasing participation among the lower classes, commercial hype, and media saturation all tended to put off educated people from higher social classes.[61]

The Influence of Television

The Netherlands Sports Federation pursued a campaign for a while with the slogan "To see is to do." Demonstrations were staged at special fairs, enabling visitors to try out a range of sports. "To see is to do" is also supposedly the effect of watching television. According to this theory, TV viewers become interested in the sports they see and decide to take them up.

The influence of the media on our behavior is extremely complicated. As Joan Chandler notes in her book about television and national sports, there is no generally accepted theory concerning the ways in which television programs influence viewers; after years of research we still do not know whether violent movies encourage children to develop violent behavior in everyday life.[62] Nor do we know whether there is any link between uneven media coverage and the differential popularization of sports. It is clear, however, that sports and the media are an ideal couple, leading Joseph Maguire to speak of the "global media-sport complex." But Maguire's analysis also reveals that the influence of the media is not constant and must always be seen in the context of wider globalization processes.[63]

One conclusion that will emerge from the following chapters is that the media function primarily as catalysts of diffusion. Throughout the world,

television keeps people informed about the latest sports news. A hundred years ago, newspapers and magazines played the same role, mediating in the national and international spread of cycling, table tennis, soccer, and baseball, for instance.[64] Today, the electronic media have become the main source of information concerning events outside our direct field of vision. Satellite and cable channels now abound internationally, acquainting many viewers with sports played in other countries. This may well inspire people to take them up and to launch their own clubs.[65]

It is doubtful whether television has an independent impact on the popularization of sports, however. Volleyball had poor television coverage during the 1970s and 1980s, yet it grew faster than basketball, which had far more games broadcast on television. Soccer and speed skating have received more Dutch television coverage than other sports for many years, yet the percentage of both in the total is declining. Nor has the Royal Netherlands Cycling Union seen any growth in its modest membership, in spite of disproportionately generous media coverage. In contrast, hockey, badminton, golf, and squash are increasing in popularity in the Netherlands, yet they all receive scant attention in the media. Whatever influence television has is most likely indirect. First, television promotes the integration of a sport into the prevailing culture, which can in turn help to cement its popularity. Second, it influences a sport's image. Reports featuring an exclusive polo club, violence on the soccer field, or the student atmosphere of a boat race will all influence viewers' opinions of these sports. But in most cases they will simply confirm existing images.

After all, should we be surprised that television fails to exert a direct influence on active participation? Spectators have very different motives from participants. A sensational and rousing report of a match is more likely to encourage viewers to tune in to the next one than to go out and play themselves. So television broadcasts can probably only boost the popularity of a sport indirectly and under certain conditions. In subsequent chapters I shall endeavor to identify these conditions.

An Alternative Approach

In general, all such explanations of the differential popularization of sports can be refuted quite simply with the aid of comparative historical analysis. Their main shortcoming is that they reify sports and detach them from their social context. Moreover, they lack the framework of a general theory, so that different explanations are advanced for the popularity of specified sports in specified countries at specified moments in time without any clarity arising as to their cohesiveness or otherwise.

Ruud Stokvis published a number of programmatic articles in the late 1980s, formulating for the first time a comprehensive theory for the differential popularization of sports. He also adopted a novel approach. Most authors tend to base their theories on the intrinsic characteristics of sports. Stokvis, however, believes that the explanation lies in the nature of the social context within which each sport is practiced. He focuses on the ranking of popularity of sports in different countries. Using a variety of theoretical traditions—from the world system theory of Immanuel Wallerstein to the modernization theories of David Landes and the theories of status distinction derived from Pierre Bourdieu, among others—he clarifies these national rankings by reference to two distinct factors: (1) the balance of power between countries and (2) class rivalries in the quest for status that intensified during the modernization process.[66] My own explanation builds on this theoretical model.

Stokvis's analysis—echoing Durkheim's famous *Le suicide*—focuses on the characteristics of collectivities, an approach that leads to a matter-of-fact, objective analysis. In my elaboration of his theory, I look more closely at the relationship between the macrosociological processes he identifies and the formation of individual sporting preferences. I examine in greater detail the social import attached to sports and how it changes in relation to wider developments in society, as well as the impact of these changes on the status-related features of sporting preferences.[67] I also focus more closely on the groups and institutions that have played a catalytic role in spreading and popularizing specific sports.

Where the status of sports is concerned, my approach is close to the ideas on "distinction" developed in the research group led by the sociologist Pierre Bourdieu. These sociologists believe that people learn to attribute different values to specific sports as part of their socialization, producing a divergence of tastes between social classes. These class-linked preferences are not based on any immutable or intrinsic value of specific sports but on the significance people attribute to the social norms associated with them. Although a sport may be played by the same basic rules everywhere, these social norms may vary widely according to context, especially where a sport is practiced by people from a wide range of social backgrounds.[68]

My approach also links up with that of several other authors, in particular that of Allen Guttmann. Independently of Stokvis and myself, he too embarked in the late 1980s and early 1990s on a study of the relationship between the diffusion of sports and the international balance of power. This work culminated in *Games and Empires: Modern Sports and Cultural Imperialism*, a masterpiece of sports history. With *Global Sport: Identities, Societ-*

ies, Civilizations, Joseph Maguire too produced an influential book on the emergence and global diffusion of modern sports. Although it cannot be denied that Maguire advances empirical data in support of his theory, *Global Sport* is nonetheless first and foremost a theoretical analysis. Conversely, while Guttmann incorporates a substantial amount of theoretical views into his work, the strength of his analysis lies primarily in his wealth of historical examples. I attempt in this book to achieve a somewhat more fluid mix of sociohistorical description and sociological theory.

Besides these general studies, Eric Dunning's analysis of the development of soccer as a world game and the research of Dunning and Kenneth Sheard into the development of rugby in England also accord well with the theory developed here.[69] This also applies to the work of Ian Tyrrell, Melvin Adelman, George Kirsch, and Richard Cashman, each of whom gives an excellent description of the rise or fall of one or more branches of sport.[70] But their explanations are different from what is asserted here. Rather than delineating a cohesive and generalized system, they tend to proffer ad hoc explanations for the popularization of a particular sport in a particular location at a particular moment in time. In contrast, this book sets out to provide a systematic explanation for the differential popularization of sports. To this end, the above theoretical influences have been used to help fashion the following model. This theoretical model cannot be applied rigidly to explain the popularity of any sport without further research. Its function is not deterministic; it aims rather to identify certain pivotal issues and generate crucial questions.

The central principle of this theory is that the differential popularization of sports, in the long term, is a relatively autonomous, "blind," and to a certain extent structured process that develops in relation to social change. Social change underlies the sporting preferences of individuals but is not susceptible to their direct influence and sometimes even escapes their conscious attention. So the popularity of sports cannot be explained by asking people why they have chosen a particular sport. Individual preferences are only "innate" to a certain extent. In the main they are products of people's experiences in certain social conditions and relations within social groups whose history stretches back for many generations.[71]

When choosing a sport, you are not merely deciding between different forms of physical exertion and competition; you are also deciding between different groups of people. Almost everyone has a vague idea of the people they expect to find practicing a particular sport, of how they behave and what kind of atmosphere prevails there. By joining a sports club, you choose a particular group. This may be because you believe you will feel at home with

these people or because you do not wish to be associated with certain groups who practice other sports. Underlying such considerations are power relations and differences of status, mainly between countries and social classes, but also between men and women, young and older people, and people from different regions.

The pursuit of sports is part of the general realm of human competition. People judge one another partly on the basis of what sport they play, how, and with whom. So insight into the relationships between sports and social groups is essential to understanding the differential popularization of sports. Groups may derive part of their identity from their shared preference for a particular sport and distance themselves from others by this means. Furthermore, the social status of sports is unequal. There is a status hierarchy of sports, which means that your choice will automatically position you in a wider social context and distinguish yourself from others.

The social status of a sport is by no means constant. It is a function of the (assumed) social background of its participants and the social etiquette they cultivate. Social background embraces nationality, city, social class, gender, and age but may also include, for instance, the school that participants attend. Higher status attracts people lower down the social hierarchy, especially social climbers. By taking up a high-status sport, they express their upward social mobility and align themselves with people who have the lifestyle they want to emulate. A major influx of such social climbers may attract those still further down the social scale, causing an overall decline in a sport's social status. This is Fallers' well-known trickle-down effect.[72] This effect does not occur automatically or in all cases. But where it does, people higher up the social ladder will often seek a different sport.

Today's popularity rankings can best be explained by investigating the prior differential diffusion and popularization of sports within the context of changing power relations and status differences and by viewing them against the backdrop of the increased interdependencies of people and nations on a global level. To understand why a particular sport became popular, we will need to look at several factors: the social background of the people who practice it in its country of origin and how they relate to other social groups; the relations between this country and the "adopting" countries; and the social groups that take it up in the "adopting" countries and how they relate to other groups.

In the first place, the international diffusion of sports is bound up with developments in international relations. Virtually all major sports in the current world sporting system originate from countries that have been among the major world powers in the past hundred years. These key countries have func-

tioned as centers of diffusion. As their spheres of influence expanded, most of the sports that had been developed within their borders spread around the world. How popular they became elsewhere depended on the nature of the relations between the countries of origin and those to which they were imported—whether these relations were characterized by rivalry or dependency, for instance. Sports from countries that have been peripheral to the world system in the past hundred years have not undergone the same diffusion and have achieved far less popularity outside their country of origin.

Within the context of these processes, the diffusion of sports was promoted by specific groups from the "dominating" countries—people involved in migration, colonization, trade, the armed forces, the church, schools, or the media.

To understand the popularization of sports within countries we must also view them in the context of changes in social relations. During the process of diffusion, sports would start off as the exclusive province of the urban elite: educated people with international ties who could journey abroad. But as relations in society changed—between classes, between men and women, and between city-dwellers and country folk—many sports spread through wide sections of the population. Which sports became popular in which areas depended on the social origins of its devotees and the social significance with which they invested their sports—again, this has to be looked at both in the countries of origin and in the "importing" countries. Each sport came with its own customs, traditions, and rules, all of which influenced its social significance. This development, which took place prior to diffusion, helped to determine the social composition of people who adopted a sport elsewhere and the way in which they could adapt it to their own society.

Taking these theoretical principles as my point of departure, I shall endeavor in the following chapters to provide a more systematic explanation for the differential popularization of sports. This will mean looking in some detail at the social history of sports: where and by whom they were developed, the specific groups among which they became fashionable, and how other groups of people responded.

3. The Provenance of Sports: Modernization and Sportization in Centers of Diffusion

THE STANDARDIZED SPORTS with the largest numbers and widest spread of participants internationally originate from a handful of countries: Britain, Germany, the United States, and Japan.[1] Of the four that are the most widespread internationally, two (track and field and soccer) come from Britain and two (basketball and volleyball) from the United States; of the next twenty-five, eight are from Britain (tennis, boxing, table tennis, badminton, archery, hockey, bowling, and squash), three from the United States (exercising/bodybuilding, triathlon, and softball), two from Japan (judo and karate), two from Germany (handball and gymnastics), and one each from France (cycling)[2] and Korea (tae kwon do). In other cases it is more difficult to trace a sport's origins to a single country (e.g. swimming, weightlifting, chess, shooting, wrestling, equestrian sports, yachting, and motor sports). Of the seven sports with the most participants, four come from Britain (soccer, track and field, tennis, and table tennis), two from the United States (volleyball and basketball), and one from Germany (gymnastics).

This strikingly small number of countries of origin provides a point of departure for explaining the differential popularization of sports. It also raises various questions. Why should most sports have arisen in these four countries? I shall seek to answer this question by looking at the distinctive features of the modernization of Britain, Germany, the United States, and Japan and their development as powerful nations. And how can we explain the difference in popularization of the major sports? To answer this I shall demonstrate a link between the social backgrounds of those who practice specific sports and social relations and trends in the four key countries.

Development of the Modern Sports Model:
Early Modernization in England

England is rightly called the birthplace of sports. This is not so much because we can find reports of sportlike activities dating from as far back as the early Middle Ages in England (jumping, horse racing, archery, stone-throwing, wrestling, and sledding, for instance); the same may be said of many other countries. It is because events in Britain took a distinctive turn in the seventeenth and eighteenth centuries, when boxing, horse racing, running, cricket, and rowing were standardized and organized at the national level. Several specific trends in English society can help explain why this country became the cradle of modern sports.

Industrialization developed in England in the latter half of the eighteenth century, several decades earlier than in other European countries. The increase in trade and industry meant that markets became more interdependent. Improvements in transportation and communication increased the range of contact between people. An extensive system of canals and roads was built in response to the need for faster transport of goods over ever longer distances.[3] Travel times were cut drastically. In 1754 an advertisement proclaimed, "However incredible it may appear, this coach will actually arrive in London four days after leaving Manchester"; thirty years later, this time had been halved.[4] Another feature specific to English society was the extent to which trade and industry penetrated the country. The renewal of society was not confined to a few population centers but was extremely widespread.[5]

A strikingly large proportion of the investors and speculators who were financially involved in Britain's trading companies, mining operations, and the building of roads, canals, and ports were from the aristocracy and gentry. This was because of the relatively small gap in lifestyle between the English nobility and bourgeoisie compared to countries on the continent. Eighteenth-century England was a fairly open society with relatively few barriers blocking social mobility and less zealously protected elites. The upper crust of English society was made up of the aristocracy and the gentry. The aristocracy consisted of a relatively small group of titled individuals, while the gentry were a far larger group of untitled landowners who owned about half of the land by the mid-seventeenth century. Both groups practiced a strict form of primogeniture. The family estate went to the first son; other sons received small inheritances and often had to work for a living. This meant that many young noblemen mixed by necessity with people lower on the social scale, as a result of which they became less disdainful of middle-class codes of behavior.

While the nobility was adopting bourgeois standards in England, the reverse trend was seen in France. There, too, the two lifestyles became increasingly entwined, but in this case it was because members of the bourgeoisie were absorbed into courtly life. They took prominent noblemen as their models, hoping that mastering courtly habits would win them acceptance in the highest circles. As a result, the nobility expanded and gained far more power than in England but was less independent in relation to the king and the central court. In England the provincial nobility maintained closer contact with the local population. In Germany and Eastern European states the primarily rural nobility tended to close ranks against the bourgeoisie and the large majority of poor farmers. Hence there was far less of a mix of bourgeois and aristocratic lifestyles in these countries than in France and England.[6]

One result of this blurred distinction between lifestyles and the closer contact between nobility and the local population in England was that the social elite became more involved with local sportlike activities than on the continent. Foreign observers were aghast to see noblemen jostling shoulders with the common folk watching horse racing, rowing, boxing, and cricket; sometimes they even competed alongside their lesser brethren.[7] The involvement of the nobility and the early start of integration processes in British society promoted the standardization of these sportlike activities. The London Season provided a significant boost; the wealthiest members of the aristocracy and the gentry lived in London while Parliament was in session, and "the sports" were immensely popular at this time. As the noblemen came from different regions, each with its own traditions, they had to agree on the rules. All this led to the emergence of the first nationally standardized sports: horse racing, boxing, rowing, and cricket.[8]

Boxing, Horse Racing, Rowing, and Cricket: The End of Patronized Sports

Before 1850, horse racing, rowing, boxing, and cricket were the most important national sports in Britain. The first three in particular flourished as spectator sports in the eighteenth century but declined somewhat in the latter half of the nineteenth century. They were characterized by patronage, competitions, crowds of spectators, and professional participants.

To measure the speed of horses—in the seventeenth century the fastest means of transport over land—the nobility organized what were called "matches against time." Rich horse owners placed bets on the time needed to cover an agreed-upon course over open ground. From 1660 onwards these races were held on specially built circular courses, which made them more

equal and increased their frequency. The Jockey Club, founded in 1752, standardized the length and width of courses, introduced age categories and handicaps, and set rules for measuring time.

Although the noblemen rode the horses themselves at the start, they soon left this to their stable-boys, who evolved into professional jockeys. They focused on buying the fastest horses, invested heavily in breeding, and bet on the races. The noblemen even organized running races between their footmen (servants who ran alongside carriages to provide assistance if the vehicle broke down) and those in the service of other rich lords. Once the circular tracks came into use, these races too were held there, to introduce variety into the day's program. Alongside the serious races, there were also events organized purely for their entertainment value. In Newmarket, for instance, bets were placed on the time an eighteen-month-old girl would take to complete the course and on the winner of a race between two men, each of whom had a wooden leg.[9]

The same combination of patronage, a large crowd, professional participants, and competitions characterized rowing. Around 1661, some ten thousand ferrymen and professional oarsmen were active in the Thames area. Their meager income was boosted considerably by the prize money that the aristocracy and gentry put up for races.

In the case of boxing and cricket—more so than with horse racing and rowing—the aristocracy and gentry themselves took an active part. Boxing became fashionable among the London elite as an alternative to fencing, which went into decline with the introduction of a ban on carrying and dueling with swords. Great fencing masters retrained to teach boxing to noblemen, who were enormously interested in learning. The involvement of the aristocracy fostered the regulation and standardization of boxing and limited the sport's violence. In 1814 the Pugilistic Club was founded as the first, albeit unofficial, administrative body for English boxing, and the new rules could be enforced at the national level. In this refined form, the boxing of the nobility distinguished itself from the many local forms of fist-fighting that existed among the lower classes. The latter would no longer be recognized as boxing today; contestants could kick and pull each other's hair and carry on fighting when their opponent was lying on the ground.[10]

Numerous pastimes are recognizable in retrospect as precursors of cricket. Games applying its basic principle (throwing a ball at a goal that is defended by someone who tries to hit the ball away) were played in many societies. But the standardization and organization of present-day cricket took place in England when the aristocrats and gentry resided in London. In 1727 they drafted articles of agreement to introduce uniformity into the rules, and

more than a century later the famous Marylebone Cricket Club refined the regulations into those that essentially still apply today.

Cricket has always occupied a special place in British culture, which has much to do with the unique quality of social relations at the cricket grounds. Noblemen not only wielded a bat and ball but in doing so mixed with butchers and carpenters. At the outset many of the players were their servants, but as time went on more and more independent professionals were taken on. "Gentlemen" and "players" associated on and around the grounds, but the social gap was undiminished. Another important feature of cricket was the focus on the participants' own enjoyment; little thought was given to ways of entertaining spectators.[11]

The patriarchal relations in these sports—and in various other areas of popular culture—collapsed when socioeconomic developments made dramatic inroads into rural life. The demand for land soared, and innovations in transportation and communications decreased local autonomy. The advent of the nouveau riche disrupted the orderly lives of the landed nobility, whose sense of security was shaken. This led, in the 1850s, to what historians have called "the mid-Victorian compromise," a period of mutual influence in which the balance of power between the establishment (aristocracy and gentry) and the socially climbing bourgeoisie was more or less in equilibrium. The aristocracy's position was further weakened in the last quarter of the nineteenth century, when land prices fell sharply as a result of the increase in imported agricultural produce.[12]

In the new social order, the middle classes had more influence than before on codes of conduct in society. They were increasingly vocal in their criticism of traditional aristocratic sports and recreations, but they attacked with no less virulence the virtually unregulated pastimes of the masses—in particular blood sports such as bull-baiting and cockfighting. They railed at the spitting, cursing, gambling, excessive drinking, and rowdy behavior that they saw as endemic to such events,[13] praising in contrast the new sports that had evolved in the latter half of the nineteenth century, with their clear regulations and superior organization.

The rise of the middle classes was a gradual development and a crucial background factor in all enduring cultural changes in Western societies, to which the increasing prominence of sport is no exception. The ideal of sportsmanship promoted during the mid-Victorian compromise was a symbiosis of the values of the aristocracy and bourgeoisie. Sportsmanship demanded a competitive attitude and a strong desire to win, combined with dignity in defeat and courtesy in victory. This ideal transcended the world of sport and replaced aristocratic notions of propriety as the central virtue in society.

The middle classes were far from monolithic; they were made up of several disparate groups. In the heavily industrialized north of England the nouveau riche, who owed their positions to success in trade and industry, acted as financiers and administrators in the professionalization of various spectator sports. In this sense they differed in attitude and orientation from the group that included bankers, physicians, and civil servants, who became particularly influential in sports in the south of England. The latter, who had been educated at private schools (the most prestigious of which are known as "public schools") and universities, joined forces with the old social elites at the end of the nineteenth century to resist the professionalism in sport that was being promoted in the north by the new industrialists. They continued to emphasize the ideals of amateurism and fair play and strove to distinguish their sports from those of the nouveau riche and lower classes. These ideals required—in the words of Bourdieu—economic and cultural capital. To the southern professionals, sport for the athletes' own enjoyment was an altogether nobler endeavor than sport for the entertainment of the public. On the one hand, this meant that players had to have a source of income outside sport, and on the other hand it meant upholding certain cultural codes taught at public school and the university: preserving self-control even in the heat of battle and valuing the competition and one's own contribution more highly than the outcome.

Professionalism was a burning issue in almost all sports. It was not so much earning money from sport that people objected to—this was common enough in the pre-Victorian era. The conflict was rooted in a combination of increased social tension in British society as a whole and the growing popularity of sport among the working classes, which high society viewed as a threat. "'Outsiders, artisans, mechanics, and such like troublesome persons can have no place found for them. To keep them out is a thing desirable on every count. The status of the rest seems better assured and more clear,'" as one commentator wrote in *The Times* in 1872.[14] One exclusion strategy was to define working-class men as "professionals" and then to bar this category from participation in competitions.

The shifting balance of power and their rising sense of insecurity meant that the aristocracy and gentry no longer consorted so easily with the lower classes; instead they applied themselves to stylizing their own distinct way of life. Consequently, they largely withdrew from the organization of patronized sports in which the "common" people played a large part.[15] Horse racing and the associated running contests declined in social status, and boxing was no longer fashionable, while cricket and rowing were restricted to exclusive circles.

The members of the Amateur Athletic Club prolonged the aristocratic tradition of boxing for a little while longer, however. In 1867 they published the Queensberry Rules (under the sponsorship of the ninth Marquess of Queensberry) which forbade wrestling, made the use of boxing gloves compulsory, and introduced three-minute rounds with a minute's rest in between and the ten-second rule after a player had fallen or been knocked down. The exclusivity and amateur regulations of this club created a select company among whom boxing was an enjoyable pastime. But prizefighting continued outside the official clubs. The involvement of businessmen and large enthusiastic crowds made these fights into big business. For young men from deprived city neighborhoods, boxing offered a way for them to literally fight their way out of their dead-end lives of poverty. As a result, boxing increasingly attracted the disdain of the cultural elite; unlike in the old days, it was definitely "not done." Meanwhile, small groups continued to practice boxing in the tradition of the Amateur Athletic Club. For some, the solution to the sport's low status lay in developing countless rules of etiquette with which they could distinguish themselves from the masses. The members of the London Pelican Club, founded in 1887, wore tuxedos to watch the bouts and did not demean themselves by cheering or jeering. Most of their peers, however, withdrew from boxing altogether. This completely changed the nature of the sport in the 1890s; it was now patronized by wealthy managers from relatively humble backgrounds, who took the lower-class professionals under their wing.

The decreased involvement of wealthy financiers and patrons spelled the demise of professional rowing. The main cause was the distinction between amateurs and professionals, which was drawn with almost unparalleled rigidity. The rowing clubs of the universities of Oxford and Cambridge wanted to avoid any association with professional oarsmen and would admit only members with a certain type of education or social background.[16] In contrast to cricket, rowing did not have an authoritative body that could declare professional rowing permissible, and the first task of the Amateur Rowing Association, founded in 1882, was to formulate amateur rules. These proved highly restrictive, partly because they were drawn up in a period of vehement class antagonism. The rules excluded from rowing anyone "'who is or has been by trade or employment for wages, a mechanic, artisan, or labourer, or engaged in any menial duty.'"[17] Although the former patrons and financiers of professional rowing on the Thames adopted a milder tone and even set up an alternative rowing organization by way of reaction, they too embraced the dogma of amateurism. Whereas in the mid-nineteenth century rowing was still popular, by the end of the 1880s it had almost vanished. The special

boats that were designed for amateur races only hastened the sport's decline. They required a completely different technique than that needed by ferrymen and sailors in their everyday work.[18]

Besides the insistence on amateur status, numerous other measures promoted social exclusivity in club membership, such as the introduction of fees, admission ballots, and strict dress codes. The limited number of rivers and canals that were suitable for boat races made it easier to confine rowing to a small elite. Oarsmen tended to be extremely loyal to their club and would often boast of its exclusivity. They ensured that well into the twentieth century rowing remained a small, socially exclusive, and geographically isolated sport, dominated by the Oxbridge and London clubs.[19] The image projected to outsiders was that rowing was inextricably linked to the elitist academic world of Oxbridge, as symbolized by the annual boat race.[20]

In cricket, the cooperation between "high" and "low" endured in spite of the altered relations between the classes. But the contrast between "gentlemen" (participants from the upper crust of society) and "players" (their lower-class associates) became sharper and more explicit, partly because matches were no longer played on the village green but on exclusive grounds. "Players" were expected not only to know their place but to show that they did. They had to take care of the grounds, serve drinks, and use separate entrances and changing rooms. These social distinctions were even reflected in the names on the score-cards: initials before a name denoted a "gentleman," and initials after the name denoted a "player."[21] These traditional distinctions meant that there was never a fierce controversy about amateurism in cricket. Gentleman were by definition amateurs and players professionals. The cricket authorities could therefore define and apply the amateur rule with more flexibility than in the case of rowing,[22] which was a boon to the uncrowned king of cricket, the physician and "gentleman" cricketer W. G. Grace.

Cricket clubs also increasingly adopted rules to exclude "undesirable elements." Competitions were spread over several days, often during the week, which would allow the elite to go away for the weekend and ensured that the public consisted not of hoi polloi but of social equals.[23] The participation of nonprofessional players from the working classes was made even harder by the imposition of fairly high fees, complicated admission procedures, and detailed dress codes and other conventions. For instance, the rules of Lancaster Cricket Club included special fines for anyone not wearing the club uniform, which consisted of white trousers, a blue and white striped sweater made of Guernsey wool, and a straw hat.[24] In spite of the changes in society as a whole, classical cricket held firm to its traditions for a long time.[25]

* * *

With the demise of patronized sports, the accent shifted from spectators to participants. In the latter half of the nineteenth century, a whole range of new sports achieved rapid popularity. These may usefully be divided into two clusters: on the one hand, sports developed within educational establishments by and for young people from the upper and upper-middle classes, and on the other hand, sports developed outside schools, in exclusive clubs, attracting a somewhat older range of enthusiasts, though also from the upper echelons of society. It was the social character of these sports that held the key to their diffusion and popularization outside England (see chapters 4 and 5).

Soccer, Rugby, and Hockey: Athleticism at the Public School and University

From the mid-nineteenth century onwards, boys' public schools and universities played an important role in the development and spread of new sports. Before that, sport had not been part of the curriculum, and teaching staffs paid little heed to students' extracurricular activities. By the end of the nineteenth century, however, this situation had changed so dramatically that some parents were complaining that there was more sport than study.

In the eighteenth and early nineteenth centuries public schools were dominated by a violent and defiant atmosphere. Rebellions were not infrequent, and in some cases troops were called in to subdue the boys. Members of the bourgeoisie who were growing in wealth and status found this situation old-fashioned, inefficient, and decadent. They attached more importance than did the aristocracy and gentry to giving their sons a sound education to prepare them for positions in the government, church, army, or commercial business. In their view, the prestigious public schools had low academic standards and abysmal discipline. They advocated reforms that would increase the powers of the teaching staff to fashion curriculum and extracurricular activities as they saw fit. Extra emphasis on sports was one of the vehicles they championed to improve discipline and the general atmosphere.[26]

The program of reforms was a huge success and sparked a sports rage that one of the headmasters described as "'extravagant athleticism.'"[27] At Lancing School it was compulsory in 1888 for boys to play soccer every day and cricket three times a week. Harrow's cricket team spent about fifteen to twenty hours a week on sports during the summer term; in the winter soccer took up virtually all their leisure hours. The sports culture came to dominate other activities at public school, creating a bizarre pecking order based on athletic

prowess.[28] A student with limited academic abilities could compensate by doing well on the sports field. Teaching staff were increasingly expected to meet sporting as well as intellectual requirements. An athletic, Christian intellectual: this was the ideal inculcated by late-Victorian headmasters. Many of them were Muscular Christians, an influential religious movement that viewed participation in sports as a fine means of fostering virtues such as self-control, loyalty, obedience, toughness, and persistence.

This emphasis on athleticism coincided with the peak of Britain's imperial power. Many Victorians and Edwardians saw a clear connection, as James Mangan puts it, between perseverance, toughness, and courage on England's playing fields and the qualities needed to be an Australian pioneer, to preach in Africa, or to fight in Burma. Sport was deemed indispensable to the training of captains of industry and leaders of the empire. It was thought to increase boys' physical strength and form their character in ways essential to military service and later positions of leadership. Furthermore, athleticism was in line with social Darwinism and the Victorian ideal of masculinity. In social Darwinism, competitive selection and the urge to succeed go together, and according to the Victorian ideal of masculinity, men should be active, brave, physically strong, and pure of mind. A universal "Tom Brown" had to be created: loyal, brave, and honest, a gentleman and a Christian.[29]

SOCCER AND RUGBY Against this background, rugby and soccer evolved from the wild and violent pastimes that were known in England as "football." Although the sports are closely related, soccer has become by far the more popular of the two—not only in England but in most other countries, the only exceptions being Wales and New Zealand. To explain this, we first need to review the different ways in which the two sports developed in their country of origin before spreading internationally. Why was soccer already far more popular than rugby in England when the two sports started being played elsewhere in the final decades of the nineteenth century?

Rugby School, just south of Birmingham, was one of the many institutions at which the bourgeoisie pushed through reforms. A relatively new public school, it recruited boys from more modest backgrounds than older and more exclusive establishments such as Eton and Harrow. Rugby's traditions were therefore less firmly entrenched, which made it easier for the headmaster, Thomas Arnold, to change the boys' lifestyles. He set stricter rules for the violent variant of football played by his pupils. Other schools soon followed suit. There was no coordination, however, and many different versions of the game coexisted.

The old boys from the various public schools mixed when they became

Oxford and Cambridge undergraduates. To play "football," they had to agree on the rules. This was easier said than done, however, largely because of the fierce rivalry between the handling game (the Rugby variant) and the kicking game (played by former students of Eton, Harrow, and Winchester). Old Etonians and Old Harrovians regarded rugby as an "obscure, Midlands establishment" with little history and less status.[30] Their own "kicking game" was infinitely superior. The Old Etonians in particular scorned the rugby players for carrying the ball.[31] These differences in tradition and social background impeded the standardization of football. Neither group had enough influence to impose its own variant on the other. During the famously ill-fated attempt to forge a single set of rules in 1863, the conflict escalated to such a pitch that the rugby supporters withdrew from the newly founded Football Association (FA). "Association Football" (later abbreviated to "soccer" in the United States) differed from rugby in several points: it allowed less physical contact, it forbade handling, and used a round instead of an oval ball; it also differed in the shape of the goal and the method of scoring points.[32]

The competition between supporters of the two variants stimulated the spread of both forms outside the greater London area. Probably each side hoped that the successful diffusion of their own game would spell the demise of the other. Thus a club was founded in Sheffield under the influence of Old Harrovians who persuaded the local players not to carry the ball. To suppress handling, the Sheffield players were required to wear white gloves and hold coins during the game.[33]

Since soccer—the "dribbling game"—was favored by former pupils of Eton and Harrow and students at Cambridge, it held more prestige than its rival variant. This prompted the elite in peripheral regions of England, who saw the leading schools and universities as their models, to adopt the FA rules and to ignore the Rugby version. The Rugby variant remained confined to the new, less-prestigious public schools, where Old Rugbians, as teachers, promoted the ideology and practice of their former headmaster. The more rapid spread of FA football was further encouraged by the early standardization of its rules at the national level in 1863, whereas it was not until 1871, with the founding of a central body with enough authority to impose binding rules on clubs and schools, the Rugby Football Union, that national unity was achieved in the rugby rules. Before this, each team interpreted the rules in its own way, as a result of which regular rugby competitions did not get off the ground.[34]

Soccer not only spread faster to elites outside greater London; it was also played far earlier (and more) than rugby outside public school circles. In the last quarter of the nineteenth century, it changed from an "old boys' sport"

to a popular sport. While in 1867 the FA had a membership of ten clubs, four years later there were fifty, in 1888 there were a thousand, and by 1905 the number had reached ten thousand.[35] This development took place in a period in which the lower-middle and working classes were acquiring more leisure time and becoming more interested in sports. One important impulse was the introduction of the free Saturday afternoon for most English factory workers; another was the extensive new state-subsidized secondary school system. By the end of the nineteenth century several regions had competitive school sports events. Soccer profited from these changes far more than rugby, for a variety of reasons linked to the issue of professionalism.

For several decades, the Old Boys from the south of England dominated competitive soccer. In 1883 a workers' club, Blackburn Olympic, won the coveted FA Cup and took it to the north of the country for the first time, beating a team of Old Etonians in the final. The Blackburn Olympic team included three weavers, a spinner, a dentist's assistant, a plumber, an iron founder, and a cotton mill worker.[36] By the 1890s the tide had turned. Soccer had achieved such popularity that the working men's teams were simply better. From 1893 to 1914 the annual FA Cup was won by working men's teams every year but one. The sole exception, Tottenham Hotspur, consisted of three Englishmen from the industrial north, five Scotsmen, two Welshmen, and an Irishman—all of them professionals.[37] Aston Villa started charging spectators an entrance fee, and others soon followed suit; these receipts became an increasingly important source of income.[38] The increased funds and the competition between clubs stimulated the quest for soccer talent and boosted players' pay. Initially they received expenses only, but they were soon being paid larger sums of money, especially in the industrial north.[39]

While soccer players increasingly came from the working and lower middle classes, the Old Boys from the south continued to dominate the boards of soccer organizations. It was they who had to decide whether the increasing trend toward professionalism was to be permitted within the FA. At first, the FA thought it could stem the tide of professionalism, but it soon took a new tack when payments threatened to continue under the counter and there was talk of alternative organizations being launched. In 1885 the FA granted professional soccer official recognition, in the hope that this would make it easier to get a grip on professional practices, as had proven successful with cricket. One of the most important men behind the recognition of professional soccer, the Old Harrovian C. A. Alcock, was also well known in cricket, one of his posts being the secretary of Surrey County Cricket Club. He wanted to resolve the problem of professionalization in soccer in the same way as it had been resolved years ago in cricket—control through legalization.[40]

In rugby, too, steps were taken in the direction of professionalization in Yorkshire and Lancashire, areas with strong industrialization and urbanization. But the rugby clubs that wanted to introduce professionalism encountered far greater resistance from the southern establishment than did the soccer clubs. The Rugby Union administrators defined the preservation of players' amateur status as the union's primary objective and held fast to a strict amateur rule. They even rejected a proposal submitted by Yorkshire clubs to compensate players solely for the loss of pay during working hours.[41]

Several reasons can be given for these opposing responses to professionalism. First, rugby club members were more attached to the amateur ideal because of the greater tension between them and players from lower social backgrounds than was the case with soccer. As a rule, the rugby administrators came from a somewhat lower social class. They were therefore more socially insecure and more sensitive to matters of status. To preserve the distance between themselves and the working class, they adopted a more exclusive stance vis-à-vis the "common people" who wanted to take over "their" sport.[42] This difference in attitude between soccer and rugby administrators was exacerbated by the fact that the conflicts about professionalism in soccer took place in the 1870s while the rugby professionalism debate was much later, in the 1890s. By this time, there was far more class conflict and segregation in British society than twenty years earlier.[43] These general trends made rugby players less willing to compete with teams lower down the social scale or to allow forms of professionalism than had been the case with soccer. The Rugby Union saw the amateur rule first and foremost as an expression of class difference, whereas the FA approached the issue of whether and how much players could be paid more pragmatically, with class differences being of secondary importance.

The position adopted by the established rugby clubs was hardened by the rivalry between the soccer and rugby establishments. The Old Etonians and Old Harrovians initially looked down upon the more violent sport of rugby. As a result, the Old Rugbians were determined to steer away from any development that could make rugby look like a sport for working men. The popularization of soccer prompted them to coin the adage, "Football is a game for gentlemen played by ruffians, while rugby is a game for ruffians played by gentlemen."[44] By preserving the social allure of their sport they could distinguish themselves from soccer, with its increasing mass appeal. The formation of a strict amateur rule was one way of achieving this; the rugby establishment's refusal to make concessions to the public was another. For many years rugby had to do without any competition system, which kept the sport out of the glare of publicity. Some clubs even refrained from giving their

players numbers on their shirts. "'This is a rugby match, not a cattle-sale,'" grunted a prominent Scottish rugby administrator when quizzed about problems of recognition that might arise.[45] It was this difference in social exclusivity that gave soccer a definite edge in popularization. While soccer grew into a sport that appealed to a wide range of the population, Rugby Union clubs largely appealed to youths from the prosperous middle classes.[46]

Soccer was the first team sport for which workers could organize without encountering obstacles. Soccer clubs offered the workers ties and loyalties in what was for many their new urban environment: they represented their streets, pubs, neighborhoods, and towns. Many of the names of the clubs founded between 1876 and 1895 attest to this. Clubs were formed largely through the main institutions where higher and lower classes met: church, school, and the workplace. Clergymen, teachers, and company managers acted as intermediaries. They saw soccer as a salutary means of giving the workers more discipline and self-control while providing recreation and enjoyment. But it was often the workers themselves who took the initiative to found a new soccer club. When Arsenal was founded—one of the best known of the factory clubs—the management gave the workers almost no help whatsoever. However—and this is at least as important—it also placed no obstacle in their path.[47]

Just before the end of the nineteenth century, rugby finally acquired its own professional variant. In the industrial counties of Yorkshire and Lancashire, where rugby matches were attracting increasingly large crowds, the majority of the sport's administrators voted in favor of the change. In the north these administrators tended to be non-public-school men working in trade and industry, whereas their counterparts in the south were mostly professional men who had attended minor public schools. As the sociologists Dunning and Sheard have shown, this gap in social background influenced the positions adopted in the debate about professionalism.[48] However, it was the southern rugby establishment that controlled the power in the union. It had little contact with the northern clubs and refused to make any concession to their desire to permit professionalization. A split in the Rugby Union was inevitable. In 1895, twenty-two clubs broke away and set up their own federation of professional rugby clubs with different rules. In 1898 this new Rugby League consisted of ninety-eight clubs. This depleted the numbers and resources of the Rugby Football Union clubs: the union's membership fell from 481 clubs in 1892 to 244 in 1903. It was not until the 1920s, when the amateur ideology enjoyed another upturn, that the number of Rugby Union clubs was back at its 1893 level.[49] The Rugby League's success was confined

to certain regions. Since rugby had developed after the professionalization of soccer, it lagged behind in the battle to attract the attention of spectators and sponsors. Furthermore, the league version acquired the image of being a rather rough workers' sport and was ranked lower on the social hierarchy than Rugby Union (middle-class amateurs) and Association Football (amateurs and professionals and socially inclusive).

FIELD HOCKEY   Although soccer grew to become the most popular sport in England, at least half of the population did not play it: soccer, like rugby, was deemed unsuitable for women. Instead, they participated in sports involving less physical contact, at least if they came from the higher social classes. Working-class girls at most attended physical education classes at primary school, but after leaving school sport was no longer an option. Women from the upper reaches of society, who attended public schools or superior boarding schools and universities, had more opportunities to take part in sports around the turn of the century. By then, fitness and physical development were no longer viewed as anathema to femininity but as supplementary qualities. At the women's colleges at Oxford and Cambridge, clubs were founded for tennis, golf, field hockey, lacrosse, cricket, cycling, croquet, swimming, and fencing. At secondary school, netball and Swedish gymnastics appeared on the curriculum.

The most popular sport at girls' schools—in spite of the considerable physical effort it required—was field hockey. Given the social pressure to behave with feminine decorum, field hockey balanced on the very edge of acceptable exertion. Some parents thought it a "violent and unladylike game," but to most it fell just within the bounds of decency. When field hockey was introduced to girls' schools and women's colleges in the 1880s, it had not yet undergone the same measure of popularization as soccer or rugby. The fact that it was deemed respectable and had not evolved into a "macho" sport fostered its development at girls' school. There were few debates over whether this was a suitable pastime for girls.[50]

The diffusion of women's field hockey was fostered, as in the case of men's soccer, by the high status of the schools and colleges where it was first played. One such was Somerville College, Oxford, whose students founded a hockey club in 1885. In 1895 the Ladies' Hockey Association was founded, following an initiative by Newnhamites (Cambridge). They applied to join the Hockey Association, but the men "turned the women down," as they put it.[51] Offended by this exclusion, the women adopted the rule that no man could ever hold an administrative position in their association. Furthermore, they

dropped the term "Ladies" from their name and called their club the All England Women's Hockey Association (AEWHA). The AEWHA took a stand against mixed hockey, arguing that each sex could play better alone, that men's participation would carry certain risks, as men ran faster and hit harder, and that women would be preoccupied with their appearance instead of scoring goals if men were around. Field hockey became a women's sport, just as soccer, rugby, and cricket were associated with men. At women's schools it became the winter alternative to tennis, just as soccer and rugby took the place of cricket in the winter months at boys' schools.

The AEWHA was soon achieving greater success than its male counterpart. The number of schools and clubs attached to the AEWHA grew from 150 in 1919 to 2,100 in 1939; by 1975 it had reached 3,800. The AEWHA was a socially exclusive organization. Weekday matches, expensive clothes, and exorbitant fees kept girls from working-class backgrounds out of the sport for many years. If they played field hockey at all, it was in one of a handful of clubs set up for them, generally founded by men or by teachers or former pupils at boarding schools.[52]

As a competitive sport, strikingly little propaganda was made for men's field hockey, in contrast to the women's equivalent, to promote its diffusion at the national or international level. At boys' schools field hockey was always far less popular than soccer, rugby, and cricket. Nor did men's field hockey receive any attention from the press. This was partly a consequence of the players' deliberate decision to make their sport as noncompetitive as possible. A few years after it was set up, the Hockey Association decided that there were to be no cups, leagues, or competitions of any kind. The specter of soccer, with its excessive popularization, played an important role in this decision. According to the editor-in-chief of *Hockey,* this policy had "'undoubtedly saved Hockey from disaster and from being sacrificed upon the altar of popular, but ruinous, competitions.'" By rejecting competition and pursuing a policy geared toward preserving a "'full-blooded amateurism,'" the hockey players hoped to prevent the popularization of their sport.[53]

It was probably partly as a deliberate way of distinguishing their game from soccer that men's field hockey remained a fairly isolated sport in which national and international matches were not built into an extensive competition system. With the exception of the Olympic Games, international competitions in men's field hockey are recent developments. The first European championships were held in 1970, the world championship has only existed since 1971, and the field hockey tournament for the Champions' Trophy was inaugurated in 1978. Even the Olympic competition was of secondary importance to the English field hockey players.

Tennis, Golf, Badminton, Table Tennis, and Squash: Middle-Class Sports in Exclusive Clubs

The rise, structure, ideology, regulations, and target group of soccer and rugby differed fundamentally from those of another group of sports that evolved toward the end of the nineteenth century. Tennis, golf, badminton, table tennis, and squash were not products of schools and universities but evolved from weekend parties held by the well-to-do bourgeoisie. These sports were for women as well as men and not so much for schoolchildren and students as for slightly older participants. Moreover, they were not geared toward physical confrontation and a robust, boisterous style of play; instead they were played with a certain serenity and restraint and without physical contact. The growing popularity of these sports coincided with the rise of a "culture of respectability," in which older, cruel modes of recreation were suppressed and civilized relaxation in the reading room, the park, and private clubs was encouraged.

TENNIS Tennis greatly resembles the recreational activities in which it had its origins. Tennis-like activities had existed centuries before, at courts and monasteries. Most of these were more like fives than tennis as we know it today, as the ball was struck with the hand over a line, against a wall, or against a sloping roof.

The net and rackets had probably been introduced at the end of the sixteenth century, creating a game that was all the rage in the late sixteenth and early seventeenth centuries. In 1596, Paris had 250 courts for what was called *jeu de paume*. It was probably this popularity that undermined its appeal to the elite, since at the end of the seventeenth century it went out of fashion, and only ten courts were left functioning as such; all the others had acquired other uses.[54] The power and influence of the French court in this period meant that its fashions and manners tended to be adopted in other countries. In England tennis also became a popular form of recreation in courtly circles, although little is known about how widespread it became in the seventeenth and eighteenth centuries. Probably England too witnessed a decline after an initial rage.[55]

In the last quarter of the nineteenth century, the old "royal" or "real" tennis reappeared. In 1874 a patent application was submitted for "A New and Improved Portable Court for Playing the Ancient Game of Tennis." The inventor was Walter Clopton Wingfield, a personal friend of the Prince of Wales (later Edward VII). Two days after the patent application, the book of rules appeared for the new creation, which Wingfield called "Sphairistiké or lawn

tennis." These rules contained numerous innovations but were still a far cry from today's tennis.

The term "lawn tennis" summed up the new game perfectly. Uniquely, it provided for a portable court that could be set up in any large garden. After the first article on the new sport appeared in *Court Journal,* others followed in *The Field,* and this form of tennis soon became known in upper-class circles. It could be played at virtually any country home and most suburban villas and was soon a regular feature of parties held by the prosperous bourgeoisie. Within the All England Croquet Club at Wimbledon and the Marylebone Cricket Club, which recruited largely from these circles, the tennis rules were refined and standardized, and the first tournaments were held.[56]

The rules of tennis distinguished, as did virtually every sport from 1870 to 1890, between amateurs and professionals. The amateur rule was not intended to exclude financial gain—a cash prize was awarded to the winner of the first amateur tournament held at Wimbledon—but as an effective means of excluding people such as laborers and servants. As with cricket, once the status of "amateur" had been acquired, it was permissible to earn money.[57]

Partly because the game was played on private premises, in the gardens of country houses and villas, women too participated. As the historian Richard Holt has observed, from a gender perspective tennis was the first truly national sport.[58] Among the well-to-do bourgeoisie, tennis provided women with the first opportunity (aside from croquet) to take part in sport outside of school. The introduction of mixed doubles in tennis tournaments in 1888 made this more striking still: to this day it is one of the few sports, along with the Dutch sport of korfball and some horse-riding events, in which men and women compete simultaneously, with and against each other. This strengthened the appeal of tennis to both men and women in the higher regions of society toward the end of the nineteenth century. Social differentiation and specialization had made relations between people more complex and more fragmented over the course of the century. Small, exclusive circles had given way to more wide-ranging networks of relationships. Sports clubs were useful for building up and maintaining these networks. In this respect mixed tennis had an advantage compared to other sports: the tennis club was an ideal place to meet an eligible marriage partner.[59] The privacy of lawns and clubs made it possible to arrange matches involving a carefully selected group of young men and women; nor did supervision pose a problem.

This did not mean that there was equality between the men and women, however. Women were allowed to play tennis, but not too energetically. The prescribed clothing, which included ankle-length skirts, restricted movement enormously. This did not change until the beginning of the twentieth cen-

tury. Suzanne Lenglen, one of the great tennis players of the twentieth century, was a key innovator in women's tennis clothes. Her game provoked controversy as well as attracting admiration and emulation. She introduced shorter skirts, used a variety of rackets, and made "unfeminine" movements on the court. The headband she wore during matches became all the rage as the "Lenglen bandeau." In 1926 "Suzanne the goddess," as she soon became known, took an even more unusual step: she turned professional, probably for the sum of a hundred thousand dollars. The sport had become such a major attraction that an American decided to exploit its commercial possibilities. He organized a series of matches between the best men and women players of the day—the start of a trend that, for all the opposition it unleashed, was never reversed. For many years, the amateur organizations continued to control the major tournaments, but the most famous players turned professional for large sums of money.[60] This is also why tennis was scrapped from the Olympic program after 1924.

The respectable and prestigious nature of tennis meant that, like golf and skiing, it was perfectly suited to advertising and sponsorship activities. Diverse groups of professionals organized under the financial wing of commercial companies and wealthy private individuals. To counter this trend, the International Lawn Tennis Federation excluded all players who signed World Championship Tennis contracts, in what we may call the last convulsions of the amateur stronghold in its fight to halt the professionalization of tennis. With incentives provided by the increasing influence of sponsors and the media, from the 1970s onwards the advance of professional tennis was unstoppable.[61]

GOLF It is illuminating to contrast developments in other middle-class sports played on private premises or at fashionable clubs—golf, badminton, table tennis, and squash—with those in tennis. On the one hand, they display certain parallels of social history, and on the other hand, there are certain differences—some subtle, some less so—that influenced the spread and popularization of these sports.

In the 1920s a booklet was published in France entitled *Tennis and Golf*. Periodicals with similar titles appeared around the same time in Germany and the Netherlands. This was no coincidence. Although the "sportization" of golf preceded that of tennis and took place in different surroundings, players and administrators belonged to similar social networks from the higher reaches of society. Both sports were played in wealthy suburban areas. So it was not strange that, at the beginning of the twentieth century, the famous Charlotte Dod should have won both the ladies' golf championship and the

women's finals in tennis, nor that the famous French tennis player René Lacoste should have married Simone Thion de la Chaume, one of the great champions of women's tennis.[62]

From the outset, golf was played by wealthy men of commerce. Just after its establishment in 1787, the Glasgow Golf Club (GGC) had twenty-five members; aside from two physicians and four army officers they were all successful businessmen. Between 1810 and 1831, twenty-six of the forty GGC members whose professions are known were businessmen. Most of the rest had similar professions, such as insurance brokers or warehouse owners.[63] In England, too, where golf was introduced toward the end of the eighteenth century, it was an exclusive sport from the beginning.

Golf required a good deal of money, time, and land. Besides the main rules, countless codes of conduct evolved, including a strict insistence on composure during matches.[64] As James Mangan emphasizes, playing on Veblen's phrase, "conspicuous consumption" went hand in hand with "conspicuous leisure" and "conspicuous resources."[65] There is perhaps no other sport in which the way it is played has become so emphatically part of what Max Weber has called "the stylization of life."[66] Matches were so long that players had to be able to take several days off work. The large estates owned by the golf clubs were a manifestation of their power and wealth. The more beautiful the landscape in which the courses were situated, the more prestigious was the club. These grounds were privately owned and fenced off from their surroundings, and nonmembers were excluded. Equally magnificent were the clubhouses—monumental mansions for which ever larger sums of money were paid. In terms of social ethos and investment in time, money, and property, golf undoubtedly surpassed tennis and the other middle-class sports. This is why it held so much appeal to the upper middle classes with newly acquired wealth. In the 1890s a new golf club was set up in England about every two weeks, largely in the industrial north and the affluent southeast.[67]

Like tennis, golf acquired a professional track early on. For two reasons, professionalism was not a burning issue. First, there was little pressure from below, as the exclusivity of this sport was already to a large extent guaranteed by the tradition of conspicuous consumption, leisure, and resources. In the second place, golf had been imported from Scotland, where a measure of professionalization had already been introduced in the nineteenth century. The first professionals in England were therefore Scottish golf instructors who were appointed to clubs and who combined their teaching with selling golf products and playing in tournaments for cash prizes.[68] Given their humble social origins, the English amateurs saw them more or less as talented servants. Club members played against them and learned their skills without admitting them

to their social circle. The professionals were a small group that existed outside regular club life.[69] Golf players from the upper crust remained true to their amateur status. It was not until the 1920s that the first upper-middle-class and former public school golf players turned professional.

The rise of women's golf was related to the tradition of seaside vacations. England's summer resorts set about creating scope for the elite to play tennis and golf during their vacation. Women accompanied their husbands to the tennis courts and golf clubs and were soon taking part in both sports. In response to this trend, independent women's clubs were set up, and in 1893 twenty of these joined to form the Ladies' Golf Union. In the higher social strata from which these clubs drew their membership, the lines between men's and women's activities were drawn less sharply than they were lower down the social scale. The park-like surroundings and moderate physical exertion associated with golf accorded perfectly with the codes for respectable behavior in public, as long as play did not become too serious or fanatical.[70]

BADMINTON, TABLE TENNIS, AND SQUASH The prestigious origins and the involvement of the social elites gave tennis and golf their high social status; this was a key factor in promoting the international diffusion and national popularization of both sports. The preferences and fashions of the English elites served as an example for the upper echelons in other countries. And these standards in turn were emulated by lower, upwardly mobile groups. Both sports have witnessed their strongest growth only recently, in response to increased prosperity and the expansion of the upper-middle classes (see chapter 4). Badminton, table tennis, and squash profited far less from these dynamic forces. Badminton and table tennis had a less respectable past and a problematic image. Furthermore, they underwent "sportization" at a later stage—not until most English sports had spread to other countries—and both had a poor organizational structure. This latter factor also impeded the spread of squash.

The precursors of badminton, such as battledore and shuttlecock, were known mainly as children's games. The sport's eventual name probably derives from the town of Badminton in Gloucestershire, where the duke of Beaufort is said to have revised the rules of the children's game in 1870. English officers developed the sport further in India, which had a badminton-like sport of its own. In the mid-1870s a set of rules was adopted in Poona, which colonials applied upon their return to England in Bath, Cheltenham, seaside resorts, and London suburbs. Badminton was largely confined to the wealthier southeast of England and is still (like tennis) relatively uncommon in industrial regions. But in contrast to the status-laden origins of tennis and

golf, badminton was seen as a children's pastime or a domestic diversion. It was not until the latter half of the twentieth century that these associations were cast off, and badminton emerged as a popular international sport.[71]

Table tennis had similar problems at the beginning of the twentieth century. It was one of a whole series of miniature games—others imitated croquet, bowling, and golf—that had evolved as parlor games in genteel circles in the final decades of the nineteenth century.[72] Table tennis started as a sort of mini-tennis that could be played indoors in bad weather or after dinner. Dining-tables were used as the playing surface, and a species of net was improvised. Entrepreneurs were quick to seize the commercial advantages of this game. Around 1870 celluloid was developed in the United States, and the sporting goods manufacturer John Jacques started producing little balls made of this material and advertising "the New Table Game of Ping-pong or Gosima." Besides being a derivative of tennis, table tennis was also promoted in a manner much like Wingfield's approach.

The distribution of table tennis products was not confined to England. Rival firms set up business, and the new sport became very popular in Europe and elsewhere under a variety of onomatopoeic names such as "Whiff-whaff" in America, "Flim-flam" in Germany, and "Pim-pam" in France. In England it was publicized in the *Ladies Home Journal* and the *Daily Mail* and became popular among the petit bourgeoisie. Ping-Pong was soon a regular feature of house parties and dinners, fulfilling the same role as tennis at lawn parties. At the beginning of the twentieth century table tennis became a true rage, and one could buy cards printed with invitations such as "We *must* have you to Ping-Pong on . . . at . . . o'clock, do come!"[73] The game's informal character meant that various versions evolved. In 1901 the journal *Lawn Tennis* called for the establishment of a table tennis organization, its goal being "the elevation of a mere drawing-room amusement up to the status of a scientific national pastime."[74] The successful model that had turned pastimes into genuine sports in the past was to be used to boost the status of ping-pong. The end of 1901 witnessed the first major table tennis tournament. Two to three hundred competitors entered, many of them fine tennis players. The women appeared in long skirts, the men in evening dress, but as tensions grew, jackets were discarded and sleeves rolled up. Not long after this, table tennis went out of fashion in these smart circles. The market was flooded with ping-pong games, and mass production undermined the game's exclusivity. Postcards now depicted maidservants grabbing their paddles to play as soon as their master left the house.[75] After 1904 table tennis was rarely mentioned in fashionable magazines.

It was not until the 1920s that table tennis was revived as a competitive

sport. Its players inherited a history with two competing images of table tennis as a competitive sport and a popular amusement. The term "table tennis" was later reserved for the competitive sport, while "ping-pong" acquired a rather denigrating undertone evocative of casual domestic recreation. Table tennis clubs had to fight against the ping-pong image. This was no easy task, as—unlike most other sports—the equipment could be purchased at toy stores. The same applied to badminton rackets. Both table tennis and badminton could be played in the garden or in your home; there was no need to join a club.

Another member of the family of racket sports is squash, an activity invented at Harrow Public School around 1850. Over the next few decades it spread well beyond Harrow, but it was not standardized until the late 1920s. Up to then, there were hardly any squash clubs, and the material and size of the rackets and balls, as well as the floors of squash courts, were all variable. In social composition, squash resembled tennis and golf. "'Squash is not a game for democracy,'" someone observed in the *Daily Express* in 1932.[76] This snobbish statement characterized the development of squash for the first few decades of the twentieth century; it was particularly popular in the exclusive West End Social Clubs. The names of other squash clubs also reflect its social milieu: the Army and Navy Club, the Conservative Club, the Public Schools Club, the Royal Air Force Club, the United Hunts Club, and the United University Club. The sport became particularly fashionable among army officers. It was they who produced most of the administrators and top-ranking players of the early decades, and also in other countries many new players were recruited in officer circles.[77]

* * *

Each branch of sport can be classified, on the basis of its history, in terms of a certain social milieu and a certain image. It is essential to bear these differences in mind if we are to understand the diffusion and popularization of these sports, which I shall describe in the following chapters. The English sports could not escape from their roots once they were taken up in other countries. They were learned in the way that was passed on by the English.

Whereas most of these sports were gradually adopted throughout the world, those invented elsewhere scarcely made any impact in England. All the most popular sports in England today are "homebred": soccer, cricket, darts, tennis, golf, table tennis, and badminton. This is quite unlike the situation in most other countries. Aside from England, it is only in the United States that the popularity of "homebred" sports surpasses that of "imported" ones (see table 7).

Table 7. Percentage by Country of Participants in Sports Originating from Britain, Germany, the United States, Japan, and Other Countries

British Sports	%	German Sports	%	United States Sports	%	Japanese Sports	%	Other Countries' Sports	%
Britain	94%	Switzerland	50%	United States	54%	Japan	15%	Austria	54%
New Zealand	84	Germany	34	Japan	42	Spain	12	Finland	40
Australia	75	(former) Yugoslavia	33	France	32	France	11	Ireland	36
Cyprus	74	Denmark	24	Italy	24	Belgium	6	Norway	34
Hungary	71	Norway	24	Bulgaria	23	Cyprus	5	Sweden	27
Belgium	69	Austria	17	Cyprus	19	Hungary	3	Iceland	23
Poland	67	Iceland	17	Hungary	17	Italy	3	Bulgaria	23
The Netherlands	66	Luxembourg	16	Spain	15	Turkey	2	Italy	23
Luxembourg	65	Sweden	12	Turkey	13	(former) Czechoslovakia	2	Switzerland	21
(former) Czechoslovakia	63	Portugal	11	(former) Czechoslovakia	13	(former) Yugoslavia	1	(former) Czechoslovakia	20
Portugal	61	Hungary	11	Sweden	11	Germany	1	France	20
Ireland	56	Poland	11	Portugal	11	Finland	1	Denmark	20
France	55	Bulgaria	10	Poland	10	Iceland	1	(former) Yugoslavia	19
Denmark	54	Spain	8	(former) Yugoslavia	9	Australia	1	Australia	18
Italy	53	France	8	Iceland	9	Luxembourg	0	The Netherlands	18
Bulgaria	51	Italy	8	Finland	8	Portugal	0	United States	14
Turkey	50	Finland	7	Germany	8	Switzerland	0	Germany	14
Iceland	49	Turkey	7	Luxembourg	8	United States	0	Spain	14
Germany	48	The Netherlands	6	Switzerland	7	Denmark	0	Japan	14
(former) Yugoslavia	48	(former) Czechoslovakia	6	Belgium	7	Sweden	0	Luxembourg	11
Spain	48	New Zealand	6	Ireland	6	Poland	0	Poland	11
Finland	48	Belgium	6	Norway	6	Norway	0	Turkey	10
Sweden	48	Ireland	5	Austria	5	Austria	0	Hungary	8
Norway	40	Japan	3	The Netherlands	3	New Zealand	0	Britain	6
United States	31	United States	2	Denmark	2	The Netherlands	0	Belgium	6
Austria	28	Cyprus	2	New Zealand	2	Ireland	0	New Zealand	5
Switzerland	27	Australia	1	Australia	1	Cyprus	0	Cyprus	4
Japan	23	Britain	0	Britain	0	Britain	0	Portugal	3

Note: Calculations are based on popularity rankings in the appendix.

Rise of the Gymnastics Movement: Accelerated Modernization in Germany

Patterns of participation in sport today reveal that in Germany, too, indigenous sports do well. In the "top six" we find English soccer, tennis, and track and field alongside gymnastics, shooting, and handball—all of them associated with German tradition. The most conspicuous is the enormous popularity of gymnastics. It is Germany's second sport and ranks only slightly behind soccer in numbers of federation members; until the 1920s gymnastics was more popular even than soccer. The growth of this peculiarly German pattern of sport can be related to developments in national and international relationships of power: the rivalry between Germany and England, the expansion of the lower middle classes, and the continuation of the sharp division between bourgeoisie and aristocracy.

In the last quarter of the nineteenth century, the sports that had been developed in England were introduced into Germany, mainly by Englishmen who were living in Germany for various reasons but in part also by aristocratic, cosmopolitan Germans who had attended school or done business in England. The petit bourgeoisie in Germany disapproved of this cosmopolitanism, regarding it as a betrayal of the strong virtues of the fatherland.[78]

Germany was undergoing rapid modernization at this time. Industrialization took place later there than in England, but it happened much faster. After about 1869 a period of unparalleled industrial growth began, primarily based on iron and steel but also on the chemical and electrical industries. By the beginning of the twentieth century, industrial development in Germany was already approaching the level of England.[79] The country was also expanding its military potential. It built up a strong position of power in Europe, largely at the expense of Austria-Hungary and France. This was achieved not only through Germany's industrial and military activities but also by more state intervention, characterized by innovations in education and by effective administration and planning. With this interventionist policy Germany hoped to boost its industrial growth and halt the increasing dominance of England.[80]

As Germany's power increased, an atmosphere of euphoric self-confidence combined with a rejection of foreign influence developed. The vigorous modernization and strong international competition was expressed among the middle classes in a profound love of all things indigenous to Germany and a strong aversion to outside influence. The strongest aversion of all was reserved for England, the country's great rival. Fritz Harkort, the pioneer of the Ger-

man manufacturing industry, expressed these feelings of rivalry when he stated passionately that he longed for the day when the German workforce was so well trained that all the English could be "'whipped out of the country.'"[81]

This rivalry meant that the Germans were dead-set against adopting English sports; sport itself was seen as un-German. Gymnastics was presented as a different sort of activity, and in the hundred years between about 1850 and 1950 it was enormously popular. The Germans were better able than other European countries to oppose the onward march of English sports and to develop their own tradition of physical education; moreover, this tradition served as a model for countries within the German sphere of influence (see chapter 4).

Turnen or Gymnastics: Sound Education and Sound Ideology

After 1807, a group of educational reformers tried to restore Prussia to its former glory on the international stage by implementing educational reform. Following in Prussia's footsteps, other German states forged ahead of England and France in education in the nineteenth century. The Germans saw schooling as the cornerstone of a morally and physically strong nation and as the backbone of industrialization and improved prosperity.[82]

The tradition of compulsory elementary schooling in Germany dates from the mid-eighteenth century, when reformers such as Johann Bernhard Basedow and Johann Friedrich GutsMuths developed new curricula out of dissatisfaction with the existing education system. They allocated a large proportion of the timetable to physical education as part of a more general moral upbringing. Physical education, they believed, would improve pupils' obedience and attentiveness in class. The new games that GutsMuths propagated in the context of physical education reflected the orderliness and austerity that underpinned the success of the bourgeois circles from which most of the pupils and teachers originated. GutsMuths detested the aristocratic tradition of privileges based on birth and social position.[83]

While Basedow and GutsMuths had a more or less international orientation, the nineteenth-century gymnastics movement increasingly radiated nationalism and patriotism. The embodiment of this trend was the "Father of Gymnastics," Friedrich Ludwig Jahn (1778–1852). In applying GutsMuths's programs, he placed even greater emphasis on standard procedures, routine repetition, and rigid structure—so much so that the movements resembled military exercises. As a true German patriot, he railed against cosmopolitanism. He reviled foreigners in general and Jews in particular. He published articles on Germany's great past and the ideal of a single German state and advocated strengthening the German language. To increase the power of the

nation, he founded a broad-based movement for the cultivation of *Turnen* (he used this German word for gymnastics instead of *Gymnastik*, with its Latin derivation). More fiercely even than Basedow and GutsMuths, he fought for greater social equality and the abolition of all aristocratic privilege. "'We know nothing of rich or poor, of title, rank or station. Gymnastics brothers are all equal, their estate is their fatherland,'" went the words of one gymnastics song.[84] A standard uniform and the habit of addressing one another as "brother" and "sister" enhanced the spirit of social equality. In the beginning, this movement had a rebellious, nationalistic air about it, and the authorities responded by trying to ban it.[85] Later on, however, it became closely associated with the dominant ideology of the government and the education system.

Jahn's gymnastics movement was enormously successful. In 1868 the Deutsche Turnbund already had 128,491 members; by 1880 there were 170,315, and by 1900 the numbers had grown to 640,000. Ten years later the first million was reached, and by 1913–14 there were 1,340,000. This was the end of the explosive period of growth. Not until the 1920s did membership return to the level of 1913, and between 1923 and 1930 it remained stable at 1,600,000. However, there was a significant increase in the number of women gymnasts. In 1900 only 15,969 women belonged to gymnastics clubs, but by 1914 there were 75,392. As the twentieth century progressed, women gymnasts considerably outnumbered the men. The Arbeiter-Turnerbund too saw its membership soar: from 9,000 when it was founded in 1893 to 187,000 in 1913–14, then to 448,000 in 1920 and 746,000 in 1930.[86]

Nowhere else in the world did industrialization, urbanization, population growth, and an overall shift in relations between the classes take place at such a breakneck pace as in Germany in the last quarter of the nineteenth century. The gymnastics clubs capitalized on this development, recruiting new members from groups that were the product of rapid industrialization and urbanization. "Typically the members were skilled workers, functionaries, and small businessmen—people with careers that were rather abruptly fashioned out of a society only recently shaken from poverty and generations of regional isolation."[87] Because of the expansion of the middle classes, within which national pride and the preservation of the German cultural heritage were key virtues, the gymnastics movement had enormous potential for growth. The new middle classes had a strongly nationalist ideology and despised the cosmopolitan lifestyle of the social elites. Their lack of political power strengthened this resentment. One way of expressing their hostility was by a moralistic repudiation of the English sports that were propagated and played by members of the upper classes.[88]

The spokespersons of the gymnastics movement singled out for criticism key characteristics of English sports such as idle pleasure and competitiveness. In their view, what mattered was not the achievement but the individual; not the distance or height of a jump but physical poise and skill. This point was driven home by setting limits to the goals pursued in German gymnastics. Surpassing these limits should not command greater admiration.[89] For the physical exercises, the content of which was specified in detail in the curriculum, the leaders of the gymnastics movement developed a range of special equipment. Some items, such as the vaulting horse, were of ancient origin. Most, however, were developed in the first half of the nineteenth century: these included the buck, tub, springboard, and horizontal bar.

The historian Richard Holt has rightly pointed out in relation to the gymnastics movement in France that gymnastics was not only in tune with the patriotism of the petit bourgeoisie and working classes, it provided relaxation and a place to make friends. Until the First World War, gymnastics clubs were among the few institutions that provided such opportunities for people relatively low on the social scale. They accommodated factory life by organizing events and training in the evening hours. Gymnastics gave young people an opportunity to wear uniforms, march in parades, travel, and go on group vacations. Furthermore it improved the size and strength of their muscles, which (as far as boys were concerned, at any rate) enhanced their status among friends.[90]

Nonetheless, the sports historian Richard Mandell is correct when he calls gymnastics an "induced sport." It was deliberately developed to improve national strength and health and was intentionally ideological, patriotic, and reliant on the state.[91] Gymnastics was less a product of those who practiced it than was the case with English sports; it was devised in educational circles and firmly supported within schools. There was a great pool of potential recruits—former pupils who had learned gymnastics at school. This provided the movement with enormous potential for growth, especially as school attendance was extremely high in Germany in the latter half of the nineteenth century in comparison to other countries.

Handball: An Alternative Team Sport within the Gymnastics Movement

The "induced" nature of gymnastics inevitably had its downside. The strict school regime was increasingly difficult to maintain, and some German pupils revolted against the suppression of freer forms of physical exertion. The sports of the elite, and soccer in particular, were attracting more and more

young men from the lower classes. Between 1883 and 1902 German federations were founded for rowing, track and field, fencing, soccer, and tennis. The pressure of these rival organizations changed the nature of gymnastics. Competitions and prizes were introduced, and the accent shifted from military drills to exercises emphasizing movement and speed. The development of "rhythmic" and "natural" gymnastics reflected some people's dissatisfaction with the traditional repertoire of exercises; they sought to forge a link between the formalism of gymnastics and the freer movements of sport. These groups changed the emphasis, in rhetoric and practice, from strength to gracefulness. This was in line with the rise of neo-Romantic ideals. Youth and hiking clubs and other groups that advocated a return to nature, such as the successful Wandervogel, attracted a large following around this time. Gymnastics too had to be dragged out of stuffy gymnasiums into the fresh air.[92]

Similar innovations led to divisions in the gymnastics movement between radical and conservative groups. A vigorous polemic arose between them, related to the criticism of English sports. The opponents of competitive gymnastics tended to oppose other sports too. Gymnasts in the tradition of Adolf Spiess, in particular, rejected any "sportization" of their art. They feared that it would lead to materialism and selfishness, unaesthetic contortions, a mania for records, and an exaggerated emphasis on performance measurement.[93] To them, sports and everything associated with them posed a threat. "'Over the past few years, a foreign plant has tried to take root on German soil in the guise of gymnastic effort, and with the deceptive dazzle of its appearance it has succeeded in turning a large proportion of young men from the better circles away from gymnastics.'"[94] In 1898 a professor and gymnastics instructor from Stuttgart published a pamphlet entitled *Fusslümmelei: Über Stauchballspiel und englische Krankheit* (Boorishness with the feet: On the shoving-ball game and English sickness), in which he warned of the dangers posed by the increasing popularity of soccer. Sports, he explained, were un-German and superficial because they were not played in the service of a "higher" ideal such as patriotism or a belief in equality, but were characterized by individualism, hierarchical relations, hero worship, and the pursuit of records. Vollert, writing in the *Zeitschrift für Turnen und Jugendspiele* in 1900, was also concerned about the "'crazed Englanders . . . who are now exerting an ominous grip on some of our nation.'"[95] The gymnasts called upon their countrymen to banish the "'poisonous plant of sport'" from German soil.[96] "'Gymnastics is closer to our nature, historically, nationally, physically, and educationally than sport.'"[97] Germans from higher social circles disagreed and defended English sport. Von Glasenapp, for instance, published the periodical *Deutscher Sport: Zeitschrift für die Interessen des deut-*

schen aktiven Gentleman-Sport (German sport: Journal for the promotion of active gentlemen's sports in Germany). Others, such as the *Landtag* representative Von Schenckendorff, adopted an intermediate position. He wanted sports to be introduced alongside gymnastics, but only their "good elements." Similar ideas were expressed in the *Deutsche Turnzeitung.*[98] But what were these "good elements"?

In spite of all the opposition, the popularity of English sports steadily increased, and eventually soccer became the most popular sport even in Germany. But gymnastics still had an enormous following, partly through its vast recruitment potential at schools, where for decades it had a monopoly. Even today it does not lag far behind soccer. In comparison to other countries, the gap in popularity between these two sports is extremely small (see the appendix).

The response of the gymnastics authorities to the rising wave of enthusiasm for English sports was twofold. First, they tried to regulate the pursuit of English sports entirely within their own organizations. By widening the scope of the gymnastics federation to include a number of "foreign" sports, such as soccer, they hoped to prevent the erosion of their authority in physical education. They hastened to stress that sports were played in a totally different spirit within their organizations. But the other sports bodies had no intention of surrendering their independence. In 1925 the gymnastics federation, forced onto the defensive, forbade its members to take part in competitions held by the national sports bodies. Four years later the ban was lifted again, as few members had kept to it.[99] Then the inevitable happened: in the birthplace of gymnastics, the gymnastics federation became part of the umbrella sports federation.[100]

The second strategy intended to stem the tide of English sport was the propagation of various "gymnastic games" such as handball and a string of more obscure activities such as *Torball, Völkerball, Haftball, Netzball, Schlagball, Prellball,* and *Faustball.* Most of these "sound alternatives" to sports were never played outside physical education classes. With the single exception of handball, none was institutionalized outside schools, so they developed none of the characteristics of the modern sports model.

Handball-like games are as old as those resembling football, but the internationally standardized form of handball dates from 1917, when the Berlin gymnastics instructor Max Heiser developed a game intended as a counterpart to soccer. Similar initiatives had been taken in the preceding decades.[101] Heiser's invention was initially designed for the ladies' branch of a gymnastics club in Berlin. Two other German pioneers of handball, Erich König and Carl Schelenz, revised his rules. In the 1920s the sport had virtually all the characteristics of today's standardized international handball.[102] New play-

ers were recruited at schools and gymnastics clubs, which meant that this "alternative to soccer," in the wake of gymnastics, eventually became one of Germany's leading sports.

The Development of the American Pattern of Sport: Relatively Autonomous Modernization in the United States

European sports occupy a secondary position in the United States; American sports dominate the scene. Of the twenty-five countries for which the popularity rankings are given in chapter 1, it is only in England and the United States that a majority of the total number of participants (94 percent and 54 percent, respectively) engage in sports developed in their own country (see table 7). This unusual pattern was possible because the United States underwent modernization fairly autonomously, and in the crucial period of sportization—the latter half of the nineteenth century—it was in many respects the equal of the dominant countries of Europe in power and prestige.[103]

As in Germany, modernization in the United States was a fast-moving process. Before 1850, the country's total industrial production was less than that of England or Germany, but by the early twentieth century it exceeded the sum of the two. In the laying of railway tracks—an important indicator of national-scale expansion and integration—it surpassed the European countries by the end of the nineteenth century.[104] But German modernization was more closely interwoven with that of other European countries. Although the United States could not be oblivious to events in Europe, its modernization was more autonomous.[105] Trade relations between the United States and Europe were less close than those among countries within Europe. By 1900 the United States had a largely self-sufficient economy with its own domestic market. Most of its inhabitants were European immigrants or their descendants, but they were far more interested in the developments within their new land than in foreign affairs.

As the United States's economic, political, and military power increased, it grew to become a major, independent hub in international relations. The government took caution as its motto, not wanting to be drawn into the intricacies of European relations and conflicts. Until 1917 Europe was of secondary, regional importance from this American viewpoint—an attitude reinforced by the factor of distance. This is not to say that American politics were doggedly isolationist. The United States built up its own sphere of influence, which stretched well beyond North America. From the beginning of the nineteenth century, the Americans expanded their influence in Latin America and the Pacific region. They annexed Hawaii in 1853, and that same

year they forced Japanese authorities to open their ports to foreign ships. In 1898 they seized power from Spain in the Philippines, and the following year they prevented other major powers from colonizing China.[106]

As the United States became a key player on the world stage, its citizens' early admiration of English culture was replaced by self-confidence in the country's own achievements and a sense of cultural superiority. In line with this, they took the liberty of reinterpreting English sports—something that scarcely happened elsewhere. The products were new sports, which they were proud to call American. A specific American pattern evolved, which is still clear today: four of the six sports with the most participants (baseball, American football, basketball, and volleyball) are homebred.

The sportization of baseball took place around 1845, forcing its rival—the English game of cricket—into the shadows as it become America's national sport. American football, too, evolved from games played by European immigrants. The various forms of football crystallized into an independent sport, the rules of which were standardized between 1870 and 1880. What made this possible? What was it that boosted the popularization of this sport in the United States so powerfully that after the Second World War it ousted baseball to become the number-one American sport?

Basketball and volleyball did not evolve from European games. Both are American inventions dating from around 1900. Basketball achieved far more rapid popularization than volleyball, and today it holds its own with the other great American sports; volleyball, however, remained (among men) a minor sport. How can these developments be explained?

Although volleyball did not prosper in its own country, it became quite successful elsewhere. Like basketball, it is played in almost all parts of the world and in this respect is the opposite of American football, which has scarcely spread outside the United States yet in its own country reigns supreme. Baseball is different again. It became tremendously popular in some countries while in others it was received with little if any enthusiasm. In the following sections I shall explain these differences by comparing the social development of the various sports in the United States and shall then examine the consequences of these differences internationally in the next chapters.

Baseball versus Cricket: The Emancipation of American Culture (Part 1)

When the first baseball club drew up the rules on which the sport is still based today, cricket was already being played on a fairly large scale in many parts of the United States. Some even referred to it as the United States's national

sport. But after 1845 so many Americans took to baseball that by the end of the Civil War it had supplanted its predecessor. This differential popularization of cricket and baseball has been much researched. Of particular interest are the studies of Allen Guttmann, Ian Tyrrell, Melvin Adelman, and George Kirsch. They all focus on the period between 1840 and 1870, and in spite of differences of interpretation, they agree on certain issues crucial to the general theory of the differential popularization of sports.[107] They show convincingly that the development of cricket and that of baseball were intertwined. In other words, an account of the rise of baseball must also explain why cricket, in spite of having arrived first, did not become the first love of American sports enthusiasts.

The early American immigrant colonies had a large recreational repertoire. Most were fairly poor families from English villages, where people amused themselves by running, playing quoits or skittles, kicking a ball, or indulging in activities that involved teasing animals. Similar games initially dominated the leisure hours of immigrants in the New World. Children's bat, base, and ball games—stoolball, "base-ball," and rounders, the precursors of modern baseball—were common in the northeastern states in the early nineteenth century. The rules of these informal and impromptu pastimes were learned from parents or friends, or from *The Boy's Own Book,* a collection of children's games that was published first in London and then in the United States. The name "Base Ball" was mentioned in one such publication as early as 1744.[108]

In spite of the political independence secured in 1783, English culture was still influential in the United States at the beginning of the nineteenth century. Books and magazines appeared in English and were largely attuned to English examples. The American sports press, too, was modeled after the English in style and content. English sports news, mainly taken from *Bell's Life in London,* was discussed in detail. Because of this, up until 1840 English spectator sports such as horse racing, running, boxing, and rowing were popular among spectators in the United States. Large-scale participation in organized sports was a later development, however. Members of the social elite in the leading Anglo-Saxon migrant areas of New York, Boston, and Philadelphia were the first to start joining clubs to practice sports, emulating the elite in England.[109]

Cricket was one of the first club sports to start focusing more on participants than on spectators. Unlike the other bat, base, and ball games played in the early nineteenth century, cricket already existed in a regulated, organized, and standardized form in England. When rich English immigrants founded the St. George Cricket Club in Manhattan, the rules and regulations lay waiting for them.[110]

The first cities to have cricket clubs witnessed the beginnings of baseball. Several of the first baseball clubs played at cricket grounds: they included St. George in Harlem, New York, and the famous Elysian Fields in Hoboken, New Jersey.[111] Between 1840 and 1860, baseball developed from a children's game into a modern sport with fixed rules and regulations, matches and competitions, a supervisory umbrella body, articles in the press, statistics, and records.

Of the baseball clubs that were founded in and around New York City after 1840, the first was the Knickerbocker Base Ball Club. Its atmosphere and social etiquette resembled that of prestigious cricket clubs like St. George, but its members had less involvement in commerce and in general earned more modest salaries.[112]

The Knickerbocker Base Ball Club served as a model to other Americans, showing how this one-time children's game could be transformed into a respectable sport. The Social Base Ball Club and the Independent Club adopted similar membership requirements and penalty clauses. The statutes of Excelsior and the Eagles were almost identical to those of the Knickerbockers. Even the players' clothes—blue woollen trousers, white flannel shirts, and straw hats—were imitated by the new clubs. The city's powerful influence prompted many young men to found clubs elsewhere to play the "New York game," as the Knickerbockers' form of baseball was called, to distinguish it from a rival variant from Massachusetts.[113]

Although baseball could not come near the popularity of cricket in the 1840s, it grew so fast between 1855 and 1865 that it overtook its older rival. This differential popularization was related to a variety of factors: the social position of the first English cricketers in the United States; nineteenth-century relations between the United States and England; relations between ethnic groups and social classes within the United States; and a special catalyst: the Civil War and the influence of the army (see chapter 1 on catalysts).

The first cricketers in the United States were high-born English immigrants who tried to keep their sport exclusive and scarcely allowed American-born countrymen to join their ranks. They did not promote the sport at schools and made little effort to interest the press in it. In a country of immigrants of such diverse national backgrounds, the English origins of cricket were not an obstacle as such. In the 1850s it was still attracting enthusiastic articles in the American press. Furthermore, toward the end of the nineteenth century other English sports, such as golf, tennis, and boxing, fared much better. The crux of the matter is that cricket was confined more or less deliberately to the English community. Its problem was not its national origins but the fact that it was controlled by an immigrant community that used it partly as a means of asserting and preserving their ethnic identity.[114]

While a combination of cricketers from "high" and "low" social backgrounds was not a problem in England, the English elite in America did its utmost to confine the sport to its own circle.[115] This was partly because of the relatively smaller social differences in the United States. American society was an open and diverse mixture of ethnic groups, without any aristocratic traditions. The status of the English immigrants who belonged to the American upper crust was therefore far more problematic than that of the aristocracy in England. This colored their attitude to lower social groups. Whereas in England the nobles had such unquestioned power that they were comfortable allowing their servants to join in cricket matches, the absence of such paternalistic relations in the United States inclined English cricketers to keep their sport exclusive; they had no desire to try combining "gentlemen and players."[116]

Baseball, however, was not confined to a select company of English immigrants. On the contrary, it became popular among poor immigrants of other national backgrounds and American-born people of lower social origins. This trend related to the second process that affected the differential popularization of the two sports: the increase in anti-English sentiments and the development of an American identity. Alongside political and economic autonomy, Americans also strove to achieve cultural independence. "'The reproduction of the taste and habits of English sporting life in this country is neither possible nor desirable,'" wrote the *New York Times*. The paper urged Americans to develop their own analogous yet original activities that would be appropriate to American life and experience. The New York Yacht Club even offered prizes for the best proposals for a suitable national sport.[117] The fact that the English tended to support the Confederacy during the American Civil War (1861–65) sharpened the nationalistic background of the rivalry between cricket and baseball.

Many baseball clubs were given names such as Young America, Independent, Union, Eagle, American, Liberty, and Pioneer. Others used their names to honor men such as George Washington, Alexander Hamilton, Thomas Jefferson, and Benjamin Franklin. Nationalistic feelings ran so high that a legend developed about the origins of baseball that completely denied its English roots. Baseball, the story went, had been invented in 1838 by an American, Abner Doubleday, in Cooperstown. This myth was so tenacious that in 1938 the leading baseball organizations prepared to celebrate the sport's hundredth anniversary.[118] In this respect baseball became the antithesis of cricket, which was associated with a group of elitist English immigrants who obstinately persisted in their identification with the mother country.

Under the influence of patriotic feelings, baseball was increasingly seen as

an archetypal American sport. This had great appeal to poor immigrants, especially those from Ireland and Germany, who had cast in their lot with their new country. To them, America was the country of opportunity, and they eagerly embraced its cultural symbols. This applied with even more force to their children. Second and later generations of immigrants felt more at home in the United States. Keen to demonstrate their loyalty, they were quick to seize new expressions of Americanization. The English resisted this trend more than other immigrants and tried to hold firm to their culture.[119]

After the Civil War, the popularization of baseball continued at an accelerated pace. Unlike cricket, it was played increasingly in lower urban milieus. In the baseball center of New York, the first clubs arose for lower-middle-class and working-class men: the Mutuals, a firemen's club; the Manhattans, a policemen's club; and the Phantoms, a club that grew out of a society of saloon keepers. In the late nineteenth century, baseball also became popular—unlike cricket—in the southern states. Although African Americans were barred from established baseball organizations until 1945, they too were keen players. Because of the long period of exclusion—the color bar lasted seventy-five years—they set up their own baseball organizations and competitions.[120]

The two sports were in different phases of development, and this also affected their popularization. The need to develop a sport to express the emerging American identity could theoretically have led to an adaptation of the cricket rules. Sports are social products; the rules and meanings are not fixed and can always be redefined. This did not happen with American cricket because it was far less malleable than baseball. While the first baseball clubs were entirely free to make and experiment with their own rules, cricket already had a long tradition and fixed rules zealously supervised by a powerful English body. The American historian Melvin Adelman identifies three phases of a sport's development. In the first, the rules, standards, and sanctions are simple, unwritten, and determined by local traditions. In the second, the entire set of rules is codified, and play is organized. In the third phase, an expansion takes place involving bureaucratization, commercialization, and professionalization, and rituals and traditions acquire a set place. By the end of the second phase, when the blueprint of rules and codes of conduct has been accepted, structural changes become more difficult; as a rule, only marginal changes are made after this. When cricket was introduced into the United States it was already in the transition from the second to the third phase, whereas baseball was still in its infancy. Because of this head start, cricket was culturally and institutionally more robust than baseball. It already existed in a regulated, organized, and standardized form before it arrived in

the United States, making it inflexible and conservative. Any calls to Americanize it were doomed to failure.[121]

Baseball's meteoric rise to success as the national sport of the United States also had to do with the aftermath of the Civil War. The sport's popularity grew at an accelerated pace once peace was restored. While on the eve of the Civil War baseball was largely played in and around New York City, after the war it attracted participants nationwide. In only one year—1866—the number of clubs grew tenfold. Each of the following years was more successful than the previous in absolute terms. The National Association of Base Ball Players grew from a small number of clubs in the vicinity of New York City at the end of the 1850s to several hundred spread over the entire country ten years later. In the major cities there was an explosion of enthusiasm.[122]

During the Civil War, cricket and baseball were part of military life. The Union generals encouraged both as training and recreation. However, baseball, with its wider social appeal, was played much more than cricket.[123] Soldiers and prisoners of war spent their free hours playing matches that local people would come to watch, learning how to play. A commentator wrote in *The Clipper* in 1865, "'When soldiers were off duty, base ball was naturalized in nearly every state in the Union, and thus extended in popularity.'"[124]

The army brought together young men from a variety of social and regional backgrounds, acquainting them with much that was unfamiliar. Not all readily accepted the newfangled ideas and customs, but whatever their response, army life promoted an integration and standardization of lifestyles, and not only in the barracks. The army units were considerably spread out, so that even people living in remote areas were confronted with new ways of doing things. After leaving the army soldiers traveled to all parts of the country as civilians, continuing some of the activities learned in the army in their new surroundings.[125]

At the end of the 1860s reports of baseball games were coming from all parts of the country. About a hundred thousand Americans were playing the game in clubs; in one season some two hundred thousand spectators came to watch the most important matches.[126] Businessmen were quick to seize the advantage. Commercialization and professionalization were a logical extension of this, in spite of the initial opposition of the baseball establishment. Newspaper proprietors soon noticed that reports of baseball games boosted sales, and the increased publicity gave the sport an added impetus. Besides covering games and reporting results, papers would contain letters to the editor explaining the finer points of the game or the best way to set up a baseball club.[127]

These trends all promoted the integration of baseball into American culture. By the end of the nineteenth century, newspapers were allocating more space to baseball than to any other cultural activity. Myths and legends, famous victories and disastrous defeats, the latest team changes, and the trials and tribulations of baseball heroes and club managers were daily topics of discussion among millions of Americans, as they are today. The makers of bats, caps, chewing gum, and beer brought baseball into their advertisements. It was the first sport to be exploited in the United States on this grand scale, and later sports had little chance of supplanting it. What is more, the business community protected baseball's image. They presented it as a respectable spectator sport for the middle classes and denounced anything that could damage this image, such as drunkenness, gambling, fighting, and corruption. Baseball was universally publicized as America's national sport, open to men of all classes and backgrounds. Immigrants soon understood that playing, watching, and talking about baseball was one of the best ways of joining the mainstream of American society.[128]

American Football versus Soccer and Rugby: The Emancipation of American Culture (Part 2)

Around 1950, baseball was toppled from its long reign as the most popular sport in the United States by American football. The difference between soccer's global popularity and American football, which is scarcely played outside the United States, has even prompted Markovits—in an allusion to classic essays by Tocqueville and Sombart on the absence of socialism in the United States—to refer to "the Other American Exceptionalism."[129]

Markovits's thesis is somewhat of an exaggeration. In the first place, soccer is played more widely in the United States than is generally assumed. In numbers of players, it occupies about fifth place. Though mainly played at the universities (where it is strikingly popular among women), it is also popular among new Asian and Latin American immigrant groups. Second, the United States is not the only country to have its own variant of football. Both Australian and Gaelic football (the latter played in Ireland) are extremely popular. Nonetheless, Markovits does raise some interesting questions. What caused the United States to develop its own variant of soccer and rugby? And above all, why did American football become so popular in its homeland and not elsewhere?

Even before the rules of soccer and rugby had been standardized in England, football-like activities were already being played at American universities. English immigrant students brought their own versions with them. And

popular novels such as Thomas Hughes's *Tom Brown's Schooldays* acquainted American students with football-type games. Matches between teams from
different years were part of the initiation rituals for students at Ivy League
schools.[130] Initially, several variants coexisted, as they had in England. But
differences in rules gave rise to problems when matches were organized between universities.

The game as played at most American universities resembled soccer rather than rugby. Harvard, however, played a hybrid form more like rugby, which
gradually spread to the smaller colleges of the northeast. Harvard's enormous
influence was felt far beyond the academic sphere. Its main rivals, such as Yale,
Columbia, and Princeton, however, were impervious to such influence; as in
the struggle between Rugby and Eton, none was willing to give up its own
version of the game. The competition between the American universities, and
particularly between Harvard and Yale, resulted in something completely new
and unforeseen. When Harvard challenged Yale to a game in 1875, the teams
agreed to abide by what they called "concessionary rules": a mixture of rugby and soccer rules in which rugby's influence was dominant. These rules,
drawn up by the two most prominent and prestigious universities, were subsequently adopted by Columbia and Princeton. On Princeton's initiative,
these four universities met in the fall of 1875 to found the Intercollegiate
Football Association, which standardized the rules. After this, each fresh
change took the sport further away from both rugby and soccer. A new scoring system, yard lines, and the rule that a team has a limited number of attempts to pass these lines increasingly gave American football an identity of
its own. By 1882, most of the characteristic rules of present-day American
football had already been established: the emphasis on the center, the scrim-
mage line, and the yardage gain and offside rules. It had come of age as an
independent sport and was recognized as such.[131]

For English players, the brief rules of soccer and rugby needed no explanation. American students, however, interpreted them in a variety of ways.
They had no long tradition to look back on, in which the eventual rules represented a hard-fought compromise between previous competing versions.
Every soccer and rugby rule had its own history. Any alteration would revive
old conflicts that standardization had finally resolved. But American students
had no older, more experienced players at their disposal to explain such
matters.[132] Their regulations had to be less ambiguous and more precise;
nothing could be taken for granted on the basis of tradition. In the words of
Riesman and Denney, there was an "etiquette vacuum" that had to be filled
with new, supplementary formal procedures.[133]

Two specific developments helped to bring about these changes to foot-

ball in the United States but not elsewhere (with the exception of Ireland and Australia). First, the American sportization of football-type activities could follow a course of its own because the United States had developed into a great nation that no longer needed to bow to the European powers. Americans emphasized their independence and cultivated their national traits. They were far less in awe of the British way of life than were the inhabitants of more peripheral (and still British-dominated) regions. Although Britain was still influential in the 1870s, the Americans possessed the cultural power to adapt rugby and soccer into their own version of the game.[134]

In the second place, the country's relatively autonomous modernization fostered the development of its own cultural products. The sportization of American football took place, significantly, when soccer and rugby were still at the beginning of the second phase of development as defined by Adelman. As early as 1869, two colleges (Princeton and Rutgers) competed in a game resembling American football. This match was played according to the Princeton rules that had been devised two years before.[135] Virtually everywhere else in the world soccer and rugby were adopted more than ten years later, around 1880, when they were already in their third developmental phase. Fundamental changes are easier to introduce at the beginning of the second phase, when the rules are still open to interpretation. Furthermore, the supervisory body, if such exists, does not yet command enough respect to enforce compliance.

The geographical distance between the United States and England was probably another factor. In spite of the numerous family ties between the two countries, they competed in fewer soccer and rugby matches before 1900 than did English and European teams. History shows that international sports events were crucial in spreading the English rules.[136] Distance also played a role in non-Western countries, but there it took far longer for the local population to gain administrative authority over the organization of these sports and the way they were played.

The diffusion and popularization of American football did not follow the same line as baseball. In the mid-nineteenth century, baseball fell several rungs on the social ladder. After this, its main support was among the lower middle classes and workers. While in the case of baseball, the army had served as a catalyst to spread the game, in the case of American football this role was played by the universities. Until after 1900, American football was played exclusively by the sons of the elite at the most prestigious universities. Only in the twentieth century did it spread to wider sections of the community, first to minor universities, colleges, and schools, and eventually to young people from lower social classes with little formal schooling.

The trickle-down effect gave American football a thrust based on the strong competition between universities and colleges to win the favor of spectators, on whom they were dependent for their funding. The competition increased the pressure on less prestigious educational establishments to copy Ivy League practices, including football; they could not afford to ignore a sport that was played so enthusiastically at Harvard and Yale. Football was one of the ways a college could prove its superiority; and for many colleges it was an easier form of rivalry than that of academic accomplishment. Football gave a school publicity and esteem and was a factor in recruiting students. It also increased students' loyalty to their colleges.[137] In 1879 the first match was held between colleges in the Midwest, and in 1889 West Coast colleges competed for the first time. By the end of the nineteenth century there were few schools and colleges without a football team.

In the latter half of the nineteenth century, a sports rage developed on the university campuses that was comparable to the craze of athleticism in England. Sports took up an increasingly large share of the program of extracurricular activities: not only football, but rowing, track and field, and wrestling were extremely popular. By this time baseball was already too much of a "proletarian" sport to appeal to students.[138]

Although around 1900 American football was only being played by students from higher social circles, as a spectator sport it soon acquired mass appeal. In 1903, Harvard University, which had about five thousand students at the time, opened a football stadium that would accommodate fifty-seven thousand spectators. Crowds of this size had never been seen before. Around 1880 the annual Thanksgiving Day match—the most important football event of the time—attracted no more than a thousand spectators.[139] Another new trend was that football matches were front-page news. The sport's entertainment value had started taking precedence over the players' own enjoyment.[140]

American schools and colleges profited enormously from the popularization of American football as a spectator sport. Aside from prestige, huge sums of money were involved. In 1903 Yale's superior football team brought in $106,000 in admission fees in a single season—one-eighth of the university's total budget for that year.[141] This financial gain was a tremendous incentive for colleges that were dependent on private income, sending them on talent-hunting expeditions outside the student circuit. It became common for gifted football players to be given scholarships, regardless of their intellectual abilities. This was a way for boys from lower social classes to gain admission to higher education, and hence to climb a few rungs higher on the social ladder. Universities that did not follow this trend no longer carried any weight in the sports competitions.[142]

As football slid down the social scale, more and more protests were voiced about the sport's increasing roughness. Some prestigious universities even abandoned football for a while: Stanford and the University of California started playing rugby instead, and for a time Columbia and Northwestern did without football altogether. In addition, the rules were adjusted to make the game less rough. This met with opposition from midwestern colleges, however. They were primarily interested in making football more attractive to spectators and were not so concerned by the prospect of a hard-fought battle.[143]

In the 1920s football was more popular at high schools than at universities. By around 1920 college students no longer had absolute control over the sport, and a split in the organization produced a professional American football competition that no longer had any connection with universities—it became today's National Football League (NFL). The clubs that participate in the NFL are commercial companies often owned by wealthy businessmen. College football still has its own competition (also professionalized these days), but even here the elite universities have long ceased to play a leading role. Until 1900 this championship was an exclusive competition between a clique of four universities: Yale (eight times champion), Princeton (four times), Harvard (four times), and Pennsylvania (twice). Since 1920, however, all these names have vanished from the honors list, the title going to "second-rate" universities such as Oklahoma, Army, Clemson, Alabama, and Nebraska (and suffering a corresponding loss of prestige).

* * *

For many decades, baseball was played far more than football outside the university campuses: it was more common at elementary and secondary school and attracted more people from lower social classes. As prosperity increased in the United States, however, this "workers' sport" lost some of its popular appeal. Especially in the second half of the century, men increasingly wanted to choose a sport with higher social status. Young people flocked to American football, while older groups gravitated toward tennis and golf. Because of its college origins, football enjoyed greater respectability than baseball and appealed more to groups that had struggled free of the working classes, where baseball was the most popular sport.[144] According to the participation figures given by Guttmann, the number of football players in interscholastic, intercollegiate, and intramural competitions doubled between 1950 and 1970.[145] In interscholastic events—which accounted for the vast majority of competitive players—football had 930,034 players in 1989, as opposed to 412,825 in baseball. In intercollegiate competitions there were

47,946 football players in 1987, as opposed to 19,481 in baseball.[146] Both sports were almost exclusively played by men. Public interest in professional competition grew at a similar rate. Between 1960 and 1970, the average number of spectators rose from 30,257 to 52,381.[147] The annual Super Bowl championship game became the most important sporting event in the United States. In 1991, the twenty most highly rated television broadcasts of all time included nine Super Bowl games. Between thirty-five and forty-two million households would tune their TV sets to the Super Bowl.[148] The sums of money that had to be paid for commercials during this championship game were beyond all comparison.

Basketball, Volleyball, and Beach Volleyball: Schools and the YMCA

Basketball ranks second in popularity, after football, in the United States. As it is played by both sexes, it has even overtaken baseball, which is very much a men's sport. Volleyball is lower down the list, at sixth place, mainly because the majority of players are women.

In concept and popularization basketball and volleyball were bound up with the YMCA, an organization based on social and religious principles. This relationship is essential to the global diffusion of these sports. The YMCA, which originated in London, was—like the Salvation Army—set up in the mid-nineteenth century to fulfill an educational role and to promote social and moral reforms. The YMCA set out to provide a "third environment"— besides home and school—for disadvantaged young people in the inner cities.[149] Although it targeted the lower classes, its clientele largely consisted of "stable young men from the clerical classes—bookmakers, stenographers, clerks, and salesmen—businessmen, a few skilled working men, and boys from the middle and upper income ranks."[150] In the latter half of the nineteenth century, the YMCA placed great emphasis on sport and other forms of physical exercise, under the influence of the Muscular Christianity movement, the aim being to mold the urban workers into "Christian gentlemen."[151]

Because of French and German influence, the YMCA's initial emphasis was squarely on gymnastic and acrobatic exercises. One historian of the YMCA movement even refers to an "Era of Gymnasium Building." While in 1869 the YMCA had no more than three indoor sports halls at its disposal, by 1887 it had 168. Canada and the United States together had a total of 466 YMCAs in 1901, with 444 indoor sports halls. Some YMCAs also had swimming pools. These facilities were often the first a town or village had ever had. With the proliferation of YMCA branches, increasing numbers of sports instructors

were needed. In 1887 there were only fifty-three "physical directors" for a total of 168 YMCA indoor sports halls.[152] The situation improved in 1885 with the establishment of the School for Christian Workers in Springfield, Massachusetts. This school, later renamed the International YMCA Training School and subsequently Springfield College, trained specialists who disseminated YMCA ideals and sports throughout the world (see chapters 4 and 5).

The success of the gymnastics movement in Germany and other European countries was linked to a strong spirit of rivalry between states and the accompanying rise of nationalism. The United States had little involvement with these conflicts, which meant that an important condition for the rise of this movement was lacking. It was becoming increasingly hard to interest the American youth in gymnastic exercises; football and track and field had far more appeal. As almost all the new sports were played outside, the exodus from the YMCA's gymnasiums was threatening their existence. The YMCA had invested huge sums in these "halls of health" and hence needed not only to widen its range of activities but also to devise alternative uses for the gymnasiums. The organization's director, Luther Gulick, therefore encouraged his staff to find indoor sports that could compete with the popular outdoor activities. This development is similar to the invention of "gymnastic games" such as handball in Germany as alternatives to English sports, although in the United States ideological differences were less prominent.[153]

BASKETBALL One of the men on Gulick's staff was James Naismith, the later inventor of basketball. Naismith had grown up in northern Canada and had studied theology at McGill University in Montreal, where he played rugby, which had been introduced under English influence. He did not miss a single match in seven years, in spite of the prevailing view that it was an unsuitable pastime for a theologist. "Football at that time was supposed to be a tool of the devil," he commented.[154] After graduating, Naismith went to the YMCA school at Springfield. He was deeply impressed by Gulick, whose personality and manner were totally unlike those of the elderly professors Naismith had known in Montreal. One of the places Gulick sent his new assistant was Martha's Vineyard College, where he was to see whether the Swedish gymnastics system taught there was worth adopting. Given Naismith's own sports background at McGill, however, he was not impressed; gymnastics had little appeal to him.[155] He experimented for a while with adaptations of American football, soccer, and lacrosse—the latter being popular in Canada—but neither he nor his students warmed to them.

He decided that the only solution was to devise a new sport for the gymnasium. In 1891 he formulated thirteen elementary rules that formed the basis

for what became the game of basketball. Dribbling and blocking opponents who were trying to score were initially forbidden. Some sneered at basketball as a "ladylike sport" or an "old man's game" because of the ban on physical contact.[156] Changes in the rules, which allowed more physical contact, soon gave the sport a different image.

By 1900 there was a national basketball championship and a professional basketball competition. This rapid development should be viewed in the context of urbanization, the growth of the youth movement, and the YMCA's support. The new sport was one of the enticements that the YMCA used to keep young men off the streets. *The Triangle,* one of the YMCA's periodicals, published the first basketball rules in 1892, and they were digested by tens of thousands of members. The new sport spread so rapidly that the YMCA was soon forced to set up a separate organization for it, as the staff were almost working around the clock arranging basketball activities.[157]

Many of those who had attended the YMCA Training School found jobs as sports instructors at high schools and colleges, where they included basketball in their curriculum. One was Charles Bernies, who set up the first college basketball team at Geneva College, Pennsylvania, in 1892. The first intercollegiate basketball competition was played three years later between Hamline College of St. Paul and the Minnesota State School of Agriculture. These were a far cry from the elite world of Yale, Harvard, Columbia, and Princeton, which played such an important role in the development of American football.[158] Rather than being spread through a trickle-down effect, basketball was deliberately propagated by the YMCA.

With the institutional backing of the YMCA and the encouragement of YMCA sports instructors working in schools, basketball grew to become the second most popular sport in the United States. As its rules had been devised with a view toward creating a responsible indoor sport, it was almost immediately classified as suitable for women. The sports instructor Senda Berenson introduced basketball as early as 1892 at Smith College in Northampton, Massachusetts, only fifteen miles from Naismith's Springfield gymnasium![159] However, she decided that in its existing form it was too strenuous and allowed too much physical contact, so she adapted the rules for women. Dividing the court into three sections, she invented a rule forbidding players from moving out of their sections. About half of the women nationwide continued to play by the men's rules, but Berenson's version was published as the official rules for women's basketball and dominated women's school and college teams until the early twentieth century.[160]

In 1989, 513,575 male basketball players were active at the interscholastic level, compared to 930,034 football players and 412,825 baseball players. With

the number of women playing basketball at 379,337, this was the most popular sport among women; only about a hundred women played football, and
around a thousand played baseball. This difference means that basketball had
a total of 892,912 players at the interscholastic level—almost as many as football and more than twice as many as baseball. Softball arose at the end of the
nineteenth century as a women's version of baseball; from 1926 onwards it
received YMCA support.

VOLLEYBALL Volleyball was developed in 1896 by W. G. Morgan, another
YMCA sports instructor. It was initially intended for somewhat older men
for whom basketball was too strenuous. It was later placed in a separate category from existing professional sports. Organizing major tournaments was
viewed as inappropriate; volleyball should remain "just a pleasant game," and
its sportization was not a priority. It was not until 1922 that the first YMCA
championships were held, using the court size and basic rules that apply today, including the three ball contacts within which the ball must be hit into
the opponents' section. And it was not until 1928 that an umbrella organization for volleyball was founded in the United States.[161]

Only in the last few decades has volleyball been professionalized and commercialized, the impetus coming from outside the United States. European
countries (Eastern and Western) took the lead in organizing major international tournaments. In the 1950s, influential IOC members from France and
Bulgaria wrote letters to Avery Brundage, their chairman, urging the inclusion of volleyball in the Olympic program. The campaign was successful:
men's and women's volleyball were both represented at the 1964 Tokyo
Games. This also improved the sport's image in the United States. In 1970, a
major university federation included volleyball in its sports program, and for
the first time universities awarded scholarships to talented volleyball players. Before that, most Americans had seen volleyball as a recreational activity for swimming pools, parks, schools, and beaches. Moreover, the absence
of physical contact gave it a reputation as a girls' sport. Women do in fact
make up the largest percentage of volleyball players—more so than in any
other major sport besides softball. In 1989 it was played by only 13,429 men,
as compared to 299,396 women.[162]

BEACH VOLLEYBALL Around 1950 a new form of volleyball played in California grew into a professionalized and commercialized sport called "beach
volleyball."[163] Its history is an interesting example of the new American sports
that have taken off internationally over the past few decades, such as surfing

and various new forms of exercising and skiing, all of which are associated with the lifestyles of young adults from the most glamorous sections of American society. The fashionable magazine *Sports Illustrated* once described beach volleyball as the perfect microcosm of the Californian lifestyle.

Beach volleyball developed from matches played on the sunny beaches of California and has since become an independent sport that bears little resemblance to its "mother" sport. Its different-sized playing field, different number of players, and the influence of sand and wind make it very different from volleyball. The first players were former top-ranking athletes from various branches of sport; they held the first championships in Sorento Beach in 1956.

The lack of beaches did not stop this Californian sport from spreading to inland areas of the United States. It had already been demonstrated in the 1970s that eighty tons of sand were enough to create a little "beach" good enough for the first World Indoor Two-Men Volleyball Championships. While beach volleyball became particularly popular in sun-drenched states such as Florida and Hawaii, inland tournaments in Scottsdale, Arizona, and Denver, Colorado, became classic events attracting huge crowds and many sponsors. In 1987 a beach volleyball tournament was even played in Calgary's ice hockey arena, with cash prizes totaling twenty-five thousand dollars. The sport's rapid spread was partly due to its association with the glitter and glamour of southern California—the home of world-famous sports and movie stars, musicians, and politicians—and the participation of big names from basketball and football. Since 1986, major tournaments have been broadcast on network television, and commercial interest has soared.

Beach volleyball seems set for a bright future. From March to October, scarcely a weekend goes by without a tournament somewhere in the United States. And in the winter months, South American countries such as Argentina and Brazil welcome this lucrative Californian sport to their shores. Australia too has expressed an interest.

The international volleyball federation (FIVB) views this development as a possible threat and is trying the defensive strategy of incorporating the new sport into its own organization. In 1987 it accepted an invitation to organize the first official FIVB Beach Volleyball World Championships on the beaches of Copacabana in Rio de Janeiro. A grand prix system with tournaments in countries including Italy, France, Spain, Argentina, Brazil, Australia, and Japan has been set up, and the FIVB has successfully campaigned for the inclusion of beach volleyball (under its own auspices, of course) as an Olympic sport, as of the games in Athens in 2004. It has already been included in the World Games, the alternative Olympiad for minor sports.

English Sports in the United States

Football, basketball, baseball, and volleyball are international sports developed in the United States. Ranked in terms of popularity, they occupy the first, second, fourth, and sixth positions, respectively. Popular sports in the United States also include several of English origin: track and field, golf, tennis, and soccer.[164]

Track and field has always had a great deal of support from schools and colleges and is mainly played by young people. This applies far less to the other three English sports. Tennis and golf became popular in the twentieth century, particularly in affluent white circles.[165] This was part of an international trend that will be discussed in more detail later on. Strangely enough, soccer developed as a women's alternative to American football. Whereas in Europe soccer is typically a men's sport in which women make up only a small percentage of players, in the United States there are 108,387 women players (as compared to 218,973 men). This puts it in fifth place in women's sports, after basketball, track and field, volleyball, and softball.[166] The U.S. men's soccer team scarcely figures internationally, whereas the women's team won the world title in 1999. However, soccer is growing in popularity among men in the United States, in spite of its poor organizational structure and an almost total lack of media coverage. On college campuses soccer has a soft but respectable image, certainly in comparison to the robust American football. It is an alternative chosen by young men who do not excel at football and baseball and by those who reject mass culture, in which these American sports are firmly anchored. More importantly, soccer's surge in popularity has to do with the influx of migrants from countries where it is the national sport. As Wagner remarks in connection with Ohio State University, soccer is being played more and more because of the increasing numbers of students of Asian origin. Outside of college campuses it is very popular among Latin American immigrants.[167] While American culture is acquiring a transnational character, soccer is acquiring the status of a global sport—including the United States.[168]

The Sportization of the Martial Arts:
Later Modernization in Japan

Japan too has evolved its own sports, which have attracted a large international following since the Second World War. At the end of the nineteenth century, the principles of Western sports started to be applied to various martial arts with a long history in Japan. They developed into judo, karate,

kendo, sumo, aikido, and kempo. The transformation of the martial arts can be explained in terms of wider-ranging changes in Japanese society and in the country's relations with the West.

In 1967 judo was the sixth most-popular sport in Japan; kendo was in eighth place.[169] This meant that Japanese sports accounted for 15 percent of the total number of participants in the country's fifteen most popular sports—more than in any other country for which sports rankings are known (see table 7). They are not only popular at home, however; like the English, German, and American sports discussed above, Japanese martial arts have acquired a fixed place in the national sports programs of other countries.

Western Sports in Japan

Japan came into contact with European soldiers and merchants as early as the sixteenth century. But fear of outside influence led the autocratic Tokugawa shogunate to drive out the foreigners—with the exception of a few Dutch and Chinese—and to restrict trade with them. The ensuing isolationist policy lasted until 1853, when an American military expedition forced the Japanese to open their ports to American merchant ships. Other Western countries were later admitted to certain ports, but their trading companies scarcely penetrated the country's interior to market their products.

The Japanese response to this American show of military force was an ambitious modernization program in the last quarter of the nineteenth century. Japan hoped that by catching up in economic and military terms, it would be able to ward off the threat of Western imperialism. Mutsuhito's ascent to the throne in 1867 ushered in the Meiji era, in which a unified state was forged and feudalism and the shogunate abolished. Modernization proceeded rapidly along Western lines and was imposed top-down by the authorities. Central government played a pioneering role in improving transportation and communications systems and introduced compulsory schooling, military service, and a national taxation system. Japan was transformed from a peasant nation into an industrial state. After 1870 its highly centralized industry underwent enormous growth, and an extensive rail and electricity network was developed. Japan's military victory over Russia in 1905 is evidence that it had already developed immense military power by the beginning of the twentieth century. This was the first time in many centuries that an Asian country had defeated a European power. Japan's military expansion also took other forms: in the last quarter of the nineteenth century it occupied several archipelagos in the surrounding seas.[170]

The Japanese elite were convinced of the need to import Western knowl-

edge if the country's autonomy was to be preserved. Students, entrepreneurs, and officials were sent abroad, and foreign specialists and advisers were invited to Japan. After a time, the foreigners could be replaced by Japanese employees who had acquired sufficient knowledge from their training abroad to take over management positions. Although the advent of Westerners and their lifestyle initially encountered considerable resistance, Western products and ideas were soon all the rage among the modernizing elite: in the last quarter of the nineteenth century the modern Japanese citizen was depicted as someone who wore Western clothes, carried an umbrella and wore a watch, ate beef, sent telegrams, and slept under sheets and blankets.[171]

This imported culture was primarily found among senior officials within the new professional bureaucracy and the managers of large companies, who were recruited from among the graduates of the new universities. The closer ties with the West also impacted on sport. Within a short time, the Japanese became acquainted with various Western sports. Between 1875 and 1889 Yokohama, Kobe, and Tokyo all acquired their own cricket, track and field, soccer, rowing, shooting, and baseball clubs.

Of all Western sports, it was particularly the American variants that caught on in Japan. Baseball actually became Japan's national sport, attracting eight times as many participants as soccer in 1967; volleyball ranked second in popularity, and basketball came in fifth. In no European country did the number of participants in American sports account for such a high proportion of the total (42 percent). Of the English sports, table tennis (third) and track and field (seventh) ranked highest. But the total number of participants in English sports as a percentage of the total of the "top fifteen" (23 percent) is less than that of any European country. The number of participants in sports of German origin is also very low in comparison to Europe (5 percent) (see table 7). How can this be explained?

In the first place, the Japanese elite, in its struggle for independence and progress, initially took the United States as its model.[172] When Japan emerged from its long period of isolationism, it was to the United States that the first major foreign missions traveled to invite experts to act as government advisers. Second, American influence was particularly strong in Japanese schools and colleges, which played a leading part in the diffusion of imported Western culture. While the majority of the English employees in Japan were engaged in building railway lines and ports and installing street lighting and communication lines, the American employees in Japan worked mainly in education. David Murray of Rutgers University was even Japan's chief inspector of education for a time. In this capacity he modeled Japanese education on American lines. The United States was also the most popular

destination for Japanese wanting to study abroad. Although the English were dominant in trade, through education American culture was more influential.[173] And in the third place, the English would not allow the Japanese to join their sports clubs; in Yokohama, the largest foreign settlement, the English Yokohama Athletic Club (YAC) denied Japanese people entry to its grounds. American teachers, however, did their utmost to encourage baseball (and later American YMCA missionaries did likewise with basketball and volleyball). In a textbook on Western sports written for Japanese pupils, the largest section was about baseball.[174] But to American teachers there would have been nothing remarkable about this emphasis: around 1880, baseball was the national sport of the United States; football was still in its infancy, and basketball and volleyball did not yet exist.

The influence of the United States on education created a foundation for the popularization of baseball. University students in Tokyo and the leading high schools were the first to take to baseball. Tokyo occupied roughly the same position in Japan as Harvard and Yale in the United States. Less prestigious universities soon emulated Tokyo's example, and secondary schools later followed suit.[175] Baseball became so popular that it was even referred to as "an obstacle to study."[176]

The adoption of baseball as Japan's national sport was not only an expression of American expansion in the Pacific region but equally an expression of Japanese resistance to their subordinate role. In a period of rising nationalism in Japan, the students of Ichiko defeated the YAC baseball team. With this victory they overturned the image of physical inferiority that Japanese intellectuals had helped to bolster. Additional victories soon followed: they won the return match against the YAC and defeated several teams of sailors from American ships. The national pride generated by these victories was felt throughout Japanese society in the ports. Whereas immigrants in the United States played baseball to appear more American, the Japanese adopted this sport to strengthen their own national identity.[177]

At the end of the nineteenth century, Japan started to orient itself more toward German development. The constitution and the education system were revised along Prussian lines. Moreover, around 1880 the Japanese government started sending the majority of students who were eligible to be educated overseas to Germany.[178] One of the elements of German ideology that was adopted in Japan was the emphasis on physical exercise to increase the strength of the nation. Among other things, this led to the introduction of daily gymnastics sessions at schools and businesses, with which almost every person in Japan is familiar today. Responses to questionnaires reveal that gymnastics or "stretching" is practiced more than any other form of

physical activity outside the framework of sports clubs.[179] Gymnastics is not popular as a club activity, however; it is seen more as a daily routine than as a sport.

Over the past few decades, the balance between English, American, and German sports has changed as a result of the popularization of tennis and golf. The new enthusiasm for these sports cannot be explained, however, in terms of the prestige of English products in the late nineteenth century. The growing number of Japanese tennis and golf players is a consequence of the high status these sports have acquired from their long association with the social elite at the international level. With the growth of prosperity in post-war Japan, they are increasingly played at commercial clubs; golf has become particularly popular among men of thirty to fifty years of age, while tennis appeals to both men and women of a younger age.[180]

The Sportization of Indigenous Martial Arts

Despite all this American, English, and German influence, Japan never set out to undergo Westernization. Western products were not adopted whole-sale but were adapted to Japanese culture. This also held true for the application of the sports model to indigenous martial arts.

From the end of the twelfth century onwards, the warrior lords were the ruling class in Japanese society. Their education and training included a variety of martial arts—with and without weapons—which were regulated and standardized, up to a point. The ordinary people had no such military pastimes: the shoguns and samurai had a monopoly on the lawful use of violence. Only sumo wrestling became a popular spectator sport.[181] The modernization of Japan dealt the deathblow to the warrior lords; in 1877 wearing a sword was officially banned. The old martial arts that these fighters had learned as ritualized combat practice became an anachronism overnight. They were revised into less violent sports, which attracted large numbers of participants.

The first of these major changes was effected by Jigoro Kano, who devised judo on the basis of jujitsu. Kano was born in 1860 on the coast near Kobe, one of the first ports opened to Western ships. In 1871 his family left for Tokyo, where he studied at the local university and took a doctorate. He was then appointed professor at the Gokohûin School, most of whose students came from the Japanese aristocracy. He undertook educational trips through Europe and the United States, where he learned more about the prevailing sports cultures.[182] Taking the model of a modern sport, he reformed the existing techniques of jujitsu. In 1882 he opened his own training school, or *dojo*,

for the new martial art, which he called *kodokan judo*. A tournament against Japan's largest jujitsu school, Totsuka, demonstrated the superiority of judo. Of the fifteen contests, his school won thirteen, with two remaining undecided. Partly as a result of this success, in 1900 Kano succeeded in having judo introduced as a compulsory subject at all Japanese schools.

This initial sportization of an indigenous martial art provoked a negative reaction from the old, traditionalist elite, but in the twentieth century judo became one of Japan's most popular sports. In 1967 the country had more than four hundred thousand judokas. Among the martial arts only kendo, with 330,000 participants, achieved a similar level of popularity. Kendo is a variant of traditional sword fighting, regulated according to the model of competitive sports. The Japanese authorities made this sport compulsory as well, though only at secondary school.[183] Later combat sports, such as karate and aikido, were not integrated into education and did not achieve such widespread popularity.

The sports model was also applied to the traditional practice of sumo wrestling. The demise of the warrior lords meant that the noble lords who had previously paid professional wrestlers to fight opponents from other courts vanished from the scene. But through sportization and commercialization, sumo was preserved as a form of professional wrestling. The result was a curious mix of a traditional Japanese martial art and the modern Western sports model. Sumo wrestling has far fewer participants than judo or kendo; it is largely geared toward the entertainment of spectators.

The successful sportization of judo and kendo encouraged numerous teachers at special schools of martial arts to adapt their techniques to the demands of sport. They invented new forms such as karate, aikido, and kempo. In the past few decades, this proliferation of martial arts has continued, in some cases through the sportization of old Asian martial arts and in others through new variants created from splits or combined forms. Karate, for instance, is a martial art originating from the island of Okinawa, which was fashioned into a sport in Japan by Funakoshi Gichin. He adopted several of the elements that had made judo into a competitive sport and demonstrated his karate techniques at jujitsu schools and university dojos. In the 1960s one of his pupils developed a variant of karate called taido. National and international organizations were set up and championships were organized for these and other new variants. In 1984, for instance, the World Taido Federation was set up, creating a new internationally organized and standardized combat sport.

Iaido, jodo, kyudo, naginata do, and kobudo are all products of the same dynamic trend. New combat sports are developed by pupils of older sports

or martial arts. This innovation is often interpreted as a painful rupture in the teacher-pupil relationship, but it can also be seen as the result of a sporting and above all commercial competitive struggle for pupils, money, and respect among martial arts specialists. This competition is a leitmotiv in the development of Eastern combat sports and still figures today in the competitive struggle between sports schools. This is why sports schools are constantly appropriating new combat sports and trying to legitimize them by seeking to link them to a certain attitude toward life (see chapter 4).

Japan was the center of the martial arts and took the lead in their sportization. But every Southeast Asian country had one or more indigenous martial arts. Using the tried and tested model first conceived by Jigoro Kano, some were fashioned into modern sports: certain wushu arts in China, bando in Burma, hapkido, tang su do, and tae kwon do in Korea, kalarippayat in India, pentjak silat in Indonesia, viet vo dao in Vietnam, and muay thai in Thailand. Several of these served in turn as a basis for new Japanese variants. After contests between Japanese karatekas and exponents of Thai combat sports, with the Japanese losing two out of three contests, the Japanese themselves developed kickboxing, a mixture of muay thai and karate. In the ongoing battle of styles, new combat sports are constantly emerging.

4. Sports in Europe: The Slow Erosion of European Dominance

The Rivalry between Two Sporting Traditions: The Basic Structure of the European Pattern of Sports until 1945

The closer the ties between countries and the more similar their social history, the more closely their national sporting patterns will resemble one another. Thus within each continent the popularity of sports displays a fair degree of uniformity—the rankings for European countries correspond to one another more closely than to those for countries in Africa, Asia, or America.

When we look at the fifteen most popular sports in European countries (see the appendix), a clear pattern emerges. In most countries, the fifteen sports with the most participants include the following eleven: soccer, track and field, tennis and table tennis (of English origin), gymnastics and handball (of German origin), volleyball and basketball (of U.S. origin), and swimming, skiing, and shooting (national origins unclear). Judo and to a lesser extent karate are the most popular Japanese sports. In addition, the top fifteen in several countries include sports that have evolved from traditional indigenous pastimes and are only played in certain regions of Europe.

The most striking common denominator in Europe is the unparalleled popularity of soccer. In Latin America and Africa, too, soccer attracts more participants than any other sport, but this is not the case in North America, Australia, New Zealand, or parts of Asia. The enthusiasm for gymnastics and handball is specific to Europe; almost nowhere else do they have such a large following. Cricket and rugby, however—in an intercontinental perspective—are only minor sports in Europe. This also applies to baseball and American football.

Before the Second World War this pattern was even more specifically European than it is today. English, German, and indigenous sports predominated; those from America and Japan did not figure at all. As Europe's international dominance decreased, this pattern faded a little. Non-European influences gained ground; American and Japanese sports arrived on the scene. Sporting trends in Europe reflect global developments today more than in the past.

Whatever the similarities between national sporting patterns in European countries, the tables also reveal noteworthy differences, which prove to be related to national origins of sports. Table 7 (pp. 68) combines the sports from the popularity rankings in the appendix into five clusters, each cluster being expressed as a percentage of the total number of participants in organized sports included in the appendix. The British cluster contains badminton, boxing, cricket, darts, hockey, golf, table tennis, tennis, and soccer. To assess German influence, sports related to the German gymnastics movement are combined with gymnastics itself: handball and shooting. The American cluster includes baseball, basketball, American football, softball, and volleyball, while the Japanese group consists of judo, karate, and kendo. The remaining sports, which are grouped together in the fifth cluster, do not originate from these four centers of diffusion: pétanque (similar to bowling) is from France, floorball (akin to indoor hockey) from Sweden, korfball from the Netherlands, camogie (a field sport played with stick and ball) from Ireland, and Australian football from Australia. This cluster also includes sports that cannot be traced to or associated with a single country of origin, such as skiing, aquatic sports/yachting, equestrian sports, bowling, wrestling, and weightlifting.

Sports stemming from the German tradition are relatively more popular in Germany, Switzerland, Austria, Sweden, Norway, Denmark, and former Yugoslavia. Sports with English roots, in contrast, are less popular in these countries. This striking discrepancy is a consequence of the rivalry between the English and German sporting traditions, which was felt in all countries that belonged to either sphere of influence.

Of English sports, soccer attracted the most players in all countries, with tennis occupying second place. Cricket, rowing, rugby, field hockey, golf, badminton, table tennis, and squash, however, were minor sports almost everywhere until 1945. Soccer's only real rival in a number of European countries was German gymnastics. In addition, handball and shooting—both associated with the gymnastics movement—were high up the charts. In every country the rise of modern sports meant the demise or marginalization of most indigenous pastimes. A few activities managed to survive against the odds, attracting a mass following in their "sportized" form.

English Sports: Popularization and Exclusivity

"We also have them in our [Dutch] dunes, those English, and yet I should not be inclined to rank them among the pinnacles of earthly hindrances—on the contrary. They would descend as winter set in, migrants by nature, identifiable from a great distance without any difficulty by . . . something that is indisputably English. Just fix your gaze upon those robust, overgrown fellows who have been formed by *sport*."[1] With this observation, Simon Gorter introduced the word "sport" (which means the same in Dutch as in English) into the Dutch language in 1866. Their pursuit of sports distinguished the English winter visitors from those around them;[2] sports did not yet exist in the Netherlands at this time. In an 1871 survey of Dutch pastimes, Jan ter Gouw named ice skating, yachting, and horse racing as the national pastimes. He also mentioned running and cycling races, billiards, archery, and rifle shooting. Traditional activities such as klootschieten, beugelen, kolven, and fives were also still popular at the regional level. Then there were violent games such as katknuppelen and palingtrekken. Strikingly, Ter Gouw's survey does not once mention the word "sport."[3] Yet only a quarter of a century later, soccer, cricket, track and field, field hockey, and tennis all had their own league competitions, clubs, and umbrella organizations.

The spread of these English sports was not an isolated phenomenon. In the mid-nineteenth century Britain towered over the other countries of Europe, economically, politically, and militarily. The country's early industrialization meant that by 1851 only 25 percent of the population were still working in agriculture. By contrast, in Belgium, the most industrialized and densely populated country of continental Europe at the time, this figure stood at 50 percent. Other competitors, such as France and Germany, were even further behind. Britain accounted for an estimated 50 percent of the total world production of iron, and 67 percent and 70 percent, respectively, of that of coal and steel. Britain was also the dominant world power. Its colonies stretched from Africa to South and Southeast Asia and from the South Pacific to North America and Australasia, and it had close commercial ties with many countries in South America.[4]

As a result of Britain's prestige as a major power, a general interest in the lifestyle of the British upper classes arose in other countries. A virtual "Anglomania" developed—a rage for English fashions, manners, customs, books, and sports.[5] Most affected were national elites with cosmopolitan attitudes, people who, because of their origins, profession, or education, were part of larger networks than the local and regional structures within which most people's lives were confined. They saw sports as highly respectable, prestigious activities with which they could distinguish themselves from the "com-

mon folk," who carried on pursuing indigenous pastimes for much longer. Their Anglo-Saxon orientation was not always based wholly on admiration; in some cases there was an ambivalent mix of resentment and awe. Some saw Britain as the trendsetter to be emulated and surpassed, while to others it was a rival evoking jealousy and fear. In either case, however, people respected the British and tried to learn from them [6]

English sports made their first entrance into continental Europe in centers of modernization: capitals, industrial and university cities, and major seaports. Cities such as Berlin, Brunswick, Bremen, and Heidelberg saw the founding of the first German clubs. In France, the first soccer and rugby clubs were started in the seaports, along the major highways linking Paris to Normandy, and in Paris itself, which had a large English colony. In Italy, sports started in Turin, Milan, Genoa, and Florence; the first Dutch centers were Haarlem, Amsterdam, The Hague, and Rotterdam. Russia's first sports clubs were founded in St. Petersburg and Moscow, followed by less highly industrialized areas such as the Ukraine.[7]

Who was responsible for the spread of these sports? In the first place, British people living abroad: entrepreneurs who set up business in Europe;[8] craftsmen employed to help countries catch up in industrial development;[9] students attending prestigious universities in continental Europe;[10] British residents of the French and Italian Riviera, who whiled away their time with sports;[11] diplomats and officials who organized matches while posted abroad;[12] and sailors who played their favorite game while on leave in foreign ports.[13] In the second place, there were two key groups in the adoptive countries themselves: wealthy entrepreneurs who made business trips to England[14] and young men from the upper classes with cosmopolitan attitudes.[15] International ties were common in these circles, and people regularly journeyed to Britain to study or to do business.[16]

The first people to play English sports in continental Europe were young— predominantly schoolboys and students.[17] Many prosperous youths were sent to be educated in the land of opportunity, which acquainted them with the most recent English school and university sports. One of the founding members of the Haarlem Football Club (HFC; founded in 1879) was Theodore Peltenburg, who had returned from Newton College two years earlier. In 1883 Pim Mulier persuaded the club to change its allegiance from rugby to Association Football, having learned the game at an English trade school. To have been to England was a feather in anyone's cap. According to the former mayor of Rotterdam, Drooglever Fortuyn, Mulier made a deep impression on his young listeners: "'He was a little older than we were, and had the aura of one who had been to England.'"[18]

To the cosmopolitan youth, English sports were superior to indigenous pastimes, which they thought outmoded and foolish. English sports represented modern times. This cultural appropriation had no objective basis, with "superior" activities supplanting "inferior" ones; it sprang from social processes in which power relations impacted on people's images of themselves and others. Nonetheless, English sports also had certain intrinsic advantages compared to existing amusements, in light of these young men's new experiences and opportunities. They existed in a standardized form, with regulations that could be adopted wholesale. This made it easier for people from different regions or countries to compete. Local pastimes, in contrast, varied greatly from one place to the next, which became more of a problem with the growth of national integration and scale expansion.

After 1870, members of social elites, especially those who owed their positions to (or expected to gain them from) social change, were more open-minded and embraced innovation more readily than preindustrial generations.[19] "We favored initiative," Mulier reflects, recalling "talks about literature and sociology" with innovators in the arts on the field where the HFC played its matches.[20] For writers and artists to be fanatical sportsmen was a sign of the times; increased physical activity was valued along with trends such as renewal, modernization, organization, an active disposition, and a wider outlook.

Once English sports had spread to other countries, their further development diverged. Until the 1930s cricket, rowing, rugby, field hockey, and golf were confined to small sections of the population. Tennis was played more widely, but soccer became the most popular English sport in all countries. Badminton, table tennis, and squash did not develop as organized competitive sports until the 1930s. These differences in popularization must be placed in the context of the prior social history of these sports in England. Whether or not a sport remained exclusive had to do with the social milieu in which it was played in Britain and that adopted it in Europe.[21] For every branch of sport Britain had already developed a full complement of traditions, symbols, and rules and regulations for clothing and play, which strongly determined the sport's social significance and the scope for preserving it for a select group. Because of this, class differences became part of the fabric of sports, and other countries could not import a sport without its history. Along with a barrage of technical features the new participants also inherited social characteristics, which each country reproduced in its own way. The new clubs adhered, sometimes in great detail, to the traditions that cleaved to the sport's roots.[22] We need only look at how teams posed for photographers to see that their whole attitude, not only their clothing, was modeled on British exam-

ples. The young men, with almost universal moustaches, adopt nearly identical poses: they sit or lie in a quasi-nonchalant style, decorated with laurels, radiating studied indifference and arrogance. This duplication of social traits sprang from the fact that the sport's proponents and first players abroad tended to belong to the same social group as participants in the country of origin and thus had a broadly similar outlook and ideology of sports. I shall illustrate this using examples from the Netherlands. Although these differ in certain respects from trends in other European countries, I believe that the Dutch developments reflect the workings of a more general mechanism.

SOCCER AND CRICKET In Europe, more people play soccer than any other sport. In several countries it has twice the number of participants as its nearest competitor. Only in Switzerland and Austria do any other sports—shooting and skiing—have a larger following.[23] Moreover, soccer has been commercialized and professionalized almost everywhere. It attracts tremendous public interest and is the dominant sport in the media. Cricket has an elitist image, however, and is played by no more than a few thousand people in each country of continental Europe. The public scarcely registers its existence, and to most people its rules are a complete mystery. John Arlott refers to the Netherlands as the most prominent European cricketing nation outside the United Kingdom. This only serves to emphasize the sport's dismal position elsewhere, since the Dutch Cricket Federation had seventy-three clubs in 1998, with a total membership of 7,180, as compared to 4,189 soccer clubs with over a million players. There is a world of difference, with virtually no overlap.

A hundred years ago all this was quite different. Many sports clubs then bore the initials "C. and F.C.," indicating a combination of cricket and Association Football; the same members played both games. The membership lists of the Netherlands Athletics and Soccer Federation and the Netherlands Cricket Federation partly overlapped. In 1890 the two federations even shared the same chairman.

This combination of cricket and soccer was not unusual at the end of the nineteenth century. In England it was common around 1880 at many private schools, universities, and clubs to play cricket from May to September and soccer the rest of the year. This led to the proliferation of Cricket and Football Clubs in continental Europe that seems so strange to us today: Austria and Italy each had their "Cricket and Football" clubs (in Vienna, Genoa, and Palermo), and in Berlin several clubs founded the German Football and Cricket Federation in 1891.

The Netherlands became conversant with the organized form of cricket in the 1870s and soccer in 1883.[24] Around 1900, soccer underwent rapid expansion, whereas the position of cricket stabilized and then declined slight-

ly. Soccer's popularization ushered in the demise of the combined "C. and F.C." clubs, as members opted for one of the two sports. Another consequence was the marginalization of cricket. This divergence of soccer and cricket was seen throughout continental Europe. But what caused it? The explanation should be sought in numerous subtle social factors that combined to keep cricket, but not soccer, a class-bound sport.

The decline of cricket in the Netherlands started in the 1890s. The pioneering clubs found their membership dwindling. The young men who had been among the first members of the cricket and "C. and F.C." clubs graduated and found jobs in which the pursuit of sport—in their minds—no longer had a place. Many moved away; some even went abroad. Cricket club memorial books are full of lamentations about the loss of members through emigration to the Dutch East Indies, making it impossible to form a team. The Leiden club Ajax lost entire teams to the Dutch East Indies.[25] The earliest soccer clubs faced similar problems. Of the 104 players who played in the Dutch national side before 1904, twenty-two later worked in the East Indies. Of the team that played for HFC in the early 1890s, more than half went to the East Indies. But soccer suffered far less than cricket, because this depletion was more than compensated for by the huge influx of new players.

Cricket's inability to attract young men had to do with the air of exclusivity it radiated. Those who had imported it to the Netherlands from England in the last quarter of the nineteenth century tended to come from aristocratic families and to be older than the first Dutch soccer players. They cultivated the elitist elements that so clearly distinguished cricket from soccer in England at this time. The English cricket tradition reeked of class distinctions, and the Dutch clubs simply adopted most of the numerous rules and regulations in which these were reflected, creating an image of cricketers as men who needed "comfortable or even luxurious facilities."[26]

In contrast, early Dutch soccer was a fairly chaotic and anarchistic affair. Some of the early matches were nothing more than two teams chasing a ball and trying to get it into the opposing team's goal. Players paid little heed to rules. To pass opponents, the HFC players initially made wily use of the trees that stood in parts of the field. Teams would sometimes consist of more than eleven men; Olympia Cricket and Football Club reportedly had "teams of 40 or 50 men on occasion, and none of them had the least understanding of the game."[27] This club even allowed nonmembers to take part in its soccer (but not cricket!) matches; it created a special section for "soccer members," who were entitled, "for the reasonable price of one guilder, to chase the ball for an entire season."[28] In short, no effort was made to make soccer exclusive, and the sport was not taken entirely seriously.

The young men who imported English sports to the Netherlands in the

last quarter of the nineteenth century came from the nobility. By contrast, the first soccer players tended to be middle-class; from the beginning, the nobles took less interest in soccer than in cricket. The aristocracy gravitated toward the exclusive culture of cricket clubs, which were preserving a microcosm of the world that was slipping away from them.[29]

In general, any gap in education and social position tends to sharpen class sensitivities.[30] In this case, the class consciousness was exacerbated by the age difference that existed between cricketers and soccer players from the beginning. While soccer attracted young schoolboys, the first cricketers were in the highest grades of secondary school. The average age of cricketers gradually increased, as fewer and fewer boys expressed an interest. Whereas the first clubs had been founded by boys aged fourteen to seventeen, in the early twentieth century the men in charge were in their twenties and thirties. Soccer players were younger. Pim Mulier had set up the first soccer club at the age of fourteen. Having procured a ball and a set of league rules, he started organizing games of rugby football in a local meadow; the better fields were already occupied by older boys playing cricket.[31] Other sports clubs were founded by young secondary school students as well. In Dordrecht, one active soccer club was set up in 1887 by four boys aged between nine and eleven.[32]

These age differences had two consequences. First, soccer players were less class conscious than cricketers and felt less of a need to keep their game exclusive, and second, even if they had wanted to, they had neither the skills nor the means to foster exclusivity. Demanding high fees would have been counterproductive. They were too young for top hats, cigars, gala evenings, and fashionable clubhouses. Cricketers, however, surrounded their game with an ethos of exclusivity. In 1884, when local high school girls presented the cricket club Red and White with a club banner, the event was celebrated with "bouquets, champagne lunches, and dinners." The founders of this club were then aged between seventeen and twenty. Two years later Red and White founded a junior section for aspiring cricketers aged twelve to sixteen. But at HFC's request this section was disbanded, and the young members joined the soccer club. It seems that the inauguration of a junior section clashed with general views concerning the age difference between players of the two sports. HFC was reproached for this policy, which deprived Red and White of "countless aspiring cricketers."[33]

Other social barriers were erected in cricket, for instance through a strict balloting system for new members. In 1888 a candidate for membership of Sparta, which started as a cricket club, had to be nominated by two members at a meeting that would then decide whether to admit him. All members were eligible to vote, and a four-fifths majority was required for admis-

sion. Utile Dulce had a rule stating that a member could be "kicked out" of the club by a general meeting if he became "a bone of contention and a liability for the club." Hercules stipulated when it was founded that only pupils of a gymnasium (the highest form of secondary school) could join.

Many cricket clubs also had a complicated system of fines and penalties and placed great emphasis on clothing. That the players of the otherwise highly respectable Hague Soccer Association did not yet have regulation clothing in 1889—they simply played in whatever old clothes were at hand— would have been unthinkable for a cricket club. Red and White prescribed the following dress: a cap with three red and white sections, a short-sleeved cotton jersey with red and white diagonal stripes, and white cotton trousers with red trimmings along the outer seams. According to a member of Hercules cricket club, the trousers must be "made of white flannel" and "spotlessly clean at the beginning of the game," another mark of the stylishness of the game of cricket.[34]

Cricket's cachet was in part a derivative of its Anglo-Saxon ethos. Rather than allowing this to fade, as in the case of soccer, the cricketers cultivated it. This heightened the game's appeal to the modernizing elites but held fewer attractions for lower social classes. In the aftermath of the Boer War in South Africa (in which the Dutch sympathized with their kinsmen, the Boers, in their struggle against Britain) this Anglophilia declined in the Netherlands, and the Anglo-Saxon aura surrounding cricket inhibited its popularization. By the time the game spread to other European countries, Britain's cricket culture was already steeped in tradition. This thoroughly British identity was far less responsive to change than relatively new sports such as soccer and field hockey. Only in countries that had undergone profound and enduring British influence could people come to see the sport as an element of their own culture. Continental Europe differed from India, Barbados, and Australia; cricket never became embedded in the national cultures of Europe, as it had in these countries.

In the Netherlands cricket retained its strong British identity. It appealed mainly to fervent Anglophiles in the social elite. They copied every detail of this identity: the special, influential role of the captain, the white jerseys, the length of matches, the communal lunches and teas, and the native terminology. Even today Dutch cricketers use the English terms and phrases "popping crease," "return crease," "pitch," "leg before wicket," "How's that?" "caught," "leg guards," "captain," "umpire," "fielder," "bowler," "batsman," "run out," "overs," and "leg-byes." In soccer, by contrast, Dutch terms were introduced for all the terms of the game. Translation was undesirable in cricket, and any effort to introduce it was immediately squashed.[35] After all, the

whole point of this sport was to move about "on English grounds, with all their English customs and English strategies . . . amid the beautiful Dutch landscape."[36]

In the 1880s English cricket teams visited the Netherlands almost every year, providing an excellent opportunity for Dutch players to observe and copy their behavior. "That superb display of striped jackets, costly, handsome, striking . . . the wonderful smell of the expensive pale yellow leather bags in which they keep their bats, gloves and leg guards. What a magnificent sight! It took our breath away. And then we had to have it all too, of course." Not all cricketers lived up to the image that the Dutch players had of them. One disillusioned writer wrote in horror after seeing Dalston Albert Cricket Club, "Great gods, what a choice bunch of disreputable ruffians!"[37] But, as is typical of all relations between the established and the outsiders, the Dutch molded their image of the English according to the trendsetters—a minority of the best.[38] These included the Blues of Newton College, who toured the Netherlands in 1888.

Instead of a small British minority that cherished cricket as an expression of their own identity, as in the United States (see chapter 3), in the Netherlands there was a small minority that expressed their admiration of British culture through the medium of cricket. The British customs and club regulations these fans reproduced were remote from the world of continental Europe. For instance, the tradition of "Gentlemen versus Players" was linked to the ways in which the English landed nobility had consorted with their subordinates in the seventeenth and eighteenth centuries. In the Netherlands and other European countries, cricket was introduced in the latter half of the nineteenth century, when these patterns of behavior were already an anachronism. The young Dutchmen wanted to keep cricket exclusive to distinguish themselves from those lower down the social scale. Their arsenal of regulations on clothing and etiquette and their fees and admission ballots were all calculated to restrict their sport to a select few.

* * *

In every country in Europe the popularization of soccer had characteristics peculiar to that country, but the same mechanism underlaid the difference in popularity between soccer and the other English sports everywhere. Since soccer's introduction to continental Europe coincided with its popularization and professionalization in Britain, it was less class-bound than other sports that were spreading to the continent around the same time. The young men from the upper crust of European society were less eager—and less able—to prevent the erosion of social barriers that had taken place in Brit-

ain. From the outset they saw soccer as a sport for the masses, unlike elitist activities such as cricket, rugby, field hockey, rowing, golf, and tennis. The ensuing difference in proprieties made soccer more accessible to the poorer classes. Soccer fulfilled the conditions for a "trickle-down" effect around 1900 more than any other English sport.

From the 1880s onward, British working men's soccer became familiar to all classes of European society, whether it was played by laborers employed in industrial regions, sailors on leave in seaports, or club teams touring the continent. Local workers and other spectators were soon fired with enthusiasm for this hitherto unknown sport. Low social status was no barrier to participation, and the elites soon resigned themselves to the increasing involvement of the poorer classes in the world of soccer; Britain had shown that this was a perfectly "normal" development.

There are several indications that the social decline of soccer started before 1900, in particular in the Rotterdam dockland area.[39] Here as in other parts of the world, the crews of British ships would play the game in their free time on the wharf or on pieces of unused land. Around 1885 several groups of Dutch boys played cricket and soccer in the neighborhoods and islands around the port of Rotterdam.[40] Here the first soccer players were probably from lower social classes than elsewhere. In any case it seems that teams from The Hague looked down on the Rotterdam players. There were only three clubs that they saw as their social equals.[41]

Rotterdam entrepreneurs succeeded in setting up a match between Sparta and an English team, Harwich and Parkstone F.C., the first against an English team in the Netherlands. By 1898 Sparta had played about another seven matches against English teams in Rotterdam and five in England. The Rotterdam fixtures attracted increasing numbers of spectators, and Sparta was one of the first Dutch clubs to start charging for admission. Cricketers, oarsmen, and hockey and tennis players saw the paying crowds of loud soccer spectators as the epitome of vulgarity. Although in 1888 twenty-five cents admission was charged for the cricket match between Utrecht and Haarlem for the Laming Cup, this practice was later condemned. After this, cricketers shrank from "profiting from the cruder instincts of the rabble. . . . No shouts of 'Wow!' and 'Come on, John!' are heard on their grounds. The baser passions are not aroused by cricket." The Dutch field hockey clubs, too, rejected admission fees on principle, emulating their British models.[42]

Soccer crowds included increasing numbers of working-class youths, many watching their first match. With their friends, fellow workers, neighbors, and relatives they set up numerous "wild" soccer teams, which competed casually at irregular hours. They frequently changed their teams' names and had

to do without clubhouses, regulation clothing, and a field of their own; they played in any field or vacant plot of land they could find. Many of these "wild" teams survived for only one or two years. They did not have the money to rent fields, buy materials, or travel.

In poor neighborhoods, "wild" soccer was a beginning; it was not a countermovement but a preliminary development. These teams hoped one day to be part of "real," organized soccer, with its framework of matches and league rules, and to have a field and clubhouse of their own. All these things were part of soccer, and it was only once you had attained them that you really counted—in the sense of being a league team and in terms of the status won for your group of friends, neighborhood, or town.[43] The first workers' soccer clubs were formed around 1900.

The members and officials of the first soccer clubs were not vehemently opposed to clubs being formed in the poorer sections of society nor to their inclusion in league matches. Even the first Dutch clubs were fairly easy-going about admitting new members and had less strict balloting rules than in other sports. When the Haarlem Football Club started playing serious matches, "no one was asked who his father was any more; the search was for sturdy fellows who ran well; they would be admitted regardless of their class, as long as they were decent, respectable lads."[44] Even so, a certain automatic selection existed anyway: only those with free time to spare, not to mention the money for clothing, membership fees, and travel expenses, could afford to play soccer. The average wage earned by workers in Haarlem at this time was barely three guilders (approximately $1.50), and child labor was still common.[45] The Dutch Football Federation did not interfere in the development of popular soccer. When the Amsterdam working-class soccer club Blue and White proposed that social class be disregarded when arranging matches, the proposal was adopted. Although the old elite clubs were not prepared to play against everyone, Cees Miermans concludes in his study of the rise of soccer in the Netherlands that working-class teams were not actively blocked.[46] Instead, the established clubs adopted a rather patronizing and indulgent attitude. "'They looked down on . . . those simple men with a certain compassion.'"[47]

In every town, Miermans assures us, soccer was played by an elite before it became an organized sport for the masses. Boys aged twelve to fifteen who contributed to the family income by taking jobs in factories and workshops would often set up soccer clubs, but they often had adult help. Elite clubs would sometimes help out by giving advice or lending them their field, or support might come from prominent citizens such as notaries, ministers, the local factory director, or the burgomaster.[48] There were also several educational institutions that might help, such as the Society Against Alcohol Abuse

and the Dutch Society for Physical Education.[49] Strikingly, soccer clubs often grew out of workers' clubs set up for a different hobby altogether, from cycling or shooting to the keeping of carrier pigeons. Nothing of this kind happened in the case of other English sports.[50]

Soccer spread at a different pace in town and countryside. When urban working-class youths were taking it up, having adopted it from the young elite, in rural regions the elite was just starting to play; the game was not taken over by lower social classes in rural areas until much later. The spread and popularization of soccer were bound up with the process of modernization. First, the rise of workers' clubs was only possible in a climate of social change. Working hours became shorter, salaries improved, and workers started to organize in numerous ways. One Utrecht working boys' soccer team called itself Strength in Unity.[51] Second, the geographical spread of the game was linked to the scale expansion and integration taking place in Dutch society. In 1919 there was not a single club in any town that lacked a railroad station.[52] How would a club in the remote district of Alblasserwaard, for example, have been able to take part in a league match? The villagers in this district had no direct link with the outside world until 1923, when they acquired a bus service.[53] After the first small-scale league matches had started up in the provinces of North and South Holland and a few isolated towns such as Deventer and Enschede, the game spread to the other provinces—starting with industrial centers such as Tilburg and major cities with institutes of higher education, such as Wageningen. Rural villages were always the last to have their own soccer team.

The more people played soccer, the less obvious the sport's English origins became. Every country evolved its own style of play and had its own soccer idols and sporting rivalries between cities and groups. English soccer terms passed out of use, and players, spectators, officials, journalists, and critics gave what had started as an English sport a distinctive Dutch flavor.[54] The best proof of appropriation was the first defeat of an English side, which Allen Guttmann describes as the "*rite de passage* of trouncing the English."[55] Such a win would be feted lyrically in the sports pages and given a prominent place in popular national soccer history. In the Netherlands this first victory is known as the "Battle of Houtrust." After suffering seven previous defeats at the hands of the English (by a total of forty-two goals to four), on March 24, 1913, the Dutch team managed to win by two to one. The sports commentators cheered in unison that Dutch soccer had finally come of age, defeating its English teachers, and had lived to see a day that the sportsmen of the Netherlands must never forget.[56] According to Jan Cottaar, it was even rumored that the ghost of the English star Vivian Woodward returned to

Houtrust in the evenings to wail and lament beside the field! That the van-
quished team were amateurs was irrelevant. The professionals were in a class
of their own—so much so as to be left out of consideration. Every country's
team set its sights on this rite of passage and celebrated it exuberantly when
it came. And not only in soccer. The Australian defeat of England's cricket
team on August 29, 1882, belongs in the same category, as does the Japanese
baseball victory against the American team by the Yokohama Athletic Club,
which made May 23, 1896, into an unforgettable date in Japanese sporting
history.[57]

A good soccer record was increasingly seen as a measure of national and
regional development. The importance attached to national and international
soccer fixtures promoted the democratization of the sport. The desire to
defeat another city's team or another country's national side meant that
quality of play overruled all considerations of background and class. As Peppard notes in reference to Russia, official soccer clubs even recruited players
from the disreputable "wild" teams if they displayed great promise.[58]

After the First World War, organized soccer underwent explosive growth
in all layers of the population as the game became the nation's most popular sport. In Germany the number of soccer club players grew from 13,644 in
1905 to 82,326 in 1910, 467,962 in 1920, and 986,046 in 1930. The number of
French teams quadrupled between 1920 and 1925, and in Russia the number
of registered soccer players soared from a few thousand in 1915 to 250,000 in
1928. As for the Netherlands, the numbers grew from a few thousand in 1904
to approximately ten thousand in 1914, fifty thousand in 1919, and a hundred
thousand in 1930.[59]

There were two primary reasons for this accelerated growth. First, soccer
benefited from the large-scale mobilization of the First World War. The army
had the effect of promoting modernization and national integration: by
bringing together young men from all parts of the country, it made urban
culture accessible to country people, to whom soccer was a new experience.
Following demobilization they started what were often the first soccer teams
in their district. Even in the Netherlands, which remained neutral, mobilization accelerated the national spread of soccer—more so than that of other sports, as the vast majority of soldiers came from the petit bourgeoisie or
working classes, and the small proportion of sports club members among
them almost all played soccer.[60]

In the second place, workers were earning more and working shorter
hours, which made it easier for them to become involved in sports. In 1919
the eight-hour working day was introduced in the Netherlands, and free
Saturday afternoons became the rule in most cities. Although wages slumped

in 1922, ordinary people's real income revived between 1925 and 1930.[61] The sports to profit most from these trends, naturally enough, were those that were accessible to workers: soccer, gymnastics, ice skating, and korfball.

The increasing dominance of the petit bourgeoisie and working classes in soccer is reflected by the changing social origins of the players for the Netherlands' national side. Cees Miermans, who distinguished three social classes, found that between 1894 and 1905, 96 percent of these national players came from the highest, 3 percent from the middle, and 1 percent from the lowest class; between 1906 and 1918, these figures were 81 percent, 15 percent, and 4 percent, respectively; from 1919 through 1929 they were 29 percent, 18 percent, and 53 percent, respectively; and from 1930 through 1940 they were 14 percent, 15 percent, and 71 percent, respectively.[62]

With the rise of workingmen's soccer, a class struggle ensued. The new workers' clubs did not greatly disrupt existing relations initially. Sometimes they were even welcomed, with slogans such as "'there is no such thing as class on the football pitch.'"[63] But as the numerical balance shifted in favor of the workers' clubs, resistance grew. Elites were averse to competing against people they would shun in everyday life. Some took steps to protect their clubs, while others abandoned soccer and took up something else. In these circles only young schoolboys continued to set up soccer clubs; they put their soccer days behind them when they grew up. Men from lower classes, however, would often carry on playing.[64]

While some elite clubs were looking for alternatives to soccer, others tried to stem this exodus. In an attempt to promote the sport among the wealthier classes, the Dutch Corinthians club was set up, named after an English amateur "old boys" club that held its own in a world of professionals for many years. Its aims were to preserve and strictly monitor amateurism, to reintroduce combined cricket/soccer clubs, to forbid transfers without the permission of the club's committee, and to extend powers to expel members. They had little success. First, the old elite clubs no longer had the power to win support for their views. Second, the Corinthians' actions had a polarizing effect; to the workers' clubs, their name was like a red flag to a bull.[65]

There was no way back to the "good old days." Anyone wanting a socially exclusive atmosphere had to find a sport where this ethos had been preserved, such as field hockey, tennis, rugby, and cricket. Cricket indeed gained a new lease on life, with the number of teams affiliated with the federation doubling between 1924 and 1929[66] and play reviving in the old "cricket and soccer" clubs. In Deventer, Utile Dulce made plans to take up "bats and balls" again. Sparta joined in the national league again after cricket had been put on the back burner since 1897, and Quick in The Hague also renewed its

enthusiasm for cricket. The Enschede cricket club Princess Wilhelmina, many of whose members were from old textile manufacturing families, had also played soccer after the merger with Enschede Football Club in the late 1890s but eventually had more success with hockey and cricket. The cricketers of Princess Wilhelmina and Quick were known for their fierce opposition to soccer.[67] The fact that they did not play soccer was part of their identity as cricketers. Attitudes to the "sport of the common people" became increasingly arrogant and condescending. Hercules's memorial book (written in 1932) commented that the Herculeans' prime interest was rightly not in "the sweaty pursuit of football."[68] Cricketers contrasted the "yelling" on the soccer field with the "summer bliss of white clothes" and "the aristocratic serenity of the cricket grounds."[69] Cricket's esoteric and exclusive qualities acquired added value. "Then we become part of the precious union of summer and cricket, we sense that we are among the initiated! Perhaps this feeling is reinforced by the small number of players in the Netherlands. To belong to this group, and therefore to share responsibility for it, makes us a little proud, but above all grateful for this privilege."[70]

Rugby, field hockey, and tennis also benefited from the growing aversion to soccer among the young elite. The numbers involved were small, however, as the vast majority of the Dutch population belonged to the petit bourgeoisie and working classes. And since they played soccer and scarcely any of the other English sports, for the reasons outlined above, soccer attracted by far the most participants of any sport in the period between the wars.

ROWING, RUGBY, AND FIELD HOCKEY In the popularity rankings of almost all the countries of continental Europe, rowing, rugby, and field hockey do not figure in the top fifteen sports. The explanation is much the same as with cricket; their prior history in England influenced their further development in continental Europe. Since the first oarsmen and rugby and hockey players outside the British Isles belonged to roughly the same social groups as their British counterparts, they tried to imitate the class-conscious elitism associated with these sports. Each of the three sports also had its own social history; each had evolved its own customs and codes, which affected the social makeup of the groups that adopted it in other countries and determined the form it took there.

The development of continental rowing was virtually a repeat of events in England. In the mid-nineteenth century the Royal Netherlands Yachting Club held rowing races based on the old English patronage system. Boats were not manned by club members but by specially hired fishermen and eel sellers. Rowing clubs such as De Maas and De Hoop gave apprentice sailors row-

ing lessons and entered the teams of sailors they trained in races. The sailors were permitted to keep two-thirds of their prize money. Three decades later, students in several university cities founded rowing clubs of an entirely different order. They adopted the exclusive English amateur rules and used the special English racing boats. These called for an entirely different technique than the sloop boats. Even if workers managed to acquire this technique, gaining admission to the Dutch Rowing Federation was out of the question for them. Elsewhere, too, rowing became associated with the values and vicissitudes of student fraternity life. Its popularity waxed and waned with the fraternities' fortunes.[71]

The first rugby clubs, too, recruited their members primarily from the student world. For decades students made up only a tiny proportion of society, and rowing and rugby clubs attracted only a fraction of this minority. These sports developed around a culture of affluent young men whose combination of rough and elitist behavior distanced them from the lifestyles and sports of schoolboys, men from lower social classes, and the older middle-class establishment. As students constituted a fairly separate community within society for decades, rowing and rugby were scarcely practiced outside of student campuses and fraternities. As a result, both are decidedly minor sports.

Given their close relationship, the sharp contrast between the relative unpopularity of rugby and the huge popularity of soccer is particularly striking. In Finland the smallest sports federation in 1985 was rugby, with a hundred members, while the largest was the soccer federation, with 365,000. For Bulgaria, the figures for 1980 were 604 and 168,318, respectively. In Germany the 8,558 rugby players in 1998 bore no comparison to the 6.2 million soccer players. The same contrast is seen in the Netherlands, with 6,407 rugby players as opposed to over a million soccer players. Before 1930 the Netherlands never had more than two hundred rugby players.

Rugby was seen in continental Europe as soccer's rough younger brother, with all the working-class connotations this implied. This meant that rugby had limited appeal to those seeking a mode of distinction. In countries where people knew little about its background (that is, outside Britain, Australia, and New Zealand) rugby was doomed to remain a small elite sport. The sport's small following was eager to nip any sign of popularization in the bud, while at the same time rugby was too rough to arouse much enthusiasm among the middle classes. It became a robust sport that failed to attract widespread interest among the lower social classes. Rugby's two faces—rough yet elitist—meant that it profited far less than hockey and tennis in the 1920s and 1930s from the exodus of the elite from popularized soccer, which had lost

its charm and distinction for them. Even the expansion of the middle classes in the 1960s and 1970s, which boosted several relatively exclusive sports,
did not help rugby.

Precisely because of their sport's roughness, rugby players were at pains
to emphasize that only men with good manners could play. Otherwise, its
social value would have soon dwindled. This risk was underscored by George
de Saint-Clair in his little book *Football (Rugby)*. According to him, most
accidents happened in the mining districts in the north of England, where
the rough men did not behave properly. If rugby were confined to men of
good breeding, it would not be dangerous at all.[72] Parents, teachers, and others
involved in boys' upbringing worried most about the sport's dangers to life
and limb. Pressured by parents, the boys of the Haarlem Football Club
switched from rugby to soccer in 1883. "The fathers did not understand,
thought five or six torn jerseys each winter at odds with the times. . . . Hence
rugby was doomed and in 1883 we changed over to 'association.' Occasionally we would still have a wonderfully wild tussle with a left-over rugby ball,
until it too was quite dead."[73] They were too young to force a different decision. In Russia a rugby match was stopped in 1886 for fear that the fierce game
would end in a riot.[74] Students were generally better able to evade this kind
of surveillance. The combination of roughness and elitism enabled them to
defy others' standards of decorum while distinguishing themselves from their
social inferiors.

France is the exception to this rule. Rugby is the country's eighth sport,
with 217,000 players; although soccer's 1.7 million is many times more, rugby's popularity in France is nonetheless anomalous. Outside Britain and Ireland this is the only country in Europe where the number of rugby players
exceeds 5 percent of the number who play soccer. This is attributable to a
variety of factors, which illustrate that even "chance" may conceal social
patterns that are anything but chance. In the first place, the popularization
of rugby in France was fostered by the dominance of Paris and its lycées.
Second, the large British colony in the Bordeaux wine region played a key
role.

Students in Paris used rugby more determinedly than their peers elsewhere
to distance themselves from soccer. This may have been related to the virtual absence of "cricket and football" clubs in France. Rugby rather than cricket
became the opposite of soccer. Boys from the French elite who belonged to
Parisian clubs such as the Racing Club de France and Stade Français initially played some soccer but were more active in rugby, rowing, and track and
field. They thought soccer unsuitable because of the working-class ethos that
was just then starting to cling to the sport in England. Richard Holt has de-

scribed the exclusivity of these two clubs. Exorbitant fees erected high barriers and automatically excluded large sections of the population. Furthermore, aspiring members had to be nominated. Considerable time and money was lavished on stylizing a distinctive culture. The difference in presentation between these clubs and the first soccer clubs, for instance in their clubhouse interiors, was highly conspicuous. Although the Racing Club de France and Stade Français are extreme examples, they underscore how differently the original players from the French elite perceived soccer and rugby. Soccer, defiled as it was by its professionalization in England, was too vulgar for them. Rugby, however, had an air of distinction.[75]

Paris has set the tone in French cultural life ever since the centralization of the state's monopoly on force and taxation.[76] There is probably no other country in Europe where one city has such an overpowering influence on public life. The sports played by elite Parisian students at prestigious clubs, such as the Racing Club de France and Stade Français, set a crucial example to the sons of the provincial bourgeoisie. At the end of the 1890s rugby had entered the lycées and universities in the more peripheral regions of France, where Parisian trends were followed avidly.[77] The aura of the Parisian lycées weighed more heavily in these young people's choice of sport than the fear that their status would be undermined in their home towns by the roughness associated with rugby.

The second significant factor in the spread of rugby was the large community of British expatriates in the regions of Bordeaux, Bayonne, Biarritz, and Pau. Some were involved in the wine trade, while others lived in colonies of affluent retirees. Their presence generated close ties between English public schools and French lycées. French pupils from Pau learned to play rugby when visiting an elite school across the channel, and prominent citizens helped to bring the sport to their own rural areas.[78] The response was such that the elite withdrew after a while, and the accent in rugby shifted to the provincial petit bourgeoisie.[79]

In 1906 soccer was still described in France as a new arrival in which elite clubs took little interest. It was not until the 1920s, with the increasing participation of workers in sport, that rugby was overtaken by soccer. In 1920 France had more than a thousand rugby clubs—about as many as soccer at the end of the First World War. But by 1925 soccer had four thousand clubs. Soccer grew fastest in the industrial centers, while rugby dominated in the industrially underdeveloped southwest.

Field hockey remained a minor sport in most of Europe, as it had in England. Male hockey players detested popularization in any form; they hardly ever organized league matches and shunned publicity. International fixtures

came later and were less frequent in hockey than in other sports. Given the dearth of propaganda and the absence of high-profile tournaments, few young European men were even aware of this sport's existence. For decades European hockey was confined to a few small enclaves. This was also true of the Netherlands, although the country has more than 120,000 hockey players today. In the late 1920s there were fewer than a thousand male hockey players in the Netherlands. Like their English counterparts, they shunned publicity and were eager to preserve their sport's exclusivity. "Our sport is not popular, and many of us are glad of it. No hockey man longs for grandstands with spectators and everything that goes with it."[80] The Dutch Hockey and Bandy Federation (NHBB) refused to admit certain clubs because "the caliber of their members" failed to meet its standards. Clubs also held admission ballots. According to the regulations of the Hague Mixed Hockey Club, any candidate whose membership was opposed by one-third of those entitled to vote would be rejected. Utrecht's Kampong club had its own informal way of vetting prospective members: in the 1930s any woman wanting to join would receive a home visit.[81] Club culture was itself an effective deterrent to outsiders. Working-class teens who did not attend a superior secondary school would not even think of joining; there was a yawning gap between their world and that of a hockey club. Not that they generally had much choice in the matter: "There are introductory days for groups, and members obviously bring their friends along. Those who fall outside this circle would perhaps not feel at home here," stated the club chairman of Le Jeune in 1981, explaining the continuing elitist character of the HOC-Gazellen Combinatie (HGC).[82]

Field hockey was particularly conspicuous at girls' schools. Relations with the independent women hockey players in England stimulated Dutch women to set up a separate hockey federation, which survived until 1941.[83] In 1927 it had almost as many affiliated clubs as the men's counterpart organization. But in the late 1920s there were still fewer than two thousand hockey players of either sex in the Netherlands, placing the sport lower on the scale than rowing or golf, for instance. After the Second World War, however, hockey soared to popularity in the Netherlands, although a steady growth had started in the decade before the war. The women's hockey federation grew from twenty-seven clubs in 1927 to 150 in 1947. In 1932 almost 1,550 women players were affiliated with the federation; in 1941 there were 6,403. The men's hockey federation grew from twenty-three clubs in 1925 to more than a hundred in 1938. In 1941, when the German occupying forces compelled the hockey federations to merge, the resulting organization numbered 8,603 men hockey players.[84]

Several factors contributed to this growth. First, field hockey benefited more than any other sport from the strong reaction of elite groups to the increased participation of workers in sport and the associated rise of the Corinthian movement in the latter half of the 1920s. Hockey was a respectable team sport that was still played on a small scale by young people from respectable backgrounds. This made it an attractive alternative to the increasingly popular soccer, which was subject to the following "unfortunate" phenomenon: "Its popularity is growing in all sections of the population except for intellectual and affluent circles. . . . It is in these very circles that hockey is providing increasingly fierce competition, and for this, soccer itself is to blame. Countless fathers, who loved soccer and were once prominent players, have encouraged their sons to play hockey instead. . . . We are forced to conclude that a worrying roughness has taken hold in soccer, the atmosphere surrounding the games is often not pure. . . . It should therefore be seen rather as a silent protest that the said circles are adopting a negative approach."[85]

The urge to practice a distinctive sport became apparent around 1925. Between 1904 and 1925, Hilversum's Mixed Hockey Club had about ninety members, but it then soared to a membership of 220 in 1933.[86] The Utrecht club Kampong played both cricket and soccer in the early twentieth century, but around 1927 it concluded that "soccer no longer has the same status as it once had in the circles from which Kampong recruits its members."[87]

This trend may have been reinforced by the attention devoted to field hockey during the 1928 Olympic Games. The success at these games—held for the first time in the Netherlands (Amsterdam)—released Dutch hockey from its international isolation. For most of the thirty thousand spectators the final against India was the first hockey match they had ever attended. Hockey also received unprecedented press coverage at these games.[88] It soon appeared in provincial areas: in the town of Venlo, fifteen young people who had watched the Olympic hockey final set up their own club.[89] The wave of enthusiasm was partly a matter of timing. The Netherlands' silver medal came in the late 1920s, when small elite sports were already booming; the Olympics helped to make hockey better known among the general public. But the underlying cause of hockey's growing popularity was its social background in combination with the exodus of status-conscious sportsmen from soccer.

Many high schools placed field hockey on their sports programs in this period, and several students' clubs were founded, such as Sport at School in The Hague, which would eventually give birth to the HGC.[90] This laid the foundation for the rapid growth of the hockey federation between 1960 and 1980 (see below). Hockey had already been introduced at several prestigious schools. The Lyceum in The Hague, for instance—once known as "the Eton

of the Netherlands"—had been playing hockey at the Lyceum Club since the early twentieth century.[91] Teachers, parents, and students at other high schools took heed of these activities, noting that hockey was a "respectable" alternative team sport. As it had always been seen as suitable for women, it drew additional benefit from the spread to high schools. Before the war, female hockey players accounted for the difference in numbers of participants between rowing and hockey. Hockey's popularity among high school students compelled the federation to set up separate youth leagues for girls and boys in 1932. Still, it was long regarded as an elite sport, and hockey clubs were found in clusters in the wealthier parts of the Netherlands.

TENNIS AND GOLF　In most of Western Europe tennis is one of the top four sports. This is mainly the outcome of a boom in the 1960s and 1970s, but tennis ranked higher than any other English sport aside from soccer in many European countries even earlier. In percentage terms, the fastest growing sport since 1980 is golf. This is a noteworthy trend, since golf—unlike tennis—used to attract a limited number of devotees. This section will look at the period up to 1945; the rapid growth of the two sports will be discussed below.

Until about 1920, golf and tennis monopolized the preferences of a specific group of sports enthusiasts: adults with high social status. In affluent circles they were both seen for decades as the final destination in people's "sporting careers."[92] Social class was a crucial factor here. Working-class boys would start by playing soccer, and upon reaching maturity they either carried on with soccer or switched to an activity like fishing. Boys from higher social classes also often played soccer in their youth, but once they went to university they took up field hockey, rugby, or rowing. And after graduating, they would bid farewell to these sports and focus on tennis or golf. Women from elite circles went from gymnastics to hockey, and then from hockey to tennis. Other sports, such as badminton, table tennis, and squash, were not possible alternatives until the 1930s because of their late sportization.

The image of tennis and golf as suitable sports for the well-to-do, even in later years, was a major factor in their appeal. Their social status corresponded to these people's social position and aspirations; the physical effort they required did not exceed accepted standards of decency for their class. Tennis and golf were a far cry from boys jostling one another for possession; they involved impeccably dressed ladies and gentlemen hitting a ball with a combination of grace and fervor. The ladies wore long skirts and hats, while the gentlemen appeared in long trousers and shirts with collars and ties.[93] Furthermore, as in England, the secluded clubhouses and grounds offered op-

portunities for the sexes to mingle.[94] While the annual ball held by the cricket club Red and White caused consternation in Haarlem, contact between boys and girls at the tennis club was far less problematic, "provided both were carrying rackets, for the sake of decorum."[95]

In its early years, tennis was played on the country estates of upper-class gentlemen. Many of the initiatives stemmed from English expatriates; they founded two Parisian clubs in the late 1870s: the Tennis Club de Dinard and the Decimal Club de Paris. They also orchestrated the first tennis tournaments and clubs in Germany, in the fashionable resorts Bad Homburg and Baden-Baden, and the first tennis club in Italy, the Bordighera Lawn Tennis Club on the Riviera. People of the same social class as these English players were likeliest to be initiated into tennis and golf—some directly but most indirectly, through friends and acquaintances of the English. The German tennis pioneer Carl August von der Meden had lived near Wimbledon in England from 1868 to 1881. Count Enrico Cigala provided the impetus for the first tennis club founded by and for Italians. His mother was English, and he often stayed in London, where he learned to play tennis. He spread his enthusiasm for the game in his circle of friends in Turin, which included several counts, marquises, and country gentlemen, and encouraged them to join his club.[96]

As a memorial book of one of the oldest clubs in the Netherlands tells us, tennis was initially played "in the seclusion of a small community with its own code of conduct and corresponding manners." This community consisted of prominent citizens, who in the earliest years included a remarkable number of aristocrats.[97] In Germany, Kaiser Wilhelm took tennis lessons. At the annual tournament at Bad Homburg, special seats were always reserved for royal visitors. Count Voss, the first great German tennis champion, came from an old aristocratic family. He wintered on the Riviera, and his summer diversions included tennis, shooting, and driving an automobile. Several Russian tsars played tennis, and they were emulated by the landed nobility and wealthy upper middle classes. The first tennis courts in Slovakia were built in the park of the Grasalkovič palace in Bratislava in 1880. Here, as elsewhere, tennis was the virtually exclusive province of the well-to-do, although the ballboys and ballgirls, who were often from humbler backgrounds, were allowed to play when the courts were free. Between the First and Second World War the Kozeluh brothers took advantage of this opportunity to develop into professional top-class tennis players.[98]

Golf, however, was just a little bit classier. Whereas tennis was also played by the middle classes, golf remained the preserve of the aristocracy and the extremely wealthy for far longer. This was partly because of the amount of

land it required. Large-scale land ownership was largely confined to the nobility, and the first golf players were mainly aristocrats and their immediate
circle. At the end of the nineteenth century the first golf championships in
the Netherlands, between the clubs of Clingendaal and Doorn, were won by
Baron Vincent van Tuyll; he later passed the title to the *jonkheer* Raymond
Schuurbecque Boeye. The first woman champion was of blue blood also—
Baroness Van Brienen, in 1906.[99] All the early golf courses in the Netherlands
were in wealthy areas; tennis clubs were more evenly spread around the country. Furthermore, tennis had more appeal to young people. Like rowing and
hockey, it was popular among gymnasium and university students. One of
the Netherlands' oldest clubs, Sphaerinda in Utrecht, was founded by students in the highest grades of the local gymnasium, who prolonged it in their
university years.[100] Nothing of this kind happened in golf.

The large expanse of land needed to play golf impeded the spread of the
sport in continental Europe. The same factor made it harder to turn golf into
a profitable enterprise. The popularization of tennis was boosted by entrepreneurs who built commercial tennis courts, making it possible to play
outside established clubs and breaking the latter's monopoly. In 1947 these
tennis courts had some twenty thousand members, as opposed to about
twenty-five thousand in clubs. Golf courses, however, remained in private
hands; exorbitant fees were charged to cover the costs, excluding "undesirable elements" from the sport.

Certain tennis clubs, too, charged fees that would automatically exclude
the majority; some charged more than thirty guilders a year at the beginning
of 1900. But the social exclusivity of golf and tennis was more a matter of
culture than money. Even clubs with relatively low membership fees scarcely attracted people from outside the aristocracy and the well-to-do upper
middle class. The Dutch Lawn Tennis Federation deliberately kept individual contributions low (one guilder) "so as to deter no one," but this did not
stop people from the working and lower middle classes from deciding that
tennis was "not for our sort."[101] As the son of a Tilburg cloth worker (born
in 1912) put it, in his world tennis and hockey were "unmentionable" and "too
highbrow." He would play soccer, like his friends and elder brothers.[102] He
had probably never even heard of golf. Most people scarcely knew anyone
who played this sport and had neither the money to play nor any acquaintances who could nominate them. Even if they had set out to gain access to
the golf courses, bridging the chasm between the world of ordinary people
and the ambience of golfing circles would have been a formidable task. All
these factors kept golf a minor sport until long after the Second World War.
In the first ten years after the founding of the Dutch Golf Federation (NGF)

in 1914, the number of affiliated clubs grew from four to seven. In the following decade, in which several clubs benefited from the fashion for distinctive sports, the number increased to sixteen, where it remained from 1935 until 1954. In 1977, twenty-four clubs were affiliated with the NGF; between 1935 and 1977 the membership of these clubs grew from 2,658 to 9,632. However, this fourfold increase took place within a climate in which the total number of sports participants increased sixfold. After 1977 the sport underwent explosive growth, and in the early 1990s the NGF had more than forty thousand members; by 1998 the membership had passed the one hundred thousand mark (see below).

TABLE TENNIS, BADMINTON, AND SQUASH Tennis was preeminently the sport of the well-to-do bourgeoisie, and before 1920 it scarcely had any competition from the other English middle-class sports. Golf was confined to noblemen and the fabulously wealthy. Badminton, table tennis, and squash scarcely profited from Britain's international prestige. When the British empire was at its peak in the latter half of the nineteenth century, none of these three sports yet existed in a standardized form. So the closer ties between the British and other Europeans did not help to spread them until the 1930s, and only after the Second World War did their popularity soar.

Before 1945 few people were familiar with squash. It did not fully develop in England until the late 1920s, and the first squash clubs in other European countries date from the subsequent decade. The handful of courts that existed in these early days were mainly on the premises of multinational companies, which intended them as recreational facilities for senior managers.[103] Squash only achieved widespread popularity in recent times.

Badminton and table tennis did not develop into international sports until the latter half of the twentieth century either. Before the Second World War, the All England Badminton Championships were virtually an all-English affair! One of the first Dutch clubs, the well-known Duinwijck, was founded as late as 1948. It grew out of Bloemendaal tennis club members' desire for a winter alternative.[104] Table tennis enjoyed a brief vogue among the well-to-do at the beginning of the twentieth century. Newspapers in several countries reported what the French referred to as "un nouveau jeu à la mode en Angleterre: Le Ping-Pong."[105] In Germany this trend led to the establishment of a table tennis club by members of Berlin's Lawn Tennis Club. There as in England, however, this was a brief vogue; soon table tennis was no more than a way of having fun. In Hungary and Germany it survived as a league sport, but it did not gain wider support until its standardization had received a fresh impulse in Britain. At the same time, the British table tennis federation took

initiatives to encourage internationalization, and soon national organizations were set up in Hungary, Czechoslovakia, Germany, Austria, and Sweden, from which the first European championships emerged in 1926.[106]

But even after the standardization of badminton and table tennis, it took several years before they achieved full recognition as sports. Many saw them as pure recreation. Badminton was something to do in the garden or on the beach, and—unlike tennis—it did not call for special clothes, courts, or clubs. Canteens in places like swimming pools and soccer clubs often had table tennis facilities; many would occasionally hit balls back and forth without giving a moment's thought to club membership. Many homes would own badminton rackets and a ping-pong table without any member of the family playing either game at a club (see chapter 3). Both were seen more or less as socially subordinate substitutes for tennis. Even when played in clubs, they had none of the glamour of tennis. And their devotees tended to be of a slightly lower class.[107]

A GENERALIST APPROACH TO SPORT   Although soccer had already undergone popularization in Britain before its spread to continental Europe, it was initially taken up by the young elite. The first sports lovers did not tend to focus on a single activity; in a sense they were generalists. The true late-nineteenth-century sportsman or sportswoman was an all-rounder who set out to master several sports at the highest level possible. One salient English example is Charles Burgess Fry, who captained Oxford's cricket, soccer, and track and field teams in the 1890s and was a good rugby three-quarter back besides. Charlotte "Lottie" Dod was equally versatile: in addition to winning the ladies' singles at Wimbledon, she was a hockey international and golf champion, an Olympic crossbow finalist, and a renowned mountaineer. Such mixes of skills inclined the first sportsmen and sportswomen elsewhere in Europe to regard English sports as a composite whole, of which they practiced several parts.

In Denmark the members of the Copenhagen Boldklub (founded in 1876) won numerous titles in soccer, cricket, and tennis. The Berlin Sports Club advertised its wide range of activities: track and field, soccer, field hockey, rugby, boxing, wrestling, fencing, gymnastics, tennis, ice hockey, figure skating, speed skating, and swimming. And then there was the Swiss "Light Athletics, Cycling, Motorcycling, Cricket, and Touring Club"! This generalist attitude gradually disappeared with the popularization of several of these sports. With the social differentiation in sport, specialization became the dominant pattern. The rise in top-class performance and the decline in the seasonal nature of sports promoted this development. The disappearance of

the generalist gentleman athlete is symbolized in France by the demise of the pluralist Union des Sociétés Françaises des Sports Athlétiques. In a period that saw increasing numbers of workers take to sport, this organization disintegrated into several autonomous compartments, each of which took responsibility for a single branch of sport.[108]

The Gymnastics Movement: Growth and Resistance

While athleticism was booming at private schools and universities, schools elsewhere in Europe had nothing more adventurous than marching exercises and a little gymnastics. The new opportunities created by the spread of English sports was a sensational breath of fresh air. "To the young people it was like a bright flame: football! So there was something else to do besides gymnastics in dusty halls."[109] Physical education teachers were far less enthusiastic about these new English products. Inclined to be suspicious or disapproving, they disliked what they saw as the new sports' elitism, individualism, and pointlessness. Instead, they propagated alternatives that they believed would improve the nation's mental or physical strength. They were fairly successful: in several European countries gymnastics became one of the most popular sports. In the eighteenth and nineteenth centuries it was elaborated and systematized, and by the mid-nineteenth century it was standardized and had spread to several other countries. Toward 1900, under the pressure of the competition with the new English sports, gymnastics increasingly acquired the characteristics of a modern competitive sport and was included as such in the Olympic program.

As will become clear, the spread and popularization of gymnastics outside Germany was fostered by various factors. First, it did well in countries with a strong German orientation. Second, the boom in the European gymnastics movement took place in a period of increasing international rivalry. Gymnastics was promoted to strengthen the nation and was more successful in countries that had suffered a military defeat, felt threatened, or were trying to catch up in socioeconomic development. The movement was dominated by the lower middle classes, where nationalist ideas easily took root. And third, the popularization of gymnastics was boosted in countries where it was given a prominent place in the army and in education. Germany had an excellent reputation in these areas. While the introduction of English sports in Europe was generally a matter of private initiative and private clubs, government played a prominent part in the development of gymnastics. The relationship between school and gymnastics meant two things. First, the inclusion of gymnastics lessons at primary and secondary schools created a

huge recruitment field of pupils who had become familiar with gymnastics at an early age. Second, it opened up gymnastics for women from lower social classes.

The systematic physical education programs were the end product of a long development. Rousseau, Johann Bernhard Basedow, Johann Friedrich GutsMuths, and Johann Heinrich Pestalozzi had written at length on the subject before the nineteenth century. Their ideas were later elaborated by people such as Friedrich Ludwig Jahn in Germany, Per Henrik Ling in Sweden, Francisco Amoros in France, and Adolf Spiess in Switzerland. A network of rival forms arose, dominated by the German variant. Developments elsewhere were to a large extent reactions to what happened in Germany, and the introduction of gymnastics in other countries reflected German influence. The Prussians Albert and Rudolf von Stephani founded gymnastics in Austria. Christiania Turnverein, the first Norwegian gymnastics club, was founded by the German Joseph Stockinger in 1855. Viktor Heikel, who is known as the father of Finnish gymnastics, studied in Germany and Sweden. He modeled his ideas on the German educational system, and in 1875 he founded the Helsingfors Turnförening. In Belgium the Belgians Legers and Isenbaert and the Germans Happel and Euler did groundbreaking work in the introduction of German gymnastics. In Greece, too, it was a German named Julius Henning who played a key role in the introduction of gymnastics around 1870.[110] In the Netherlands, several of the names adopted by the first gymnastics clubs reflected German influence: "Friedrich Ludwig Jahn" in Edam; "Jahn" in Stadskanaal, Westzaan, and Rotterdam; "Siegfried" in Drachten and Groningen; "The German" in Landsmeer and Tilburg; "Kaiser Otto" in Naarden; and "Adolf Spiess" in Veenhuizen.

While the adoption of English sports was bound up with awe and admiration for English elite lifestyles, German gymnastics spread rather from a combination of fear of and fascination with Germany's achievements. British foreign policy—especially in a military sense—was directed beyond Europe far more than that of Germany. Europeans tended to perceive Germany's power as more of a threat than Britain's expansion, not least because of the wars it had fought in the latter half of the nineteenth century against Austria, Denmark, and France and the Prussian *Kulturkampf* in Poland. At the same time, Germany stood for modernization and civilization.[111]

Germany's success encouraged all the other countries in the German sphere of influence to strengthen their nation by similar methods: this applied to parts of the Austro-Hungarian dual monarchy, with its large German and German-speaking minorities; to Switzerland, Sweden, Denmark, and up to a point the Netherlands; to Belgium, Luxembourg, France, Ice-

land, Norway, and Bulgaria. In all these countries gymnastics grew explosively after about 1850, and it is currently among the ten sports with the most participants. There as in Germany, the gymnastics movement became an organizational vehicle for nationalist groups, and in all these countries it was also largely controlled by the petit bourgeoisie. Where this class was not large, there was no breeding ground for the growth of gymnastics. Unlike English sports, gymnastics was often imported by older men, many of whom were involved in education, the army, or workers' organizations. While the elite turned to English sports, the petit bourgeoisie and workers took up gymnastics.[112]

Gymnastics exercises promoted physical and mental development. They therefore became part and parcel of the teaching curriculum and were incorporated into a more general "civilizing offensive" among the population in the latter half of the nineteenth century. In the Netherlands the first gymnastics clubs were founded in the 1860s, and in 1868 several of them formed the Dutch Gymnastics Federation. Like their German predecessors, the proponents of gymnastics were active on two fronts. They encouraged primary and secondary schools to incorporate the subject into their physical education curriculum and propagated it through clubs. Special courses were set up to train gymnastics teachers for schools.[113]

A fierce struggle ensued between the supporters of the English sports and the gymnastics movement. Physical education teachers played a key role here. In the first place, their vehement opposition to the English sports sprang from the perceived threat to their jobs. More physical activity outside school would undermine the purpose of their subject and further erode their already low social status. In the second place, there was friction between these lower-middle-class educators and the enterprising and cosmopolitan elite youth, who were constantly straining for greater independence. The teachers, who wanted to keep physical education within the school's control, were infuriated by the efforts of pupils from the upper crust of society to organize and play English sports outside school.[114]

The struggle between the two worlds was very much an ideological clash. Gymnastics supporters saw the English sports as unproductive, anti-utilitarian, and elitist. They disliked the strong emphasis on performance, league matches, prizes, records, and league tables, fearing that it would foster individualism. Rather than measurement and tables they believed in accentuating form and style. Moreover, the teachers bemoaned the lack of "competent" leadership in sports clubs.[115] Sports without proper supervision, in their view, produced fanaticism, to the detriment of homework and students' futures.[116] In schools and the army, gymnastics was an ideal form of mass rou-

tine exercise. If pursued on the same scale, English sports would drive up costs for schools, given the time, space, and facilities they required.

Other countries adopted the clear-cut and orderly mass gymnastics exercises as well, along with the nationalist ideology and patriotic mysticism that clung to them. But since nationalist movements always applied the German model to their own national objectives, gymnastics acquired a unique identity and significance in each country. Quarrels arose, fueled by national and ethnic rivalries, as to the "true" ideological basis and the "correct" way of doing the exercises.

The best-known example of a gymnastics movement that developed along an entirely separate path is the Sokol. The Sokol (Czech: falcon or hawk) society originated in Prague in 1862 and later gained wide support among other Slav peoples, providing them with an outlet for nationalist sentiments. In Czechoslovakia, the Sokol openly opposed German domination and the class differences associated with it. The large German minority (25 percent of the population) monopolized the best positions in society. German literature was accorded a dominant place in the school curriculum, and Czech intellectuals were encouraged to master its language and emulate German culture.[117] In 1867, Czechoslovakia became part of the Austro-Hungarian Empire and had a German-speaking government. The Czechs followed their own national and nationalist Sokol movement in opposition to the German style. They expressed their national aspirations and their resistance to German dominance in mass demonstrations with flags and uniforms. The transformation of German Turnen into Czech Sokol is part of a general pattern in which sports spread from "high" to "low" in the international power hierarchy, undergoing a change in meaning along the way. Dominated countries appropriate cultural products in a manner that reflects their relations with the dominant country. The Czech Sokol society had more than two hundred thousand members in 1914, and by 1930 the numbers exceeded 350,000.[118] This success may be ascribed to the movement's nationalist foundations and the social pressure exerted on all "right-minded" Czechs. One of the movement's slogans was "To be Czech is to be a Sokol."[119]

Any military threat or defeat fueled the propaganda activities of the nationalist gymnastics movements and their popular support. In Sweden, educational reform and the increasing emphasis on the importance of physical education was linked to the military defeats that had forced the country to surrender the Baltic region to Prussia and Finland to Russia. Under the leadership of Per Henrik Ling, a completely separate form of gymnastics developed. Like the program of his German contemporary Jahn, Ling's Swedish gymnastics was full of patriotic and paramilitary motifs. Ling was prob-

ably familiar with the work of the Germans GutsMuths and Vieth, and he imported gymnastics equipment from Germany. But he departed from the German model. He simplified the exercises, reduced the use of equipment, placed more emphasis on free movement, and rejected even more resolutely any form of competition or differentiation according to levels of proficiency. His form of gymnastics was made compulsory at Swedish schools in the early nineteenth century.[120]

In France too it was a lost war, in 1870, that increased pressure to improve the discipline and strength of the nation. Although gymnastics had been compulsory at school for decades and was taught to the troops, club gymnastics soared in popularity in the ten years following France's defeat by the Prussian army. In 1873 a handful of clubs founded the Union des Sociétés Françaises de Gymnastique. By 1914 it included more than a thousand clubs with about 350,000 members. If the introduction of English sports in France was the result of Anglomania, then the adoption of gymnastic models from Germany may be called the result of Germanophobia. Patriotism, national anthems, flags, and other national emblems became associated with the pursuit of gymnastics. At gymnastics displays, speakers would assure the spectators of their hatred of Prussia. The desire for revenge and the fear of renewed German aggression are also clear from the names chosen by gymnastics clubs: "La Revanche," "La Patriote," "La Régénératrice," "France." "Il nous faut du muscle" was the patriotic slogan.[121]

Shooting benefited from the same ideological background and international rivalry. The Norwegian Central Federation for the Promotion of Physical Exercise and the Use of Arms (whose motto was "protect your country") is an example of organizations in Germany, Denmark, Norway, France, Serbia, Romania, and Switzerland that combined gymnastics and shooting. Because of this combination, shooting is still very popular in all these countries, especially in Switzerland, Germany, and the former Yugoslavia. Partly because of the existence of a large volunteer army, the two sports were compulsory military exercises for Swiss schoolboys. In 1895 boys aged sixteen to nineteen received at least sixty hours of instruction in gymnastics and shooting annually. This tradition survived well into the twentieth century,[122] which explains the continuing popularity of shooting in Switzerland today.

Although patriotism and national rivalries boosted the inauguration of gymnastics and shooting clubs, bonding with a group was equally important. In contrast to the exclusive clubs for English sports, gymnastics clubs offered members from lower social classes opportunities for recreation, amusement, an amicable atmosphere, companionship, travel, and physical development. Furthermore, membership in a gymnastics club enabled them to distinguish

themselves, as respectable members of the working class, from the lumpen, who took no part in such activities.[123]

The popularization of soccer put the gymnastics movement under immense pressure. The mass gymnastics exercises were less playful, more monotonous, and allowed less scope for individual initiative. Furthermore, soccer enjoyed far more social prestige. It came from England and was initially played by the elite. In the course of time it also appealed to the petit bourgeoisie and working classes, the traditional recruitment ground of the gymnastics movement.[124] To survive, gymnastics had to make concessions.[125] A variety of gymnastic games were devised to retain the youth's allegiance. These alternatives were promoted with especial vigor in countries with a strong gymnastics movement that was under increasing pressure from English sports. Where this pressure was less in evidence, no such efforts were made.

Handball was one of these new alternatives. For many years it was not recognized as an independent sport but was included in the gymnastics program and organized and practiced under the auspices of the gymnastics or track and field federation.[126] The Dutch Federation for Physical Education introduced this "movement game" at various schools where soccer was forbidden. And in Switzerland teachers were still promoting handball out of an aversion to soccer in the 1950s.[127] Because of the link between handball and gymnastics classes, in many European countries handball is in the top fifteen sports in terms of numbers of participants.[128] This is striking, as it has scarcely gained a footing in other parts of the world. German culture has little influence outside Europe, and handball has accordingly remained confined to this continent.

As the sports promoted within the gymnastics movement were developed with a view toward physical education and educational training, there was far less resistance to girls joining in.[129] Because of this, even today school sports are most popular among women. In 1990 in the Netherlands, more women than men participated in gymnastics, handball, volleyball, korfball, and swimming. Led by general stereotypes of female behavior, teachers ensured that play was not too vigorous or competitive, that it did not involve physical contact, and that it was not exposed to public view. Sports that were less amenable to control within a school regime were less accessible to women. For many decades women were actually forbidden to play sports such as soccer. Russia and Denmark both banned women's soccer; the game would damage women's breasts and legs, the Danish federation explained.[130] Toward the end of the nineteenth century the Dutch soccer federation banned a soccer match between Sparta's women's team and a team from London. With-

in clubs, too, men tried to prevent women from playing soccer. In 1910 male employees at a cloth factory in the province of Twente set up the Rijtersbeek sports club, mainly to play soccer. In 1926 several female fans (and employees?) stated their desire to form a women's soccer team and applied to join the club. The club's committee frustrated this initiative, explaining that soccer was unsuitable for women. "Try korfball instead" was their advice.[131]

* * *

The struggle between the English and German models of sport followed a different course in each country, depending on its international position and relations between the classes in its society. The result is today's national sporting pattern (see table 8).

Because of its own strong position, Britain was influenced less by its rival Germany than any other European country. The eight sports with the most participants in Britain do not include any of German origin. And it is scarcely surprising, given their historically close ties with Britain, that Australia, New Zealand, and Ireland display little interest in these sports. (The problematic nature of the close relations between Britain and Ireland is reflected in the large number of indigenous sports in the latter country; English sports are less popular than Celtic games. This again illustrates the point that a sport's national provenance and tradition provide a channel for expressing national identity.)[132] On the other side stands Germany, together with the countries within its sphere of influence: in particular Switzerland, Austria, (former) Yugosla-

Table 8. Quotient Indicating the Number of Participants in Sports of British and German Origin in Various Countries

Australia	0.00	Spain	0.15
Cyprus	0.00	Portugal	0.16
Britain	0.00	Poland	0.17
United States	0.02	Bulgaria	0.22
Ireland	0.04	Japan	0.23
Finland	0.05	Luxembourg	0.24
Italy	0.06	Sweden	0.25
New Zealand	0.07	Iceland	0.34
Belgium	0.08	Denmark	0.45
(former) Czechoslavakia	0.09	Norway	0.60
The Netherlands	0.11	Austria	0.63
France	0.14	(former) Yugoslavia	0.67
Turkey	0.14	Germany	0.70
Hungary	0.15	Switzerland	1.84

Source: Calculations are based on the popularity rankings in the appendix.

Note: For these calculations sports were classified according to the same clusters as in table 7.

via, Norway, Denmark, and Sweden. Because of the specific social constella-
tion at the end of the nineteenth century, characterized by a small and isolated elite and a large class of farmers and small businessmen, the reaction against
English sports was vehement in Switzerland, where "sports" stood for "foreign influence" and dreaded "cosmopolitan trends."[133] Switzerland is the only
country in which sports of German origin attract more participants than those
from Britain. Uniquely, gymnastics is ranked higher than soccer. However,
even gymnastics is surpassed by shooting, thanks to the Swiss volunteer army
and the long tradition of instruction in using firearms.

Denmark and the Netherlands have been influenced by both traditions.
The modern history of these countries has been heavily determined by their
geographical proximity to the two rival powers. The gymnastics movement
had already secured a place in sporting life when ties with Britain were promoted by industrialization and English sports took root. In both countries,
English sports became more popular in urban centers, while gymnastics and
handball flourished in the countryside. Gymnastics had spread to all the
provinces of the Netherlands by 1900, because of the early establishment of
schoolteachers' organizations. At the beginning of the twentieth century there
were about twelve thousand gymnasts in the Netherlands, making it probably the second sport after ice skating.[134] In 1914 the gymnastics federations
totaled almost thirty thousand members, and in 1924 the numbers exceeded
forty thousand. It was not until the early 1920s that gymnastics was overtak-
en by soccer, which attained fifty thousand participants by about 1925. It remained the second sport until the 1950s, only slightly behind soccer: in 1947
there were 178,565 gymnasts as compared to 263,519 soccer players. Handball
attracts less interest in the Netherlands than in Denmark and other countries influenced by Germany—possibly because of the popularity of korfball,
another sport promoted by educationists and supported by the gymnastics
movement. Although korfball was long confined to the west of the country,
with handball enjoying more popularity in regions bordering on Germany,
they appealed to roughly the same groups.[135] The launch of the Dutch Handball Federation prompted the following headline: "Watch out, korfball players! The Dutch Handball Federation is out to draw players away from Korfball clubs!"[136] Together the two sports occupied fourth place in 1998, with
153,196 members, after soccer, tennis, and gymnastics. (This would produce
a quotient of 0.18 in table 8.) In Denmark soccer ranks first, with badminton third and tennis fourth, while handball and gymnastics are at second and
sixth place, respectively. Table 8 reveals a fairly large difference between the
two countries because soccer and tennis dwarf all other sports in popularity
in the Netherlands.[137]

In France, German influence was less lasting. Here the gymnastics movement bloomed after the country's military defeat by Germany. The first gymnastics clubs were founded in regions under German influence, whereas sports clubs sprang up in Paris and in ports that had close ties with Britain. Here, too, English sports were initially confined to the elite, while gymnastics clubs attracted the poorer classes. This meant that the popularization of soccer and rugby posed a threat to the gymnastics clubs. Many club committees responded by starting soccer and rugby within their own organizations in a bid to retain their influence on their members and to stop them from drifting away to other clubs.[138]

Ice Skating in the Netherlands: National Popularization and International Marginalization

In several countries, one or more "sportized" pastimes have survived the competition with imported sports: in Ireland there are Gaelic sports like hurling and camogie, in France *pétanque,* in Austria *Eisschiessen* (akin to curling) and *Heeressport* (like shooting), in the Scandinavian countries orienteering, in the Balkan states wrestling, and in the Netherlands ice skating. Compared to the German and English sports, these activities tend to be enormously popular in their "home" country without having spread or been popularized much elsewhere. Speed skating is an interesting Dutch example.

TRADITIONAL DUTCH PASTIMES   Writing in 1871, Jan Ter Gouw called horse racing, ice skating, and yachting the national pastimes of the Dutch. Most other traditional activities were solely regional: tilting at the ring in Zeeland, klootschieten in Twente, fives in Friesland, beugelen in Limburg, and kolven in North Holland. In addition there were numerous violent pastimes such as katknuppelen, vogelknuppelen, palingtrekken, ganstrekken, and bekkesnijden.[139]

In the nineteenth century some of these pastimes came under the paternalistic scrutiny of nobles and the well-to-do bourgeoisie, who were intent on promoting national prosperity and a more civilized society. The Dutch Fives Federation was set up by affluent citizens who saw the new organization as a vehicle in their efforts to curb drinking, swearing, and spitting on and around the fives courts. In addition, a sense of national identity was taking hold in these circles. The integration and scale expansion taking place in society made people want to transcend regional boundaries and think Dutch. If fives was to command respect, it had to be organized at the national level.[140]

With its early organization, regulation, and standardization, fives to some

extent evaded the fate of most traditional Dutch pastimes: demotion to ridiculed amusements leading a marginal existence in a few small regions. Frisian *fierljeppen* (pole vaulting over a canal) makes people laugh, whereas pole-vaulting high jumps are taken seriously and much admired. The difference is the degree of integration within the international sports world. Fierljeppen never progressed beyond Frisian canals, whereas pole vaulting secured a place in the track and field program and is practiced in major stadiums around the world. It survived and won acceptance because it adopted the characteristics of modern sports—something that fierljeppen, kolven, beugelen, and klootschieten basically failed to do. By the end of the nineteenth century their popularity was confined to farming circles and a few pockets of old-fashioned citizenry. Unable to transcend their provincial origins, they were marginalized as imported sports came into fashion.[141]

Speed skating is an exception to the rule: uniquely, it transcended its traditional Dutch origins to become a major competitive sport. In 1998 the Royal Netherlands Ice Skating Federation had 162,418 members, making it the country's fourth most popular sport.[142] Internationally, however, it is a different story; speed skating is in much the same position as korfball, another Dutch product.

SPRINTS, LONG-DISTANCE, AND SHORT-TRACK SKATING: REGIONAL, NATIONAL, INTERNATIONAL The Netherlands is the only country in Europe, and probably in the world, where speed skating is one of the ten sports with the most participants. Climate and geographical factors obviously play a role here. Before the advent of artificial ice rinks (the first indoor rink was built in London in 1876; the Netherlands had none at all until the eve of the Second World War, when it acquired *one*),[143] skating was wholly dependent on natural conditions. But these conditions were far from unfavorable: the Netherlands is overlaid with regional systems of ditches, rivers, canals, and lakes that allow skaters to cover considerable distances; there is less snowfall than in countries further north; the flatness of the land means weak currents; and the winters often permit skating without being so severe as to make it into torture. The Scandinavians have the disadvantage of what are often very cold winters, besides frequent heavy snowfall that impedes skating; they can skate there almost every year, however. Dutch skaters watch the weather forecasts each year in anxiety. Yet even this uncertainty can add to the fun. In the nineteenth century the first skating of the year meant races and festivities on the ice, followed by evenings of music and dance in the inns.[144]

Still, the uniqueness of the conditions in the Netherlands should not be overstated. Other countries too have areas with excellent skating conditions.

The Fens near Cambridge in England are a traditional skating district; for decades "fen skating" was a common term for speed skating. There are excellent lake districts in Scandinavia, in Germany to the east of Hamburg, in northern Poland, and in the Baltic states. Russia, North America, and various Asian countries (including China and Japan) also provide good skating conditions. In the nineteenth century many English businessmen took winter vacations in Scandinavia to enjoy the ice. In fact people skate in every country that has frozen lakes and waterways: in Scandinavia skating is documented from the eleventh century, and in China it probably existed earlier still.[145]

The popularity of skating today may be partly attributable to the huge ice festivities that astonished foreign visitors in the eighteenth and nineteenth centuries.[146] The image of the Netherlands as a skating nation was probably reinforced by the paintings of these festivities by Dutch artists. Since international ties were few and far between, and those that did exist were confined to national elites, such pictures were an important factor in image-making, and Dutch painters were world-renowned. Moreover, the historical achievements of the Republic of the United Netherlands attracted international attention. Foreign observers noted that the festivities were relatively free of class distinctions. High and low, young and old—everyone joined in the frolics on the ice. True, the upper classes preferred figure skating while village men favored speed skating; but everyone was out on the ice all the same. It was not so everywhere. In Germany, women were excluded from skating for decades, and in Louis XVI's France, skating was an elite activity.[147]

In the Netherlands, skating was a truly national pastime. Innkeepers and landlords were happy to organize races and festivities on the ice in light of the business they would do, just as the staging points in today's races are often at cafés and restaurants. The leading citizens of a village would often take it upon themselves to organize races. In skating as in other popular pastimes, these gentlemen tended to have a "hidden agenda" of improving prosperity and spreading civilized practices. The purpose of the ice and skating clubs they set up was twofold: to promote recreation on the ice and to maintain ice courses. By hiring unemployed laborers for the necessary work, they would often be providing a significant source of income.[148] From the outset, the races were held for prizes, whether in cash or in kind. These prizes were valuable and often significantly boosted the income of farmers, sailors, and fishermen forced to abandon their work for weeks during a severe winter. Winners would receive bags of flour, pieces of meat, gold watches, lumps of peat, articles of clothing, or cap brooches.

Skating is still a popular national pastime, albeit in a different form. Weath-

er permitting, the Dutch grab their skates and flock to the nearest ditch, canal, river, or lake. But what concerns us here is identifying the reasons for this
enduring popularity. It will not do to cite historical continuity, for two reasons. In the first place, almost all the other popular amusements of the past
have been marginalized. This includes sprinting along a 160-meter straight
course—in the nineteenth century the kind of speed skating that the Dutch
loved most. It was imported sports that won the people's hearts in the twentieth century, not indigenous pastimes. In the second place, the Dutch skating tradition has led only to a nationwide passion for long-distance skating.
Judging by the popularity of sports such as figure skating, ice hockey, and
short-track skating, the influence of this tradition has been relatively minor,
certainly when compared with countries such as Canada, the United States,
Russia, Sweden, Germany, and (former) Czechoslovakia. Two questions thus
remain. First, why has the old tradition of skating in the Netherlands endured
only in long-distance skating? Second, why is the great enthusiasm this sport
arouses in the Netherlands not matched by any comparable interest internationally?

When the skating clubs and associations organized international amateur
competitions in the latter half of the nineteenth century, their activities in-
terfered with the aims and nature of local skating clubs.[149] Much the same
thing was happening with rowing. Cosmopolitan young men from elite milieus preserved what had once been a popular pastime in a new form, with a
distinctive cachet, in clubs that certainly did not welcome everyone. The first
elite skating clubs were founded in England around 1840. On the initiative
of one of the pathfinders' clubs, the National Skating Association of Great
Britain was established in 1879, with the Duke of Devonshire and the Earl of
Leicester as its first presidents. It made amateur status compulsory for the
races it organized and introduced longer distances, which was a departure
from popular tradition. They were also more concerned with the participants'
preferences than those of the public. While in popular events the winner was
determined in an elimination race between skaters starting together, according to the new regulations of the skating association the winner was determined by time alone. This removed much of the excitement for spectators.
Crowds were an essential part of traditional races, both for the cash prizes
collected from entrance fees and for the innkeepers' turnover. The new amateur rule was a blow for impoverished folk who had used their skates to add
to their meager incomes every winter. The best amateurs, such as Charles
Goodman Tebbutt, were wealthy men of standing and education, who skated, as the expression goes, for pleasure, not for money.[150]

At the end of the nineteenth century the skating association set about

organizing international skating fixtures with kindred spirits and men of other nationalities but of similar social standing. Thus was born the Dutch Skating Association (today's KNSB), following an invitation by the English. In spite of the Netherlands' long skating tradition, the Dutch accepted the draft regulations—albeit after making a few minor alterations—provided in 1882 by the British Skating Association. The British regulations pointed the way; the distances skated in the first semiofficial world championships held in Amsterdam were measured in miles instead of kilometers! But since each club regulated its own races with a fair degree of autonomy, there was soon a bewildering chaos of records and championships. To put an end to this, delegates from several countries founded an international skating association, on the initiative of Pim Mulier. The new body stipulated that races would be on an amateur basis, in pairs and against time, on an oval course and over distances of five hundred, fifteen hundred, five thousand, and ten thousand meters. With this international harmonization, the national skating associations broke free from traditional forms of skating in their countries. The new mode of skating clearly put "professional" skaters at a disadvantage; always having raced over short distances on straight courses, they now had no chance of winning.[151]

Local traditions such as fen skating in England and sprinting in Friesland endured, but eventually became marginalized—the fate of all onetime popular pastimes. The first Western city-dwellers to take up the international form of skating derided them as "backward," "provincial," and "old-fashioned." Writing in the Frisian daily newspaper the *Leeuwarder Courant,* Baron de Salis described sprinting as a kind of speed skating that belonged in a century that put physical strength before talent "and not in our own." He depicted it as an obsolete kind of fairground game. A president of the association later added, "The professional races were left to their own devices; that clawing away at a sprinting course, often in primitive attire, would always have a certain appeal for the general public, and nothing could be done to change that, but the Amateur races, that was where there was work to be done, and people were eager to do it."[152]

A yawning gap opened up between the KNSB, which represented international competitive skating, and the numerous local and regional skating clubs, which were in charge of sprints, noncompetitive skating, and ice festivities. The KNSB withdrew from any involvement with sprinting, and from 1904 it suppressed professionalism by disqualifying skaters who took part in races organized outside its authority. For a long time sprinting and long-distance skating survived separately from one another, with the latter, modern form of competition far less dominant than it is today. In fact, the regional

and provincial clubs often had more members than the national association.[153] The two groups each had their own demarcated territories. The KNSB
did not manage to obtain a monopoly on organizing races, nor to enforce
the amateur rule. The skating clubs held races according to their own rules,
having no desire to conform to standards imposed by a small group of officials from the urban communities in the west of the country; but when it
came to international fixtures, they had no say whatsoever.

The KNSB's mightiest weapon, its monopoly on national and international
races, was not yet strong enough to carry the day. Plenty of skaters still attached
more importance to winning money, goods, and prestige in their own communities than to national and international titles and medals. In 1928–29
Geeske Woudstra claimed to have won about two thousand guilders in sprinting. But as Dutch unification progressed and people started to identify more
strongly with the nation as a whole, sprinting gradually lost its appeal. The
first national sprinting championship, held in 1924, was too late to reverse the
trend. Local traditions lost out to new national and international agreements.
In addition, social provision had improved, rendering obsolete the function
of traditional speed skating to use entrance fees to buy "nutritious food for
the poor."[154] After the Second World War, long-distance skating attracted large
numbers of spectators away from the sprinting races, and with them the most
talented competitors. In 1954 sprinters were defeated even over their own distance by their long-distance rivals. In 1963, the province of Friesland abolished
cash prizes in a bid to stop standards from declining further, as it would enable exchanges of skaters over short and long distances.[155]

The construction of artificial rinks in the 1960s dealt the death blow to
sprinting. These circular four-hundred-meter courses imposed compliance
with the international rules. To young people the new rinks emphasized that
sprinting was outmoded. Thus the building of an artificial rink prompted
Atje Keulen-Deelstra, a renowned sprinter in Friesland, to try her luck skating longer distances, in which she went on to triumph internationally. Her
regional reputation became national fame, but she remained a "local hero-
ine." Dutch speed skaters are famous only in their own country.[156]

Although sprinting has vanished into the background, skating has remained a national pastime in the Netherlands—so much so that many Dutch
people learn to use racing skates. Moreover, the sport's long popular tradition helped to erase the slightly elitist image of long-distance skating, which
was initially associated with the major cities. The skating association had no
wish to foster exclusivity; on the contrary, it wanted to wean as many people
as possible away from sprinting to longer distances. Nor did the general public
view the new variant as a special, fashionable type of skating.

As skating's roots lay in the countryside, it never became an urban workers' sport like soccer, but remained a sport for the "ordinary" man or woman in small Dutch villages. Whereas artificial rinks are found only in big cities, many of the top-class skaters of the past fifty years have come from the polders and rural regions.

In spite of all the Netherlands' international success, the KNSB's membership has been declining steadily since 1960. Yet this downturn in long-distance racing has been accompanied by a resurgence of skating tours. International ties and influences have reinvigorated the romanticism of national folklore. Whatever the weather, when the ice is there, the Dutch don their skates en masse. Refreshment stands, medals, journeys of 40, 60, or 120 kilometers past the rushes, under bridges, trudging over the roads: what to a foreigner is totally obscure folklore is part of the Dutch national identity.[157] About fifty years ago the speed sprinting that once played such a large part in regional life was finally ousted by distance skating, which is organized at the national level. Yet the latter variant has not caught on internationally, and its significance is therefore waning as integration and identification increasingly acquire global parameters. While the Dutch focus single-mindedly on this one variant, a rival form is emerging—short-track skating, which uses the infrastructure of indoor rinks built for figure skating and ice hockey. These facilities give short-track skating the edge as far as development is concerned, as distance racing needs four-hundred-meter courses that are not so easy to find outside the Netherlands.

Short-track is not a retrograde step, despite the slashing of distances. While long-distance skating is increasingly seen as a traditional Dutch pastime, short-track is a new international variant from the United States and Canada. It has spread rapidly and already has Olympic status, while long-distance skating is languishing. In this unequal battle, the Netherlands and Norway are pitted against the United States and Canada.[158]

Speed skating was already having a hard time in the winter arena. Even the prominent sports of ice hockey and figure skating and the rising star of short-track are now overshadowed by skiing, which reigns supreme over the winter sports. While speed skating became a sport for the masses, skiing was long the prerogative of the rich. It has what long-distance skating lacks: ties with the affluent classes and fashionable winter sports resorts. With the expansion of the middle classes and increased prosperity, skiing is now more widely accessible, which is an additional blow to skating. In traditional skating nations such as Norway and Finland, skating is losing ground to skiing. The same trend is perceptible in the Netherlands, albeit to a lesser extent. Prestigious skiing is in the ascendancy, but people still feel affection for skating, as

that typically Dutch sport with typically Dutch refreshments by the side of the frozen canals, with Frisian bands thumping away and a new world champion every year.

New Relations, New Sporting Preferences: Trends since 1945

The Erosion of Europe's Power and the Rise of Non-European Sports

In the late nineteenth and early twentieth centuries, Germany and Britain dominated the European scene. France had been compelled to take a step back, but remained a key player. Over the course of the twentieth century the influence of these powers was gradually eroded by non-European states: the United States, the Soviet Union, and Japan.

The intervention of the United States in the First World War reflected the weakened position of the great states of Europe. The far-reaching consequences of the collapse of Wall Street also showed that the European powers' autonomy was a thing of the past. The Second World War made it clear once and for all that they could not solve their problems alone: American aid was essential for the reconstruction of Western Europe. The dollar became the unit of currency against which the worth of all other currencies was measured. Throughout the world, colonies shook off the yoke of European domination.

The old relations made way for a new order in which two superpowers, the Soviet Union and the United States, dominated the world stage. The formation of the opposing alliances NATO and the Warsaw Pact and organizations such as the European Economic Community and Comecon confirmed the division of Europe into west and east, a situation that endured until the collapse of communism in the late 1980s. Western Europe relied on American support, while Eastern Europe was subsumed into the Soviet Union's sphere of influence. The cultural life of the east was influenced by Russia and that of the west by the United States. The defeated nations Germany and Japan, disencumbered of their military machines, set about rebuilding their ruined industries. Both did so with such phenomenal success that they grew into economic superpowers in the latter half of the twentieth century.[159]

THE SOVIETIZATION OF SPORTS While the countries of Western Europe tried to restore continuity with the prewar era, those of the eastern bloc experienced a radical break with the past. Each country became integrated into

one of two power blocs that stockpiled arms while locking horns in ideological rhetoric. This division also drove a cultural wedge between the blocs, although, to borrow a phrase from Jacques Rupnik, the Iron Curtain was located further to the east in culture and lifestyle than in political terms. In the countries of the Eastern bloc, ties with Western culture were temporarily severed. In their place came a Sovietization of culture, in which art, literature, music, and sports all served political ends.[160] This trend led to several differences in sporting patterns between east and west, the most striking element of which was the relative neglect of tennis, golf, badminton, and squash in the east.

Russia was not in the business of developing or exporting sports in the latter years of the nineteenth century. The country lagged far behind the West in numerous respects. With its largely agricultural economy, it was characterized by a huge gap between the cities and rural areas and was heavily dependent on imported technology. In its desire to modernize it looked west, inviting entrepreneurs from Britain, Germany, and France to help, and it was these guests who introduced the new sports in the latter half of the nineteenth century.[161]

In Russia these sports long remained the province of the elite, and after the 1917 Revolution they came under heavy fire. The Marxist-Leninist criticism echoed the gymnastics movement's rejection of "bourgeois sports." As late as 1929 the Central Committee of the Communist Party issued a decree condemning the pursuit of records. This attitude changed in the 1930s. Organizations for physical education and sports were enlisted in the sweeping socioeconomic changes implemented under Stalin. Industrial productivity and sports were linked, and it was thought that sports would bind people more firmly to companies, unions, and the party. The membership of sports organizations soared; if the Soviet statistics are to be believed, they went from 250,000 in 1924 to 6.5 million in 1934.[162] This fresh accent on sports was related to the increasing rivalry with the West and the public's increasing interest in sports. To encourage sportsmen and sportswomen and to help them catch up, a ranking system of sporting levels was introduced. State support primarily targeted first-class athletes whose achievements would boost the Soviet Union's international prestige. In 1948 it was decreed that the USSR's leading athletes had the task of "'securing first place in the world in the most important sports over the next few years.'"[163] To this end, Soviet sports organizations finally joined the "bourgeois" international federations after the Second World War. In 1946 the Soviet Union joined the organizations for soccer and weightlifting, and in 1952 it took part in the Olympic Games at Helsinki, for the first time since the Revolution.

The Soviets emphasized the amateur sports in the Olympic program. Other Communist countries took a similar line. As the party controlled the media, the education system, the sports clubs, sports instruction, and the provision of facilities, these sports were given far more scope. This was particularly marked in the former German Democratic Republic. If an Olympic medal could be gained in a particular sport, its pursuit was stimulated, good facilities were created, and talented athletes recruited and trained. Tennis, golf, badminton, and squash did not receive such support as they did not belong to the select field of Olympic sports.[164] Moreover, they symbolized the capitalist elite, and as such were at odds with "the interests of the working class." Alongside this direct influence, Soviet domination also contributed indirectly to the neglect of these sports. In the West their popularization increased with the growth of prosperity and the expansion of the upper middle classes. The socioeconomic stagnation in the Eastern bloc meant that general levels of prosperity rose far more slowly. Thus the most important factor promoting the growth of these sports was absent behind the Iron Curtain.

Tennis in the former Czechoslovakia was the sole exception to this rule. No research has been done into this phenomenon. However, the theory of the differential popularization of sports unfolded in this book provides a hypothesis that could explain the anomaly. It is important to look at the long tennis tradition in the Czech territories. Although Sovietization suppressed the popularization of tennis in Eastern Europe, both directly and indirectly, it did not eradicate the sport's existing popularity in Czechoslovakia. Tennis's greater popularity in Bohemia and Moravia before Sovietization than in other parts of Central Europe or the Balkans is related to sharp differences in economic development. Prior to the Communist invasion, the Czech territories were relatively advanced in industrial terms. Around 1900 they had belonged to the most industrialized part of the Austro-Hungarian Empire.[165] This meant that they had closer ties with Britain than the surrounding territories and a larger contingent of wealthy bourgeoisie. Among the latter, tennis was the English sport with the greatest appeal. Thus the tennis tradition that had grown up in Czechoslovakia before the Second World War continued during the phase of Soviet domination.

THE DIFFERENTIAL POPULARIZATION OF AMERICAN SPORTS Even before 1900, articles had appeared about the increased influence of the United States in Latin America and the Pacific region. It was far longer before this influence started to make itself felt in Europe.[166] As a result, baseball, basketball, and volleyball did not spread through Europe until people in Latin America and

parts of Asia were quite familiar with them. The sports had a few isolated enthusiasts in Europe around the turn of the century, but it was not until the intervention of U.S. troops in the First World War that they won a substantial following, and several decades more elapsed before they achieved mass popularity. The critical period was between 1950 and 1980, when U.S. power and prestige rose to unprecedented heights. In the Netherlands, the membership of clubs playing American sports rose from 6,860 in 1950 to 196,707 in 1980. American sports club membership grew 425 percent between 1963 and 1980, compared to an overall growth of 181 percent for all sports. In 1963 not one of the American sports belonged to the Netherlands' "top ten," and only volleyball was in the top twenty. Twenty years later, volleyball had risen to number four, and basketball and baseball had both entered the top twenty. Italy displayed the same pattern, with an increase in the number of volleyball and basketball players from 211,291 in 1974 to 468,407 in 1983, a growth of 122 percent, while total sports club membership figures rose by 49 percent. In 1983 these two were the most popular sports after soccer.

Despite this trend, European sports continued to dominate the scene. The most popular sports in the United States, baseball and American football, attracted few devotees. This relative lack of interest in American sports stands in sharp contrast to the success of other elements of American popular culture, from Levi's and Coke to *Ally McBeal* and the music of Michael Jackson. Two reasons may be advanced for this. First, the Americanization of culture cannot be separated from the media saturation of society. The main catalysts of cultural dissemination to have gained power spectacularly over the last few decades of the twentieth century are the electronic media. Through electronic channels, more people in ever-widening circles are aware of new trends that would have otherwise passed them by. In the late 1920s, radios became part of virtually every household in Western countries. After the Second World War they were joined by television, which started appearing in European living rooms in the 1950s. Simultaneously with the rise of radio and television as mass consumer goods, the power and prestige of the United States increased. The concept of the American way of life that was conveyed was heavily determined by the reports and images that the Europeans received through these channels. With the advent of commercial channels, program production increasingly came into American hands, which strengthened the influence of television as a disseminator of American cultural products. American sports, too, receive more media coverage than in the past.[167] This boosts TV ratings for matches, but it does not encourage Europeans to go out and play the sports themselves. The media coverage is not geared toward boosting participation; on the contrary, it focuses on the

top professional matches and treats them as spectacles. That is where the media's interests and objectives lie. This function of the media can even inhibit the popularization of a sport. The presentation of American football can create the impression that it is a TV sport, practiced by present-day gladiators. American football is a modern spectacle that you can enjoy at home, with beer and popcorn within easy reach: a sport to watch, not to play, like speed skiing and professional wrestling. The media spread images of sport, but they are far less significant when it comes to boosting participation. Dozens of baseball and American football games are now shown on European television, and sales of T-shirts, jackets, and caps with the logos of famous American teams have soared in Europe, yet neither sport is played much there. Instead, it is volleyball, the American sport with the least commercialization and media coverage in its mother country, that has the most players in Europe.

Second, relationships of power between Europe and the United States were less unbalanced than elsewhere. True, the Second World War had dramatically weakened European countries, but it had not destroyed their positions of power. On the contrary, they revived astonishingly fast, formed economic and political alliances, and renewed their influence in the global political arena. After the war, European cultures received a fresh impulse, and many Europeans are still proud of them. There was no question of the United States practicing a form of cultural imperialism, promoting its own culture over indigenous forms as a "civilizing" influence or in order to further its own political and economic objectives.

American sports had to compete in Europe with a whole range of established sports that had the edge in many ways. European sports were already integrated into the fabric of everyday life; they had a sophisticated organizational structure and an impressive infrastructure; the game rules were fairly well known; some were included in school curricula; the media had specialist reporters for them; the most important fixtures and the comings and goings of the leading sports stars were routinely discussed over lunch. In southern Europe, where modernization came later, this sports culture was less firmly entrenched, and young people were more receptive to outside influences. This explains why American sports gained their largest European following, relatively speaking, in Turkey, Bulgaria, Italy, and Spain (see table 7). The same probably applies to Greece, where basketball in particular is enormously popular.

BASKETBALL AND VOLLEYBALL Having overcome their initial disadvantage, basketball and volleyball are now high up in the popularity league tables in

Europe—far more so than baseball or American football. This popularity can be explained by looking at the influence of three catalysts: the YMCA, the army, and schools.

YMCAs played an essential role in the introduction of basketball and volleyball. During and after the First World War they organized matches in these sports as a form of relaxation for the troops. Young men from European armies came into contact with them for the first time through the YMCA or by watching American soldiers play. Following an initiative by Elwood S. Brown, the physical director of the YMCA and the head of the sports division of the U.S. armed forces, the Inter-allied Games were held in Paris in 1919, with five hundred thousand people watching matches in twenty-four branches of sport. For the first time, basketball and volleyball, the sports of the liberating armies, were shown to large crowds of European spectators.

The link with the army meant that basketball and volleyball were organized first in countries that had been most closely involved in the war effort. It was Central European countries that launched international basketball and volleyball federations. The first contest for the volleyball world championship took place not in the United States but in Czechoslovakia. The Soviet Union captured the gold medal, the host country won the silver, and Bulgaria won the bronze. In the women's event the first three places were won by the Soviet Union, Poland, and Czechoslovakia. During and immediately after the war the YMCA set up secretariats and schools to promote and organize sports in various countries and regions, including Estonia, Latvia, Poland, the former Austria-Hungary, Italy, and the Balkans. By the end of 1919, more than two hundred thousand Italian soldiers were using YMCA facilities. In the same year, James Naismith, the inventor of basketball, toured the U.S. bases in Europe and saw a basketball game between American soldiers inspire a group of French spectators to practice throwing the ball into the basket. A few years later, hundreds of teams throughout the country were playing the new sport.[168] Basketball and volleyball were more successful in countries that had fought than in those that had remained neutral or saw little of the conflict. In the Netherlands and Scandinavia, both sports were introduced years later—also by the YMCA.[169]

The Second World War saw another surge in the popularity of volleyball and basketball, again fostered by the presence of American troops. In Germany, basketball developed rapidly in areas close to U.S. bases after the war. The first clubs sprang up in the American zone in southern Germany, where the sport spread faster than in the British or French zones.[170] Volleyball's major breakthrough in the Netherlands also coincided with the arrival of American and Canadian troops.[171]

While the involvement of the YMCA and the army helped to spread basketball and volleyball relatively early on, it could not guarantee that the
momentum of popularization would be sustained. The rapid growth in the
number of participants took place in the early 1960s and was attributable to
two quite different factors. First, the power of the United States reached its
zenith at this time, and many American products and habits were crossing
the Atlantic. Second, the close ties between the American YMCA and the
European gymnastics movement promoted the popularity of basketball and
volleyball. Both of them—especially volleyball—fitted perfectly into the tradition of what Richard Mandell has called "induced sports." The YMCA, like
the European gymnastics movement, put up a struggle in its early years
against the sports that were drawing its clientele away. In response to this
threat, just as the gymnastics organizations had invented new sports like
handball and korfball, the YMCA promoted basketball and volleyball, indoor
sports that could be played in the increasingly idle gymnasiums. Many leaders of the European gymnastics movement were happy to adopt the YMCA's
sports. They had similar interests and ideological positions and targeted the
same recruitment groups.[172] Basketball and volleyball helped make physical
education classes more colorful. There was little desire to revive the mass
marching drills and other exercises that had been aimed at inculcating discipline and order, because of their Nazi associations. Moreover, with the
greater freedom young people expected in the 1960s and 1970s, they wanted
new, modern sports attuned to their lifestyles. In short, volleyball and basketball filled a need in the curriculum and acquired an important place in
physical education classes.

The relationship between the popularity of volleyball and basketball in
different countries (see table 9) was in part a derivative of the strength of the
gymnastics movement. Basketball was approached with more caution, as—
unlike volleyball—it had been commercialized and professionalized early on.
Since volleyball was as yet "untouched" by these developments when it was
adopted in Europe, it corresponded more closely to the ideology of European
gymnastics. In countries where the gymnastics movement was strong, volleyball became more popular than basketball. Furthermore, this relationship
also meant that more girls took up volleyball.[173]

BASEBALL Like volleyball and basketball, baseball was imported into several countries before 1920, though it did not start to become really popular
until after the Second World War. Even then, it prospered in only a handful
of countries. It lacked the support of the YMCA, was welcomed less enthusiastically by the gymnastics movement, and was scarcely incorporated into

Table 9. The Ratio between the Number of Volleyball and Basketball Players in Europe

Finland	3.3:1	Portugal	1:1.2
The Netherlands	3.2:1	Sweden	1:1.4
Norway	3.2:1	Belgium	1:1.5
Germany	2.6:1	Cyprus	1:1.5
Austria	1.9:1	Hungary	1:1.6
(former) Czechoslovakia	1.8:1	(former) Yugoslavia	1:1.9
Denmark	1.5:1	Iceland	1:2.1
Italy	1.4:1	Spain	1:2.7
Bulgaria	1.3:1	Ireland	1:12.3
Switzerland	1.3:1		
Poland	1.2:1		
Turkey	1.1:1		

Source: Calculations are based on the popularity ranking in the appendix.

school sports. (In contrast, softball—another sport that received YMCA support in the United States—did find its way into physical education classes in some countries). Baseball had the additional disadvantage of low social status; its position in America was analogous to that of soccer in Europe. It had been popularized and professionalized early on (around 1870) and was known as a workers' sport. In Europe, too, its appeal was largely to the poorer classes, and the first Dutch baseball clubs started as sections of soccer clubs in Amsterdam, Haarlem, and (later) Rotterdam.[174] But it could not undermine soccer's status in these circles as the real "people's sport."

Baseball has had a certain amount of success in Italy and the Netherlands, while Finland has developed its own variant of the game, *pesäpallo,* which has become enormously popular.[175] The uneven fortunes of baseball in Europe are hard to explain on the basis of the available information. Its introduction in Belgium, France, Sweden, Germany, and Spain followed much the same pattern as in the two European baseball countries. In most cases it was imported between 1910 and 1925, either by Americans or by Europeans who had visited the United States.[176] The discrepancies are most likely attributable to differences in baseball and softball instruction in school, but as yet it is unclear how and why these differences arose.

AMERICAN FOOTBALL American football grew to become the most popular sport in the United States and yet made no impact at all on Europe. The lack of interest in playing this sport is a global phenomenon, and so any explanation for this striking contrast must adopt a global perspective.[177]

The development of American football is reminiscent of that of rugby, in that both are seen as soccer's more violent "brothers." The social elite were

put off by the roughness of American football, while the majority of the middle and working classes were already devoted to soccer. An added factor was that the global spread and popularization of soccer had taken place when American football was almost unknown outside Ivy League college campuses. Other countries tended to view it as the American equivalent of rugby rather than as a new branch of sport. For Europeans, Association Football was part of their national and continental culture. To them, theirs was the true football; the Americans played some strange variant.

By the time American football reached Europe, its association with Ivy League universities was a thing of the past. It had developed into the new All-American sport, professionalized and commercialized to the hilt. This limited its appeal to the elite youth. At this stage it mainly attracted young men from poorer classes who wanted a rougher sport to distance themselves from soccer, which was becoming almost bourgeois. Those who had been successful in spite of their humble origins, however, preferred an unimpeachable sport like tennis, as part of a lifestyle suited to their new social position.

In Europe, American football has done best in Britain, where it had sixteen thousand registered players in 1988. True, this is meager compared to half a million golfers and more than a million soccer players, but it is a beginning. It could presage developments elsewhere in Europe. Alternatively, it could reflect Britain's idiosyncratic sports culture. First, British society is in general more strongly influenced by the United States than are its European neighbors. Second, rugby is a school sport in Britain, and it has therefore always attracted more players there than on the continent. In Britain, American football seems to appeal largely to the young elite. Hence its success is not at the expense of soccer—as some might expect—but of Rugby Union. In continental Europe the elite has never taken much interest in rugby, and the same indifference afflicts American football today. This is probably due in part to the sport's commercialization in the United States and to the way it is promoted in Europe (on commercial television, aimed at a mass audience).

Compared to other sports, few people are involved in promoting American football beyond the shores of its homeland. The YMCA, which promoted "its own" volleyball and basketball worldwide, has never been enamored of American football. The sport's roughness is rather at odds with the organization's educational ideology; besides, the YMCA encourages active pursuits and sees American football as primarily a spectator sport. Nor could the sport ride on the waves that had spread soccer and baseball. Both were enormously popular in their countries of origin when they became known throughout the world, and sailors, soldiers, and workers had played a major part in their dissemination. In contrast, American football was for years

confined to Ivy League campuses. Around 1900 it was still a small sport, scarcely played in the army or by workers or sailors. In this respect it most resembled cricket and rugby; they too flourished at schools and universities attended by the sons of the elite. They were propagated by British-educated army officers, teachers, and senior officials. Unlike Britain, the United States had no colonial empire, and so it lacked the network of elite colonial schools that taught the rulers' culture (see chapter 5).

The National Football League has accorded high priority to the internationalization of American football, partly in response to pressure exerted by commercial companies such as Anheuser-Busch, who make Budweiser beer. Companies that have linked their brands to the sport in the United States hope to expand their European market if American football attracts more interest and is televised.[178] But this will be no easy task. The NFL, Anheuser-Busch, and other interested parties have two problems connected to the image of American football. I have already pointed out that the emphasis is less on participation and more on watching top-class games. But people are generally more likely to watch a sport if it is played in their surroundings. So the whole idea of trying to build up TV audiences for American football in a vacuum is ill-conceived from a commercial viewpoint. It would be more effective to stimulate participation, which would indirectly create a larger potential audience. As Janet Lever concluded in 1983, "We overlook the importance of youth leagues as training grounds for future fandom. . . . Professional sport establishments make a wise investment wherever they support youth leagues. When they permit girls to play too, they potentially double the ranks of future committed fans."[179]

More televised games will not necessarily boost participation. Despite all the NFL games shown on commercial TV and booming sales of clothing with names or logos associated with American football, few people actually play the game. The Netherlands is an interesting case in point. A group of Amsterdam youths founded the country's first American football club after they had been asked to take part in a game with American tourists in the Vondelpark, Amsterdam's main city park. After this, teams sprang up in other major cities, including the Utrecht Vikings, the Zwolle Bulldogs, and the Meppel Scorpions. Each club has its own cheerleaders, and a few have an American coach. They play in a Dutch league, and the final for the Veronica Bowl has been televised several times. Dutch and other European viewers can also watch a fair number of U.S. college and professional football matches on commercial TV. Even so, in 1998 the Dutch American Football Federation had precisely 633 members, compared, for instance, to the 23,900, 45,000, and 145,000 people who play baseball, basketball, and volleyball, respectively.[180]

DISSEMINATION AND ENTRENCHMENT: THE JAPANESE MARTIAL ARTS The introduction of the sportized martial arts, which initially spread from Japan and later from other parts of the Far East, is in a sense the reverse of what happened a hundred years ago. Whereas Asians once adopted European sports, Europeans are now flocking to sports imported from Asia.

In the early twentieth century Japan developed into a power that could compete with the West in many areas, but it has only become an economic superpower in the past few decades. Its level of industrialization, while remarkable in a regional context, was relatively low by European standards until 1914. The period of greatest growth occurred after 1945, with an unprecedented decline in the proportion of the population involved in agriculture: in 1955, 37.9 percent of the population were still working in the agricultural sector; by 1980 the figure had shrunk to a mere 9.8 percent. In the same period, the service sector grew from 35.5 percent to 55.4 percent. By about 1960 Japan was one of the seven richest countries in the world. Growth then accelerated at a staggering rate, with the gross national product doubling every five years. Japan became a political and economic world power and served as a model for the West.[181]

Japan's prestige in the West was an unprecedented phenomenon for a non-Western nation. Just as had happened previously with Britain, Germany, and the United States, the rise of Japan as an international superpower increased interest in the country's culture. People wanted to know not only about the latest technological innovations but also about the country's etiquette, social relations, work and culinary habits, and its sports culture. One result was the large-scale pursuit of the martial arts that had evolved from Japanese pastimes.

It was after Japan had been forced to open up its ports that Europeans had first come into contact with Japanese culture. The inventor of judo, Jigoro Kano, had been sent to Europe in 1889 to study European traditions of combat. Whenever he had the opportunity, he demonstrated his own martial art. His Japanese pupils and Westerners who had lived in Japan also helped to spread judo and jujitsu. At the beginning of 1900, the first publications on the subject appeared in England. The Health and Strength Library published, for instance, *The Textbook of Ju-Jutso, as Practiced in Japan*.[182] The Japanese martial arts instructors especially set out to interest soldiers of all ranks, sailors, and police officers.[183] They used judo and jujitsu techniques to teach self defense and the exercise of controlled force.

For the hypothesis argued here, that a close relationship exists between the international balance of power and the differential popularization of sports, it is significant that although judo was introduced into Europe and the United

States around 1900, it did not achieve international popularity until after the Second World War. The postwar period saw the transformation of judo from a rather esoteric and marginal Japanese form of combat into a large-scale international sport, in contrast to jujitsu.[184] The first contest for the world title took place in 1956, and in 1964 judo was incorporated into the Olympic Games. Although the sport had already been known for half a century, its popularity soared during this period in Europe and in the United States. Before the Second World War, only a few hundred Germans at most practiced judo; by 1966 the judo federation had more members than those for hockey, golf, or badminton. And in France, Spain, Portugal, and Belgium, judo became—almost overnight—one of the ten most practiced sports.[185] In the Netherlands, although P. M. C. Toepoel was already teaching the jujitsu techniques he had learned in London in 1910, for decades such activities were confined to small clubs and martial arts schools. It was not until the 1950s that club membership suddenly increased: from 1,497 in 1950 to 42,500 in 1969 and 54,023 in 1980, after which it stabilized. The men who embraced judo in the early stages of this boom often had a more general interest in Japan. Regarding it as a spiritual haven, they learned to speak the language, lived there for a while, and married Japanese women.[186]

Judo's success was worldwide. Thirty years after its foundation, the International Judo Federation had ninety-seven members: thirty-three in European countries, fifteen in Asia, twenty-four in America, twenty in Africa, and five in Oceania. National judo federations existed from Malta to Mongolia and from Senegal to the Solomon Islands. Other martial arts developed along similar lines later on. They increasingly acquired the characteristics of modern sports and were included in the global system of sports competitions. Besides judo and karate, smaller martial arts also underwent internationalization, such as the Japanese arts of kickboxing, aikido, and kendo, Korean tae kwon do, and Indonesian pentjak-silat.

Several underlying dynamic forces have led to a proliferation of Oriental martial arts in the past few decades. First, as already noted, this period witnessed an enormous surge in Japan's economic power and international prestige, and to a lesser extent in that of other East Asian countries, stimulating interest in their sports. The internationalization of ties has acquainted Westerners with an ever-increasing variety of newly evolved martial arts. The postwar stationing of American and European troops in Japan and South Korea, for instance, also played a part.[187] Another factor was the growing influx of Asian migrants into Europe and the United States, especially between countries with historical colonial ties. Thus pentjak-silat is more popular in the Netherlands than anywhere else in Europe because of its sizeable

Indonesian and Moluccan minorities, and viet-vo-dao has the most devotees in France because of the large Vietnamese community.[188] Finally, the "battle of styles" stimulated the development and spread of a constant stream of new combat techniques (see chapter 3). Almost nothing has been written about this competition between the various martial arts in Europe. The following brief discussion of its importance and impact shall be based on the (equally scarce) information on developments in the Netherlands.[189]

Most martial arts were initially practiced not within sports clubs but in specialized martial arts schools or *dojos,* which resembled the boxing, swimming, cycling, and fencing schools of the Netherlands in the early twentieth century.[190] As judo increasingly acquired the characteristics of a Western sport, it was incorporated into the regular Dutch sports structure, and in 1939 the Dutch judo federation was founded. Whereas later martial arts, taught in miscellaneous one-man businesses, largely evade the influence of officialdom, the judo federation has managed to bring a large proportion of the total number of judoists within its ranks. In the 1960s and 1970s the judo federation expanded enormously, profiting from the lowering of the minimum age for sports club members. It was one of the first to allow members from the age of six. As a result there was an enormous influx of youngsters from six to fifteen years of age, many encouraged by their parents who sought a responsible means of enhancing their children's fighting spirit. In 1998, 74 percent of judoists were junior members—the highest percentage of all sports. An unintentional consequence of the preponderance of youngsters was that the sport lost its appeal for a large proportion of martial arts enthusiasts— secondary school boys for whom the masculine aura of martial arts is their most attractive feature. "Judo has become a children's sport" was their verdict.[191] Many boys who had taken up judo at an early age switched to alternatives: mainly karate, the second Japanese sport to be imported into the Netherlands.

Schools for the martial arts are competitive businesses, and to maintain a distinctive profile and hold on to their clients they have to keep updating the program. These schools mushroomed in the 1970s, when newly qualified physical education and sports instructors found their chosen profession saturated and set up their own schools as a way of avoiding unemployment.[192] Institutes in turn capitalized on this trend by setting up new courses for exercise coaches and martial arts school managers.[193] The new coaches and managers built on the success of their predecessors, many of whom were judoists and karateists who now ran schools of their own. These pioneers had visited Japan during their active sporting career, taking part in competitions and visiting dojos. Many had lived there for extended periods and encoun-

tered other Eastern martial arts, which they then introduced at their own establishments in the Netherlands. As managing these schools became an increasingly lucrative business, martial arts champions and instructors turned into entrepreneurs, for whom visits to East Asia were partly business trips to seek out new combat styles to offer their clients.

As the number of martial arts schools increased, competition became fiercer, and with it came the need to keep varying the program. The product differentiation this generated was more marked than in traditional organized sports and has led to an extremely diversified range of options, from ante-natal exercises to ultimate fighting. Many proprietors have drawn addition-al inspiration from the American rage for exercising. While retaining mar-tial arts as their primary focus, they have found fitness and strength training and to a lesser extent aerobics and exercise classes to be lucrative extras. Under the pressure of this commercial competition, traditional gymnastics too has altered course, embracing fashionable activities (originating in the United States) such as aerobics, jazz ballet, and calisthenics, which mix elements of sport, physical exercise, and dance.[194]

By adjusting rapidly to the latest developments in the martial arts and exercising, these private schools have attracted a larger and more diverse cli-entele. In 1984, an estimated three hundred thousand people frequented schools for the martial arts in the Netherlands. In the same year, 60,111 mar-tial arts practitioners were attached to a recognized federation—only 20 percent of the total number using martial arts schools, but nonetheless a sevenfold increase relative to 1950. Teaching self-defense and exercise classes helped justify these schools' existence. The former was a response to increas-ing feelings of insecurity in society, while the latter addressed concerns about the unhealthy lifestyles associated with postindustrial society.[195]

Outward appearance is another aspect of social differentiation. Among the lower social classes, martial arts schools are mainly used for training and body-building to create muscular bodies and enhance fighting ability, whereas the middle classes primarily visit classes that will help keep their bodies fit, slim, and healthy.[196] While one man is concerned to improve his physical appear-ance, to gain respect, and to impress his friends, girlfriends, and strangers, the other sets out to counter the stiffness produced by the daily intellectual working routine. Even in the middle classes, however, weight training has gained a cer-tain respectability. What was a fairground attraction in the nineteenth centu-ry is now practiced by thousands of people every day. Bodybuilding is still unacceptable in affluent circles, but running, working out on exercise bicy-cles, and "body maintenance" with relatively light dumbbells are all widespread today. Private fitness and/or martial arts schools have something for everyone.

Some instructors had other reasons for introducing new martial arts, unrelated to commercial competition. Their admiration of Japanese society and culture included a desire to emulate its hierarchical relations. A new combat style would almost always be accompanied by rules of conduct based on these relations. Pioneers of new branches of the martial arts longed for the moment at which they no longer had to practice humility but could be called "master" or "teacher" in their own right. By starting a new school or promoting a new combat technique they became teachers instead of pupils and hoped to receive the kind of admiration they had felt for their own instructors. Daily rituals would serve to confirm their new position of power. Instruction manuals on new combat styles would often include a personality cult. They also proclaimed and promoted a new lifestyle purporting to derive from Japanese philosophy. The specific combat rules were combined with the initiator's behavioral guidelines and covered with a very weak Oriental sauce.

In general this battle of styles went with a toughening of the martial arts, with later variants becoming increasingly violent. Underlying this trend was sporting as well as commercial competition. Schools could prove their worth by ensuring that their pupils defeated those from rival institutions. This competitive spirit was also seen between different martial arts. The question was not only which school produced the best karateist, but also whose style was best and which school could produce an all-round martial arts champion. This rivalry between martial arts goes back as far as the early sportization of judo. Jigoro Kano demonstrated the superiority of his new judo combat style by defeating pupils of the largest Japanese jujitsu school. Kickboxing arose when Japanese karateists lost to men practicing Thai muay-thai and, impressed by its ferocity, created a new adaptation of traditional karate. The Dutchman Tom Harinck decided, after being heavily defeated by muay-thai boxers, to alter his own Chakuriki style to counter Thai supremacy.[197]

What makes certain people switch to new, more violent martial arts? In general, these sports attract boys with little education, who hope to distinguish themselves from their peers through their prowess in fighting, a quality valued more highly in their circles than among the educated classes. They reject judo and official karate as "soft options," bourgeois variants in which violence has been tamed and regulated. Furthermore, judo and karate are far more closely integrated into the organizational structure of Dutch sport, which constitutes a particular barrier for ethnic minorities (see chapter 1). Martial arts schools are independent businesses. Unlike sports clubs, they do not insist on membership, making them more accessible to ethnic minorities.[198]

The newest martial arts were always more violent, which was appealing,

as it stretched the bounds of the permissible. Practitioners could score toughness points among friends and rivals: the martial arts career leads from the
soft to the tough path, for instance from judo to karate and then to kickboxing, free fighting, or even ultimate fighting. The reverse is never seen. Individual careers of this kind reflect the chronology of imported martial arts.
Some champions in established styles carried on in their old style precisely
because they could not countenance a loss of status, while others transferred
to a different technique because the competition was getting too stiff. One
could keep practicing in the hope of improvement or adopt a new style in
which established reputations would have to be proven all over again.[199]

The strictly regulated, "civilized" or "soft" martial arts, such as judo, karate, and aikido, have the most participants; they are increasingly popular
among the Dutch white middle classes. Tougher variants such as savate,
muay-thai, kickboxing, full-contact karate, and free fighting tend to be popular among lower-class boys, among whom they attract a relatively high percentage of ethnic minorities.[200] These boys and men are willing to undergo
the physical torture and tough, intensive training these techniques impose
to achieve the coveted goal of manly, muscular bodies and physical strength.

Only a small number of young men opt for the toughest variants. As spectator sports, however, they are more popular than "softer" sports. The main
professional contests are grouped together in gala events that the bourgeois
middle classes would not dream of attending. They are repelled by the an-
ticipated violence, the suspected presence of underworld figures, and the
association with heavy drinking, gambling, and uncontrolled behavior. Not
that they have ever witnessed any of this first-hand, but have they not read
that these sports are for teenage dropouts, watched by crowds of "blonde,
high-heeled ladies and muscular fellows glittering with fake jewellery . . . who
are mainly occupied with jeering and screaming"?[201]

Nonetheless, martial arts are also popular among the highly educated classes. Indeed, they have a magnetic appeal. Anything that revolts the lower middle classes they see as a challenge. To do something that ordinary people do
not understand; to embrace an element of lower-class culture rejected by the
bourgeoisie, but to give it a different interpretation, a different form, is an
expression of superiority. It cannot jeopardize their social standing; in language, appearance, behavior, and clothing they are too far removed from
underworld figures to be associated with them. They dabble in the martial
arts but do so selectively and not too seriously. Too many injuries could dis-
turb the precarious balance between distinction and loss of esteem. Nor do
they have the time to devote themselves to hardening their bodies sufficiently
to practice Thai boxing or full-contact karate. Judo, however, they find too

soft, considering it more suitable for the lower middle classes or their own children. Their preference is for something in between, like karate (as long as the toughest fellows have already abandoned it for new variants). Other popular choices, though less daring, are aikido (which lacks the element of competition) and tae kwon do (in which participants wear good protective gear and which forbids punches to the head): "the price that a martial art with classical views must pay to win recognition in society."[202]

Changes in Class Relations and the Increasing Popularity of Status Sports

The introduction of the five-day work week and huge wage increases in the Netherlands boosted the demand for sports and recreation. As part of a general expansion of public welfare provisions, the public authorities tried more actively to meet this demand by funding sports grounds and building parks and other outdoor recreational facilities. This in turn created the conditions for an explosive growth in sporting activities, both casual and in clubs. Between 1963 and 1990, in which the Dutch population grew by 25 percent, the number of sports club members grew by 160 percent, from 1.57 to 4.08 million.

Some sports profited more than others from this general trend. The previous sections explained why American and Japanese sports grew faster than the average. This final section on the differential popularization of sports in Europe focuses on two different groups of sports that grew at an above-average and below-average rate, respectively. The fast-growing cluster consists of sports associated with (and practiced by) the elite. Mountaineering, bridge, golf, field hockey, equestrian sports, rowing, skiing, squash, tennis, and yachting all grew far more rapidly in the last quarter of the twentieth century than other sports. The surge in popularity of bridge, hockey, and tennis started in the mid-1970s, while mountaineering and rowing took off in the 1980s. Hockey and tennis leveled out somewhat in the 1990s after a period of above-average growth, while bridge, mountaineering, and rowing continued to increase in popularity. Golf, equestrian sports, and squash continued to grow even more rapidly than before in the 1990s.

Meanwhile, certain sports associated with lower social classes—gymnastics, handball, ice skating, soccer, and swimming—lost some of their appeal. These sports had below-average growth until the late 1970s, after which their membership actually started to decline in absolute terms. If a value is ascribed to each sport on the basis of participants' average income, a status hierarchy of sports can be constructed (see table 10 for the Netherlands).[203]

Table 10 shows clearly that the sports in the former group occupy the high-

Table 10. Status Ranking of Sports in the Netherlands

Rank	Sport	Index	Rank	Sport	Index
1	squash	2.73	17	gymnastics	2.13
2	surfing	2.71	18	cycling	2.11
3	field hockey	2.70	19	rowing	2.08
4	golf	2.69	20	soccer	2.03
5	skiing	2.67	21	track and field	2.03
6	yachting	2.63	22	running	2.02
7	equestrian sports	2.44	23	weightlifting	2.00
8	korfball	2.41	24	indoor soccer	1.95
9	tennis	2.40	25	ice skating	1.94
10	chess	2.38	26	auto racing	1.92
11	badminton	2.28	27	handball	1.86
12	checkers	2.27	28	swimming	1.86
13	table tennis	2.23	29	motorcycle racing	1.86
14	baseball	2.20	30	martial arts, bodybuilding	1.84
15	basketball	2.17	31	water polo	1.71
16	volleyball	2.16	32	billiards	1.63

Source: Data are from Inter/View, *Sports Scanner* (processed by the author).

est positions while those in the latter group are all in the bottom half of the table. Of the thirty-two sports, gymnastics, handball, ice skating, soccer, and swimming all occupy positions between seventeen and twenty-eight. These are old sports, which are largely associated with and played by skilled workers, small entrepreneurs, and junior management. In 1963, 70 percent of total sports club membership related to one or more of these pursuits. By 1980 this percentage had fallen to 54 percent, and by 1998 it was as low as 39 percent. The ten sports with higher social status, however, grew enormously in popularity in this period, from 12 percent in 1963 to 24 percent in 1980 and 37 percent in 1998. The other fifty-eight sports that are organized nationally in the Netherlands exhibited a variety of patterns, but as a whole they did not undergo significant growth. As table 11 makes clear, most of the gain clearly went to the ten high-status sports. This table compares the popularity of mountaineering, bridge, golf, field hockey, equestrian sports, rowing, skiing, squash, tennis, and yachting (high-status sports) in 1963, 1980, and 1998 to that of gymnastics, handball, ice skating, soccer, and swimming (low-status sports) and of the other fifty-eight sports practiced in the Netherlands.

In other Western countries, too, the number of people playing high-status sports increased more rapidly than the average rate of growth. In Sweden the total number of clubs increased by 13 percent between 1963 and 1980; low-status sports lagged 4 percent behind average levels of growth, whereas more prestigious ones grew 45 percent faster than average. In Germany, the share of soccer, gymnastics, and handball in the total number of sports club

Table 11. The Social Status of Sports and
Changing Levels of Participation

	High-Status Sports	Major Low-Status Sports	Other Sports
1963	12%	70%	18%
1980	24	54	22
1998	37	39	24

Sources: Data are from Nederlandse Sport Federatie,
Ledentallen, 1963 and 1980; NOC*NSF, *Ledentallen,* 1998
(processed by the author).

members declined by 10 percent between 1966 and 1990, whereas tennis, ski-ing, and golf collectively increased their share of the total from 6 percent to 14 percent. In Belgium, squash, golf, bridge, and skiing were among the ten sports with the biggest growth in numbers of clubs between 1978 and 1988. In Western Europe, tennis even seriously rivaled soccer for popularity. The ratio between devotees of these two sports changed dramatically within a brief space of time. In 1963 there were 5.4 times as many soccer as tennis play-ers in France; by 1989 there were only 1.3 times as many. And a similar story unfolded in Denmark: the ratio fell from almost 10 to 1 in 1953 to 3 to 1 in 1990.

A number of related social changes since the late 1950s can help explain these trends. In the first place, the size of each sport's traditional recruitment group altered along with society's changing class structure. General levels of education and prosperity increased sharply between 1960 and 1980, and the working class gradually accounted for a smaller proportion of the workforce. The middle classes (minus the self-employed) grew larger, however, keeping pace with the expansion of the machinery of government and higher edu-cation. More and more university graduates entered the workforce, many finding employment in the burgeoning service organizations, in fields such as health care, social welfare, education, culture, recreation, and the environ-ment. The rise of this "new class" was balanced by a corresponding decline in traditional services with low social status, such as the domestic service branch. The number of small entrepreneurs (particularly traditional shop-keepers) and wage-earners in agriculture and industry also declined.[204]

In short, the number of people whose education, income, and profession placed them in the social classes among which high-status sports were pop-ular in the past became much larger, swelling these sports' recruitment groups. Boys and girls from poorer social classes discovered they could join in sports that their parents could not have contemplated. After completing their education they tended to abandon low-status sports such as gymnas-

tics, handball, soccer, and swimming in favor of activities more in tune with their new positions. Hockey benefitted most from the growth in secondary and higher education in the Netherlands, as the most prestigious sport to which high school students were introduced.[205] Growing prosperity made vacations in snow-covered mountain resorts accessible to more people than ever before, boosting skiing. In more mountainous regions, competitive skiing became popular; the flat landscape of the Netherlands restricted most Dutch people's skiing to winter trips abroad. The Netherlands Skiing Association cleverly exploited this trend by introducing an inventive recruitment policy, including good deals on special exercise programs, practicing on artificial ski runs, and vacation insurance, as well as free subscriptions to the association's journal and discounts on hotel bookings and skiing events. Between 1978 and 1988 the association's membership actually grew more rapidly than the number of skiers: by 212 percent compared to the 111 percent increase in the number of skiers.

In the second place, the general level of prosperity rose fastest, in relative terms, in the lower social classes, reducing income differences and hence eroding class-related behavioral differences.[206] The middle classes became less reticent about taking up elite pursuits: police officers, nurses, and bookkeepers ventured onto the tennis court. Upwardly mobile groups in particular adapted their lifestyles seamlessly to their new, higher social positions, which included sports with the appropriate status. The young man who had seen his father's modest furniture store grow into a successful business for modern interiors, the entrepreneur whose father had once been a factory worker, and the arts student whose parents had only attended a few years of elementary education were particularly keen to acquire the right symbols. Tennis was the most obvious choice, partly because it was not even necessary to join a club, as commercial courts abounded.

This does not mean that virtually all sports have been fully democratized—that today's tennis players are no different from the kind of people who play soccer or handball. Superficially it looks as if people of all classes are on the courts. However, research reveals that social differences between sports are alive and well (see tables 10 and 12).

Tennis has dropped only a few rungs on the social ladder in the Netherlands over the past few decades. This shows that the expansion of the middle class has boosted tennis rather than more interest among lower social groups.[207] Thanks to this expansion, one in twenty-two Dutch people belong to a tennis club, as compared to one in two hundred in the early 1960s. And more than a million Dutch people (out of a population of fifteen million) regularly play without joining a club.[208] With numbers like these, the sport

Table 12. Breakdown by Social Class of Dutch Nationals and
Participants in Various Sports (Organized and Informal), 1988

Social Class	All Dutch Nationals	Hockey	Skiing	Tennis	Soccer
A (highest)	16%	37%	38%	32%	14%
B1	12	9	16	19	14
B2	17	27	22	21	20
C	39	22	21	25	46
D (lowest)	16	4	2	2	6

Source: Inter/View, *Summo Scanner.*
Note: Social class is determined by education, income, and home ownership.

itself can scarcely serve as a mark of distinction. Instead, it is all about where
you play—on a hired court or at a club. And a long-established club like
Sphaerinda has far more cachet than a recent arrival like Willpower.[209]

When the tennis boom started to slow down in most Western countries
in the early 1980s, golf in particular surged to unprecedented heights of popularity. The two trends are related. People from circles formerly associated
with tennis now found that the relatively unknown and more exclusive sport
of golf provided the atmosphere, relationships, and social contacts they
sought. Forty-six percent of golfers responding to a questionnaire in 1988 said
that they used to play tennis, but only 26 percent of them still did so. They
had also played more hockey in the past than at the time of the survey (36
percent as opposed to 10 percent), but this change was probably largely age-
related.[210] Among highly educated young people in senior management, the
popularization of tennis triggered a revival in squash.[211]

The rise of golf is perhaps the most striking development of all. In 1955
there were twenty-seven hundred golf club members in the Netherlands,
putting it in twenty-seventh place. By 1980 golf club membership had grown
to 10,735, but golf had nonetheless dropped to thirty-third place, because
many other sports had grown faster in the interim. After 1980 the expansion
of golf outstripped that of all other sports: in the space of sixteen years, the
Dutch Golf Federation grew tenfold to more than a hundred thousand members. In 1998 golf became one of the ten sports with the most participants in
the Netherlands. This is an international trend; golf is the sport with which
highly educated, prosperous middle-aged people with good social positions
can boost their image in international circles. The highest percentage of golf
players is found in the wealthiest countries. The golf boom started in the
United States in the 1970s, with Japan following in the early 1980s, and Europe toward the end of the 1980s. In France the number of golf licensees
quadrupled between 1983 and 1989 from about 46,000 to 160,000, and Swe-

den, Germany, and Denmark witnessed similar trends. Growth has lagged behind in less prosperous countries.[212] This trailing development applies equally to the other status sports that have done so well in Western Europe; they flourish less in countries such as Turkey, Portugal, and the countries of Eastern Europe, where standards of living are rising more slowly, the middle classes are expanding less dramatically, and class differences are more resistant to change.

The vogue for golf also has to do with the aging of the population. In 1988 only 8 percent of golfers were twenty-four years of age or less; 33 percent were aged between twenty-five and forty-four, and 44 percent were between forty-five and sixty-five. This means that golf is benefitting more than other sports from the aging of society. However, the age and social range of golfers are widening to some extent, especially in metropolitan areas. A market research study revealed that potential golfers are younger than those already active in the sport (20 percent are twenty-four years of age or less; 20 percent are aged twenty-five to thirty-four; 28 percent are aged thirty-five to forty-four; 16 percent are aged forty-five to fifty-five; and 16 percent are over fifty-five), have a slightly lower income (72 percent have an above-average income, as opposed to 85 percent among active golfers), a distinctly lower level of education (47 percent are highly educated compared to 77 percent of active golfers), and are less likely to come from the upper echelons of society (77 percent from class A or B compared to 91 percent of active golfers).[213] Golf's heightened prestige also brought the percentage of women golf club members more or less up to the level of other elite sports. While women accounted for only 22 percent of members in 1963, by 1990 they were at 43 percent. The ratio will probably stabilize at fifty-fifty, in common with other elite sports.

As a result of all this interest, new golf courses are being built by the dozen, and play is becoming cheaper. What is more, there are relatively more public golf courses than before, although in 1988 the majority of golf facilities were still members-only.[214]

* * *

The popularization of tennis, badminton, and hockey mainly ensued from the expansion of the middle classes and was strengthened by the democratization and growth of informality in Dutch society in the 1970s. Ten years later, this invasion of what had once been an elite cultural good led many to seek other ways of enhancing their status—hence the rapid growth of golf, bridge, rowing, and mountain-climbing.[215] This thirst for distinctive sports went with a tendency toward greater formality in the 1980s, accompanied by a widening gap between rich and poor. After the blossoming of untold democrati-

zation and emancipatory movements in the 1960s and 1970s, when behavioral codes slackened and open expressions of authority were reviled, the 1980s saw something of a reaction, with a revival of respect for law and order and etiquette and expressions of class differences becoming more acceptable again.[216] One result of this trend was a revival in student fraternities, which indirectly boosted rowing. In 1963 the Royal Netherlands Rowing Federation had 11,140 members; by 1981 it had acquired only 576 more, whereas the total number of people active in sports more than doubled in this period. It caught up in the 1980s, though: while overall sports club membership grew by a modest 10 percent, the rowing federation grew by more than 40 percent.

This process of encroachment followed by an exodus to sports with higher status is a specific example of a more general trend. Especially during periods of rapidly growing prosperity, declining social differences, and increased social mobility, lower social classes have more scope to adopt elite codes of behavior and are less timid about doing so; this popularization creates the need among the elite to seek new ways of distinguishing themselves from the newcomers.

This process was first seen in the Netherlands in the late nineteenth century. Far more children were attending school, and wages had risen such that many workers could afford nonessential items such as recreational club fees. By promoting and playing the new English elite sports, the upper crust initially distinguished and distanced themselves from the masses. The exclusivity of these new English sports endured for several decades, but that of cycling, for instance, soon crumbled. This had to do with the mass marketing of products: from cookies to clothing—and bicycles too—numerous articles were now being turned out on assembly lines.[217] In about 1880, when the first cycling clubs were founded, owning a bicycle was still a mark of distinction. The first cyclists were all from the upper classes. But the mass production of bicycles and the commercialization and professionalization of track cycling ushered in a rapid popularization of this sport.[218] As more people from the poorer classes appeared on the tracks and in the stands, the elite's interest waned. In the early twentieth century they transferred their allegiance to a sport that was still exclusive—auto racing.[219]

Between 1925 and 1930, "'the good years preceding the Depression,'"[220] the Dutch sports world witnessed a new drive to achieve distinction. The national economy was booming, certainly in comparison to the disastrous time that followed.[221] Another key factor was the increase in organized workers' sports in the 1920s, one consequence of which was the founding of the Dutch Workers' Sports Federation in 1926. In 1933 the sports with the most participants

within the federation were, in descending order, gymnastics, swimming, soccer, korfball, track and field, and handball.[222] In other organizations, too, these were the most popular sports among workers. With so many workers actively joining in, playing a sport no longer automatically enhanced status. Two consequences ensued. In the first place, some of the elite, especially the most highly educated, became more critical of sports, which had been introduced by their own ancestors a mere fifty years earlier. In the second place, the choice of sport became increasingly significant. As workers embraced korfball and soccer, the more fashionable clubs in these two sports found their membership dwindling.[223] The rise of the Corinthian movement and the growth of elite sports that no one had heard of a few years before similarly reflected the status rivalry of the time. The number of teams affiliated with the cricket federation doubled between 1924 and 1932, hockey's rapid growth started around 1927, while the number of golf clubs also grew faster in the 1920s than in the previous and following decades.

The current drive to achieve distinction through sport differs from these previous ones in several respects. In the first place, elite sports are attracting far more people than ever before. And in the second place, the commercial exploitation of this trend is more marked. That the social composition of so-called elite sports is already far more heterogeneous than this label would seem to suggest is immediately apparent to any new initiate. While tennis, hockey, skiing, golf, squash, horse riding, bridge, gliding, mountaineering, rowing, and cricket are still mainly the preserve of highly educated people with above-average salaries or good prospects, the narrowing of the income and lifestyle divide, enhanced social mobility, and the expansion of the upper middle classes have greatly attenuated their elitist qualities. Even so, their enduring prestige, fueled by their historically rooted public image, still exercises great appeal. The popularization and commercialization of a sport will prompt some to go elsewhere. This is why different, minor sports labeled "elitist" are constantly being discovered or rediscovered. Are appearances deceptive, or is cricket too making a comeback? It is not history that repeats itself, but the underlying social mechanism.

Popularization changes a sport's image and its nature. The advent of new types of golfers puts pressure on all sorts of customs and etiquette that used to distinguish golfers from participants in other sports. Crowds now congregate around the greens of the major tournaments, a professional golfer who has made a successful putt raises his hands in delight; the public applauds and occasionally shouts and whistles. All this changes golf's image, and not even the distinguished amateur who plays his eighteen holes in the serenity of an exclusive club can shrug it off. True, golf champions do not yet leap into

the air at the moment of victory, nor do they set off on a lap of honor to display their medal, flowers, and national flag to rows of cheering spectators. But if the game makes its entrance into the Olympic Games at some point in the future, would such spectacles be so improbable?

The development of tennis is a perfect example of the erosion of class-bound codes of conduct and customs that inevitably accompanies popularization. This sport is now a hybrid of elitist and popular characteristics. We see tournament players wearing colored shirts, unpressed soccer shorts without pockets, cycling pants as undergarments, and Hawaiian-style shorts. Gone are the days in which tennis was confined to sedate gravel courts at exclusive clubs whose members knew one another not only from the clubhouse but also from their shared suburban social life, committee meetings, lunches, and receptions. Many tennis clubs have become larger, more diverse, and more anonymous. The sport is played on concrete, at indoor sports centers and in the street. Joining in seems less daunting. Professional tennis stars like John McEnroe and André Agassi have banished the image of the tennis player as a gentleman in white shirt and shorts. And during matches, umpires are fighting a losing battle in their efforts to curb the enthusiasm of the huge crowds. "Silence, please!" The peace and quiet they are asking for is not a prerequisite for concentration but a relic of the sport's prestigious past. After all, competitors of all kinds need concentration: from the soccer player running to take a decisive penalty to the ice skater turning into the home stretch to the athlete speeding to a new high jump record. But for them you will not find any referee or loudspeaker booming, "Silence, please!" As yet, the noise at tennis matches is confined to isolated shouts of encouragement and a bit of yelling, but sometimes, as in Davis Cup matches, things are already getting a little rowdier. It still sounds a little timid, but calling "Olé, olé" and "Come on, Holland" is no longer unacceptable. Spectators are gradually becoming fans, in spite of the umpire's urgent requests for "Silence, please!"

5. Differences in the Global Sporting System

BUOYED BY WESTERN international expansion, sports spread fast to all corners of the world. Wherever traders, migrants, and colonial officials settled, they set up sports clubs in order to meet other Westerners in foreign parts, to sustain cultural ties with their mother country, and to relax after the day's work. Only fifty years after British colonials founded the first cricket club outside Britain—in Calcutta in 1792—there were clubs on every continent. German gymnastics clubs sprang up in the mid-nineteenth century not only in Europe but in Windhoek (in what was then German South West Africa) in 1861, in Hong Kong in 1863, in Valparaiso, Chile, in 1870, and in Alexandria, Egypt, in 1873. Following an American initiative, basketball was first played in Tientsin, China, in 1896, only four years after the sport's invention in Springfield. Two years later the Americans introduced basketball to Chile and the Philippines.[1] These countries and cities are only a few random examples of the globalization of organized sports in the second half of the nineteenth century. It would be easy to find a similar string of examples for virtually all the organized sports that existed at the time.

Modern sports only flourish if the necessary transportation, organizational, and communications infrastructure exists at the national level. This is why competitive sports have gained ground fastest in countries that are relatively far advanced in processes of scale expansion and integration. In this respect Britain developed earlier than France, France earlier than Greece, Greece earlier than Korea, and Korea earlier than Mali. The rise of sports federations within each country follows a classical model of innovation and diffusion. Expressed as a graph, it appears as an elongated S-shape: after a phase of slow initial development comes a short and rapid climb, which then tapers to a period of far more gradual growth.[2]

Wallerstein's theory of the world system applies here too: each sport spreads from a core country to areas further from the center and from there to the periphery. The chronological order in which national soccer federations arose in Europe reflects this rule. Between 1860 and 1873 federations were founded in England, Wales, Scotland, and Ireland; between 1889 and 1910 in the Netherlands, Denmark, Germany, Switzerland, Belgium, Italy, France, Austria-Hungary, Czechoslovakia, Norway, Sweden, and Finland; and after 1910 in Russia, Spain, Portugal, the Baltic States, Poland, Yugoslavia, Bulgaria, Greece, Romania, and Albania. This broadly reflects the chronology of modernization and relations between core countries and the periphery in the latter half of the nineteenth century.[3] Geographers call this "hierarchical diffusion." Another term, "contagious diffusion," is used to explain phenomena such as the early spread of soccer to Ireland.[4] Neighboring countries will adopt a sport sooner than those further away. Geographical proximity facilitates the diffusion of all innovation; oceans or mountain ranges tend to impede these processes.

The popularization of sports in non-Western countries has followed the same pattern as in Europe. The dissemination of sports between and within countries reflects the international balance of power and national processes of modernization. In British colonies a different pattern of sports evolved than in American protectorates, which was different again from that in countries that preserved their independence. The first sports organizations were founded in centers of political and economic development. In general the initiative came from Westerners, whether working in government, trade, or the army. Before long the first "locals" became involved. They belonged to modernizing elites who had been educated either in the West or at schools based on Western principles and saw sport as part of a modern lifestyle and material progress. In the next phase, some sports became accessible to groups lower down the social scale, first in urban centers and later in the countryside. The more peripheral a country in the world system, the more slowly sports catch on, especially in rural areas and among lower social groups and mature adults, and the longer the resistance to women's participation tends to persist.[5] The spread and popularization of Western sports puts pressure on indigenous pastimes. The pursuit of, say, Malay *sepak takraw* and Indian wrestling lasted longest in regions and among groups who were least involved with modernization.[6]

At the end of the nineteenth century no country could withstand the military and economic supremacy of the West. The unequal balance of power resulted in the unequal "import" and "export" of cultural goods and affected attitudes when cultures met. Most white Europeans had a sense of innate

superiority and believed that disseminating Western culture was a boon for the indigenous population of non-Western societies. Furthermore they hoped that if colonized nations adopted their values and goals it would help preserve Western domination.[7] Western achievements reaped admiration in other parts of the world. In some countries the elite saw Western modernization as a model for development, without which their nation was doomed to second-class citizenship, while others feared the threat to their own culture and identity. The adoption of Western sports and the sportization of traditional pastimes also meant copying Western lifestyles—not just terms, rituals, symbols, and clothes but also standards of organization, regulation, standardization, secularization, specialization, training, quantification, and the effort to break records. All this meant adopting more goal-oriented behavior and the long-term bureaucratic coordination and planning that Max Weber describes as characteristic of the development of Western societies.[8]

Some, concerned to protect their own cultural heritage, tried to stem the tide of Western sports and associated lifestyles. However, in trying to preserve indigenous pastimes, they tended to adopt strategies based on the success of modern sports: they regulated, standardized, and organized them along Western lines, thereby depriving them of much of their traditional character and appeal. The net result of their efforts was a renewal of these pastimes that increased the diversity of the global sporting system.[9]

No Tabula Rasa: The Differential Popularization of Sports in the "White Dominions"

After a long history as British colonies, Canada, Australia, and New Zealand finally achieved independent status in the period between the wars. Their close cultural ties with Britain distinguish these "White Dominions" from other colonies. The immigrants who drove out or subjected the indigenous inhabitants in the nineteenth century were almost all of European origin, and most were British.[10] They were less subservient to the "mother country" than other British colonies, and their societies were more egalitarian. These dominions had no small long-entrenched indigenous elite that sought to ally itself with colonial administrators and distance itself from the rest of the population by imbibing British education and behavior: most inhabitants of the "white settler societies" felt British, and many were intent on preserving British culture.

Because of these differences, the British influence on sporting patterns took a completely different form in the White Dominions than in colonies in Asia, Africa, and the West Indies. In these territories it was not only British offi-

cials, businessmen, officers, and soldiers who introduced and propagated English sports but the entire population with British roots who had already become acquainted with English sports or their precursors before emigrating. As Richard Holt comments, these countries were no tabula rasa on which the British could write as they pleased.[11] Here, people did not learn the sports from strangers but from each other. Older sports, such as cricket and horse racing, and the pastimes from which new sports such as soccer and rugby emerged, along with all their nuances in social significance, were as familiar to these people as to the British.

The sports culture was oriented toward Britain. The pioneers simply continued their old culture in a distant country. Government, the army, and schools also played an important role. The curricula of the elite schools allowed plenty of time for rugby and cricket. Many headmasters had attended or visited British public schools and adhered to the ethics prescribed by *Tom Brown's Schooldays,* which influenced the youth for generations.[12] Furthermore, in spite of the enormous distances involved, cricket and rugby matches were often held between these countries and Britain, which hoped for a strengthening of mutual ties.[13] For the inhabitants of the Dominions these matches had another function: besides nurturing a sense of cultural affinity with people on the other side of the world they were also a channel for venting feelings of national rivalry and the urge for independence. This ambivalent attitude reflected the split loyalties of many individual immigrants. Allegiance to the old culture, where their roots lay, vied with a commitment to their new country, which held their future. This mixture of comradeship and rivalry gave the matches against the British a special flavor and imparted a unique emotional charge to moments of victory.[14]

Australia and New Zealand

Because of their close ties and similar social structure and history, Australia and New Zealand have similar sporting patterns. Both are totally dominated by English sports, with nine out of the top eleven sports originating in Britain: soccer, cricket, indoor bowling and lawn bowling, golf, netball, tennis, rugby, squash, and field hockey. If we focus on the proportion of sportsmen and sportswomen who play English sports, New Zealand occupies second place (84 percent) and Australia third (75 percent), behind the United Kingdom itself, but ahead of all other European countries, the United States, and Japan (see table 7, p. 68). From an international perspective the popularity of rugby, cricket, and netball in Australia and New Zealand are the most striking. Also noteworthy are the high score of Australian football and the

relative popularity of American basketball.[15] In New Zealand, long known as "the Britain of the South" because of its affectionate attachment to British culture, the typically English sports still rank highest.[16]

Australia and New Zealand were from the outset averse to snobbishness. Most immigrants came from Britain's lower classes, and their emigration was largely motivated by a desire to do well in an open, more egalitarian society. Such attitudes led to the rapid democratization of rugby and cricket, sports that were elitist elsewhere. In New Zealand both are now widely played among the poorer sections of society. Australian cricket did not develop the sharp distinctions between "players" and "gentlemen" that were so marked in Britain. Here Rugby League—the professional variant—caught on far more than Rugby Union, and the popularization of Australian football soon did away with class barriers.[17]

For two reasons, rugby became more popular in New Zealand and Australia than in Britain. First, many immigrants came from the British Midlands, where rugby had originated and was most popular. Second, status was far less of an issue: rugby players did not put on airs in these fair-minded countries.[18] Rugby is New Zealand's national sport, with about two hundred thousand club members as opposed to soccer's seventy thousand. This popularity was already well established a hundred years ago. Many clubs immediately adopted the Rugby Union rules when they were published in about 1870. By 1890 there were already some seven hundred clubs affiliated with sixteen regional unions, while the membership of New Zealand's Football Association stood at only 109 clubs around 1900.[19] Rugby has about 250,000 players in Australia (Union and League combined), while soccer (indoor and outdoor combined) has twice this figure. But both have to compete with Australian football, which is almost as popular as soccer.

The development of Australian football can be explained by much the same factors that nourished American football: it was partly attributable to the vast distances between Britain and Australia and partly because the first football clubs were founded before soccer and rugby were standardized in Britain. What emerged in Australia was a variant that most resembled rugby as played at Harrow but was unique for Australia. The first clubs were founded in the smart suburbs of Melbourne, but the game soon spread to poorer neighborhoods.[20]

While boys learn rugby and cricket at school, girls are taught netball and field hockey. Netball is so widespread at girls' schools that it occupies third place in New Zealand. It is played almost exclusively (98 percent) by women. In this regard it resembles gymnastics in Europe. As far as the proportion of women participants is concerned, field hockey follows in New Zealand

at 64 percent, then horse racing at 64 percent and softball at 52 percent. In Australia and South Africa, too, netball is popular among young schoolgirls while field hockey tends to attract female high school and university students. The great majority of players in both cases are between ten and nineteen years of age. These figures are similar to those for the United Kingdom.

South Africa

In South Africa, British influence dates from the early nineteenth century, when the British annexed the Cape of Good Hope to safeguard their route to India. In the 1820s thousands of British colonists poured into South Africa, English became the official language, and the English legal system was adopted. Here, too, this influence has made an indelible stamp on today's sporting patterns; nine out of the eleven most popular sports are of British origin. Soccer has pride of place, followed by tennis, track and field, and rugby. Badminton, squash, swimming, field hockey, golf, netball, and basketball are all prominent.[21]

The apartheid system also had a strong influence on sports. Wealthy whites traditionally play tennis, golf, and squash, while middle-income whites have tended to prefer rugby, swimming, netball, field hockey, track and field, and cricket. The large Indian community plays more cricket and field hockey (as in India itself) than other groups. Among blacks, "persons of mixed race," and other Asians, soccer became the most popular sport, causing many whites to avoid it. In 1977 there were about 330,000 registered black soccer players as opposed to 40,000 whites, putting soccer in only eighth place among whites, which is very low from an international perspective.[22] Afrikaners prefer rugby, which in South Africa is no longer an elite sport, though it is almost exclusively white.

Students at the Universities of Stellenbosch and Cape Town were the first to start playing rugby in South Africa. From these trendsetting institutions the sport soon spread among the white population. Rugby's status-ridden British past made it perfectly suited for appropriation as an exclusive white sport. Soccer had no such airs. Brought to South Africa by British soldiers, it soon became popular in mining areas. As the first players came from the poorer classes, the apartheid barriers were far easier to dismantle than in the case of rugby.[23]

Canada

Because of its proximity to the United States and greater ethnic diversity, Canada acquired different sporting patterns than those of the other domin-

ions. The largest ethnic group was French-speaking, and rivalries with English-speaking immigrants impeded the spread of British culture.[24] This new multicultural society was engaged in a quest for its own identity. Its need for symbols to express this identity resulted in Canada acquiring its own pattern of sports, distinct from those of Britain and the United States.[25]

In the mid-nineteenth century the Canadian pattern of sports in the British colonies still bore the imprint of the mother country, with horse racing and cricket ranking highest. Cricket's popularity peaked in the 1860s, when extra British troops were sent to Canada to defend the colony against the threat posed by the American Civil War. The most enthusiastic devotees of these first organized sports were found at army garrisons among officers who had attended English public schools and at elite schools modeled along English lines.[26] According to Richard Gruneau, the popularity of English sports waned at the end of the nineteenth century as the proportion of English-born Canadians started to decline, the colonial class structure crumbled, and the influence of American culture grew stronger. Gradually the Canadian pattern of sports became more like that of its powerful neighbor.[27]

The shift from British to American influence also had to do with the increase in transportation and communication lines between Canada and the United States. Since these north-south connections were faster, better, and cheaper than those between east and west, American influence forestalled the autonomous development of a Canadian sporting pattern modeled on British precedent. As American influence grew stronger, baseball, American football, volleyball, and basketball became popular, first in the western provinces with their strong orientation toward the United States, then in southern parts of Ontario and Nova Scotia, and eventually throughout the rest of the country. Americans also became involved in the development and commercial exploitation of Canadian ice hockey, baseball, and football, which meant that these sports too became Americanized. Of the British sports, only soccer, tennis, and golf remained really popular. Tennis and golf provided the elite with a refuge as other sports were invaded by the masses. Soccer remained popular, thanks to the influx of increasing numbers of immigrants from soccer-loving countries. Among the country's 350,000 soccer players (in 1990) those who were born in Canada are in the minority.[28]

Rivaling these were a number of other sports that evolved within the country to impart a unique quality to Canadian sporting patterns: ice hockey (which grew to become Canada's national sport), curling (introduced by the Scots and now played by half a million enthusiasts), and to a lesser extent lacrosse (an Indian pastime that was "sportized" by Canadian immigrants). Curling has more players in Canada than anywhere else in the world. (This

does not justify calling it Canada's national sport, however, as some have done: in numbers of participants and spectators and in terms of media coverage this honor clearly belongs to ice hockey.) Hockey is Canada's "'national religion,'" the "'Canadian metaphor.'"[29] In 1984 there were a staggering 250,000 registered players under twelve years of age. In terms of sales, hockey skates have been at the top of the Christmas shopping list since 1927.[30] Hockey's popularization followed broadly similar lines to that of American football in the United States. It was first regulated and organized in Canada in 1879 by students at the prestigious McGill University in Montreal. From there it gradually spread to other universities and colleges, to lower social classes, and from urban areas to the countryside. By about 1900 most Canadian towns had their own ice hockey clubs; Montreal, the main hockey center, had more than a hundred.[31]

Another of Canada's "national sports" is lacrosse. The reason why it has sometimes been given this label is not because of the number of participants but because it developed out of a North American Indian pastime, baggataway. In the 1830s immigrants adapted it to the model of English team sports. French immigrants named it "la crosse"; British influence was reflected in the introduction of a football-like goal and in the names for the sections of the field, derived from cricket. In 1856 the Montreal Lacrosse Club made its appearance. Within ten years there were eighty clubs in total, with some twenty thousand players, all affiliated to the national lacrosse federation. While the popularization of ice hockey recalls that of American football, lacrosse developed along roughly the same lines as baseball. Both were presented as symbols of national identity, in opposition to the English cricket; in both cases, patriots spun myths intended to cement belief in their local origins. But the difference between the two sports is equally significant, as it brings out the difference in the balance of power between Canada and the United States. While baseball became extremely popular in Canada, lacrosse hardly made any impact on the United States; indeed, lacrosse scarcely managed to spread beyond Canada, while baseball is played throughout the world.

* * *

Smaller ethnic groups also made their mark on sporting patterns in the dominions. But these are clearly subordinate to British influence—much more so than in continental Europe, for instance. In Australia gymnastics does not figure among the top twenty sports. In New Zealand, which had a great many more German settlers, it stands in seventh place. Handball has few devotees in either country. Shooting and swimming, which can also be linked to the gymnastics movement, are also far less popular in these countries than in Europe.

Only in recent decades have American and Japanese sports started to catch on. The explanation of this internationalization of Australian sporting patterns should be sought, as Allen Guttmann notes, in the "postwar influx of European immigrants who are not particularly interested in an Australian replication of British life."[32] Because of this, Australia and New Zealand have evolved into highly differentiated, ethnically diverse, and multicultural societies. The once-dominant British culture succumbed to a wider range of influences—especially from the United States and Japan. The first baseball and basketball games in Australia (between American teams) were held in the nineteenth century. But in spite of the Americans' promotional efforts, "the domain of sports," as Allen Guttmann has called it, "continued to be steadfastly British."[33] It was not until the last few decades of the twentieth century that there was a change in the air. Basketball now has some two hundred thousand participants in Australia, making it one of the ten most popular sports. Moreover, substantial sponsorship contracts have been negotiated with Japanese and American firms, enabling a professional baseball league to be formed, and major league games from North America are now televised. Because of this, cricket has been put on the defensive.[34] The recently introduced Eastern martial arts are also doing well. Karate, with more than thirty thousand participants, and tae kwon do, with twenty thousand, are already in the middle group of Australian sports. Judo has declined somewhat, as it has in Europe; in 1985 there were about ten thousand registered judoists.

It is not only numbers that have changed; global developments have also transformed the form and content of sport. The once-dominant amateur stronghold has been overtaken by professional organizations. Managers, sponsors, and marketing and public relations experts are pushing the "old boys'" network of officials into the background. Multinationals such as Pepsi Cola, Toyota, Shell, Dunlop, and Wang increasingly sponsor sports teams and events. Under American influence, show and spectacle have gained in importance, and the focus of attention has shifted from players to the public. The annual Rugby League and Australian Rules Football finals now resemble the NFL Super Bowl, and rugby, soccer, and basketball games are brightened up with cheerleaders, giant mascots, and live bands.[35]

Spurned and Embraced: The Differential Popularization of Sports in Asia

The sporting patterns of most of the countries of Asia, Latin America, and Africa display a number of similar features. In the first place, the dominant influence of Britain and the United States is reflected in the popularity of soccer, track and field, hockey, cricket, baseball, basketball, and volleyball. Of

these sports, soccer and baseball are generally played most. This is because they had already become the national sports of Britain and the United States before they spread to other continents. This meant that it was not only Europeans and Americans from elite groups that disseminated them but also Western sailors, soldiers, and workers. It was from these visitors that the local population learned soccer and baseball, which had none of the exclusivity that characterized some of the other sports.[36]

Second, the enormous gap in popularity between baseball and soccer on the one hand and tennis, golf, squash, field hockey, and other elite Western sports on the other hand has survived longer in Asia, Africa, and Latin America than in Western Europe, where increased prosperity and education have boosted the latter category since the 1960s and 1970s. In most non-Western countries, much of the population is still engaged in agriculture, fewer attend higher education, and standards of living are lower: all these factors go with a slower growth in the upper middle classes—the recruitment group for elite sports. This is in contrast to the huge proportion of the population for which soccer and baseball have a natural appeal. Thus the international tennis federation of Bangladesh has sixteen hundred registered players, while the FIFA records (with rather suspect precision) the existence of 138,995 soccer players in Bangladesh.

Another shared feature is the lack of popularity of gymnastics, handball, and other sports associated with the German gymnastics movement. This is not only because of the lack of any German political or military influence, but also because of the small size of the lower middle class—the mainstay of this movement in its native land. German influences are confined to isolated immigrant communities in a few countries, and gymnastics clubs are in general little more than meeting places for people with German roots.

Besides these similarities, however, we can point to several sharp distinctions. These are greatest in Asia; national sporting patterns in Africa and Latin America are more homogeneous. India is a nation of cricketers, Japan is devoted to baseball, and China is a table tennis stronghold. Virtually every Asian country has its own preferred martial art: there is pentjak silat in Indonesia, muay thai in Thailand, tae kwon do in Korea, wu-shu in China, and judo in Japan. Two reasons account for these differences between Asia and the other continents. First, Western influence was more diverse in the early period of the global spread of sports: while Africa was almost completely under European domination and much of Latin America had achieved political independence, Asian countries were ruled by a variety of administrations. There were British (Pakistan, India, Malaysia, Burma), French (Vietnam, Laos, Cambodia), Dutch (Indonesia), American (the Philippines), and

Russian (northern Asia) colonies or protectorates. Afghanistan, China, Siam (Thailand), and various countries in the Middle East retained their independence; Japan grew to become a political, economic, and military superpower by the early twentieth century, which the Western powers ignored at their peril and which had imperial ambitions of its own. It colonized the Bonin, Ryukyu, and Kuril Islands, Formosa (Taiwan), Korea, and parts of China and Manchuria.

Second, Asian cultures were less vulnerable to Western influences than those of Africa, as the balance of power was less unequal. The Europeans discovered that Asia was a continent of sharp contrasts—appalling poverty coexisted with Oriental splendor. The Indian maharajahs, the Japanese shoguns, and Chinese viceroys radiated an air of wealth and power that impressed the Europeans more than the power of elites in other parts of the world. The Asian intelligentsia enjoyed a strong position and could invoke a centuries-old written culture that was much respected in the West. The colonial administrators made it possible for the intelligentsia to be educated along European lines. Though this tended to facilitate the spread of Western products, techniques, ideas, organizational structures, and codes of conduct, it also gave the local elites thus educated the tools to resist the Westernization of their culture. While regarding the advantages of a Western-style modernization model as the key to progress, they wanted to preserve their country's independence. No large intelligentsia of this kind existed in the countries of Africa and Latin America.[37]

These variations in dependency generated certain fundamental differences between Asian states: in former British colonies, such as India, Pakistan, Burma, and Malaysia, almost all the sports to attain popularity were English; in countries like the Philippines, the United States was influential and American sports did better than elsewhere; in more or less politically autonomous states, such as Thailand, China, Korea, and Japan in East Asia, and Iran and Yemen in West Asia, soccer gained a stronger hold and cricket and field hockey attracted less enthusiasm than in former British colonies.

The precise ranking of these sports cannot be given for Asia with the same precision as for Europe, as the statistics are incomplete and unreliable. Still, we can gain a rough idea. India has four major sports: Indian wrestling, soccer, cricket, and (probably to a lesser degree) field hockey. The international hockey federation would not go beyond estimating the number of field hockey players in India at "tens of thousands" for 1990, while in 1979 an IOC publication had quoted a figure of 4.5 million. In both cases it is unclear what criteria these figures were based on. According to FIFA, India has about 8.27 million soccer players. No figures are available for the number of cricketers,

but the Indians themselves regard cricket as their national sport. Whether it does or does not exceed soccer in popularity is not really so important; it is clear that cricket is played more in India than anywhere else in Asia,[38] while in Asian countries that largely retained their independence, soccer's dominance is far more striking. In China, only the ten million table tennis players are anywhere in the region of the 20.5 million soccer players. In Korea the only rival to soccer—at 3.3 million players—is track and field, while in Thailand no other sport has anything like the 1.2 million soccer players. Where the influence of the United States has been stronger, fewer people play soccer and more gravitate toward basketball, volleyball, and baseball. This trend has already been discussed in relation to Japan. The Philippines has few soccer players in comparison to other Asian countries—only 142,800 according to FIFA; this is fewer than Korea or Thailand, in spite of the country's larger population. No figures are available for basketball and volleyball, but both are probably more popular in the Philippines than soccer.[39]

Given the impossibility of dealing with each country in detail, I shall focus on a few examples that are illustrative of these general relations of interdependency: British India, the onetime American protectorate of the Philippines, and China, which has never lost its independence.

India

How is it possible that cricket grew to become India's national sport, whereas in the United States and continental Europe it has always been marginal? Worldwide it may be said that in countries with which Britain had close trade relations, soccer is far more popular than other sports, whereas cricket, field hockey, and rugby have done particularly well in countries over which Britain has had political and military dominion. Generally, the longer and more intense this British influence, the likelier it was that cricket would eventually gain a following outside the British community and would come to be seen as part of the country's own culture. In India this succeeded so well that Ashis Nandy once joked that cricket was an Indian sport that had accidentally been discovered by the British![40] In contrast to the White Dominions, rugby did not catch on in India, whether among the "high" or "low" sections of society. Besides cricket, soccer and field hockey also prospered; polo, golf, tennis, and squash never went far, although they are quite popular among the elite.[41]

Britain's export of cricket to India may be regarded, up to a point, as a case of cultural imperialism. The colonialists saw the sport as a good way of building ties with the local ruling classes while almost surreptitiously administering a dose of British lifestyle. At the elite schools they taught carefully selected members of the young elite the principles of sportsmanship: how to play the

game, the appropriate customs and rituals, and the precepts of clothing and conduct.[42] Sport in general and cricket in particular was an exercise in "the art of being 'British.'"[43]

The young elite were particularly receptive to what they saw as modern influences. They had no desire to return to the old order; they wanted progress toward a new, independent society with modern lifestyles, which they saw as reflected in sports. Sports appealed to the imagination of a succession of princes and their vast retinues. Taking part in a cricket match was a way of distinguishing themselves from traditional elites and the rest of the population. Membership in a sports club represented status, respectability, and influential social contacts. As sports were taken up primarily by youths, it was cricket and field hockey rather than the more sedate tennis and golf that became popular. Cricket became the prime symbol of the English public school culture, and therein lay much of its appeal to Indian princes.[44]

At the end of the nineteenth century cricket was still a fashionable game in India, played by the British and British-educated and British-oriented elite: the Parsees, the feudal Gujaratis, and the upper-class Maharashtrians. But unlike tennis and especially golf, cricket was accessible to lower social groups. The British cricket culture was characterized by relations and codes of conduct that easily fitted into the mores of Indian society. It was the only sport in which it was possible for "gentlemen" and "players" to mingle without the social distinctions being eroded. This tradition was repeated in India, first in the relations between British and Indian players and subsequently in those between higher and lower Indian castes.[45] This tradition enabled men of humble origins to forge their way to the top ranks of the sport, albeit they were never allowed to forget their "place."

Between 1930 and 1950 the Indian cricket team included several princes, along with captains of industry and Oxbridge-educated senior officials. After this the sport spread throughout a wider area, geographically and socially, although it is still less common in regions lacking the patronage of a rich elite. According to Nandy, the influx of players from working-class backgrounds means the average height of the Indian cricket team is now approaching the national average. Another change is the number of regional dialects spoken by the players, sometimes necessitating the use of interpreters. Once most cricketers had an independent source of income, but today the majority is dependent on government or commercial sponsorship. With the development of cricket as India's national sport, ministers of state, actors, and big businessmen like to be seen at important matches, and the country's leading cricketers are public figures, comparable to "Bollywood" film stars. Several test match players have married famous actresses.[46]

Field hockey too was introduced to India by the British elite and popularized among local princes through the school system. But it differed from cricket in two respects. First, it never conquered the entire social spectrum of Indian society. And second, it remained confined to a few regions in the Punjab and northern India. Its popularity was based in the Sikh community.[47] To gain a better understanding of these developments, more research is needed on the way in which field hockey spread from Britain to India, the characteristics and regional ties of the British and Indian players concerned, and this sport's institutionalization in India.

Rugby had none of the appeal to Indians that it exercised in the White Dominions. This had to do with the relations between the colonialists and the local population. As a contact sport, rugby was regarded as suitable only for social equals; matches between whites and Indians were out of the question. This was equally true in the White Dominions. In Australia, New Zealand, and especially South Africa rugby became one of the most popular sports among whites. Interracial rugby matches were virtually unknown. In India there was the added factor that rugby clashed with prevailing views of the desirable degree of physical contact and with notions of cleanliness and filth. The British themselves saw it as a sport for "gentlemen ruffians," a label sought by neither senior British officials nor Indian princes. The struggle in the mud with a leather ball was not their sort of thing, not even among themselves, let alone between "high" and "low." In contrast, cricket did not impose rough physical contact or extreme physical exhaustion, nor did it call for direct contact with unholy things, incompatible with princely dignity.[48]

Among army officers, polo and later squash were popular, but outside the barracks they commanded little interest. In Britain, too, squash was popular among the military, and polo had a long tradition of association with warriors. Give the knight-at-arms a sword instead of a stick and the practical usefulness of polo immediately becomes apparent. It trained horsemanship with only one hand on the reins, so that the other was free for the sword in situations that called for agile maneuvering while fighting off an assailant. Poems and drawings attest to polo's centuries-old popularity under a variety of names in Persia. But it was a very different game from today's standardized polo. The opposing teams could contain up to a hundred contestants, and although the fight was generally between two teams, there were sometimes four. It appears to have been an extremely rough affair, given the many reports of fatal injuries sustained by participating nobles. Perhaps it was these accidents, in combination with the pastime's ever-widening popularity, that prompted early efforts in the direction of sportization. In Persia and Tibet attempts were made at an early stage to regulate and tame it.[49] Still,

a wide range of variants continued to exist, with sharp local distinctions. It was not until the latter half of the nineteenth century that polo became a modern sport and assumed its current form, after the British had regulated and organized it more strictly and had set up umbrella organizations that monitored compliance with the standard rules at the international level. In this new form polo has ousted all its various precursors. Even in countries that once had their own polo-like games, the elite—landowners and army officers in particular—promoted the British variant, which ended up prevailing everywhere.[50]

By the end of the nineteenth century soccer was no longer an elite sport in Britain. *The Times* scarcely deigned to cover it, and, taking their cue from such indifference, the colonial officials of the British empire saw the game as beneath their dignity.[51] It was common folk—soldiers and sailors who belonged to the soccer-loving classes in Britain—who brought soccer to India. Its popularization in its native land meant that soccer had far fewer of the rules and traditions that appeal to the snobbishness of the elite and discourage the masses. Soccer was presented in such a way that it was easy for ordinary Indians to take it up. In 1889 a British trading society launched the Trade Football Cup, which was renamed the Indian Football Association Shield four years later. The cup was first won by an Indian team in 1911, when the barefoot players of Mohum Bagan Football Club defeated a regimental side from the British army. This "rite of passage" horrified the British, who saw it as a humiliation that tarnished the superiority of the colonial rulers and the white "race" in general. A crowd of at least eighty thousand spectators watched the match in a period of considerable social unrest. Local papers described the victory as a sign of Indian development, equality, and even superiority. One commentator wrote of the pride and joy that filled every rice-eating, malaria-ridden, barefoot Indian, now that they had been shown the better of the beef-eating, Herculian, well-shod John Bull. After the result of the match was announced, the white inhabitants of Calcutta judged it best to remain indoors for the time being.[52] As organized sports as such remained confined to the elite for much longer than in Europe, it was not until the late twentieth century that organized soccer was played in large numbers. Soccer did not have the resources of cricket, which enjoyed the patronage of wealthy Indians who financed matches, clubs, and facilities, so it took longer to reach the poorer classes.

The differences in sporting patterns between Asia's various former British colonies spring from the size of the British-educated elite and the duration and intensity of the colonial period. If these factors were not substantial, cricket and hockey did not take hold, and soccer fared better. This

applied, for instance, to the later Burma and Malaysia. In the British crown colonies of Malacca, Penang, and Singapore, relations were different from those in India. These territories remained under the control of the British authorities in India until 1867, when they were placed under Colonial Office rule as colonies. The British renewed the infrastructure and centralized government but used these colonies as much as possible as lucrative resource-rich areas involving a minimum of administrative expenditure.[53] Other parts of what later became Malaysia were British protectorates; here, British officials were less conspicuous still. The significant catalysts as far as sports were concerned were the army and commerce rather than schools and officialdom. For these reasons soccer became by far the most popular sport in these regions, leaving cricket far behind; the latter is played there primarily by men of Indian origin.[54]

The Philippines

While India still bears traces of Britain's former domination, sporting patterns in the Philippines reflect American influence. At the end of the nineteenth century the United States ousted the Spanish rulers of the Philippines and made it an American protectorate. As the years went by, basketball, volleyball, baseball, and softball all gained a substantial following.[55] American officials and army units along with the YMCA acted as the main catalysts in this assimilation process.

The YMCA was closely involved in the introduction and organization of modern sports in the Philippines. It helped to build gymnasiums and swimming pools, launched courses to train physical education instructors, sent local students to the YMCA training institute at Springfield, and organized matches between schools, universities, and commercial companies.[56] Unlike the sports policy of the British colonialists, which was initially geared toward a select elite, the YMCA set out explicitly to make sports accessible to ordinary people. "Everybody in the game" was the ideology underlying the YMCA's guidelines.[57] These guidelines also reflect a thrust toward sportization. Philippine coaches and sports officials were encouraged to cover the country with a web of sports organizations, in which the YMCA officials themselves took up key positions.[58] Americans urged local sports officials to adhere to the amateur rule, though without applying it so strictly as to make sports inaccessible to the masses.[59] The Far Eastern Championship Games—which initially included participants from China, the Philippines, and Japan—were another YMCA product. They gave many spectators their first opportunity to watch major events in volleyball, basketball, track and field,

baseball, soccer, swimming, and tennis. The first games were held in Manila in 1913, the second in Shanghai, and the third in Tokyo.[60]

In their dedicated efforts to get the locals to play sports, the YMCA promoted volleyball and basketball—their "own" sports—with the greatest fervor. Every Springfield-trained physical director was well aware that these two games bore the YMCA seal of approval. In consequence, they spread almost immediately after their invention and were more successful in areas in which the United States in general and the YMCA in particular had the most influence.

Where baseball was concerned, it was U.S. army units that were most influential in exporting the game to countries such as the Philippines—which they did before the end of the nineteenth century. Since troops were permanently garrisoned there, the soldiers soon cleared vacant plots of land near their camps and made them suitable for baseball matches; they even organized their own league. Young Philippine men working in or around the barracks would watch the matches, and soon they were infecting friends with their enthusiasm and forming their own teams.[61]

Americans tended to organize sports in schools rather than private clubs, just as they did at home. Only elite sports such as tennis, golf, and polo were played in exclusive circles. The Department of Education included volleyball, basketball, baseball, and track and field in the secondary school curriculum as early as 1903, so everyone who attended school soon had an opportunity to play these sports competitively. For children from the poorest classes, however, such opportunities were few and far between. If they managed to play any sport at all, they naturally gravitated toward one least associated with clubs and schools: boxing, soccer, or baseball. Three well-known top-class Philippine sportsmen from the mid-twentieth century reflect these social distinctions: the boxer Gabriel Elorde was born in 1934 into a poor family at Bogo and did not get beyond the third grade of elementary school; the basketball player Carlos Loyzaga (b. 1930), however, attended several colleges. The tennis player Felicismo Ampon was at the other extreme compared to Elorde. Born in Manila in 1920 as a member of a prosperous family including many tennis lovers, Ampon was rich enough to reject successive attractive deals offered by people eager for him to go professional.[62]

American football was not one of the YMCA's favored games, neither in the Philippines nor anywhere else. The inclusion of football in the Far Eastern Games was immediately followed by an announcement that "English rules shall govern."[63] It is not entirely clear why the YMCA never promoted the American variant, although several plausible hypotheses may be suggested. First, football's reputation had plummeted in the United States in the early years of the twentieth century, especially among those—including the

YMCA—who advocated "clean" sports. Several players had been carried off wounded from college matches, and there had even been some deaths, so that university officials—and later on even the White House—considered banning the sport altogether.[64] The sport's roughness did not accord with the YMCA's ideas concerning the upbringing of young people from the poorer urban classes (its main target group). Furthermore, by 1900 American football had already become a spectator sport, whereas the YMCA's preference was always for active participation.[65] And last but not least, the popularization of American football in the United States constituted a direct threat to the success of basketball and volleyball. The lack of YMCA support meant that American football was not included in the school curriculum in countries where the organization was influential. The YMCA was content to see the local population developing a taste for English soccer, which they had learned from sailors on leave, rather than adopting any other variant.[66]

China

Around the beginning of the twentieth century, the great European powers were threatening to divide China among themselves. France claimed the southern provinces, and Britain countered by conquering the Yangtze region. But the Europeans found themselves facing a different political reality here than in Africa. In this part of the world, the United States, Russia, and Japan were all directly involved. As a result, China retained its independence amid numerous Western influences. Western courses of education became popular with the Chinese elite; where Western lifestyles and behavior had previously commanded nothing but distaste, they now started to exercise a certain fascination.[67] Increasing Western influence meant the advent of modern sports.[68] The introduction of these sports followed four main channels: the American YMCA and Chinese who had studied in the United States gave China basketball and volleyball;[69] British sailors, businessmen, diplomats, and missionaries introduced the Chinese to soccer, cricket, tennis, and badminton; German and Japanese teachers and physical education instructors brought gymnastics equipment and forms of rhythmic gymnastic exercise; and contacts with Japanese merchants were important in disseminating table tennis and baseball. This diversity of influence has led today to a varied pattern of sports that differs from that of India and the Philippines. High on the Chinese popularity tables are the English sports soccer, table tennis, badminton, and track and field; the American sports basketball, volleyball, softball, and baseball; the German-linked gymnastics, shooting, and swimming; and a number of martial arts that have sprung from the country's own fighting traditions.[70]

In 1916 China had more than seven thousand church centers, YMCAs, and

missions. Missionaries played an important organizational role in the introduction of Western sports. One of the best known is the British "Muscular
Christian" Archie Liddell, the Olympic four-hundred-meter champion of
1924 who was immortalized in *Chariots of Fire*. American YMCA officials too
had a good deal of influence at the beginning of the twentieth century—so
much so that the China regarded the YMCA as synonymous with physical
education. If a state school or city council wanted to launch a physical education program, they would immediately ask the YMCA for advice. In China as in the Philippines the organization combined evangelical and human-
itarian work. Besides programs for training and for feeding the malnourished
it promoted participation in sports, organized and coordinated sports
leagues, and trained coaches and physical education instructors. At the Chinese YMCA physical education school, the curriculum included not only a
great many sports and allied disciplines such as anatomy, physiology, and
hygiene but also Bible studies, English language, and the history of Western
physical education. After graduation, students went to other parts of China
and took over the leadership of sports organizations when most American
specialists left China in the early 1920s. But the YMCA itself concentrated its
activities in the cities and did little in outlying regions.[71]

The most distinctive feature of the Chinese sporting pattern is the enormous popularity of table tennis, which ranks in the country's top three sports,
together with basketball and soccer, while volleyball probably occupies fourth
place.[72] The dominance of table tennis is not, as has sometimes been suggested, the result of a centuries-old tradition. Sports dictionaries that identify
China as the country of origin of ping-pong are in need of correction. Table
tennis is not a traditional Chinese pastime; it was imported in the twentieth
century from Britain, and possibly also from Japan.[73] Nor is the sport's great
popularity attributable to the superlative international achievements of
Chinese table tennis champions, which did not occur until the latter half of
the twentieth century. Rong Guotuan, the first Chinese world champion, won
the title as recently as 1959. Six years later China achieved world supremacy,
winning five world titles and being represented in every single final in the
world championship. Yet the great popularity of table tennis had been noted by one commentator earlier, in 1956: "Which is the most popular sport?
Undoubtedly basketball. . . . Second most popular? You may be surprised at
the answer; table tennis."[74]

Although today's vast numbers of table tennis players are hard to explain
on the basis of the available information, two factors probably played an
important role: first, the influence of Japan, where table tennis had been fairly
popular since the 1920s, and second, the rise and gradual spread throughout
the country of the Red Army. Until 1930 table tennis was a marginal phenom-

enon in China; in rural areas it was quite unknown. It was played only in a few major trading cities where Europeans and Japanese introduced a variety of Western sports. In Shanghai, Japanese enthusiasts started a table tennis club, which organized its first matches in 1924.[75] Eleven years later a national table tennis association was founded, uniting clubs from Shanghai, Zhejiang, Jiangsu, Nianjing, Quingdao, Hong Kong, and Macao. The YMCA promoted the sport here, too, especially among elementary and secondary school pupils.

From these trading cities, table tennis spread to rural areas. Given the important role that the army played in disseminating baseball in the United States and soccer in Europe, it is fair to assume that the Red Army had an unwitting catalytic effect. This supposition derives support from the famous travel journal of the American journalist Edgar Snow, who journeyed through northwestern China in the mid-1930s, defying a ban by the Chinese authorities: "Many people had been amused to hear about the Reds' passion for the English game of table tennis. It was bizarre, somehow, but every Lenin Club had in its center a big ping-pong table, usually serving double duty as dining table. The Lenin Clubs were turned into mess halls at chow time, but there were always four or five 'bandits,' armed with bats, balls, and a net, urging the comrades to hurry it up; they wanted to get on with their game. Each company boasted a ping-pong champion."[76]

By this time the Red Army had already secured a strong power base, especially in the countryside, where the vast majority of the population lived. Table tennis was not a compulsory military exercise, like the long jump, running, hill-climbing, grenade-throwing, and marksmanship; it was a voluntary recreation in the Lenin Clubs, the army's social and cultural centers. It was an ideal form of relaxation in the evening after the busy days that Red Army soldiers always had, even when there was no fighting.[77] Through the Red Army, table tennis acquired a larger following in the Chinese hinterland than most other sports. As a result, there was soon an enormous pool of potential talent, many times larger than in other countries, giving China a head start that made it invincible for a long time.

Further investigation of these factors could not only help explain the popularity of table tennis in China but might also reveal the factors that suddenly shot Chinese table tennis to the top in about 1960. International conflicts kept Chinese table tennis players out of international competitions until 1953, when they first took part in the world championships. Between 1959 and 1987 they took more than fifty world titles, alongside forty second and seventy-four third places. The first Chinese world champion in the men's game, Rong Guotuan, did not come from one of the major trading cities but from Zhong-shan in the province of Guangdong. The game was already taking the coun-

try by storm before his championship match, and the trend continued afterwards, partly because the Chinese government seized on these successes to promote national unity and boost the country's international image. It invested in a national table tennis infrastructure unlike anything elsewhere and provided far better facilities than were available for many other sports in China. Players from all parts of China were involved in national selection matches and were given the opportunity to gain experience in national and international competitions. The succession of trophies also encouraged the Chinese to see table tennis increasingly as part of their cultural heritage with which they distinguished themselves from other nations.[78]

Independent Dependence: The Differential Popularization of Sports in Latin America

Spanish colonization brought sports-like pastimes such as bullfighting, pelota, and fencing to Latin America. As modern sports had not evolved in this protracted colonial period, Spanish influence on present-day sporting patterns is not very marked. Around 1800 most Latin American countries gained political independence. Economically, however, they remained dependent on the major Western powers—above all on Britain, which had numerous investment and trade links with the region, and on the United States, which had a wide range of ties with its southern neighbors.[79]

Since it was economic rather than political or military ties that were dominant in most Latin American countries,[80] sports spread along different lines than in Asian or African colonies. Most of the contacts with the foreigners were in commerce, and so the sports that grew fastest were soccer and baseball—the former in British-influenced countries such as Argentina, Brazil, and Chile, and the latter in countries such as Colombia, Venezuela, Panama, Cuba, Nicaragua, the Dominican Republic, and parts of Mexico, which had strong U.S. involvement.[81] The main characteristics of the pattern of sports in Latin America can be explained by a closer analysis of these relations of dependency.

Immigration and investment brought other European influences. Chile had many gymnastics clubs, for instance, that had been set up by German immigrants. Gymnastics was a compulsory school subject in this country at the end of the nineteenth century, a period during which the Chilean army was being reformed along Prussian lines, and all Chilean army officers were required to learn German as part of their training. Germans also founded gymnastics clubs in Argentina, Uruguay, and Brazil. Swiss immigrants too had their own meeting places, centering on a distinctive sport. The Sociedad Tiro Suizo de Buenos Aires is only one example of the many Swiss shooting

clubs that were set up in Argentina, Chile, and Uruguay in the last quarter of the nineteenth century.[82] Gymnastics and shooting clubs offered people a chance to meet fellow expatriates and strengthened ties with the mother country. But these clubs exercised no influence beyond their own commu nities.[83]

British Influence

The differential spread of sports is bound up with the nature of bilateral relations. In countries colonized by Britain, the difference in popularity between soccer, the sport of the "common folk," and that of the typical colonial sports cricket, rugby, and hockey was less great than in countries that only had trading relations with Britain. Argentina, Brazil, and Chile witnessed no mass influx of highly educated British immigrants, nor did they acquire schools modeled on British lines. Sports were spread by sailors and the employees of commercial companies, and in these groups, soccer was the most popular sport.[84]

As industrialization started to transform many major cities in Latin America around 1900, a new urban elite emerged and became part of the international economic system.[85] These upwardly mobile entrepreneurs soon adopted the lifestyle of businessmen and officials from the core countries of the world system. While some were content to join existing sports clubs that had been set up by foreigners, others launched exclusive clubs of their own.[86] The members of the Regata Club and the Lima Riflery Club were primarily Peruvians—they owned factories, haciendas, mines, and newspapers. The prototype of the *conocido* (eminent) sportsman was a dynamic, athletic member of a wealthy, prominent family. At the end of the nineteenth century this new elite was active in just about every sport that was flourishing in Britain. The Peruvian Unión Cricket Club, for instance, participated in cricket, tennis, rowing, fencing, horse racing, golf, polo, track and field, and soccer.[87]

With the single exception of soccer, these were all sports then being played by the elite in Britain. So when the elite in Latin America took them up, they happily set up the same exclusive organizational structures. Soccer developed along different lines. While it was still being played in Europe at elite generalist sports clubs and by boys at fashionable public schools, it was on the decline in these circles. Its center of gravity was increasingly shifting toward the working classes.

This popularization in soccer's home country had two specific consequences for the way this sport spread. First, soccer was imported by all social classes. At one end of the social scale were British-educated local boys and wealthy British schoolboys living in Latin America because of their fa-

thers' jobs. At the other end were British sailors and workers, who were present in large numbers—sailors because of the close commercial ties that existed with these countries and workers because they were hired to help build railroad lines and other elements of the industrial infrastructure.

The second consequence of this popularization was that soccer could not be kept exclusive. With other English sports, most local people encountered social barriers keeping them out, but in soccer all such barriers had already been eroded in the mother country. Several factory directors helped to set up soccer teams among their personnel. Elite clubs did little to discourage lower social classes from taking up the game, even helping to set up organizational structures and professionalization for working men's soccer. True, this development prompted the membership of the elite clubs to give up playing soccer themselves.[88] Not even the conocido sportsmen could stop the crew of a British ship playing a demonstration match for the inhabitants of Callao, the poor harbor town where soccer took root as a workers' sport in Peru. British sailors were soon competing frequently with Callao's dockworkers and fishermen. It started with games in the street, in town squares, or on the beach—barefoot if need be, with two stones denoting the goal. "Every neighborhood had its own casual team. You could see them play from 8 A.M. to 8 P.M. All those teams!" a Peruvian worker recalled about those first years. Soon they were starting their own soccer clubs.[89]

Elsewhere in Latin America, too, the oldest soccer clubs are found in ports visited by British sailors and traders where Britain had big commercial interests: Sao Paulo and Rio de Janeiro in Brazil, Rosario and Buenos Aires in Argentina, Montevideo in Uruguay, and Valparaiso in Chile. Many of these clubs were originally British, set up as a recreational resource for the crews of merchant ships.[90] Toward the end of the nineteenth century hundreds of British ships were calling at Montevideo, Uruguay, every year. In 1898 their crews founded the international soccer club I Zingai—the name means "the Gypsies" and stands for people who have no fixed abode and are at home in all countries of the world. Many ships from the British navy lay at anchor in Coquimbo, north of Santiago. Here, the first games took place between the sailors and the British trading folk who had settled in the town.[91]

Soccer also spread from British schools. Encouraged by their teachers, the sons of British expatriates competed, for instance, against fellow countrymen employed by the railroad company. Valparaiso, a small Chilean port that became Europe's gateway to Chile in the nineteenth century, had three clubs in 1892: two for schoolboys (the English Athletic Mackay and Sunderland School and the English Academy Robinson Club) and one for men working for a leading British tea importer (Rogers Football Club). The British teach-

ers and pupils who introduced soccer to the area translated the rules to encourage the local youth to join in.[92]

In Brazil, too, soccer was first played by British sailors on the wharves of
Rio de Janeiro and Sao Paulo. But it was the local-born son of the British
consul in Sao Paulo who introduced club soccer after leaving the school he
had attended in Southampton, England. He brought to Brazil official soccer
and an "established rule book." To set up a regular league he founded several clubs and persuaded the Sao Paulo Athletics Club to add soccer to their
activities. He was also involved in starting soccer teams among employees of
the English Gas Company, Sao Paulo Railways, and the London Bank.[93] At
around the same time, men at both ends of the social scale in Brazil's ports
and major cities were also taking up soccer, the elite in exclusive clubs and
the lower classes in irregular groups. In the hinterland it took much longer
before soccer spread from the local elite to the common folk.

In South America as in Europe this popularization led the more status-
conscious of the elite to seek a different sport. In Rio de Janeiro not a single
team with "colored" players won a championship until 1922. The turning-
point came the following year when Vasco da Gama, frustrated by poor results in its first seven years, signed on several "colored" players that the press
described as scarcely able to sign their names. When Vasco da Gama then won
the championship for two successive years, other teams soon followed suit.
Once this trend was set, the snobbish *clubes finos* had to bend or break; if they
stuck to their guns they would soon face relegation. The choice was stark—
distinction in social allure or in sporting quality. They could not have both.

The same competitiveness led to the introduction of professionalism in
1933, which further hastened soccer's social decline. Brazilian officials finally abandoned the amateur principle when they found the country's talent
being picked off by professional European and Argentine clubs. Enormous
public and media interest had made soccer into a lucrative business.[94] Some
clubs opened their doors to workers, the elite withdrawing to the committee rooms. Other clubs bade farewell to soccer altogether and shifted to other sports, which still offered the exclusivity they wanted.[95]

The gap between soccer and the other British sports is wide. Soccer is the
only British sport that counts. Although South Americans were familiar with
polo, golf, and tennis before 1900, these sports never went beyond the small
group of hacienda owners, factory directors, city councillors, professors, law-
yers, and doctors. They have not crossed the class barriers as in Europe, for
the simple reason that the class differences are greater in Latin America. Such
sports are beyond the reach of most workers, small entrepreneurs, and lower
public servants, let alone the millions of unemployed, slum-dwellers, and inhabitants of remote villages where organized sports are totally nonexistent.

American Influence

Amid the Latin American soccer nations are several countries where not soccer but baseball is the most popular sport—for analogous reasons. Baseball had already gone through the process of popularization before it was imported, and it was therefore a sport for the common folk from the start. Local people saw baseball from the beginning as a sport for everyone. It prospered in countries that were influenced more by the United States than Britain: Cuba, Puerto Rico, Nicaragua, the Dominican Republic, Panama, Venezuela, and Colombia. (There is one noteworthy bastion of baseball in Brazil—in Sao Paulo, which has the largest Japanese minority community in the world).[96] Baseball was introduced in Latin America at a time when American economic and political/military influence in the Caribbean region was greatly increasing in strength.

A comparison between Nicaragua and Belize indicates the impact of the dominance of these two world powers on the differential popularization of baseball and soccer. Nicaragua was for a long time a Spanish colony, but after achieving independence in 1821 it came under strong American influence. Nearby Belize, in contrast, was still part of the British empire until the 1980s. The countries' sporting preferences reflect these different histories. In Nicaragua baseball is the national sport, while in Belize this distinction belongs to soccer. In a questionnaire, 29.4 percent of Nicaraguan respondents named baseball as their favorite sport, while only 8.4 percent preferred soccer; the corresponding figures in Belize were 4 percent and 28.1 percent, respectively.[97]

In Cuba baseball was spread by students returning from the United States and through relations with American soldiers. Cuban longshoremen started playing baseball in Matanza in 1866 after the crew of an American ship had invited them to a demonstration match. In the early 1870s the first clubs sprang up in Havana and several other cities, and soon they were competing in their first league matches.[98]

Baseball was seen in Cuba, as indeed everywhere else, as a classless sport. It was never confined to private clubs—you could learn the game at the docks, in open fields, and in the street. Baseball had no rules of decorum in the United States, so it acquired none elsewhere. Although certain wealthy Cubans did play in exclusive clubs, they did not impede street baseball.[99] Baseball thus grew to become Cuba's most popular sport, with basketball and volleyball following some way behind, but still ahead of track and field and soccer, sports that had originated outside the United States. In 1978 there were 2,181 baseball facilities, 1,317 for basketball, 1,256 for volleyball, 402 for athletics, and 313 for soccer.[100]

In Mexico, British involvement in industrialization and modernization was

initially greater, but investors from the United States gradually became more important. At the end of the nineteenth century, American and British experts and investors competed for contracts to build railroads and to work mines as part of the enormous social and economic transformation wrought under Porfirio Diaz (1876–1911). These external ties and the influx of foreign capital promoted technological and cultural innovations that also led to the rise of organized sports. Wealthy British and American businessmen gravitated toward exclusive clubs for cricket, golf, and polo, while among the lower echelons—miners, low-ranking technicians, and railroad employees—the British imported soccer, and the Americans baseball. Some of the Mexican elite were admitted to the exclusive foreign clubs, but a Mexican worker could count himself lucky if he knew any foreigners to teach him soccer or baseball; this was likeliest in the railroad and mining companies, because of the large numbers of British and American employees, and this was where the first clubs were formed.

Soccer and baseball are the most popular sports in Mexico today, with soccer ranking first in most regions. In the Yucatán Peninsula, however, which is closer to Cuba than the rest of the country, baseball has the largest number of players. It was probably introduced at the end of the nineteenth century by Cuban workers and guerilla fighters who were looking for a safe haven in their struggle against Spanish rule. Boys from working-class neighborhoods in the capital of Mérida and the port of Progreso learned baseball from them and played the game in the streets, barefoot and—more striking still in the case of baseball—with bare hands, and were little concerned to apply the rules strictly or to devise real leagues. The first baseball clubs were set up by the local elite at a time when Yucatán was undergoing considerable industrial change, partly through the influence of its northern neighbors. Soon there were workers' clubs too. A twine factory at Mérida started a baseball club for its workers, El Fénix, in the early 1900s. In the same town the railroad workers founded the baseball club La Plancha, while dockworkers from Progreso launched the Club Colón.[101]

Baseball was classless, and it was an American product, two factors that made it soar to popularity among the poorer classes in the Caribbean. The United States was a dominant presence in the region in the late nineteenth century, and a large proportion of the local population looked up to it. By adopting elements of its culture, they could bask in America's reflected glory. Standing on a baseball diamond or wearing a baseball cap gave some young hopefuls the illusion that they were a little closer to the wealth of an American.[102]

But this is not the only reason for the sport's success in the Caribbean, as

Allen Klein points out in his book on baseball in the Dominican Republic. There was no question of an eager and unquestioning imitation of American culture. For the Dominicans the Americans were not only the most powerful and developed nation but also—from 1916 to 1924—the occupying power. So American hegemony also prompted resistance, which the locals expressed by adapting baseball to their own culture.[103] Occasionally, as in the case of cricket in the Trobriand Islands, such adaptations lead to alterations in the basic rules of the game, creating a new sport. But in most cases they are confined to the development of a particular national style of play and national customs, rituals and symbols, and heroes and personalities. Such changes in the culture of a sport, however gradual, eventually detach it from the country of origin.

Compared to some of the Asian countries influenced by American sporting patterns, the popularity of basketball and volleyball in Latin America long lagged behind that of soccer and baseball. This is because the influence of the YMCA—the great promoter of these two sports—was less marked here. According to one historian of the YMCA, the Catholic countries of Latin America were among the most impenetrable regions for this Protestant organization. Though Argentina, Chile, Uruguay, Brazil, Peru, Cuba, and Mexico all had YMCA branches, none of them flourished. The center of gravity of the YMCA's foreign mission was in East Asia.[104] It was not until after the Second World War, when the United States had become the major world power, that the demand for American products increased throughout the world, and basketball and volleyball became far more popular in Latin America, as in Europe.

In the Periphery: The Differential Popularization of Sports in Africa

Within a short space of time the major European powers colonized the entire continent of Africa. While in 1876 they only controlled one-tenth of the continent, by 1900 they laid claim to nine-tenths of the territory. The vast majority of this power was in British hands. Then came France, while Germany, Belgium, Italy, Portugal, and Spain all had to make do with far smaller slices of the pie. Neither the Soviet Union nor the United States possessed any colonies, and it was not until after the decolonization era that they acquired any appreciable influence in Africa.[105]

The colonial powers took a different attitude toward Africa than toward their Asian colonies. African societies were less stratified. The elite was smaller, nor was there any prosperous merchant class or a sizeable civil service. Where-

as the Europeans respected Asian achievements in art and science and were
impressed by the power and wealth of the social elite, they regarded Africa
as a "dark" and "embryonic" continent, which had neither history nor culture.[106] To the average Victorian Englishman, Africans were primitive barbar-
ian children in need of education and upbringing. It was far less prestigious
to work in Africa than to belong to the Indian Colonial Service. A British
official in Africa was seen as nothing more than "'an underpaid schoolmaster in an overpopulated school.'"[107]

Besides this difference in attitude, the nature and degree of the Europeans'
involvement in Africa was different from that in Asia. Most African countries were colonized more than a hundred years later than those in Asia.
Moreover, there were fewer Europeans in Africa than in Asia, and they tended to stay for shorter periods of time. Compared to Asia they collaborated
less with local elites, and their level of investment and infrastructural innovation was far lower, especially in the hinterland.[108]

These differences had several consequences for the development of African sport in general and for the differential popularization of specific sports.
In the first place, Africans came into contact with modern sports later than
Asians, and so they went without the boost of international sporting events
for a long time. Clubs and federations that could build up the necessary ties
developed far later here than elsewhere. In this regard, British colonies were
somewhat better off than their Francophone counterparts. The first soccer
clubs in the French colonies of Togo, Mali, and the Ivory Coast were founded
thirty years after the launch of the first soccer club in British-ruled Ghana. This
was partly because these French colonies were located in more peripheral
regions. But it was also because the British made a greater effort to educate
the elite in their colonies, which included inculcating Western lifestyles.[109]

In the second place, the gap between Europeans and the African elite meant
that most sports—especially those belonging to the elite English category—
remained an exclusive white preserve for far longer. The local elite who gained
admission to exclusive schools and clubs was far smaller than in Asia, and
they were not welcomed into the pursuit of sports with such alacrity. Indeed,
many sports organizations were for "whites only." The Europeans competed only against each other and were very reluctant to countenance mixed
sports. Interracial matches were a rare occurrence; they were confined to
small cultural enclaves of rich Africans who succeeded in adopting Western
lifestyles and scarcely consorted with the majority of the local population or
to regions where Europeans were not numerous enough to form entire teams
and members of the local elite had to be co-opted if matches were to be possible at all. For Africans of Indian origin, sports were somewhat more accessible than for blacks.[110]

All European sports clubs enthusiastically promoted their own exported sports with their specific rules, regulations, customs, and traditions. As the British controlled about 50 percent of the population in Africa, the English sports were in the best position for eventual popularization. The British started far more sports clubs than other Europeans in Africa.[111] But since it was inconceivable for the local elite to play a large part in these clubs' activities, as in India, golf, tennis, squash, and above all the typical colonial sports of cricket and hockey never achieved the same popularity as in Asia. This did not apply so much to areas that had British schools for the local elite or large communities of Indian migrant workers. Hockey and cricket are played in Kenya, Nigeria, and Ghana more than in Botswana, and far more than in Zaire, Senegal, or Egypt.[112]

To the administrative and military British elite, it was self-evident that rugby, cricket, tennis, polo, and squash were for whites only. It was not until after independence that black African officers started to take them up. Even then, they did so far from mainstream society, in accordance with the large divide between themselves and the African population at large.[113] Soccer— and to a lesser extent track and field (especially running) and boxing—gained the largest following among Africans.[114] The popularization of soccer was possible mainly because the white elite saw it as a socially inferior sport. So they initially left European soldiers and small groups of white skilled workers to organize it and did not protest when the black population started playing the sport informally. In southern Africa, for instance in Botswana and Zimbabwe, soccer thus became the counterpart of the "Boer sports" rugby and cricket.[115] In the second place, the increasing number of soccer players among the black population was related to the only institutions where they came in contact with organized sports: the army, the police, and schools.[116] The first African soccer club was launched in 1903, at the instigation of an English teacher in Cape Coast, Ghana.

In Togo and Senegal, too, schools were breeding grounds for soccer clubs. The presence of British army units was another factor in the popularization of soccer among the African population. In South Africa the British army recruited mule and donkey riders and scouts from the local population; the new recruits learned to play soccer while serving with the British infantry, and the most talented black players were sometimes included in battalion teams. Soccer and track and field were practiced at the regimental level in black battalions such as the King's African Rifles and the Royal West African Frontier Force. At the end of the colonial period and after independence, many military teams competed against local civilian teams. Blacks serving in the police—as carriers, for instance—learned the rules of soccer by watching Europeans playing the game.[117]

After independence, it was through schools and the army, not through clubs, that most Africans participated in national and international sports venues. Of the participants from central Africa in the first African Games in 1976, 56 percent came from schools and colleges, and 24 percent came from the military.[118] And in 1989, Jimu Tembo commented that every good soccer player in Malawi had been trained either abroad or at one of the mission schools.[119]

Sports played a far greater role in the British army than in the French or German forces, for instance. The foreign legion's official training program consisted mainly of boxing, wrestling, running, and fencing. The time that the British spent on sports, the French devoted to marching. It was not until after the war that French military authorities in Senegal and the Ivory Coast also started organizing sports events for soldiers. In Gabon the Ligue Militaire Omnisport set up soccer matches between the army, air force, police, fire department, and junior civil servants.[120] German influence in Africa was fairly minor. But wherever Germany did colonize a territory, the familiar struggle emerged between sports and gymnastics. However, gymnastics did not prosper, mainly because of the absence of a large middle class, the mainstay of the gymnastics movement in Europe.

American sports did not get off the ground in Africa until after decolonization. With the end of European control, American and Russian influences started to make themselves felt. In Malawi the arrival of American peacekeeping troops brought basketball and volleyball to the country. When the Americans departed, sports instructors remained, who introduced the sports into the elementary school curriculum. In Zaire, too, people learned basketball and volleyball when American U.N. troops were stationed there in the 1960s. Basketball in particular has become enormously popular in Zaire in the past few decades—it still has far fewer players than soccer, but more than any other sport.[121]

Roughly speaking, the most popular sports in Africa today, in descending order, are soccer, track and field, basketball, and volleyball. These are also the most popular and most widespread sports worldwide. Part of their attraction lies precisely in this global spread. With the passage of time, national rivalries and sensitivities have come to play a less important role in these sports, as they are increasingly seen as truly international and noncolonial pursuits.[122] Everyone who takes part is linked to the global sporting system, which means that for a brief moment they can transcend, at least symbolically, their own limited geographical borders.[123]

6. Competition between the Lines

GLOBAL SPORTS ARE WHAT most interest today's *homo ludens;* pastimes that lack the aura of globalization have less appeal. This is a recent development. Not much more than a century ago, the rules of sportlike games and the way they were played were still determined locally and agreed upon only in the barest outline. Competitions at anything beyond the regional level were virtually nonexistent. People were familiar with their own local pastimes and shook their heads at the customs of those in the next county. Within the space of a century, a sports system has come into existence that links people from all corners of the earth. A century ago as yet unknown and unloved, today known throughout the world: Association Football, track and field, basketball, volleyball, tennis, and other sports are played all over the planet according to the same basic rules. It is this development from local variation to global standardization that is the most fundamental difference between modern sports and the sportlike activities of the past.

The internationalization and spread of most sports were related to general processes of scale expansion and integration in society. In England and Scotland, these modernization processes accelerated earlier than elsewhere, enabling pastimes to be organized, regulated, and standardized at the national level for the first time. This made it possible to arrange competitions to find the country's best performer in a sport. Annual competitions gave this struggle for glory a seasonal character, and matches were planned long in advance; the contests soon attracted regular crowds of spectators.

Most sports spread within a single generation after the establishment of regulatory bodies in all continents. This was not only a derivative of countries' increasing interdependency but also stemmed from the competitive

thrust that is inherent to modern sports and that inevitably generated an internationalization of sporting ties. Modern sports—like forms of art and music and certain modes of dress—are a universal, cohesive phenomenon. This global sporting system is internally differentiated and subject to constant change. By applying the model of existing sports—which includes not only organizational structure, regulation, and standardization but also contests, quantification, and the effort to break records—to activities both old and new, branches of sport are constantly being added to the global system. And within this system the popularity of individual sports varies and changes over time.

Theory of the Differential Popularization of Sports

None of the numerous explanations that have been suggested for the diverse and changing popularity of the various branches of sport can withstand the test of comparative historical analysis. The main problem with most explanations is that they focus on the different rules by which sports are played. In this book (following in the footsteps of Ruud Stokvis) I have taken an entirely different line: the key to explaining the differences in popularity between sports and the changes to which they are subject lies not in the intrinsic characteristics of sports but in the social framework within which they originate and are spread. I have elaborated this approach into a number of related hypotheses, which served as an interpretative model. I started out from two basic premises: first, that the current differences in popularity between sports must be interpreted by reference to the development of the global sporting system; and second, that the differential popularization of sports is a blind process that displays a certain structure and is bound up with wider social trends. In a nutshell, this model is predicated on the assumption that people's different and changing preferences for a given sport are based on the social and cultural meanings they attribute to each sport, meanings that alter in response to changing relations between groups of people, in particular between countries and social classes.

Underlying this theory is the notion that in the world of sport, alongside the open, sporting fight to win, a completely different kind of competition is going on "between the lines." This hidden competition relates to people's desire to bind themselves to certain groups and distinguish themselves from others by their choice of sport.

In drawing up this theoretical model I was convinced that it was possible to reduce the multiplicity of differences and changes in the popularity of sports to a single cohesive problem. I set out to structure the chaos of ques-

tions prompted by the enormous variations in the popularity of sports and to answer them consistently in their mutual relations and from a single clearly defined perspective.

The Diffusion of Sports and the International Balance of Power

The theoretical model I have described concerns the impact of social factors on psychological responses. This goes to the heart of the development of sociological theory. It touches on the classical sociological question about the link between major trends in society and individual emotions, behavior, and preferences.[1] This link exists even at the highest level of social integration, that of international relations: there is a clear connection between countries' international positions of power and their spheres of influence and the spread and popularity of sports. There is no question of objective differences of quality, with "better" cultural expressions ousting lesser ones; at issue are social processes in which power relations between people affect the way they judge their own sports and those of others.

That individual sporting preferences should be related to the international balance of power may at first seem an odd idea. But in fact we can see it happening all around us every day. Just think of the imbalance in ties between, say, Dutch and Americans. Many Dutch readers are familiar with the *New York Times,* but it will be a rare American who reads the Dutch newspaper *NRC Handelsblad;* Dutch TV viewers tune in to CNN, but Americans have no knowledge of Dutch channels; American terms are often incorporated into Dutch vocabulary, whereas this scarcely happens the other way around; basketball is played in the Netherlands, but you are unlikely to find anyone playing korfball in the United States. In the final analysis, the dominant direction in the spread of cultural goods mirrors the power relations between states.[2]

Today's world sports system is largely dominated by sports originating in countries that have occupied positions of international power since the mid-nineteenth century: Britain (track and field, cricket, field hockey, rowing, rugby, tennis, and soccer), Germany (gymnastics and handball), the United States (basketball, volleyball, and baseball) and Japan (judo, karate, and other martial arts). The mother country of modern sports is Britain. It was there that the first sports (notably boxing, horse racing, rowing, and cricket) underwent national organization and standardization. Modernization accelerated faster in Britain than elsewhere, largely because of the country's early industrialization. This soon led to a higher level of national integration, an essential precondition for the standardization of sportlike pastimes with all

their local and regional variations. Furthermore, the differences in lifestyle between the nobility and the bourgeoisie were less marked in Britain than in the countries of the European continent. This was reflected, for instance, in the fact that the British nobles took quite an interest in the pastimes of the local population. Many lived in London residences for part of the year, and there they founded clubs that, for the first time, had a say over rules and regulations at the national level, enabling standardization. In the latter half of the nineteenth century their middle-class successors applied this model to other sportlike pastimes, some familiar and others new: the elite schools and universities developed soccer, rugby, and field hockey; young adults from elite circles, already established in society, developed tennis, badminton, table tennis, squash, and (in Scotland) golf.

Because of Britain's power and prestige in the late nineteenth century, cosmopolitan elites in other countries took an interest in the lifestyles of the British upper class and adopted the modern sports that they played. As a result, the English sports spread throughout the world, following a pattern that can be understood in terms of two distinct processes: first, the sports spread initially to core countries, then to semiperipheral, and finally to peripheral countries, and second, they caught on faster in countries that lay within Britain's sphere of influence. The nature of the relationship with Britain was a key factor: where it was largely based on rivalry, the English sports never attained the same popularity as in British colonies. Furthermore, the latter favored different sports than countries whose dependence on Britain was largely based on commerce.

The introduction of these sports to continental Europe coincided with the powerful modernization of Germany, which developed into Britain's main competitor in continental Europe, especially in the last quarter of the nineteenth century. As Germany became more powerful, its citizens became more averse to foreign influence, and this included English sports. Instead they favored Turnen or gymnastics, which became one of the most popular sports in Germany and all the countries within its sphere of influence. The struggle that developed between the propagandists of gymnastics (and related sports, notably handball) and the supporters of the English sports raged for a long time in many other countries, though it was fought most vehemently in countries under strong German influence. Most of these were in Europe, which explains why the success of the gymnastics movement scarcely went beyond this continent.

In the United States, too, indigenous sports arose (baseball, American football, basketball, and volleyball) whose popularity has long since outstripped that of the English sports. Again, key factors were the country's vigorous

modernization and its rise to become Britain's main rival. But equally important was the fact that the United States underwent modernization relatively autonomously from Europe. So there was no violent struggle against the English model of sports, as in Germany; American sports simply grew increasingly popular, ousting all other contenders from the center. Soon these sports were spreading around the world: first to countries that the United States had dominated politically and militarily before the Second World War or with which it had close economic ties, and later worldwide, as the United States became one of the two superpowers. At this point, volleyball and basketball also climbed several places in the European popularity rankings.

Since about 1950, the Japanese martial arts have spread throughout the world. Though the sportization of traditional martial arts in Japan was partly due to Western influence, it was also an expression of the country's powerful (later) modernization. They did not flourish internationally until Japan became an major economic power, after the Second World War.

To explain the pattern of distribution of sports, we have to examine the immediate sphere of influence of each of the four main countries of origin and the nature of their relations with the countries they dominated. Whether or not relations were tight-knit, whether they were colonial or commercial, and the degree of competition all helped to determine which sports were adopted. Sports associated with countries that have little power on the world stage have never attracted much enthusiasm internationally, however many people actively pursue them at home (for example, Australian football, lacrosse in Canada, pétanque in France, floorball in Sweden, and korfball in the Netherlands).

Dominated countries can do little to change the fact that influence tends to be one-way, especially in periods of scant migration: the cultural balance of exchange is inherently unequal. While people from the dominated country study the political, military, and cultural characteristics of the dominating power, representatives of the dominating country travel the world to demonstrate and profit from their superiority. This imbalance does not mean that a dominated country will unquestioningly replace what are seen as expressions of its own culture with "alien" cultural elements. The very inequality of the relationship creates a mixed bag of responses: resistance and admiration, resentment and awe. Alien elements are always adopted selectively and adapted to the indigenous culture. While Indians embraced cricket, Dominicans baseball, and South Africans rugby, each country incorporated these sports into their own culture so firmly that with the passage of time more and more people came to see them as their own cultural heritage and even as symbols of their successful struggle against cultural domination.

Other inhabitants of the dominated country may derive from the military and economic dominance of the greater power a sense that their own culture is inferior. For instance, korfball—one of the few internationally standardized sports whose roots are in the Netherlands—enjoys little social esteem in its home country. One well-known journalist called it "fantastically blah, Dutch bourgeois through and through, it smells of cabbage and gravy."[3] And this deprecatory attitude is quite common. Korfball has attracted derision ever since its invention, partly because of its Dutch origins and its negligible spread to other countries. In the core countries that have dominated international relations, people view their own cultural products very differently. "Undeutsch" (un-German) has a negative sound to it in Germany, but "on-Hollands" (un-Dutch) has positive connotations in the Netherlands, where "Dutch" stands for pettiness and short-sightedness, for the refusal to look beyond national frontiers.[4]

The Popularization of Sports and Changing Class Relations

That English sports became particularly popular in territories within Britain's sphere of influence does not explain the differences that arose between them. Why did soccer, for instance, and not cricket or rugby become by far the best-loved sport in many Latin American, European, and African countries? And why have the latter two done so much better in India and New Zealand, respectively? Simply invoking the international balance of power will not suffice to explain the differential popularization of sports. There are other key factors: in particular, which groups dominated and promoted the various sports in their countries of origin, which groups appropriated them elsewhere, and the latter's positions within their society's class structure.

Looking at sports from the vantage point of social development, we can divide them roughly into four groups. First, there are two groups that were initially monopolized by the upper and upper middle classes. The first consists of a large number of sports that remained the exclusive province of the elite for a long time. Most originate from Britain: they include golf, field hockey, rowing, rugby, squash, and tennis. The second group consists of sports that started off as elitist activities but soon slid down the social scale: soccer, baseball, and American football. Their social development cannot be explained simply by invoking the trickle-down effect: for why should this effect operate so much more strongly in some cases than in others? In general, the trickle-down effect was more apparent in sports played primarily by young people and in those attached to institutions such as schools and the armed forces and less in those confined to private clubs. Throughout the

world, inclusion in school physical education curricula has always boosted the spread of a sport.

Then there are two groups that have little to do with social elites. One consists of sports developed and promoted by individuals and organizations to enhance the physical and moral fiber of the nation, especially the youth. This includes the German gymnastics movement, handball, the obliquely related shooting and swimming, and the YMCA sports volleyball and basketball. Their proponents targeted the whole population, but their prime appeal was to the lower middle classes and skilled workers. The last group consists of sports developed by the working classes, such as snooker and darts. In contrast to the "downward social mobility" of the second group, these sports have tended to remain within their original working-class environment.

Soccer and baseball had already undergone popularization in their home countries before modern sports spread worldwide at the end of the nineteenth century. This had various consequences. First and most importantly, it meant that they were spread in part by people of little education and low social status (such as soldiers, workers, and sailors). Second, it meant (indirectly) that soccer and baseball—in contrast to other British and American sports—achieved more popularity in countries with which Britain and the United States had strong commercial ties than in their colonies. Cricket, rugby, and field hockey did best in British colonies, where organizing sports was largely the province of officials, army officers, and private school teachers. And third, prior popularization influenced the way a sport was presented, organized, and played elsewhere. Baseball and soccer had none of the exclusivity of certain other sports that were being propagated at the same time and were therefore easily accessible to the masses.

When British elite sports such as golf, squash, polo, and tennis were imported, they tended to be played in private clubs; their devotees preserved and cultivated the social distinction associated with them in their country of origin. People from lower social classes had little opportunity to join in. They were scarcely likely to know anyone who could nominate them, nor did they have much interest in joining clubs whose members had a totally different lifestyle. In most cases this meant that such sports scarcely underwent popularization until their potential recruitment group grew larger, a consequence of increased prosperity, the expansion of the bourgeoisie, and the narrowing of class divisions in society.

The growth in popularity of German gymnastics stemmed from different causes. It started around 1900 with the expansion of the petit bourgeoisie and benefitted from the trend for skilled workers to indulge in organized leisure activities. The spread of gymnastics was less dependent on individual initi-

atives than that of the English sports because it was incorporated into the school curriculum. It was promoted by the intellectual spokespersons of the lower middle classes—teachers, preachers, and doctors. In countries that had little German influence and a relatively small lower middle class, there was no seedbed for the mass growth of gymnastics. In a period of strong national rivalries and rising nationalism, the popularization of gymnastics was largely confined to the European continent. Its ideological origins, based on the desire to ennoble and strengthen the nation, appealed to feelings of patriotism and ideals of healthy living among the lower middle classes.

Of the American sports, volleyball and basketball did best in areas where the YMCA was influential. Wherever the United States intervened militarily, the YMCA was involved in educational reform and in the sports program of the American military. In Europe the YMCA introduced both of these sports in the wake of American intervention in the First World War, but they did not achieve mass popularity until after 1945, when the power and prestige of the United States had grown considerably, and they could supplant the discredited gymnastics movement.

The international spread of Japanese martial arts is a variation on the general pattern. But there is also a significant difference. Unlike other sports, they are practiced in Europe within commercial organizations, which has generated a huge diversity in the range of martial arts that are offered, with increasingly "tough" variants being introduced all the time. Less integrated into the dominant sports structure, they are less bourgeois and less associated with the "establishment," giving them an especial appeal to outsider groups. Judo and karate, over which the umbrella federations have more say, tend in Europe to attract young people from the white middle classes.

One indication of what I have called "hidden competition" is that the popularization of a sport tends to be followed by an exodus of those who want to distinguish themselves from the masses. As the "snob value" of cycling and soccer, and later tennis, has been undermined, people from elite circles have abandoned them for smaller, more obscure sports, where they can still find the ambience they seek. Their quest for "distinction" is not always a conscious choice to elevate themselves above others. The point is that no one can escape from the distinguishing effects of social conduct. By opting for a particular sport, you attach yourself to a particular group of people and distinguish yourself from others. This choice, though determined by individual taste and preference, is far from random in social terms—the distribution of social groups among sports reveals a distinct pattern. Individual choices are made within the context of social trends and relations and cannot be separated from them.

To choose one sport is—partly consciously, partly unconsciously—to reject others. A golfer will not mind an acquaintance seeing him working his way around the links. He will probably be less happy, however, to be discovered on the korfball pitch, in the canteen of the local martial arts school, or enjoying snooker, bowling, or tug-of-war. No one can escape from the status value of sports. This does not mean that it is the prime reason for someone taking up a sport; quite different factors may play a role. But the choice of a particular sport always leads to a certain positioning in society, whether you like it or not.

A sport's social status, as based on the expected income and education of participants, is part of its wider image. Other elements of this image include the sport's national origins, the degree to which certain groups have been excluded from it, and the degree to which it has responded to changes in society. Comparison of the social histories of sports helps us understand the relations between them.

Most people come into contact with a variety of sports, mainly through their parents, friends, schools, and the media. They invest a sport with a certain significance on the basis of what they see and hear, regarding the partly institutionalized culture that has evolved around it and the kind of people they associate with it. The image of tennis, as it was once played in exclusive clubs, in spotless white attire, is quite different from tennis played at a local sports center, in brightly colored, fashionable clothes. Cultural characteristics of this kind influence people's ideas of a sport, from how it is played to how they will be expected to behave as participants and spectators, the kind of atmosphere they will find there, how the body is used and the degree of physical contact that is considered acceptable and customary, and the extent to which tension and emotions are expressed openly. Often there is a vague consensus about such matters, and a majority of people will agree in classifying a particular sport as modern or old-fashioned, elitist or working-class, masculine or feminine, or as suitable for older or younger age groups.[5] In periods of social transition, contrasting views of a sport will clash, and tastes will waver.

The point here is not whether gymnastics is "really" a women's sport or whether cricket is quintessentially English, but the fact that these images exist. To ethnocentric Britons, it was once self-evident that cycling went with Frenchmen, gymnastics with Germans, and baseball with Americans. And their own sports were part and parcel of the national image they had of themselves and projected to the outside world and part of how others saw them.[6] Although precursors of cricket, soccer, rugby, field hockey, and golf existed in many countries, in their new, standardized form they were regarded as

British cultural products. And though baseball started life as a variation on the English game of rounders, everyone agreed that it was an American sport.

The same applies to the connection between sports and social classes. To rephrase a maxim of Norbert Elias, we could say that a sport is exactly as "civilized" as the surrounding society or social class.[7] Golf as played on an eighteen-hole course by someone wearing special shoes and using trolleys and golf clubs of a British or American brand, amid flora and fauna and within a historical, exclusive, rural club, is worlds apart from golf played by someone in a tracksuit and Adidas trainers on a vacant plot of land next to the highway that some enterprising individual has converted into a nine-hole course. It is not the technical characteristics of golf (or of boxing, soccer, tennis, cricket, cycling, or volleyball) that are responsible for the class associations each one evokes. The status value of golf to today's golfers will no doubt wane if it is inundated by members of lower social classes. While the basic rules will stay the same, the rules of social decorum will change, and it is this that gives the sport its special significance. The same applies to boxing. It is not this sport's focus on physical contact that determines the class with which it is associated, but the way it is practiced and its partly institutionalized customs. While boxing is nowadays associated with the lower classes, at the end of the eighteenth century it was particularly popular among the English aristocracy. It is the atmosphere, mode of play, clothing, social etiquette, symbols, and rituals that determine what class a sport is associated with, not whether people participate as individuals or in teams, inside or in the open air, or with or without balls, rackets, bicycles, or boxing gloves.[8]

The Aura of Globalization

Globalization did not suddenly come about in recent times; rather, it is the outcome of a proliferation of interdependencies over several centuries. In this long-term process, a succession of countries have held sway in political, economic, military, and cultural life. The spread of standardized and organized sports took place in the most recent phase of this process, in which many cultural goods were disseminated throughout the world.

Although there was a definite connection between the spread of sports and the prestige of the countries where they originated, this significance has been eroded by time; indeed, even the association with a particular country has weakened, partly because language plays a minor role.[9] In some cases the association with higher social classes has survived. The importance of the British origins of golf and tennis has declined in comparison to the early 1900s; what counts today is their global association with the highest social

groups from prominent regions. It is not only in Europe and the United States that the popularity of tennis and golf is increasing. In Korea, for instance, these are the sports that people say, when asked, they would most like to play "in the future."[10] The increased popularity of tennis and golf is being felt in prosperous countries in all parts of the world. But globalization has also boosted sports such as soccer and track and field, despite their lesser status. It endows them with a new air of modernity and perpetuates their popularity. Sports confined to countries with a nondescript international image are gradually coming to be seen as elements of national folklore. They can still arouse plenty of enthusiasm within their national frontiers, but elsewhere they lack the global allure without which people of other countries will not respond to their charms.

The sports structure is embedded in a system of competing states. Every standardized sport has its own national organizations to arrange league competitions, to determine national champions, and to select the country's national teams. At the Olympic Games, sportsmen and sportswomen represent their nation; flags are displayed and national anthems played. All such events are products of the process of state formation and national rivalries that existed between 1880 and 1914. As the global spread of sports took place during the heyday of the nation state as the central unit of government and identity, the power of states was related to the spread of sports in numerous ways. Today, while nations do their utmost to safeguard their international position, economic and cultural trends are increasingly becoming detached from national borders.[11]

In the past, national elites played a leading role in importing sports from other countries. But the expansion of the media and the growth of tourism, commerce, and migration have weakened their role; the electronic media have become the main catalysts in the process of distribution. It looks as if snooker, for instance, is being spread from the working classes of one country to the same classes elsewhere, without any intervention on the part of national elites—a near-impossible pattern of distribution in the late nineteenth century, when there was no television. Nowadays the medium is the mediator. Gone is the dominance of national elites, whose main interest was in adopting sports associated with the lifestyle of the English upper middle classes.

Television has not brought equality in the exchange of cultural traditions and inventions. Still, something new has happened. A transnational culture has been born, which is rapidly spreading around the globe, by satellite, via cable television and the Internet. Itself an amalgam of expressions of culture from all parts of the world, it is incorporated selectively into local culture

everywhere.[12] Although Anglo-Saxon elements predominate, other cultural traditions are increasingly mingling with them. This is partly because the media are less exclusively bound to superpowers, and because their reporters and cameramen are standing by in almost every part of the world. And partly it is attributable to increased "bottom-up" influence: large-scale migration from poor to richer regions means that people in prosperous countries are increasingly encountering new cultural phenomena, from areas about which they were previously quite ignorant.

The concept of universalism appeals to everyone, including the young and poor who cannot travel around the world: by taking part in cultural activities that transcend national borders they escape—symbolically, at any rate—from the restrictions on mobility that are imposed by their age or financial resources.[13] In the late nineteenth century, the pursuit of sports united large groups of people from different villages, towns, and regions at the national level, before this kind of national integration had been achieved in many other areas. The geographical circles within which people participated in sporting events gradually expanded, strengthening the sense of national unity on several fronts. Today, a similar renewed realization of collectivity is making itself felt on a global scale. The universal popularity of sports has created the possibility of a shared experience for the world's inhabitants, whose increasing interdependence at the supranational level is not yet liberally supplied with appropriate global symbols.[14]

Appendix: Participation in Organized Sports in Twenty-five European and Four Non-European Countries

In the following tables the sports with the most participants are listed for each country, based on the number of club members. Although the use of membership figures as an indicator of the popularity of sports has certain disadvantages (see chapter 2), it nonetheless provides the clearest picture of differences in popularity of organized and largely competitive sports from one country to the next.

The following points should be borne in mind in relation to these rankings:

—Hunting, fishing, motor sports, and walking have not been included in the tables, for reasons of noncomparability.

—The periods of time covered by these figures vary from one country to the next. Statistics for several years were obtainable only for a few countries.

—Rankings are most reliable in the case of countries where most sports clubs belong to federations, which are in turn mostly affiliated with the National Olympic Committee or national sports federation. This applies, for instance, to Germany, Italy, and the Netherlands. Several countries have more than one sports federation.

—Where it was impossible to ascertain the membership of all the existing federations, as in the case of Denmark, those with the largest were used. It may be assumed that the smaller federations would have little influence on the ranking of the fifteen organized sports with the most participants.

—The ranking and number of participants for Sweden is based on a representative survey in which people were questioned about their participation in organized sports.

—The rankings provide the least comprehensive picture in the case of countries in which sports tend to be organized in the framework of the school system rather than clubs, notably Britain and the United States.

—As sports in the United States are largely organized through the school system, the rankings and figures for the United States are based on data supplied by the

National Collegiate Athletic Association (NCAA) for the 1986–87 academic year and by the National Federation of State High School Associations (NFSHSA) for the year 1988–89. The fragmented organizational structure outside schools makes it extremely difficult to construct an overall picture. As these rankings are based on participation among school and college students, sports with relatively high levels of participation among older people—in particular, tennis and golf—are lower down the scale than would be expected in a comprehensive picture.

European Countries

Austria (1988)

1	Skiing	542,297
2	Soccer	255,000
3	Gymnastics	163,978
4	Tennis	120,087
5	Eisschiessen	95,603
6	Shooting	80,938
7	Swimming	66,095
8	Cycling	45,496
9	Tobogganing	24,000
10	Heeressport	23,282
11	Table tennis	22,283
12	Equestrian sports	21,310
13	Track and Field	20,305
14	Handball	18,380
15	Volleyball	13,609

Source: Bundes-Sportorganisation Österreich, *Sport 87/88.*

Belgium (1987)

1	Soccer	383,951
2	Tennis	64,900
3	Basketball	62,230
4	Volleyball	41,085
5	Judo	35,887
6	Swimming	31,598
7	Gymnastics	31,455
8	Track and Field	26,642
9	Squash	25,625
10	Table tennis	20,970
11	Balle pelote	13,670
12	Shooting	13,352
13	Golf	11,600
14	Badminton	11,081
15	Karate	10,656

Source: Sport Information Bulletin 13 (1988).

Bulgaria (1980)

1	Soccer	168,318
2	Track and Field	148,195
3	Volleyball	80,788
4	Basketball	64,314
5	Wrestling	52,924
6	Chess	49,199
7	Table tennis	46,479
8	Swimming	45,741
9	Handball	39,925
10	Gymnastics	25,777
11	Skiing	13,608

Cyprus (1991)

1	Soccer	10,000
2	Track and Field	2,100
3	Basketball	1,800
4	Volleyball	1,200
5	Table tennis	602
6	Karate	500
7	Tae kwon do	450
8	Badminton	431
9	Judo	400
10	Bowling	350

Source: ISI/CONI, *Challenges Ahead.*

Bulgaria (1980), Con't.

12	Shooting	13,438
13	Weightlifting	5,324
14	Cycling	4,834
15	Tennis	3,724

Source: Haralampiev, *Physical Culture and Sport.*

(Former) Czechoslovakia (1985)

1	Soccer	563,043
2	Skiing	80,467
3	Volleyball	76,014
4	Ice hockey	67,783
5	Tennis	63,751
6	Table tennis	63,423
7	Track and Field	44,701
8	Basketball	41,754
9	Handball	41,571
10	Chess	34,419
11	Judo, karate	29,037
12	Gymnastics	28,224
13	Swimming	23,558
14	Bowling	15,758

Source: Kamphorst and Roberts, eds., *Trends in Sports.*

Denmark (1990)

1	Soccer	336,022
2	Handball	177,976
3	Badminton	167,333
4	Swimming	123,194
5	Tennis	122,083
6	Gymnastics	110,663
7	Equestrian sports	72,807
8	Yachting	60,345
9	Shooting	44,249
10	Golf	39,132
11	Track and Field	30,560
12	Volleyball	23,439
13	Rowing	21,638
14	Table tennis	18,931
15	Orienteering	17,884

Source: Dansk Idraets-Forbund, *DIFs Medlemsopgorelse.*

England (1980)

1	Soccer	1,150,000
2	Darts	1,400,000*
3	Golf	514,000
4	Tennis	244,000
5	Bowling	240,000
6	Table tennis	200,000
7	Badminton	107,000
8	Cricket	80,000

*Includes Scotland, Wales, and Northern Ireland

Source: Centre for Leisure Research, *Digest of Sports Statistics.*

Finland (1985)

1	Soccer	365,467
2	Track and Field	207,251
3	Skiing	205,617
4	Volleyball	79,769
5	Orienteering	70,957
6	Ice hockey	68,127
7	Pesääpallo	65,979
8	Yachting	33,344
9	Shooting	30,231
10	Tennis	27,452
11	Basketball	24,154
12	Biathlon	23,338

Finland (1985), Con't.

13	Swimming	17,305
14	Judo	15,782
15	Skating	15,770

Source: Finnish Society for Research in Sports and Physical Education, *Sport and Physical Education.*

France (1997)

1	Soccer	2,056,684
2	Tennis	1,062,786
3	Judo	543,016
4	Basketball	473,263
5	Péétanque	455,633
6	Handball	343,673
7	Skiing	303,213
8	Golf	261,058
9	Rugby	255,872
10	Yachting	226,126
11	Equestrian sports	211,153
12	Karate	205,000
13	Gymnastics	182,390
14	Swimming	179,578
15	Table tennis	160,768

Source: Sport Information Bulletin 14 (1998).

Germany (1998)

1	Soccer	6,216,233
2	Gymnastics	4,715,312
3	Tennis	2,114,892
4	Shooting	1,589,079
5	Handball	838,409
6	Track and Field	830,644
7	Equestrian sports	724,472
8	Table tennis	722,277
9	Skiing	671,878
10	Swimming	627,843
11	Mountaineering	596,084
12	Volleyball	535,627
13	Golf	296,370
14	Bowling	269,570
15	Judo	264,909

Source: Deutsche Sportbund, *Mitgliederzahl Spitzenverbände.*

Hungary (1988)

1	Soccer	85,990
2	Handball	16,384
3	Track and Field	11,771
4	Basketball	9,030
5	Table tennis	7,122
6	Tennis	5,989
7	Volleyball	5,782
8	Swimming	5,200
9	Wrestling	4,377
10	Judo	4,335

Source: ISI/CONI, *Challenges Ahead.*

Iceland (1983)

1	Soccer	20,040
2	Skiing	11,400
3	Handball	8,973
4	Track and Field	8,673
5	Swimming	5,122
6	Basketball	4,883
7	Badminton	3,697
8	Gymnastics	3,442
9	Golf	3,100
10	Table tennis	2,393
11	Volleyball	2,362
12	Weightlifting	1,077

Iceland (1983), Con't.

13	Yachting	1,049
14	Judo	829
15	Shooting	520

Source: Sport Information Bulletin 12 (1988).

Ireland (1983)

1	Celtic sports	306,600
2	Soccer	218,760
3	Golf	103,646
4	Squash	103,400
5	Track and Field	90,292
6	Basketball	69,550
7	Camogie	66,211
8	Badminton	47,480
9	Swimming	34,997
10	Field hockey	30,469
11	Handball	28,443
12	Tennis	23,000
13	Cricket	22,200

Source: Sport Information Bulletin 12 (1988).

Italy (1991)

1	Soccer	1,232,632
2	Volleyball	415,811
3	Basketball	291,844
4	Tennis	217,507
5	Winter sports	188,929
6	Bowling	135,631
7	Track and Field	126,707
8	Wrestling, judo	81,537
9	Yachting	73,104
10	Cycling	63,970
11	Gymnastics	63,158
12	Swimming	56,212
13	Equestrian sports	48,589
14	Golf	35,131
15	Handball	32,582

Source: Comitato Olympico Nazionale Italiano, *In Movimento.*

Luxembourg (1998)

1	Soccer	26,894
2	Tennis	8,898
3	Gymnastics	6,628
4	Basketball	5,189
5	Bowling	4,373
6	Table tennis	4,251
7	Golf	4,139
8	Shooting	4,044
9	Cycling	3,136

Source: Sport Information Bulletin 51 (1999).

The Netherlands (1998)

1	Soccer	1,022,288
2	Tennis	724,021
3	Gymnastics	246,788
4	Skating	162,418
5	Swimming	152,927
6	Volleyball	144,792
7	Skiing	140,769
8	Equestrian sports	137,864
9	Field hockey	129,054
10	Golf	119,994
11	Bridge	108,231
12	Yachting	100,823
13	Korfball	96,217

The Netherlands (1998)

14	Track and Field	84,755
15	Badminton	82,383

Source: NOC*NSF, *Ledentallen* (1998).

Norway (1984)

1	Soccer	270,953
2	Skiing	193,146
3	Gymnastics	111,310
4	Handball	88,567
5	Track and Field	86,567
6	Orienteering	38,748
7	Shooting	28,957
8	Swimming	28,230
9	Yachting	25,404
10	Volleyball	23,150
11	Tennis	23,128
12	Equestrian sports	10,644
13	Cycling	9,510
14	Skating	9,385
15	Ice hockey	8,521

Source: *Sport Information Bulletin* 13 (1988).

Poland (1972)

1	Soccer	280,898
2	Track and Field	47,797
3	Shooting	32,407
4	Volleyball	29,007
5	Handball	25,640
6	Basketball	23,990
7	Chess	18,410
8	Table tennis	12,200
9	Weightlifting	10,922
10	Swimming	8,531
11	Skiing	7,631
12	Wrestling	6,957
13	Boxing	6,654
14	Canoeing	5,768

Source: Sieniarski, *Sport in Polen.*

Portugal (1989)

1	Soccer	80,846
2	Handball	12,470
3	Basketball	8,254
4	Track and Field	6,984
5	Volleyball	6,834
6	Judo	3,745
7	Swimming	3,680
8	Tennis	3,530
9	Table tennis	2,853
10	Gymnastics	2,426

Source: ISI/CONI, *Challenges Ahead.*

Spain (1997)

1	Soccer	597,039
2	Basketball	195,367
3	Golf	121,771
4	Judo	121,771
5	Karate	90,070
6	Tennis	82,570
7	Track and Field	77,279
8	Handball	75,059
9	Volleyball	71,793
10	Mountaineering	61,924
11	Winter sports	61,643
12	Shooting	55,940
13	Tae kwon do	41,274
14	Cycling	38,055
15	Underwater sports	36,721

Source: *Sport Information Bulletin* 50 (1999).

Sweden (1993)

1	Soccer	820,000
2	Track and Field	370,000
3	Floorball	360,000
4	Ice hockey	250,000
5	Golf	240,000
6	Basketball	230,000
7	Shooting	190,000
8	Skiing	180,000
9	Gymnastics	170,000
10	Volleyball	160,000

Source: ISI/CONI, *Challenges Ahead.*

Switzerland (1978)

1	Shooting	546,624
2	Gymnastics	316,162
3	Soccer	309,473
4	Tennis	125,459
5	Skiing	116,000
6	Ice hockey	67,655
7	Mountaineering	57,674
8	Cycling	52,455
9	Equestrian sports	51,000
10	Swimming	36,000
11	Handball	32,000
12	Boxing	18,500
13	Track and Field	18,000
14	Table tennis	16,000
15	Volleyball	14,000

Source: Steinegger, *Sport '78.*

Turkey (1987)

1	Soccer	143,687
2	Volleyball	76,468
3	Basketball	68,522
4	Track and Field	50,942
5	Table tennis	32,279
6	Handball	29,561
7	Wrestling	23,847
8	Swimming	7,928
9	Judo	7,225
10	Tae kwon do	5,793
11	Karate	4,468
12	Boxing	3,256
13	Shooting	3,225
14	Yachting	1,070
15	Skiing	806

Source: Sport Information Bulletin 32 (1993).

(Former) Yugoslavia (1990)

1	Soccer	186,822
2	Shooting	110,886
3	Handball	32,518
4	Basketball	28,729
5	Volleyball	14,779
6	Tennis	12,742
7	Track and Field	12,538
8	Skiing	11,939
9	Swimming	11,376
10	Judo	9,680
11	Table tennis	9,092
12	Gymnastics	6,877
13	Equestrian sports	4,626
14	Wrestling	4,380
15	Yachting	4,002

Source: Comitato Olympico Nazionale Italiano, *Practica Sportiva.*

Outside Europe

Australia (1984–85)

1	Soccer	520,042
2	Cricket	504,050
3	Australian football	491,100
4	Bowls	489,952
5	Golf	432,000
6	Netball	347,000
7	Tennis	300,000
8	Rugby	256,110
9	Squash	216,955
10	Basketball	196,977
11	Field hockey	176,181
12	Touch football	125,000
13	Yachting	108,030
14	Baseball	89,000
15	Bowling	89,000

Source: Australian Sports Commission, *Annual Report.*

New Zealand (1983–84)

1	Rugby	224,700
2	Netball	114,210
3	Golf	113,867
4	Bowls	84,407
5	Cricket	77,821
6	Soccer	77,316
7	Gymnastics	65,200
8	Tennis	61,500
9	Yachting	54,000
10	Squash	53,450
11	Bowls indoor	50,300
12	Field hockey	42,700
13	Softball	36,101
14	Track and Field	35,835
15	Basketball	29,650

Source: Kamphorst and Roberts, *Trends in Sports.*

Japan (1967)

1	Baseball	824,728
2	Volleyball	612,180
3	Table tennis	526,035
4	Paddleball	492,836
5	Basketball	413,770
6	Judo	407,782
7	Track and Field	368,220
8	Kendo	329,299
9	Softball	178,958
10	Gymnastics	152,801
11	Golf	114,178
12	Shooting	103,588
13	Soccer	103,204
14	Mountaineering	101,677
15	Swimming	100,408

Source: Guttmann, *From Ritual to Record.*

United States (1986–1987, 1989)

1	American football	999,724
2	Basketball	915,771
3	Track and Field	836,999
4	Baseball	433,317
5	Soccer	347,705
6	Volleyball	322,777
7	Tennis	279,170
8	Cross-country	275,310
9	Softball	258,481
10	Wrestling	249,081
11	Swimming/diving	184,285
12	Golf	163,466
13	Hockey	53,167
14	Lacrosse	34,974
15	Gymnastics	32,831

Sources: NCAA, *Sports and Recreational Programs* (1987); NFSHSA, *1989 Sports Participation Survey.*

Notes

Chapter 1: A Global Panorama of Sports

1. My analysis of the global system of sports is a variation on the global system of culture as discussed by Abram de Swaan; see De Swaan, *Perron Nederland,* 93–120.

2. Stokvis, *De sportwereld,* 16.

3. This term was introduced by Norbert Elias, albeit in a slightly different context and with a slightly different meaning; see Elias, "Genesis of Sport," 92.

4. Guttmann, *From Ritual to Record,* 15–55.

5. Brailsford, "1787."

6. On the development of these football-like activities, see Walvin, *People's Game,* 9–30; Dunning and Sheard, *Barbarians, Gentlemen, and Players,* 21–45; Elias and Dunning, *Quest for Excitement,* 175–90.

7. Weber, *Peasants into Frenchmen,* and Knippenberg and de Pater, *Eenwording van Nederland,* are interesting studies of these changes in France and the Netherlands, respectively.

8. Bale, *Sport and Place,* "International Sports History," and *Sports Geography.* For the Netherlands, see Spaans, "Sociale geschiedenis," 54. See Guttmann, *From Ritual to Record,* 61–62, on the relationship between sportization and industrialization: "The spread of modern sports organizations correlates with the rise of industrialism. The first nations to industrialize were also the first to establish national organizations for modern sports, in almost the same order." See also Clignet and Stark, "Modernization and the Game of Soccer," 81–98; Guttmann, *Games and Empires,* 53 and 200 n. 37.

9. In 1787 boxing had a large, enthusiastic public and something approaching a national championship. The first boxing hall opened its doors as early as 1719, and boxing regulations were first written up in 1743. By this time Wetherby's famous Racing Calendar had long been publishing the most important horse races. The Jockey Club was founded around 1750, and by the end of the century it was the most important supervisory body for horse racing. Commerce, gambling, breeding, and training were already inextricably connected with these races. See Brailsford, "1787," 217–22.

10. Holt, *Sport and Society in Modern France,* 4–5.

11. See Giddens, *The Nation-State and Violence,* 261–64.

12. See Weber, *Peasants into Frenchmen,* 199; MacAloon, *This Great Symbol.* The same discrepancies existed in other parts of Europe. While inhabitants of the Netherlands with a fixed address probably travelled no more than ten to twelve kilometers from their homes on an everyday basis around 1880 (Knippenberg and de Pater, *Eenwording van Nederland,* 53–54), Pim Mulier, the man who was largely responsible for introducing sports to the Netherlands, journeyed to countries including Britain, Belgium, France, Germany, Scandinavia, and the Dutch East Indies between 1880 and 1900. Money was no object for him. He came from a well-to-do family and was a man of private means.

13. *Kolven* resembled hockey; *beugelen* was played with an eight-pound ball and a bat; in *palingtrekken* the aim was to pull the head off a live eel tied to a post; *katknuppelen* involved throwing sticks at a barrel containing a cat until the barrel burst and the cat ran off in terror. Another Dutch pastime, *klootschieten,* involved rolling an oval ball or disk along the ground.

14. De Swaan, *Perron Nederland,* 102–7.

15. Stokvis, *Strijd over sport,* 12–17, and *De sportwereld,* 52–53.

16. Thus in 1887 there was some public indignation in the Netherlands when an Englishman and an American organized contests to find the world champion in swimming (Stokvis, *Strijd over sport,* 18).

17. Mulier, *Athletiek en voetbal,* 1894.

18. See *Nederlandse Sport,* February 7, 1885; Stokvis, *Strijd over sport,* 18.

19. Stokvis, "International and National Expansion of Sports."

20. The rules for the winter Olympics are less strict. The IOC takes "widely practiced" to mean "a) national championships or cup competitions, regularly organized by the respective national federations; b) international participation and organization of regional and/or world championships in the respective sports" (International Olympic Committee, *Olympic Charter,* 24).

21. Guttmann, *Whole New Ball Game.*

22. Information derived from international sports federations and the IOC.

23. Korfball is a mixed team sport, combining elements of basketball and netball. Netball is played by two teams of seven players trying to throw a ball into an open-ended net.

24. Not all sports receive an equal amount of attention. Sports whose social history has not yet been written, in particular, are somewhat neglected. These are often practiced by a relatively small group. Games such as chess and checkers have also been largely left out of consideration. Future research will have to establish whether the differential popularization of these sports and games is explicable in terms of the theory developed in this book.

Chapter 2: The Popularity of Sports

1. Stokvis, *De sportwereld,* 130–35.

2. Inter/View, *Sport Scanner.* Participation in sports in the past is the most significant variable in explaining the composition of the sporting public; see McPherson, "Sport Consumption and the Economics of Consumerism," 239–75; Van de Brug, *Voetbalvandalisme,* 145; Guttmann, *Sports Spectators,* 84.

3. The ideas of the American sociologist Ernest W. Burgess are particularly valuable in clarifying the spatial and social divisions within towns and the dynamic relationship between them; see Park, Burgess, and McKenzie, *The City.*

4. During the process of socialization people also become familiar with the technical features of sports and learn to value them to a greater or lesser extent. They become acquainted with the atmosphere, the way matches are played, and the ins and outs of clubs and players in relation to some sports more than others. Thus the number of participants of each sport depends on its tradition in a particular country or region.

5. See for example Manders and Kropman, *Sportdeelname, Sportbeoefening, drempels en stimulansen,* and *Sport, ontwikkeling en kosten.*

6. See Renson, "Sport voor allen."

7. See Deutscher, *What We Say/What We Do.*

8. Merton, *Social Theory and Social Practice;* Jolles, *Verenigingsleven in Nederland,* 27.

9. Following a joint initiative by the Italian CONI (Comitato Olympico Nazionale Italiano) and UK Sport and Sport England, the COMPASS project is currently in progress. It is to culminate in a coordinated monitoring of participation in sports in Europe.

10. Van Galen and Diederiks, *Sportblessures,* 11–12, 19–26. The differences between the questions asked makes it extremely difficult to compare levels of participation in sports. See for example the participation percentages for eight sports that emerged from five French surveys (*La Lettre de l'Economie du Sport* 87 [29 August 1990]):

	INSEE (1983–84)	CESP (1984)	INSEP (1985)	INSEE (1987–88)	CESP (1989–90)
Swimming	18.1 (1)	16.5 (1)	22.5 (3)	13.0 (3)	23.7 (1)
Tennis	8.6 (4)	12.0 (2)	12.8 (5)	8.3 (5)	13.8 (5)
Gymnastics	3.6 (6)	10.8 (4)	26.3 (1)	15.1 (1)	10.7 (6)
Running	3.6 (6)	8.9 (5)	12.7 (6)	4.8 (6)	16.3 (3)
Rambling	11.7 (2)	7.0 (7)	24.9 (2)	10.7 (4)	16.8 (2)
Cycling	9.2 (3)	11.2 (3)	15.4 (4)	13.9 (2)	14.1 (4)
Table tennis	1.0 (8)	8.0 (6)	3.9 (8)	3.1 (8)	10.2 (7)
Soccer	4.2 (5)	6.6 (8)	6.8 (7)	3.7 (7)	7.4 (8)

Key: INSEE = L'Institut de la Statistique et des Études Économiques; CESP = Centre d'Étude des Supports de Publicité; INSEP = Institut National du Sport et de l'Éducation Physique

11. A recent Dutch survey reveals that 96 percent of competitive sports participants pursue their sports in clubs. In the case of people referred to rather misleadingly as "recreational sports participants" (after all, most competitive players would also claim to be engaged in recreation), 61 percent practice their sport without joining a club (Van Galen and Diederiks, *Sportblessures,* 23).

12. Goudsblom, *Sociologie van Norbert Elias,* 33–34 and 215 n. 22.

13. Seehase, *Der verein,* 66–67.

14. In the Netherlands fewer members of ethnic minorities belong to clubs than Dutch nationals of the same age and education. But outside the framework of clubs, male members of ethnic minorities probably participate in sports to almost the same extent as Dutch

males (Hoolt, *Sportdeelname van etnische groeperingen;* Beeltje, *Opties met betrekking tot de sportbeoefening*).

15. See Jolles, *Verenigingsleven in Nederland.*

16. For rowing, see Widdershoven, "Stagnerende groei." For the information on the Coca-Cola survey I am indebted to an employee of Coca-Cola, Frank W. Bean.

17. See for example Hart and Birell, *Sport in the Sociocultural Process,* 676; Elias and Dunning, *Quest for Excitement,* 39–40; Stokvis, *De sportwereld,* 690.

18. Durkheim, *Le suicide.*

19. Lever, *Soccer Madness,* 35.

20. Krämer-Mandeau, *Sport und körpererziehung auf Cuba,* 29.

21. Holt, *Sport and the British,* 211.

22. Sodusta, "Historical Development of Sport in the Philippines," 727.

23. "Football could be played by anyone, regardless of size, skill and strength"; "tall, short, stocky, or slim—anyone can play [soccer], unlike [American] football, rugby, or basketball, where particular body builds give some a distinct advantage" (Lever, *Soccer Madness,* 34); "The [soccer] player did not need to be possessed of extraordinary physical characteristics" (Mason, *Association Football and English Society,* 1).

24. See for example De Vries, "Aanbod van sportaccommodaties"; Bowen, *Cricket,* 120; and Eziakor and Nwali, "Trends in Sports in Nigeria," 369.

25. Manders and Kropman, *Sportbeoefening, drempels en stimulansen.*

26. Van de Wouw, "Realiteit en Utopie."

27. Between 1970 and 1985 the number of tennis courts increased from 2,870 to 8,579, an increase of 5,709. The total number of pitches and courts for soccer, korfball, hockey, handball, rugby, track and field, and baseball increased in the same period by only 4,694 (Centraal Bureau voor de Statistiek, *Statistisch zakboek,* 148).

28. *Sport Information Bulletin* 21 (June 1990), 1487, and 23 (December 1990), 1701.

29. Soccer has been described as "the much simpler and inexpensive game" (Baker, *Sports in the Western World,* 134); it was "inexpensive to play and could be played almost anywhere, even in the streets of towns" (Mason, *Association Football and English Society,* 1), it "could be played year-round; it required little equipment" (Levine, "Sport and Society," 236), and it "can be played by the poorest children in an empty lot with rolled-up stockings in lieu of a proper ball" (Lever, *Soccer Madness,* 34).

30. See Guttmann, *From Ritual to Record,* 97.

31. Taks, *Sociale gelaagdheid in de sport,* 327–28.

32. Ibid.

33. See also Sleap and Duffy, "Factors Affecting Active Participation"; Bourdieu, *Distinction.*

34. Buytendijk, *Het voetballen,* 17–23.

35. Guttmann, *From Ritual to Record,* 128.

36. Miermans, *Voetbal in Nederland,* 81–105.

37. "It was, and is, a simple game, easy to play and follow" (Mason, *Association Football and English Society,* 1); "the popularity of soccer . . . is due to the fact that this game is easy to play and many people get a lot of fun out of it" (Jimu Tembo, "Historical Development of Sports in Malawi," 492); "it was simple to play, easy to grasp, and could be played on every surface under any conditions, by indeterminate numbers of men. It needed no equipment but a ball, and could last from dawn to dusk" (Walvin, *People's Game,* 45–46).

38. Netherlands Cricket Federation (hereafter NCB) memorial volume (1933), 244. The same has been said of the difference between baseball and cricket in the United States. Baseball is simply easier to learn, according to Kirsch (*Creation of American Team Sports,* 99).

39. See Guttmann, "'Our Former Colonial Masters,'" 102.

40. Pietersen, *Sociologie van de sport,* 139.

41. Rijsdorp qtd. in ibid., *Sociologie van de sport,* 46.

42. Pietersen, *Sociologie van de sport,* 139.

43. Diem, *Weltgeschichte der sports,* 872–73.

44. Qtd. in Guttmann, *From Ritual to Record,* 95–97.

45. Qtd. in Kirsch, *Creation of American Team Sports,* 94.

46. Tyrrell, "Emergence of Modern American Baseball," 207–8; Adelman, *Sporting Time,* 92 and 113.

47. *NRC Handelsblad,* March 18, 1989.

48. Überhorst, ed., *Geschichte der Leibesübungen,* vol. 6, 10.

49. Van Maanen and Venekamp, *Sporters in cijfers;* Venekamp and Wolters, *Sporters in cijfers;* NOC*NSF, *Ledentallen.*

50. See for example Spel en Sport, *Jaarbericht 1987;* Telegraaf Tijdschriften Groep, *Sportmarkt in ogenschouw,* 78.

51. See for example Zijderveld, *Culturele factor.*

52. Van Maanen and Venekamp, *Sporters in cijfers.*

53. It is more likely that individualization may influence the number of people who practice sports without joining clubs. They not only avoid having to engage in official ties with others, they may well choose sports that can truly be practiced on an individual basis and more or less independently of others, such as running, cycling, and surfing. But here I am focussing on the effect of individualization on organized sports.

54. Lüschen, "Interdependence of Sport and Culture."

55. See Van Bottenburg, "Individualisering en populariteitsontwikkeling."

56. See for example the English hockey coach in *NRC Handelsblad,* March 24, 1989; and Zhou Yuan, *China's Contemporary Sports,* 8, on table tennis in China.

57. Stokvis and Minee, "Olympische Spelen van 1992."

58. Lenk, *Leistungssport,* 45; see also Guttmann, *From Ritual to Record,* 98–99.

59. Wirth, "Wo Manager umsonst arbeiten," 69.

60. Van Tijn qtd. in Boogman et al., *Geschiedenis van het moderne Nederland,* 46.

61. Miermans, *Voetbal in Nederland,* 154; De Swaan, *De Olympische hoogte,* 26; Stokvis, *De sportwereld,* 27–31.

62. Chandler, *Television and National Sport,* xv.

63. Maguire, *Global Sport,* 144–75

64. Miermans, *Voetbal in Nederland,* 106; Seymour, *Baseball,* 33; King, "Sexual Politics of Sport," 73–74; Friederich, "Untersuchungen," 59–60.

65. Stokvis, "Populariteit van sporten," 120.

66. Stokvis "Populariteit van sporten" and "International and National Expansion of Sports." See also Stokvis, "Continuities in the Theory of the Differential Popularization of Sports."

67. See Blumer, *Symbolic Interactionism.*

68. Bourdieu, *Distinction,* 208–25, *Chose dites,* 203–16, and "Program for a Sociology

of Sport." See also *Actes de la Recherche en Sciences Sociales* 79 and 80 (1989), esp. Waser, "Marché des partenaires," 2–21.

69. Dunning, *Sport Matters;* Dunning and Sheard, *Barbarians, Gentlemen, and Players.*

70. Tyrrell, "Emergence of Modern American Baseball"; Adelman, *Sporting Time;* Kirsch, *Creation of American Team Sports;* Cashman, "Cricket and Colonialism."

71. Mennell, *All Manners of Food,* 15.

72. Fallers, "A Note on the 'Trickle Effect.'"

Chapter 3: The Provenance of Sports

1. When defining the provenance of a sport, the main criterion is where the development and standardization of the rules occurred that are central to the way the sport is played at the international level today.

2. However, this sport also had roots in England.

3. The first Turnpike Act was introduced as early as 1663; the major growth of toll roads set in around the mid-eighteenth century. Four hundred fifty-two such acts were passed between 1760 and 1774, by which time fifteen thousand miles of toll roads covered almost the entire country. See Briggs, *Age of Improvement,* and *Social History of England;* Pope, *Atlas of British Social and Economic History,* 99.

4. Qtd. in Briggs, *Social History of England,* 207; see also Pope, *Atlas of British Social and Economic History,* 98.

5. Landes, *Unbound Prometheus,* 41–123.

6. Hobsbawm, *Industry and Empire,* 13; Landes, *Unbound Prometheus,* 66–70; Schöffler, *England das Land des Sportes,* 50–72; Jansen, "De Sterke en Flexibele Staat," 54–55.

7. See Kloeren, *Sport und Rekord,* 120–293.

8. See Stokvis, "Sports and Civilization," 129–30; cf. the introduction to Elias and Dunning, *Quest for Excitement.*

9. Kloeren, *Sport und Rekord,* 145–53, 240–61.

10. Later on, boxing was described in the same way as sixteenth-century fencing, as "the noble art of self-defense" (Kloeren, *Sport und Rekord,* 148–49; Schöffler, *England das Land des Sportes,* 30–42. For a detailed description of the long-term development of boxing, see Sheard, *Boxing in the Civilizing Process*).

11. Bowen, *Cricket;* Chandler, *Television and National Sport,* 112–14.

12. Bailey, *Leisure and Class;* Holt, *Sport and the British,* 44–50.

13. Ibid., 31–33.

14. Qtd. in ibid., 109.

15. Ibid., 98.

16. Rowing had become popular at these universities in the 1820s, and by the mid-nineteenth century it was a standard item on the curriculum.

17. Qtd. in Halladay, *Rowing in England,* 3. In spite of the changes sweeping through society, the clubs retained this discriminatory amateur rule until the late 1930s. The *London Times* welcomed the decision to scrap the amateur rule as the end of "'this anachronism, reminiscent of obsolete social distinctions'" (Qtd. in Halladay, *Rowing in England,* 167–77).

18. Ibid.; Stokvis, *Strijd over sport,* 31. Just as university rowing clubs distinguished themselves from the centuries-old tradition of professional rowing by their own adherence to amateurism, university athletics clubs adopted a similar strategy vis-à-vis footmen's run-

ning races. Nineteenth-century Oxbridge students and graduates saw the latter as plebeian and associated them with gambling and dirty tricks. To distance themselves from all such practices they founded exclusive clubs with a strict amateur rule, within which they developed most elements of today's athletics.

19. Speak, "Social Stratification"; Halladay, *Rowing in England;* Page, *Hear the Boat Sing.* The number of clubs actually decreased. Whereas in 1890 there had been 457 rowing clubs in England (301 of which were in the greater London area), by 1925 there were scarcely more than two hundred, although this probably does not imply any decline in membership (Dodd, "Rowing," 291).

20. Halladay, *Rowing in England,* 137–38. The role of the London rowing clubs is underestimated in this account (see Page, *Hear the Boat Sing*). By the end of the 1960s more than half of the 460 rowing clubs had some connection with an educational establishment. Partly for this reason, even today most oarsmen come from elite groups; most clubs are in the southeast of England in affluent districts (Bale, *Sport and Place,* 157).

21. Chandler, *Television and National Sport,* 117; Williams, "Rugby Union," 119–20; Holt, *Sport and the British,* 107. According to Holt, a scorecard of this kind was corrected at Lords as late as 1961: "'Your cards show, at no. 8 Middlesex, F. J. Titmus, that should read, of course, Titmus, F. J.'" (107).

22. Halladay, *Rowing in England,* 2.

23. Chandler, *Television and National Sport,* 118; Holt, *Sport and the British,* 175–76.

24. Speak, "Social Stratification," 50.

25. A professional variant, league cricket, evolved in the industrial north, but it was always disparaged (Hill, "League Cricket," 123). It was at a disadvantage from the start, as county cricket had the prestige to attract leading professional cricketers. In the 1960s, "limited over" matches were organized to make cricket more attractive for spectators. These matches were decided within the space of one day at most, while county matches would take three days to complete (Chandler, *Television and National Sport,* 119–20).

26. Dunning and Sheard, *Barbarians, Gentlemen, and Players,* 46–57; Holt, *Sport and the British,* 75–79.

27. Qtd. in Mangan, *Athleticism,* 207.

28. Holt, *Sport and the British,* 81.

29. Mangan, *Athleticism,* 80–87, 129–38, and *Games Ethic and Imperialism,* 18; Holt, *Sport and the British,* 74–98.

30. Dunning and Sheard, *Barbarians, Gentlemen, and Players,* 99.

31. Walvin, *People's Game,* 40.

32. Ibid., 38–49; Dunning and Sheard, *Barbarians, Gentlemen, and Players,* 100–129.

33. Walvin, *People's Game,* 40.

34. Ibid., 48; Dunning and Sheard, *Barbarians, Gentlemen, and Players,* 101; Mason, *Association Football and English Society,* 23.

35. Mason, *Association Football and English Society,* 31; Holt, *Sport and the British,* 154–57.

36. Walvin, *People's Game,* 74.

37. Baker, *Sports in the Western World,* 124–25.

38. Between 1872 and 1884, fewer than ten thousand spectators attended the FA Cup finals; between 1884 and 1891 the numbers were scarcely above twenty thousand. The

numbers rose to more than forty thousand in 1893 and an extraordinary 110,000 in 1901. Many spectators were workers; most were skilled and had a regular source of income (Mason, *Association Football and English Society,* 142–58).

39. The first generation of professionals were skilled workers. Some were recruited with advertisements in sports magazines and newspapers. Their pay was fairly meager. Only the six hundred highest-paid footballers earned more than factory workers; in the 1901–2 season the FA set a maximum wage of 208 pounds a year. We can safely assume that top-class players earned more, but in the first few decades of the century few could earn a decent living (ibid., 90–123, 135–36 n. 165).

40. Walvin, *People's Game,* 78–79; Mason, *Association Football and English Society,* 75. The ties between soccer and cricket were of a more general nature. When bats, balls, and wickets were stored away in the fall at the end of the cricket season, out came the football; soccer was the game to play until spring, when the next cricket season began. A great many of these cricket and football clubs eventually focused exclusively on soccer—famous examples being Sheffield Wednesday and Everton (Mason, *Association Football and English Society,* 31). One advantage of the combination was the presence of a suitable playing field. Other aspects of cricket were also adopted in soccer. In the early years, for instance, county matches and competitions were organized, following the example of cricket. More strikingly, when clubs first turned professional, amateurs were always chosen to captain their teams (Mason, *Association Football and English Society,* 76).

41. Dunning and Sheard, *Barbarians, Gentlemen, and Players,* 145–46; Holt, *Sport and the British,* 135.

42. Dunning and Sheard, *Barbarians, Gentlemen, and Players,* 139–42 and 175–200; Holt, *Sport and the British,* 106; Stokvis, "De populariteit van sporten," 678.

43. Dunning and Sheard, *Barbarians, Gentlemen, and Players,* 190–98.

44. Allison, *Association Football and the Urban Ethos,* 214.

45. Qtd. in Holt, *Sport and the British,* 106.

46. Dunning and Sheard, *Barbarians, Gentlemen, and Players,* 232–40. Which sport came first is of secondary importance. The important point is how much a sport benefitted from this initial period. In Manchester and Wales rugby was introduced before soccer. Manchester's first rugby players kept their sport so exclusive that soccer soon became more popular. In Wales, with its totally different social makeup (including a small middle class with little power), there was far less opposition to the popularization and professionalization of rugby. Welsh rugby administrators were far more willing than their counterparts in England to allow the best players to be paid. The Welsh Rugby Union, like Association Football in England, won the hearts of the workers (Williams, "Rugby Union," 310; Holt, *Sport and the British,* 105).

47. Walvin, *People's Game,* 45–73; Mason, *Association Football and English Society,* 29; Holt, *Sport and the British,* 138–79.

48. Dunning and Sheard, *Barbarians, Gentlemen, and Players,* 188.

49. Williams, "Rugby Union," 313. Until recently, parts of Yorkshire still observed a subtle distinction in secondary school rugby: "grammar schools" (whose pupils are in principle prepared for higher education) played Rugby Union, and "secondary moderns" played Rugby League. Such differences show how historical distinctions may be reflected in today's practice, and how physical education teachers may semiconsciously help to perpetuate social patterns in sports.

50. Before 1850 only a handful of boys' schools played anything resembling field hockey. Around 1860 a few "old boys" from one such school drew up new rules for the game and founded the Blackheath Football and Hockey Club. In 1886 they managed to reach an agreement with others on the standardization of field hockey rules (Miroy, *History of Hockey*, 35–90, 193; McCrone, *Sport and the Physical Emancipation*, 44, 128, 169).

51. See Miroy, *History of Hockey*, 113.

52. Ibid., 197; McCrone, *Sport and the Physical Emancipation*, 128–37; see also Holt, *Sport and the British*, 129.

53. Qtd. in Miroy, *History of Hockey*, 95; see also 112.

54. Mandell, *Sport*, 130; Baker, *Sports in the Western World*, 86. One of these indoor courts, near the Louvre, was used for many years in the twentieth century as a museum of impressionist art.

55. Birley, "Bonaparte and the Squire," 27; Gillmeister, *Kulturgeschichte des Tennis*.

56. Gillmeister, *Kulturgeschichte des Tennis*, 223.

57. Clerici, *Ultimate Tennis Book*, 69; Gillmeister, *Kulturgeschichte des Tennis*, 242.

58. Holt, *Sport and the British*, 126.

59. See Holt, *Sport and Society*, 177, and *Sport and the British*, 126; McCrone, *Sport and the Physical Emancipation*, 156–66; Stokvis, *De Populariteit van sporten*, 682.

60. Arlott, ed., *Oxford Companion to Sports*, 608.

61. Chandler, *Television and National Sport*, 153–74.

62. Clerici, *Ultimate Tennis Book*, 69; Walker, "Lawn Tennis," 247; Gillmeister, *Kulturgeschichte des Tennis*, 236–37.

63. Holt, *Sport and the British*, 71.

64. Arlott, ed., *Oxford Companion to Sports*, 432–35.

65. Mangan, *Athleticism*, 100.

66. Weber, *Wirtschaft und Gesellschaft*, 537. This is reflected today in the numerous specialist stores targeting golf players.

67. Mangan, *Athleticism*, 100; Lowerson, "Golf," 192.

68. In 1900 more than half of all British professionals were of Scottish origin (Lowerson, "Golf," 196).

69. Ibid., 204.

70. McCrone, *Sport and the Physical Emancipation*, 166–77; Lowerson, "Golf," 191–205; Holt, *Sport and the British*, 130–31.

71. Arlott, ed., *Oxford Companion to Sports*, 43; Bale, *Sport and Place*, 93–109.

72. The social history of this sport has received little attention, but what little information is available allows us to gain a reasonably reliable picture of its development. This section on table tennis is based on studies by Horst Friederich ("Untersuchungen" and *Ping-Pong*).

73. Friederich, "Untersuchungen," 46.

74. Two such associations were founded, each using different rules and recognizing a different champion. One was the Table Tennis Association, with sixty-five clubs affiliated in 1902, which chose *Lawn Tennis* as its official organ (ibid., 44–48).

75. Ibid., 77.

76. Qtd. in Horry, *History of Squash Rackets*, 148.

77. Ibid.

78. See Goudsblom, *Taal en sociale werkelijkheid*, 71.

79. Landes, *Unbound Prometheus*, 231–359; Kemp, *Industrialization*, 189–92; De Vries and Righart, "Van Achterblijver tot Koploper," 180–206. Between 1861 and 1913 coal consumption increased by a factor of thirteen in Germany. In absolute terms this brought it up to the same level as Britain, which consumed six times as much as Germany at the beginning of this period. Coal consumption in France and Belgium increased by a factor of four in the same time span, but in 1913 their combined consumption was less than half that of Germany (Landes, *Unbound Prometheus*, 293). Furthermore, in 1913 Germany accounted for two-thirds of Europe's steel production and used more kilowatt-hours of electricity than Britain, France, and Italy together. Allgemeine Elektricitäts-Gesellschaft and Siemens had already grown into leading multinationals by this time. Industrialization dramatically reduced the proportion of people working in agriculture. In 1880, 50 percent of the workforce was employed in agriculture and livestock breeding, 30 percent in trade and industry, and 20 percent in the service industries. By 1914 these percentages had changed to 35 percent, 40 percent, and 25 percent, respectively (Stone, *Europe Transformed*, 160; Joll, *Europe since 1870*, 1–2).

80. Gerschenkron, *Economic Backwardness*; Stone, *Europe Transformed*, 106; Joll, *Europe since 1870*, 2.

81. Qtd. in Landes, *Unbound Prometheus*, 149.

82. Willink, *Burgerlijk sciëntisme*, 163–219. A few statistics may serve to illustrate the German lead in education. In the 1860s school attendance in Prussia and Saxony exceeded 97 percent, while in Britain it was only about 50 percent (Landes, *Unbound Prometheus*, 339–46). In 1900 illiteracy in Germany was a mere 0.05 percent, while in Britain it was 1 percent and in France 4 percent (Joll, *Europe since 1870*, 143–44).

83. Mandell, *Sport*, 159–61.

84. Qtd. in Eichberg, *Leistung*, 236.

85. Jahn served several custodial sentences for inciting to riot.

86. Überhorst, *Frisch*, 351; Van Dalen and Bennett, *World History of Physical Education*, 213; Buchner, "Untersuchungen zur Entwicklung," 40; Dixon, "Prussia, Politics, and Physical Education," 133.

87. Mandell, *Sport*, 166.

88. Joll, *Europe since 1870*, 59; Förster, "Der Einfluss Englischen Sports," 34. The new middle classes in Germany grew from five hundred thousand in 1880 to two million in 1905 (Stone, *Europe Transformed*, 122).

89. Eichberg, *Leistung*, 143–49.

90. Holt, *Sport and Society in Modern France*, 50–59.

91. Mandell, *Sport*, 158–77.

92. Eichberg, *Leistung*, 150–68.

93. Überhorst, *Frisch*, 51; Eichberg, *Leistung*, 149.

94. J. Sauerbrey qtd. in Buchner, "Untersuchungen zur Entwicklung," 27.

95. Qtd. in Förster, "Der Einfluss Englischen Sports," 80.

96. Theodor Kleber qtd. in Förster, "Der Einfluss Englischen Sports," 81.

97. Qtd. in Bernett, "Drei athletische 'Meetings,'" 105.

98. Förster, "Der Einfluss Englischen Sports," 33–84.

99. Stokvis, *Strijd over sport*, 63.

100. Eichberg, *Leistung*, 168.

101. In Denmark the gymnastics teacher Holger Nielsen introduced a handball-like game at his school in 1898. This *haandbold* was similar to the Central European *hádzená*, as was the game that an Irishman introduced into the United States in 1870 and for which a championship game was held in Los Angeles in 1919. Montevideo, too, had a handball-like game in the same period (Bosma, *Voordat het Gras Verdwenen Is,* 13–14).

102. Bosma, *Voordat het gras verdwenen is,* 13–14.

103. Stokvis, "Populariteit van sporten," 682–87.

104. Hobsbawm, *Industry and Empire,* 294–95; Barraclough, *Introduction to Contemporary History,* 99. Until 1850, the total length of the railroad network was half of what had been laid in Europe. Between 1850 and 1870 the length of the rails grew at the same rate, and in the following decade the Americans extended their rail network by 30 percent relative to the Europeans (Hobsbawm, *Industry and Empire,* 93).

105. For instance, the United States remained outside the gold standard agreed upon by the major European states between 1863 and 1874 (Hobsbawm, *Industry and Empire,* 115).

106. Barraclough, *Introduction to Contemporary History,* 101–10.

107. Guttmann, *From Ritual to Record,* 91–116; Tyrrell, "Emergence of Modern American Baseball"; Adelman, *Sporting Time,* 91–183; Kirsch, *Creation of American Team Sports;* Guttmann, *Games and Empires,* 15–20. These theories are unusual in that they are based on a comparison between the two sports rather than an isolated history of baseball, unlike, for instance, Harold Seymour, *Baseball.*

108. Seymour, *Baseball,* 5; Rader, *American Sports,* 2–9; Adelman, *Sporting Time,* 91.

109. Rader, *American Sports,* 18–21; Mandell, *Sport,* 178–79; Lewis, "Cricket and the Beginnings of Organized Baseball," 320.

110. Cricket clubs existed in America before this, probably as early as in 1786, but they were not organized on a durable basis and had little influence.

111. Lewis, "Cricket and the Beginnings of Organized Baseball," 317–26; Kirsch, *Creation of American Team Sports,* 57.

112. Seymour, *Baseball,* 16; Adelman, *Sporting Time,* 123. Although the gentlemen members of this club had been meeting to enjoy sporting activities in an amicable atmosphere since 1842, the club was not officially established until 1845. Historians of the sport acknowledge that baseball teams existed before this year but ascribe a pioneering role to the Knickerbockers.

113. Seymour, *Baseball,* 20; Adelman, *Sporting Time,* 122; Kirsch, *Creation of American Team Sports,* 71.

114. Kirsch, *Creation of American Team Sports,* 97. Some did try, of course, to dispel the atmosphere of English exclusivity surrounding the game; the American Cricket Club, for instance, confined membership to Americans. But most cricket clubs tried to preserve the English heritage (Adelman, *Sporting Time,* 105–9).

115. Tyrrell rightly observes that the American development of cricket differed in this respect from that in India. The English administrators in India transmitted their culture to the Indian elite, wanting them in turn to promote English policies and lifestyles. This started at school, where Indian princes learned the English language and became acquainted with English manners, sports, and modes of dress (Tyrrell, "Emergence of Modern American Baseball," 213–14).

116. Kirsch, *Creation of American Team Sports,* 107–8. There were few towns where workers played cricket. One was Newark, where more than 80 percent of the local cricketers (as opposed to 45 percent of baseball players) were from the working classes in the period from 1855 to 1860. National origins were a more crucial factor in Newark than social background. While 45.3 percent of Newark's cricketers came from England, this was true of only 6.6 percent of the city's baseball players. But Newark was exceptional in its large numbers of working-class cricketers. In most cities, such as New York, Brooklyn, Boston, and above all Philadelphia, "white-collar workers" prevailed. Even among them there were more English immigrants than Americans, although the difference was less marked (Kirsch, *Creation of American Team Sports,* 111–42).

117. See Adelman, *Sporting Time,* 135; Lewis, "Cricket and the Beginnings of Organized Baseball," 327. New Yorkers in particular tended to be nationalistic and anti-British. The English were only one of many ethnic minorities in New York. In 1855, only 22,713 out of Manhattan's total of 325,645 immigrants were of English origin (Manhattan's total population at the time was 622,924).

118. Seymour, *Baseball,* 11; Kirsch, *Creation of American Team Sports,* 93.

119. Lewis, "Cricket and the Beginnings of Organized Baseball," 321; see also Guttmann, *Whole New Ball Game,* 59.

120. Seymour, *Baseball,* 24; Rader, *American Sports,* 95–96; Adelman, *Sporting Time,* 138–56; Guttmann, *Whole New Ball Game,* 59.

121. Adelman, *Sporting Time,* 114–16. See also Tyrrell, "Emergence of Modern American Baseball," 207–11. Because of the standardization and organizational structure already achieved in England, the cricketers in the United States also had less need to organize nationally. The lack of an umbrella cricket federation until 1878 in America put the sport at a disadvantage compared to baseball: a good organization could help settle local disputes, combine and represent participants' interests, arrange competitions, and coordinate contacts with the media.

122. Seymour, *Baseball,* 41–46; Adelman, *Sporting Time,* 129; Kirsch, *Creation of American Team Sports,* 102, 215.

123. Kirsch, *Creation of American Team Sports,* 79–81.

124. Qtd. in ibid., 202.

125. See Guttmann, *Games and Empires,* 73. See also the role that Eugen Weber attributes to the army in the process of modernization in France (Weber, *Peasants into Frenchmen*).

126. Adelman, *Sporting Time,* 157; Kirsch, *Creation of American Team Sports,* 230.

127. Seymour, *Baseball,* 33.

128. Tyrrell, "Emergence of Modern American Baseball," 221; Kirsch, *Creation of American Team Sports,* 263.

129. Markovits, "The Other 'American Exceptionalism.'"

130. Falla, *NCAA,* 5–6; Rader, *American Sports,* 81.

131. Baker, *Sports in the Western World,* 127–31; Rader, *American Sports,* 81.

132. According to Walter Camp, the "father of American football," qtd. in Riesman and Denney, "Football in America," 156.

133. Ibid., 156.

134. Maguire, "More Than a Sporting Touchdown," 233.

135. Mandell, *Sport,* 187.

136. Some sports matches did take place between British and American teams. In 1873, for instance, Yale defeated an Eton team by 2–1, which also indicates that the Yale players had no difficulty adapting—even at the international level—to the official rules of the English Football Association (Baker, *Sports in the Western World*, 127).

137. Rader, *American Sports*, 76; Stokvis, *De sportwereld*, 23.

138. Rader, *American Sports*, 74; Mandell, *Sport*, 187; Chandler, *Television and National Sport*, 51.

139. Rader, *American Sports*, 82; Mandell, *Sport*, 188.

140. This is a sociological reinterpretation of the notion that prior to commercialization top-class players liked sport for its own sake, whereas later their main interest was in the money it would earn them (see Stokvis, "Nieuwe sportmoraal").

141. Rader, *American Sports*, 85.

142. Betts, *America's Sporting Heritage*, 129; Chandler, *Television and National Sport*, 47–54.

143. Falla, *NCAA*, 14; Rader, *American Sports*, 142–43; Park, "Sport, Gender, and Society," 15.

144. See Chandler, esp. her quotations from Lewis (Chandler, *Television and National Sport*, 50).

145. Guttmann, *From Ritual to Record*, 142.

146. National Federation of State High School Associations, *1989 Sports Participation Survey*; National Collegiate Athletic Association, *Sports and Recreational Programs*, 1986–87.

147. Falla, *NCAA*, 72.

148. Meserole, *1991 Information Please Sports Almanac*, 407–8.

149. Johnson, *History of YMCA Physical Education*, 47; Stokvis, *De sportwereld*, 23.

150. Rader, *American Sports*, 151–52.

151. The YMCA's sports administrators tended to come from a theological or medical background. Gulick was a missionary's son and graduated with a degree in medicine in 1889. The inventor of basketball, James Naismith, was a theology graduate and also took a degree in medicine later in life (Johnson, *History of YMCA Physical Education*, 16–21 and 55; Stokvis, *De sportwereld*, 43–47 and 158–60).

152. Johnson, *History of YMCA Physical Education*, 28–70.

153. Ibid., 70; Stokvis, "Populariteit van sporten," 686.

154. Naismith, *Basketball's Origins*, 15.

155. Ibid., 28.

156. Johnson, *History of YMCA Physical Education*, 89.

157. Baker, *Sports in the Western World*, 170; Rader, *American Sports*, 152–53; Guttmann, *Games and Empires*, 99.

158. Basketball competitions between Ivy League schools started after 1897.

159. Guttmann, *Games and Empires*, 99.

160. Baker, *Sports in the Western World*, 170; Rader, *American Sports*, 167–68. See Van Bottenburg, "Als 'n man met een baard op 'n bokkewagen," for the relationship between American women's basketball and Dutch korfball, which also divides the court into three sections.

161. Brandel, *Volleyball-Weltgeschichte*, 19.

162. These statistics refer to the interscholastic level (National Federation of State High School Associations, *1989 Sports Participation Survey*).

163. The information on beach volleyball in this section has been taken from Brandel, *Volleyball-Weltgeschichte,* 174–85.

164. In the latter half of the nineteenth century, German immigrants founded a number of *Turngemeinde* (gymnastics associations) in the United States, but the sport never attracted much enthusiasm. On the background factors, see Guttmann, *Games and Empires,* 153–56.

165. Davidson, "Social Differentiation," 201–2; Rader, *American Sports,* 68.

166. All the 1989 statistics relate to the interscholastic level (National Federation of State High School Associations, *1989 Sport Participation Survey*).

167. It is unclear whether the second generation will continue to this tradition, or if they will opt for the old symbols of Americanization.

168. Wagner, "Sport in Asia and Africa," 401; Maguire, "More Than a Sporting Touchdown," 233.

169. Guttmann, *From Ritual to Record,* 150. In 1978 baseball was still Japan's most popular sport by far (Tsukuda, "Entwicklung des Sports in Japan," 133).

170. De Graaff, "Inleiding" and "De Vlucht naar Voren"; Romein, *De eeuw van Azië,* 28–29.

171. Sansom, *Western World and Japan,* 382–83.

172. Romein, *De eeuw van Azië,* 30–31.

173. Of the 550 students sent abroad between 1868 and 1874, 209 were sent to the United States, 168 to England, 82 to Germany, and 60 to France (see Burks, "Japan's Outreach" and "Role of Education in Modernization").

174. Roden, "Baseball and the Quest for National Dignity," 513–19.

175. Stokvis, "Populariteit van sporten," 687; Wildt, *Daten zur Sportgeschichte,* vol. 4, 68–74.

176. Whiting, *Chrysanthemum and the Bat,* 3; Saeki, "Sport in Japan," 54–55.

177. Roden, "Baseball and the Quest for National Dignity."

178. Tadashi, "Contributions of David Murray"; De Graaff, "De Epistemologische Revolutie," 447.

179. *Nieuws uit Japan,* March 1977; Saeki, "Sport in Japan," 52.

180. Saeki, "Sport in Japan," 56–76.

181. Wildt, *Daten zur Sportgeschichte,* vol. 4, 50–64; Saeki, "Sport in Japan," 52–53.

182. Leeflang, *Budo,* 17–23.

183. Saeki, "Sport in Japan," 54; Mitchell, *Alles over vechtsporten,* 23.

Chapter 4: Sports in Europe

1. Gorter, *Letterkundige studiën,* 54.

2. Simon Gorter evidently transmitted his enthusiasm to his son, Herman Gorter, who became a fanatical sportsman as well as an excellent poet.

3. Ter Gouw, *Volksvermaken;* Van der Molen, *Levend volksleven,* 128–45; Stokvis, *Strijd over sport,* 1.

4. Landes, *Unbound Prometheus,* 187–88; Hobsbawm, *Industry and Empire,* 110.

5. Muller, "Anglomanie"; for examples outside the Netherlands, see Sandblad, "Sport

and Ideas," 130, for Norway; Weber, "Gymnastics and Sports," 83, for France; Förster, "Der Einfluss Englischen Sports," 80, for Germany.

6. Landes, *Unbound Prometheus,* 124, in relation to the economic developments. See also Weber, "Gymnastics and Sports," 97; Stokvis, *Strijd over sport,* 14–15.

7. Weber, "Gymnastics and Sports," 84; Wildt, *Daten zur Sportgeschichte,* vol. 2; Riordan, *Sport in Soviet Society;* Guttmann, *Games and Empires,* 44–45.

8. One of the first sports clubs in the Netherlands consisted almost exclusively of English employees of Amsterdam firms. The sole exception was a Dutchman whose mother was English (Miermans, *Voetbal in Nederland,* 88).

9. For example, the English engineers recruited to build the rail network in Denmark who brought cricket with them (Idorn, "History," 25).

10. The countries of continental Europe were ahead of Britain in some ways, in spite of having lagged behind in the Industrial Revolution. This was especially true in science and education (Landes, *Unbound Prometheus,* 125).

11. For example, the people who launched the Bordeaux Athletic Club in 1877.

12. In 1887 a British vice consul founded Norway's first tennis club (International Tennis Federation, *75 Years,* 93); the diplomatic corps in St. Petersburg founded the Superior Society of the British Colony, a club that played tennis, soccer, and cricket (Riordan, *Soviet Sport,* 110).

13. See for example Fisek, "Genesis of Sports Administration in Turkey," 625; Miermans, *Voetbal in Nederland,* 59.

14. For example, the businessman Eduardo Bosio from Torino, who founded the renowned club Juventus in 1887 after a business trip to England (Guttmann, "'Our Former Colonial Masters,'" 55).

15. In 1898, for instance, "'nombreux jeunes gens de la bourgeoisie marseillaise, frais émoulus de leurs études en Grande-Bretagne'" (many middle-class young men from Marseille, full of the enthusiasm generated by their recent studies in Britain) launched the famous Olympique de Marseille (qtd. in Bromberger et al., "Allez l'O.M.!" 15).

16. The sports were introduced earliest in the most industrialized countries of Western Europe. In other countries, such as Spain, Portugal, Greece, Romania, Bulgaria, and Russia, it was not only British visitors and members of national elites who imported them. Other Western Europeans also played a part—members of colonies of foreigners where sports had already become common and regarded as part of modern life. (For a discussion of Russia in this regard, see Peppard, "Beginnings of Russian Soccer.")

17. "Fast alle Gründungen in der Schweiz waren das Werk von Akademikern" (In Switzerland almost all the clubs were founded by academics; Pieth, *Sport in der Schweiz,* 134–35). "There can be no doubt that it was the *lycéens,* both at school and as old boys, who spearheaded the movement to introduce English sports into France" (Holt, *Sport and Society in Modern France,* 65). In Germany the founding of the Akademischer Sporting Club and Football Club Universität symbolized the same pattern.

18. Qtd. in Miermans, *Voetbal in Nederland,* 90.

19. Stokvis, *Strijd over Ssport,* 9–11.

20. *De HFC'er,* special issue (1965), 10–12.

21. Stokvis, "Populariteit van sporten," 679.

22. See Pieth, *Sport in der Schweiz,* 35, on the adoption of English sports in Switzerland;

see also Riordan, *Soviet Sport,* who observes in relation to Russia that "The amateur snob-
bery . . . was applied to the letter" (112).

23. In Ireland Celtic sports enjoy greater popularity, but these consist of an unseparat-
ed collection of sports.

24. At this point the Haarlem Football Club switched from rugby to soccer (Mulier,
"Oprichting van de Haarlemsche Football Club," 13).

25. NCB memorial volume (1933), 36, 309.

26. Feith, "Cricket," 40.

27. Hague Soccer Federation (hereafter HVV), memorial volume (1908), 5.

28. Ibid., 4.

29. Miermans, *Voetbal in Nederland,* 254. See also Van Bottenburg, "Het bruine monster," 10–11.

30. Wilterdink, *Vermogensverhoudingen in Nederland,* 203.

31. Mulier, "Oprichting van de Haarlemsche Football Club."

32. Stokvis, *Strijd over sport,* 9–10.

33. Red and White memorial volume (1831).

34. Hercules memorial volume (1932).

35. In 1885 the notion of translating these cricket terms into Dutch was rejected in *De
Nederlandsche Sport,* the Netherlands' only sports magazine at the time.

36. Schröder in NCB memorial volume (1933), 282.

37. Mulier in NCB memorial volume (1933), 255 and 259.

38. Elias and Scotson, *Established and the Outsiders,* 11–12.

39. Van Bottenburg, "Het bruine monster," 18–20.

40. Sparta memorial volume (1948).

41. Miermans, *Voetbal in Nederland,* 142.

42. Adriani Engels, *Honderd jaar sport,* 189; *Hockey Sport,* October 8, 1938, 26.

43. Miermans, *Voetbal in Nederland,* 123–25; Meijs, "Over neutralen en katholieken,"
41, 87.

44. Mulier in *De HFC'er,* special issue (1965), 12.

45. Haarlem Football Club (hereafter HFC) memorial volume (1979).

46. Miermans, *Voetbal in Nederland,* 111.

47. Qtd. in ibid., 114. See also Mulier's memories of workingmen's soccer: "I once picked
up a ball that was out, when a bony athlete from the other side snarled at me with heav-
ing chest: 'Keep off! Damn it, that's my ball!' lunging at the innocent object with his coarse
night porter's hands. Now set a good example, I thought to myself, with altruistic, ambi-
dextrous, autopsychological didacticism, as a good university entrant would say. This I
said with the utmost affability to the wild stranger, holding out the coveted thing: 'Here
you are, dear, don't cry, you can play with it'" (HFC memorial volume [1919], 3).

48. For example, at the founding of Sneek, Rimburg, Delft, and PSV (Eindhoven) soccer clubs.

49. For example, at the founding of NEC, Schoonhoven Sports Club, and Helder soccer club.

50. Micrmans, *Voetbal in Nederland,* 109–14.

51. Ibid., 109–13.

52. Spaans, "Sociale geschiedenis," 54.

53. Ibid., 54 and 57; Verrips, *En boven de polder.*

54. Allen Guttmann pointed this out to me at the conference "Diffusion of Sports: Globalization and Americanization" in Amsterdam, on June 12, 1992; see also Miermans, *Voetbal in Nederland,* 119.

55. Guttmann, "'Our Former Colonial Masters,'" 53.

56. Adriani Engels, *Honderd jaar sport,* 226–28.

57. These examples derive from Guttmann, "'Our Former Colonial Masters,'" 52–53. In a sense we could also see the euphoria in Cameroon following its achievements in the 1990 World Cup and Nigeria's gold medal at the Atlanta Olympic Games in 1996 as rites of passage for African soccer countries, which conclusively erased Africa's second-class status in relation to Western countries and undoubtedly heralds other, greater triumphs. For a theoretical reflection on these rites of passage, see also Guttmann, *Games and Empires,* 179–82.

58. Peppard, "Beginnings of Russian Soccer," 153; see also Metcalfe, "Organized Sport and Social Stratification in Montreal," 96.

59. For Germany, see Arz, "Situationsanalyse des Fussballsports," 35; for France, see Holt, *Sport and Society in Modern France,* 80; for Russia, see Peppard, "Beginnings of Russian Soccer," 166, although it should be borne in mind that Soviet officials were generally not averse to slightly exaggerating statistics on participation in cultural life. The figures for the Netherlands are taken from Miermans, *Voetbal in Nederland,* 248–49; see also the comments in Spaans, "Sociale geschiedenis," 84, and his appendices on soccer.

60. See Van Bottenburg, "Het bruine monster," 29–30.

61. De Regt, *Arbeidersgezinnen en beschavingsarbeid,* 35–39.

62. Miermans, *Voetbal in Nederland,* 252.

63. Krips qtd. in ibid., 112.

64. Ibid., 112–24. This probably still holds true today in the case of soccer, which may explain why many men from the affluent classes continue to follow premier league soccer with enthusiasm, even though they tend not to play themselves. The active pursuit of a sport at an early age is an important condition for passive interest later on (see chap. 2 n. 2).

65. Ibid., 148–59.

66. NCB memorial volume (1933), 167.

67. NCB memorial volume (1933), 288.

68. Hercules memorial volume (1932), 41.

69. De Monchy, 'Eens cricketer, altijd cricketer!' in NCB memorial volume (1933), 304.

70. Van Manen, in NCB memorial volume (1933), 248–50.

71. Stokvis, *Strijd over sport,* 31; Pieth, *Sport in der Schweiz,* 112; Holt, *Sport and Society in Modern France,* 180; Widdershoven, "Stagnerende Groei."

72. Qtd. in Weber, *Gymnastics and Sports in Fin-de-Siècle France,* 87.

73. Mulier, "Oprichting van de Haarlemsche Football Club," 13.

74. See Riordan, *Soviet Sport,* 110.

75. Weber, "Gymnastics and Sports," 86; Holt, *Sport and Society in Modern France,* 66–67.

76. Elias, *Höfische Gesellschaft.*

77. In Nantes the Parisian example led to the launch of Stade Nantais; in Perpignan a

former student of the Lycée Michelet in Paris introduced the sport into Catalonia, a region that later became a major rugby stronghold. Charles Péguy introduced soccer into the grammar school in his city of Orléans, but when he moved to another town he switched to rugby because this was the sport of the Parisian lycées. Weber, "Gymnastics and Sports," 87; Holt, *Sport and Society in Modern France,* 67.

78. Holt, *Sport and Society in Modern France,* 68. In Bayonne rugby was introduced by a notary's son. He persuaded a rowing club(!) to start playing rugby, a move that ultimately produced the celebrated rugby players of Aviron Bayonnais. The example set by Paris and the strong English influence in the southwest of France molded this region into the bastion of rugby. Weber, "Gymnastics and Sports," 87; Holt, *Sport and Society in Modern France,* 68.

79. Weber, "Gymnastics and Sports," 85–88; Holt, *Sport and Society in Modern France,* 72.

80. Qtd. in Royal Netherlands Hockey Federation (hereafter KNHB) memorial volume (1988).

81. Dona, *Sport en socialisme,* 132–33; Kampong memorial volume (1902–52), 102; HGC memorial volume (1904–81), 11.

82. HGC memorial volume (1904–81), 77. Bloemendaal Hockey Club also has a committee to watch over the club's "quality," as its chairman put it in 1991. Introductory days and committees are subtler variations of the committees that used to vote on the admission of new members. The "HOC" in HOC-Gazellen Combinatie is an acronym for HHV-ODIS Combinatie, which includes acronyms for Haagsche Hockey Vereniging and Ons Doel Is Scoren.

83. There was certainly a need for women to achieve independence: in 1907 the Amsterdam Hockey and Bandy Club would not allow women's hockey more than once every two weeks, for instance, and then only on Tuesdays and Thursdays. And in 1911 the board of the Dutch Hockey and Bandy Federation (NHBB) made it clear that the gentlemen hockey players did not wish to merge with the ladies. KNHB memorial volume (1988).

84. The effect of the South Holland Hockey Federation joining is unclear. NHBB memorial volume (1938), 26.

85. Kammeijer, "Hockey," 53–54. In 1946, Quarles van Ufford, who played soccer at the Haarlem Football Club as a veteran, commented, "'That cheerful, civilized atmosphere is the great attraction of hockey. . . . A world of difference from soccer'" (qtd. in ibid., 84–85).

86. Hilversum Mixed Hockey Club (hereafter HMHC) memorial volume for De Bult (1904–79).

87. Kampong memorial volume (1902–52).

88. Adriani Engels, *Honderd jaar sport,* 301. This surge of public interest posed a threat to the sport's elitist ethos and dismayed many players: "'What are these people doing here? People who did not know how to spell the word "hockey" or that the game is played with a stick, people who yell when the ball rolls into the goal from outside the circle. How can hockey benefit from interest from such quarters? It will bring nothing but trouble and strife. Fortunately, the players have been debating the matter so intensively that we can add the necessary provisions to the regulations in September to stop matters getting any worse'" (Qtd. in Van der Zee and Boerop, *Holland Hockeyland,* 90).

89. Van der Zee and Boerop, *Holland Hockeyland,* 39.

90. HGC memorial volume (1906–81), 16.

91. Founded in 1908 by seventh-grade pupils of the Hague School Club (HLC), HLC memorial volume (1908–83).

92. The term "sporting career" was probably coined by Sjoerd Rijpma. D. Nieman wrote the following in 1949: "Seventeen years passed by. The toy cart was exchanged for a hoop, the hoop for a football, and the football for a tennis ball" (*Lawn Tennis* special issue [1949], 48).

93. *Lawn tennis* special issue (1949), 11.

94. See for example Guttmann, *Women's Sports,* 130.

95. Red and White memorial volume (1931).

96. Clerici, *Ultimate Tennis Book,* 132–39; Gillmeister, *Kulturgeschichte des Tennis,* 271–83.

97. Haarlem Lawn Tennis Club memorial volume (1885–1985), qtd. in Dahles, *Lokale Helden,* 4; see also Leimonias memorial volume (1988).

98. Clerici, *Ultimate Tennis Book,* 132–39; Gillmeister, *Kulturgeschichte des Tennis,* 271–83; Guttmann, *Women's Sports,* 130. In the Netherlands, too, before the Second World War professional players were often former ballboys from poor backgrounds. They made their careers as tennis coaches (Dahles, *Lokale Helden,* 4 n. 6).

99. Del Court tot Krimpen, "Golf," 113–25; Adriani Engels, *Honderd jaar sport,* 91–92.

100. Hercules memorial volume (1932).

101. *Lawn Tennis* special issue (1949), 18; Spaans, "Sociale geschiedenis."

102. Meijs, "Over neutralen en katholieken," 124–26.

103. Horry, *History of Squash Rackets,* 53–60.

104. De Duinwijcker memorial volume (1948–73), 11.

105. Friederich, "Untersuchungen," 59–62.

106. Ibid., 180–90.

107. For the Netherlands, see table 10, p. 157. For Belgium, see Vanreusel et al., "Is Golf-spelen een Dure Manier van Biljarten?" And for Germany, see Lüschen, "Interdependence of Sport and Culture," and Schlagenhauf, *Strukturelemente.*

108. Holt, *Sport and Society in Modern France,* 80.

109. Amsterdam Football Club memorial volume (1895–1945).

110. Steine, "Norwegen," 68; Verhagen, "Belgien," 122–23; Strohmeyer, "Österreich," 290–93; Szymiczek, "Greichenland," 371; Finnish Society for Research in Sports and Physical Education, *Sport and Physical Education in Finland,* 8; Guttmann, *Games and Empires,* 141–48.

111. Rupnik, *Het andere Europa,* 42.

112. See Nordlund, "Scandanavia," 197; Weber, "Gymnastics and Sports," 71; Stokvis, *Strijd over sport,* 40–89; and Mandell, *Sport,* 177.

113. Miermans, *Voetbal in Nederland,* 72–73; Stokvis, *Strijd over sport,* 72–73.

114. Stokvis, *Strijd over sport,* 71–75.

115. Miermans, *Voetbal in Nederland,* 97; Diem, "Federal Republic of Germany," 128–29; Weber, "Gymnastics and Sports," 71; Mandell, *Sport,* 168–69.

116. Similar objections to "bourgeois sports" underlay the founding of the Dutch Workers' Sports Federation in 1926, over half of whose membership were gymnasts (see Dona, *Sport en socialisme,* esp. 42–43 and 157–59).

117. Riordan, *Sport in Soviet Society*, 47; Stone, *Europe Transformed*, 309–10.

118. This did not include the more than 275,000 young people who underwent compulsory Sokol training, nor the 250,000 members of Sokol-affiliated organizations (Jandacek, "Sokol Movement in Czechoslovakia," 56–58).

119. Ibid.; Blecking, *Slawische Sokolbewegung*.

120. Halldén, "Schweden," 29; Mandell, *Sport*, 170–73.

121. Weber, "Gymnastics and Sports," 97; Holt, *Sport and Society in Modern France*, 12 and 40–49. The gymnastics movement served a variety of ideologies, but the emphasis was always on strengthening the group. The German Marxist party and the Italian Fascist party also founded gymnastics clubs. Marxist doctrine rejected competitive sports with their mania for records, commercialization, and "trafficking in humans." From this point of departure, after the 1917 Revolution in Russia gymnastics evolved into a state-supported movement (Riordan, *Sport in Soviet Society*). At the end of the nineteenth century there was also a flourishing Jewish gymnastics movement with a nationalist and Semitic undertone, which aimed to strengthen Jewish awareness and to be part of what Max Nordau called "Muskeljudentum" (Mandell, *Sport*, 174–76).

122. Burgener, "Schweiz," 273. Danish shooting clubs mushroomed in areas bordering on Germany after the 1848–50 war against Prussia. The threat of renewed conflict hung in the air. Here too a broad-based patriotic movement promoted shooting with government support (Idorn, "History," 135–36).

123. Weber, "Pierre de Coubertin," 73; Holt, *Sport and Society in Modern France*, 52–59, 182.

124. Teachers did not share pupils' love of soccer; it was "'glorified by the youth, but cursed by many a schoolmaster,'" in the words of one secondary school teacher in Amersfoort in 1896 (qtd. in Miermans, *Voetbal in Nederland*, 94; see also 95–101).

125. Thus the big Swiss gymnastics associations responded to the popularization of soccer by adding track and field, handball, and skiing to their program (Pieth, *Sport in der Schweiz*, 124).

126. In Belgium handball was part of the Workers' Gymnastics and Sports Movement. Neutral handball associations did not come into existence in Belgium until after the Second World War, and it was not until 1958 that handball was detached from the workers' movement in an institutional sense and an independent handball federation was founded (Verhaegen, "Belgien," 137).

127. Bosma, *Voordat het gras verdwenen is*, 17; and Pieth, *Sport in der Schweiz*, 304 n. 135.

128. Research has shown that sports played during someone's years at school greatly influences their choice of sport in later years (Manders and Kropman, *Sportbeoefening en zijn organisatiegraad*, 123–24, 138). Comparative international research with respondents from Spain, France, Belgium, Denmark, and Sweden revealed that people who did gymnastics, track and field, handball, volleyball, and basketball had largely been encouraged to take up these sports at school, whereas table tennis, badminton, tennis, squash, cycling, golf, soccer, and rowing were almost always picked up from friends or relatives (Claeys, *Sport in European Society*, 38–39).

129. Regarding women's participation, sports may be divided into three groups. First, there are sports from which women were initially excluded and in which they are still a small minority. In the Netherlands these include boxing, soccer, ice hockey, billiards,

checkers, chess, crossbow archery, and auto racing. Women are still excluded from three track and field events: pole-vaulting, throwing the hammer, and triple jump. Then there is a group in which women are in the majority: gymnastics, handball, volleyball, and swimming, all of which are related to physical education (Stokvis, *De sportwereld,* 37). Finally, there is a group of sports in which men and women participate in roughly equal numbers. In the Netherlands these are primarily sports that recruit their members from the higher social classes: tennis, hockey, rowing, and golf.

130. Riordan, *Sport in Soviet Society,* 322–23; Idorn, "History," 50.

131. Rijtersbeek memorial volume (1926–76).

132. See Holt, *Sport and the British,* 236–79.

133. Pieth, *Sport in der Schweiz,* 88 and 135.

134. Spaans, "Sociale geschiedenis," 95–101.

135. Idorn, "History," 25–28; Stokvis, *Strijd over sport,* 40–89.

136. See Bosma, *Voordat het gras verdwenen is,* 38.

137. Little is known about the history of badminton in Denmark. It was imported into Denmark much later than the other English sports, in 1925, by a Danish businessman who had been to London. A few English players staged demonstration matches in the late 1920s. The popularization of this sport in the next ten years followed the government's decision that every city's school should have its own gymnasium. Badminton probably benefited from the enormous growth in medium-sized indoor sports facilities (Idorn, "History," 56–57). In the early 1930s the Danish Badminton Federation was founded, and many teams and individual players took part in games in Britain. As early as 1939 a Dane won the All England Championships, the top event in badminton. After that, the Danes were regular competitors in international badminton, and they also took the sport to other Scandinavian countries.

138. Holt, *Sport and Society in Modern France,* 57.

139. The latter list involved cruelty to cats, birds, eels, and geese, respectively, while the last, *bekkesnijden,* was a knife game in which opponents tried to slash each other's faces. Ter Gouw, *Volksvermaken;* Van der Molen, *Levend volksleven.*

140. Kalma, *Kaatsen in Friesland;* Stokvis, *Strijd over sport,* 5–6.

141. Ter Gouw, *Volksvermaken;* Sagers, "Kaatsen, Kegelen, Kolven, Beugelen," 71.

142. With about a hundred thousand players, korfball too is a successful Dutch sport, but in contrast to speed skating there was no pastime that could be identified as a precursor. It was devised at the beginning of the twentieth century by a Dutch teacher and was played in an organized and standardized form from the start. Elsewhere I have discussed the connection with the problematic image of korfball and the sport's Dutch origins (see Van Bottenburg, "Als 'n man met een baard op 'n bokkewagen").

143. Polednik, *Sport und Spiel auf dem Eis,* 83.

144. Kleine et al., *Niet over een nacht ijs,* 85.

145. Van Buttingha Wichers, *Schaatsrijden,* 29; Brown, *Ice-Skating,* 136–39.

146. Polednik, *Sport und Spiel auf dem Eis,* 10–22; Brown, *Ice-Skating,* 28–29.

147. Polednik, *Sport und Spiel auf dem Eis,* 19, 30.

148. Stokvis, *Strijd over sport,* 3; Kleine et al., *Niet over een nacht IJs,* 83.

149. Kleine et al., *Niet over een nacht ijs,* 84.

150. Bloom, *Skaters of the Fens,* 29; Brown, *Ice-Skating,* 121–24.

151. In 1890 a race was organized on the initiative of Baron de Salis (the secretary of the Amsterdam Sports Club and subsequently the chairman of the Dutch Skating Federation for nine years) that would determine "once and for all" who were faster, the amateurs or the professional skaters. The well-trained amateurs easily won the two-mile race, with the first professional skater finishing fourth (Van Laer, *Gedenkboek,* 18–20, 58–59).

152. Kleine et al., *Niet over een nacht ijs,* 41–42.

153. Ibid., 20.

154. Ibid., 53. See also Bloom, *Skaters of the Fens,* 94–101.

155. Kleine et al., *Niet over een nacht ijs,* 47–49.

156. Atje Keulen Deelstra belonged to a new generation of fêted Dutch skaters. From the 1960s onwards, as the Netherlands focused more on long-distance skating, it did increasingly well at the international level. Between 1905 and 1960, Dutch skaters achieved very little in the international arena: in all those years they came second once and third twice at the world championships and captured one bronze and three silver medals at the Olympic Games. After the advent of artificial rinks spelled the demise of sprinting, while skating tours were more closely integrated into the Dutch Skating Association, the pool of potential international skaters greatly expanded. Long-distance skating profited more than before from the Netherlands' long tradition of skating as a popular pastime.

157. This boom is also due in part to organizational and social change. The KNSB succeeded in integrating skating tours largely into its own organization. On the eve of the Second World War the KNSB was still against recognizing "skating tourism" as one of its policy areas. The officials wanted the ANWB (Royal Dutch Touring Club) to take responsibility for it. Today, the KNSB supervises at the national level the safety, registration, and efficiency of the tours, issues cards, and awards medals and diplomas. All this information is widely publicized. Most people now own cars, making the starting places in polders and on the banks of lakes more accessible. If no tours are available nearby, devotees can travel to another province.

158. The emphasis on speed skating is typically Dutch. Internationally it is a marginal event; figure skating—once the province of the elite—has long been more prominent. Speed skating was originally a sport for the masses. Books on skating published outside the Netherlands in the eighteenth and nineteenth centuries dealt exclusively with figure skating.

159. Joll, *Europe since 1870,* 324–465.

160. Rupnik, *Het andere Europa,* 120, 183.

161. Riordan, *Sport in Soviet Society,* 43; Stone, *Europe Transformed,* 197 and 230; Joll, *Europe since 1870,* 210.

162. Van den Heuvel, *Sport in de Sovjetunie,* 23.

163. Qtd. in ibid., 24.

164. Even in Olympic sports this support was far more geared toward the small minority of top-class performers than on encouraging large-scale participation.

165. Rupnik, *Het andere Europa,* 160.

166. Barraclough, *Introduction to Contemporary History,* 75; Joll, *Europe since 1870,* 313.

167. See Maguire, *Global Sport.*

168. Johnson, *History of YMCA Physical Education,* 189–95 and 243–47. For similar YMCA and army influence in other countries, see Verhaegen, "Belgien," 140–41; Baker,

Sports in the Western World, 213–14; Netherlands Volleyball Association (hereafter NeVoBo) memorial volume (1947–72), 5.

169. In 1927 the Danish YMCA organized a major sporting event, the YMCA World Games, providing the Danes with their first large-scale experience of both sports (Idorn, "History," 46 and 84; Johnson, *History of YMCA Physical Education,* 247). In the Netherlands the two sports were introduced in 1928 on the initiative of the chairman of the General Society for Young People (AMVJ), whose roots and goals were much akin to the YMCA's. He invited a youth sports leader from the English YMCA to Amsterdam for a basketball and volleyball demonstration. This initiative was more effective than that of Father S. Buis, who had had several volleyball courts built at his St. Willibrord mission at Uden. He had learned about this sport in the United States after a stay in Illinois. Missions and seminaries in the area also adopted volleyball, but the sport did not spread any further (NeVoBo memorial volume [1947–72], 6).

170. Hensen, "Entwicklung des Basketballs," 97–102.

171. The great promoter of Dutch volleyball, Kees van Zweden, took up the sport at the encouragement of Roosje, the "minor sports" instructor at the Christian Institute for Physical Education in The Hague, "But it was from the Canadian military after the war that we learned real volleyball." After the war two enthusiasts in Utrecht founded SOS, a volleyball and softball club. One had learned softball and the other volleyball from Canadian soldiers; the club played the former in summer, the latter in winter (NeVoBo memorial volume [1947–72], 6–19).

172. The relationship between the YMCA and the European gymnastics movement also generated influence in the reverse direction. It was the YMCA that founded the national handball federation in the United States (Johnson, *History of YMCA Physical Education,* 317).

173. Whereas women account for 34 percent to 36 percent of basketball players in Denmark, Germany, and the Netherlands, the figures for volleyball are much higher: 47 percent, 49 percent, and 57 percent, respectively.

174. Sparta memorial volume (1888–1998), 151.

175. This variant of baseball was constructed in 1920 by the Finnish professor Lauri Phkala. It continued to exist as a separate branch of sport in Finland but met the same fate as korfball in the Netherlands—substantial but declining popularity in its own country and unknown elsewhere. In 1985 it was still played by about sixty-six thousand Finns, but this was ten thousand fewer than a decade earlier.

176. Belgians learned baseball from Japanese sailors; it had become Japan's foremost national sport in the early twentieth century.

177. Stokvis's explanation of the lack of interest in American football in Japan is unsatisfactory, as it implies that the popularization of this sport should proceed far more easily in Europe ("Populariteit van sporten," 688).

178. Maguire, "More than a Sporting Touchdown."

179. Lever, *Soccer Madness,* 112.

180. This explanation does not predict that the sport has no future in Europe. It does clarify, however, why the popularization of American football is such a slow process, in spite of its American origins and the promotion of certain companies and commercial TV stations.

181. Barraclough, *Introduction to Contemporary History,* 54; Fukutake, *Japanese Social Structure.*

182. This book was written by Uyenishi, an instructor at the Japanese military academy for officers and a police academy in Osaka. In England, Kano demonstrated his new sport at the end of the nineteenth century for representatives of the British navy (Essink, *Elseviers judo-boek,* 17).

183. At the beginning of the twentieth century, judo and jujitsu were also part of the training at the U.S. Naval Academy in Annapolis; in France, judo was first practiced by the Parisian police force (Van Nieuwenhuizen, *Jiu Jitsu en judo,* 22–25; Essink, *Elseviers judo-boek,* 17; Arlott, ed., *Oxford Companion to Sports and Games*).

184. Goodger and Goodger, "Judo in the Light of Theory"; Arlott, ed., *Oxford Companion to Sports and Games;* Lagendijk, "Zwarte band van etnische minderheden," 48.

185. Sometimes other Eastern martial arts are also subject to the authority of the judo federation, but no detailed figures on this are available.

186. Goodger and Goodger, "Judo in the Light of Theory," 12–23; Reid and Croucher, *Oosterse krijgskunst,* 202–4; Johnson, *History of YMCA Physical Education,* 343.

187. Reid and Croucher, *Oosterse krijgskunst,* 198–222.

188. Lagendijk, "Zwarte band van etnische minderheden," 52.

189. In writing this section I drew extensively on the work of Eric Lagendijk, for which I owe him a debt of gratitude. The majority of books on the martial arts are richly illustrated treatises on technique and tactics.

190. Stokvis, *Strijd over sport;* Kok, "Schermen," 164; Burkens, "Wielrijden," 240. The word "school" was apt, as for years the emphasis was more on instruction than competition.

191. Leeflang, *Zen in actie,* 48.

192. Stokvis, *Strijd over sport,* 113.

193. In 1987 twenty-four thousand sports clubs were registered with the chamber of commerce. One-seventh of them (1,630) consisted of schools for the martial arts and fitness centers (Centraal Bureau voor de Statistiek, *Sportclubs en sportscholen,* 16).

194. TERP, *Verkennend onderzoek,* 18; Stokvis, *De sportwereld,* 94.

195. TERP, *Verkennend onderzoek,* 16; Lagendijk, "Lichaamscultuur in beweging," 73.

196. Featherstone, "Lifestyle and Consumer Culture," 129; Bourdieu, *Distinction,* 218.

197. *Karate en andere Oosterse vechtsporten* 1:3 (July/August 1989): 24. Harinck developed the Chakuriki style in response to traditional karate. Whereas in traditional karate participants are not meant to touch one another, full-contact boxing is based on the principle that the harder you hit your opponent the better it is. Training and fighting methods are relentlessly hard and intensive. The arms of the Chakuriki school displays a yellow sun with a red bull terrier in it, holding an olive branch in its jaws. Harinck urges the Chakuriki man to be like this dog (Harinck, *Ontleende kracht Chakuriki*).

198. Hoolt, *Sportdeelname van etnische groeperingen,* 10–11.

199. Lagendijk, "Zwarte band van etnische minderheden," 51.

200. Hoolt, *Sportdeelname van etnische groeperingen,* 23; Lagendijk, "Zwarte band van etnische minderheden," 50. Kickboxing has been particularly popular among Surinamese and Moroccans in the Netherlands ever since its introduction (Lagendijk, "Zwarte Band van etnische minderheden," 49).

201. Luuk Blijboom in the daily newspaper *Haarlems Dagblad,* June 27, 1989.

202. Thoutenhoofd, *Taekwondo,* 187.

203. This status hierarchy is based on data gathered by the Inter/View agency. A total of 4,485 people who (according to information they supplied themselves) were members of sports clubs were asked which sports they practiced in clubs and to indicate whether their income was below average, average, or above average. Using a modified version of the method that Günther Lüschen used in the late 1950s to construct a similar status hierarchy of sports, I used these Inter/View data to calculate a status indicator for each sport, using the formula

where:

V_{si} = index value of sport i

N_{si1} = number of participants in sport i belonging to income category 1 (below average)

N_{si2} = number of participants in sport i belonging to income category 2 (average)

N_{si3} = number of participants in sport i belonging to income category 3 (above average)

As this hierarchy relates to participants' income, rowing occupies a lower position than it would if people were asked to indicate its status. This is because it is particularly popular among students, whose income is low. Nor does the high position of korfball accord with the sport's image among the general public, who associate it with the petit bourgeoisie. It would be incompatible with this general image to incorporate korfball into the comparison as a high-status sport. For a discussion of the social background of korfball, see Van Bottenburg, "Als 'n man met een baard op 'n bokkewagen."

A few other comments are in order concerning this status hierarchy. In the first place, although the total number of respondents is quite large ($N = 4,485$), the number of participants for each sport is too small to be able to extrapolate to all the participants of a given sport. In the second place, the table links status solely to participants' income. No data were available on other indicators, such as their education or their parents' income or education. Third, this table took no account of people's own opinions of the status of individual sports. Even so, comparison with similar rankings in Belgium and Germany reveals that the research used here provides a reasonably reliable indication of the status hierarchy of sports in the Netherlands in 1986. Although researchers from other countries each pursued their own methods, the results do not greatly diverge from the hierarchy presented here. (For Belgium, see Vanreusel et al., "Is golfspelen een dure manier van biljarten?"; for Germany, see Lüschen, "Social Stratification"; and Schlagenhauf, *Strukturelemente.* The work of Vanreusel et al. is particularly interesting because they compare the stratification index of sports for the years 1969, 1979, and 1989.

204. Varekamp, "Verandering van de Samenstelling"; Stokvis, *De sportwereld,* 31–33.

205. This also greatly boosted the popularity of volleyball.

206. Ultee et al., *Sociologie,* 54–74; Wilterdink, *Vermogensverhoudingen in Nederland.*

207. Vanreusel et al. measured the stratification index of sports for 1969, 1979, and 1989. It reveals that skiing, hockey, yachting, tennis, and golf scarcely declined in status between

1969 and 1989 (Vanreusel et al., "Is golfspelen een dure manier van Biljarten?"). See also Van Bottenburg, "Individualisering en Teambinding," where I compare the 1986 status index to one for 1962 based on club sports in Amsterdam.

208. Telegraaf Tijdschriften Groep, *Sportmarkt in ogenschouw,* 66.

209. See Suaud, "Espace des Sports"; and Waser, "Marché des partenaires."

210. Nederlandse Golf Federatie, *Behoefte-onderzoek Golfsport Nederland,* appendix 24.

211. Suaud, "Espace des Sports," 15–19.

212. *Sport Informatie Bulletin* 21 (June 1990): 1487, and 23 (December 1990): 1683; see also Nederlandse Golf Federatie, *Ontwikkeling golfsport in Nederland* (February 1986): 7–9.

213. Nederlandse Golf Federatie, *Behoefte-onderzoek Golfsport Nederland,* 24, appendix 36–37.

214. *Sport Informatie Bulletin* 23 (December 1990): 1683; Nederlandse Golf Federatie, *Behoefte-onderzoek Golfsport Nederland,* 31.

215. The international growth of mountaineering merits further study. The membership of the Royal Dutch Alpine Association (KNAV) has soared since 1981. It is interesting to compare its members with those of the Dutch Mountaineering Association (NBV). Whereas the KNAV largely attracts an elite membership, the NBV appeals to somewhat lower social classes. The alpinists largely go on individual expeditions to the Swiss Alps, with the accent on sport, whereas the NBV membership favors group trips in the mountains of Austria. Some Alpinists regard the latter as hiking rather than "real" Alpinism. In light of this class distinction, the government-imposed merger of the two associations was fraught with difficulties.

216. Wouters, *Van minnen en sterven,* 96–149; Wilterdink, *Vermogensverhoudingen in Nederland.*

217. Boogman et al., *Geschiedenis van het moderne Nederland,* 262.

218. In 1897 one out of every 140 Dutch people owned a bike, in 1900 it was one in forty-five, and in 1911 one in ten (Baudet, *Een vertrouwde wereld,* 17); France had fewer than thirty thousand bicycle owners in 1890, but by 1893 there were 130,000 and in 1901 about a million. To expand their share in this booming market, bicycle manufacturers made large sums of money available for cycling races. Moreover, these races were moved from the roads to special tracks in an attempt to make a profit out of the public's interest (Maso, *Het zweet der goden,* 26).

219. Burkens, "Wielrijden," 254; Holt, *Sport and Society in Modern France,* 94; Stokvis, *De sportwereld,* 26; Maso, *Het zweet der goden,* 11–30.

220. W. J. van de Woestijne qtd. in Boogman et al., *Geschiedenis van het moderne Nederland,* 387.

221. The real national income, per capita consumption, and volume of labor were fairly constant from 1921 to 1925 and from 1933 to 1936. Between 1925 and 1930, however, they rose sharply, with a decline in the early 1930s. Industrial production expanded and import and exports increased; the number of unemployed was minimal in the second half of the 1920s (Boogman et al., *Geschiedenis van het moderne Nederland,* 377–91).

222. Dona, *Sport en socialisme,* 42–43 and 157–59.

223. For korfball, see Van Bottenburg, "Als 'n man met een baard op 'n bokkewagen"; for soccer, see Van Bottenburg, "Het bruine monster en de 'king of sports.'"

Chapter 5: Differences in the Global Sporting System

1. Kolatch, *Sports, Politics, and Ideology in China*, 8; Wildt, *Daten zur Sportgeschichte*, vol. 3, 230, 258, 261; Wildt, *Daten zur Sportgeschichte*, vol. 4, 18, 44, 130, 143–44, 163–64; Sodusta, "Historical Development of Sport in the Philippines," 726.

2. Bale, "Adoption of Football," *Sport and Place*, "International Sports History," and *Sports Geography*; Guttmann, *From Ritual to Record*, 61–62. In countries where modernization started around the same time and progressed at the same pace, the growth of umbrella sports federations followed similar lines (Bale, "International Sports History"; see also Bale, *Sports Geography*, 50–62).

3. For the spread of sports, see Miermans, *Voetbal in Nederland*, 64; Bale, "Adoption of Football" and "International Sports History." For the theory of the global system in this context see Wallerstein, *Modern World System*, vol. 1; Chirot, *Social Change in the Twentieth Century*; and Bergeson, ed., *Studies of the Modern World System*.

4. See Bale, *Sports Geography*, 57–60.

5. Brahim Errahmani, "Le sport juvenile en Algerie," 53; Clignet and Stark, "Modernization and the Game of Soccer"; Mandell, *Sport*, 275; Bale, "International Sports History" and *Sports Geography*.

6. Joseph, "India," 250; Douglas, "Sport in Malaysia," 174.

7. Stoddart, "Sport, Cultural Imperialism, and Colonial Response."

8. See Guttmann, *From Ritual to Record*; Beezley, "Bicycle, Modernization, and Mexico," 22–25.

9. A form of "creolization" (Hannerz, "World in Creolization"; see also De Swaan, *Perron Nederland*, 105–6).

10. While Australia and New Zealand had a population of only 250,000 in 1860, by 1910 it had grown to more than 12.5 million (Barraclough, *Introduction to Contemporary History*, 88). The first large group of British colonists to settle in what is now South Africa, five thousand people in total, arrived in 1820; in 1914 The Cape and Natal had more than 760,000 colonists of British origin (Hyam, *Britain's Imperial Century*, 300; Porter, *Atlas of British Overseas Expansion*, 85). In Canada the flow of immigrants started earlier. Here, the population trebled between 1821 and 1851 to a total of 2.3 million and doubled again in the following half-century (Redmond, *Sport and Ethnic Groups in Canada*, 23; Morrow, "Historical Development of Sport in Canada," 40).

11. Holt, *Sport and the British*, 227.

12. Mangan, *Games Ethic and Imperialism*, 159.

13. Holt, *Sport and the British*, 227; Inglis, "Imperial Cricket," 155.

14. See Holt, *Sport and the British*, 229–31.

15. Cushman, "Trends in New Zealand," 157; Leck, *South African Sport*, 32.

16. Holland Rose et al., *Cambridge History of the British Empire*, 243.

17. Smith, "Sports Involvement in Dunedin," 21–22.

18. Turner, "Emergence of 'Aussie Rules,'" 259.

19. Wildt, *Daten zur Sportgeschichte*, vol. 4, 197.

20. See Turner, "Emergence of 'Aussie Rules,'" 261–70. The difference with the United States was that the latter was more independent and had a more equal standing in rela-

tion to Britain than Australia. So a relatively autonomous sporting pattern could develop in America but not in Australia.

21. Human Sciences Research Council, *Sport in the RSA*, 43 and 50–51; Leck, *South African Sport*.

22. Rugby comes in first place among young white men but occupies eighth place among black male students, whereas soccer occupies first place among black males and sixth among whites. See Leck, *South African Sport*, 18; and 1980 Census, cited in Human Sciences Research Council, *Sport in the RSA*.

23. Leck, *South African Sport*, 6–18.

24. Holt, *Sport and the British*, 223. With about seven hundred thousand immigrants, the English were less numerous than the Irish. Then there were five hundred thousand Scots and two hundred thousand Germans, as well as many smaller groups (Redmond, *Sport and Ethnic Groups in Canada*, 23).

25. Redmond, *Sport and Ethnic Groups in Canada;* Mangan, *Games Ethic and Imperialism*, 162–65.

26. Morrow, "Historical Development of Sport in Canada," 40.

27. Gruneau, *Class, Sports, and Social Development*, 104; see also Mangan, *Games Ethic and Imperialism*, 163.

28. Redmond, *Sport and Ethnic Groups in Canada*, 44–48.

29. Qtd. in ibid., 31.

30. Nederlandse IJshockey Bond, *IJshockey!* 7.

31. Mangan, *Games Ethic and Imperialism*, 163. The causes of this slow dissemination merit further investigation.

32. Guttmann, *Games and Empires*, 95.

33. Ibid., 94.

34. Ibid., 95–96.

35. McKay and Miller, "From Old Boys to Men and Women."

36. See Holt, *Sport and the British*, 236–37.

37. Romein, *Eeuw van Azië*, 4; Barraclough, *Introduction to Contemporary History*, 153–98; for the relationship with sport, see Überhorst, *Geschichte der Leibesübungen*, vol. 6, 11.

38. See for example Cashman, "Phenomenon of Indian Cricket"; Nandy, *Tao of Cricket*.

39. See Beran, "Physical Education and Sport in the Philippines," 149–59.

40. Nandy, *Tao of Cricket*, 1.

41. Cashman, "Phenomenon of Indian Cricket"; Nandy, *Tao of Cricket*.

42. Stoddart, "Sport, Cultural Imperialism, and Colonial Response," 654.

43. Holt, *Sport and the British*, 236; Lord Harris, the governor of Bombay, believed that cricket could inculcate a sense of political responsibility if the Indians had a proper understanding of the codes of the game. Lord Willingdon, a former English county cricketer and later the governor of Bombay and Madras and viceroy of India, also believed in the virtues of cricket as an instrument of moral instruction. So did Sir Stanley Jackson, one of the best British players around 1900 and in the 1930s the governor of Bengal (Stoddart, "Sport, Cultural Imperialism, and Colonial Response," 658).

44. Cashman, "Phenomenon of Indian Cricket," 189; Wildt, *Daten zur Sportgeschichte*, vol. 4, 23; Stoddart, "Sport, Cultural Imperialism, and Colonial Response," 662–63; Nandy, *Tao of Cricket*, 69, 107.

45. Cashman, "Phenomenon of Indian Cricket," 195–97. This was not specific to India. The "gentlemen and players" tradition gave cricket an ethos that made it possible for European immigrants and aboriginals to play the game together in Australia. After missionaries had taught cricket to the people they described as "Australian savages," as part of a drive to civilize them, an Aboriginal team, the Poonindie Eleven, played against a side of the colonial elite, the team of St. Peter's College, in the 1870s (Daly, "New Brittania in the Antipodes," 169–70).

46. Cashman, "Phenomenon of Indian Cricket," 182–96; Nandy, *Tao of Cricket*, 86–88.

47. Cashman, "Phenomenon of Indian Cricket," 182.

48. Ibid., 195; Cashman, *Patrons, Players, and the Crowd*, 259; Guttmann, *Games and Empires*, 35–39.

49. Wildt, *Daten zur Sportgeschichte*, vol. 4, 14–16, 37, 77–86, 102–6, and 129.

50. Stoddart, "Sport, Cultural Imperialism, and Colonial Response."

51. Holt, *Sport and the British*, 236–37.

52. Wildt, *Daten zur Sportgeschichte*, vol. 4, 18–22; Stoddart, "Sport, Cultural Imperialism, and Colonial Response," 667–68.

53. Bingham et al., *History of Asia*, 182–202.

54. In these crown colonies rugby preceded soccer, but it was monopolized by Europeans. In the 1920s and 1930s only one Asian player made it to the national team, which had hitherto consisted entirely of Europeans; he had attended school in Scotland and learned rugby there.

55. Beran, "Physical Education and Sport in the Philippines."

56. Bocobo-Olivar, *History of Physical Education in the Philippines*, 103; Sodusta, "Historical Development of Sport in the Philippines," 729; Beran, "Physical Education and Sport in the Philippines," 152.

57. Tutherly, *World at Play.*

58. The same applies, for instance, to Korea, where the president of the YMCA also presided over the umbrella sports federation (Mulling, "Sport in South Korea," 88).

59. "Combine all existing organizations, however small, into a national federation, however weak . . . and conduct national contests at stated periods. . . . Working through the federation, organize schools, colleges, government bureaus, and groups in every community, into clubs, each entitled to representation. Combine these groups into larger associations, which will gradually absorb the voting rights of the smaller units in the federation. . . . Make the amateur requirements light, and their administration flexible. Assume that everybody is an amateur on a certain date, and insist that thereafter he must play for sport, and not for money or its equivalent. . . . Seek to popularize sport for sport's sake; arouse the athletic interest by local, national, and international competition; make athletics easy, available and attractive" (Tutherly, *World at Play*).

60. Ibid.; Bocobo-Olivar, *History of Physical Education in the Philippines.*

61. Bocobo-Olivar, *History of Physical Education in the Philippines*, 46.

62. Ibid., 42–45, 62, 165–69; Mulling, "Sport in South Korea," 87–88; Sodusta, "Historical Development of Sport in the Philippines," 731.

63. Tutherly, *World at Play.*

64. Falla, *NCAA*, 13–14; Baker, *Sports in the Western World*, 143.

65. This organization was unenthusiastic about the commercialization and profession-

alization of sports; see Naismith, *Basketball's Origins;* and Johnson, *History of YMCA Physical Education.*

66. In the Philippines, for instance, the YMCA played a key role in organizing the Far Eastern Championship Games. When they were held for the first time, the program included track and field, swimming, tennis, baseball, basketball, volleyball, and soccer. American football was the only American sport absent from the program, while soccer (an English sport) was represented (Kolatch, *Sports, Politics, and Ideology in China,* 53–54). Soccer was played in 1895 by British men living in Manila, after which the locals started playing too. There were also Philippine students who propagated soccer after having studied in the British colonies of Singapore and Hong Kong (Wildt, *Daten zur Sportgeschichte,* vol. 4, 28).

67. Ch'en, *China and the West,* 70.

68. The organizers, coaches, and referees of the first sports matches were almost all foreigners. As late as 1923, an American spoke on China's behalf at the opening ceremony of the sixth Far East Athletic Games (Knuttgen, *Sport in China,* 17).

69. Most Chinese students who attended educational courses abroad later left for Japan; of the Western countries, the United States was the preferred destination (Ch'en, *China and the West,* 158, 207).

70. Kolatch, *Sports, Politics, and Ideology in China;* Zhou, ed., *China's Contemporary Sports.*

71. Kolatch, *Sports, Politics, and Ideology in China;* Ch'en, *China and the West,* 134; Brandel, *Volleyball-Weltgeschichte,* 24.

72. Zhou, ed., *China's Contemporary Sports,* 10–14; Willcox, *Acrobats and Ping-Pong,* 28–29; Rizak, "Sport in the People's Republic of China," 101.

73. See Knuttgen, *Sport in China;* and Friederich, "Untersuchungen."

74. Montagu, "Sports Pastimes in China," 150–52.

75. Friederich, "Untersuchungen," 85. In 1916 the YMCA youth branch in Shanghai installed table tennis facilities (83).

76. Snow, *Red Star over China,* 281–82 (see also 278–83).

77. Stone, *Europe Transformed,* 279; Kolatch, *Sports, Politics, and Ideology in China,* 82.

78. Knuttgen, *Sport in China,* 125; Friederich, "Untersuchungen," 17.

79. Hopkins and Wallerstein, *World-System Analysis,* 20, 46; Chirot, *Social Change in the Twentieth Century,* 24.

80. Chirot, *Social Change in the Twentieth Century,* 24, 51.

81. Wagner, "Sports," 139–40; Beezley, "Bicycle, Modernization, and Mexico"; Arbena, ed., *Sport and Society in Latin America;* Levine, "Sport as Dramaturgy," 138.

82. See chapter 4 for the popularity of shooting in Switzerland.

83. Piñeyrúa, "Geschichtliche Entwicklung," 12–13; Wildt, *Daten zur Sportgeschichte,* vol. 3, 238–52; Jürgens, "Beitrag zur Geschichte," 49.

84. Baker, *Sports in the Western World,* 133–34; Wagner, "Sports," 139–40. One of the few Latin American countries where cricket did become the national sport is Barbados. This is not an exception to the rule, however. Like India, Barbados—sometimes called "Little England"—was annexed by Britain early on, in 1627. This fulfilled an important condition for the adoption of this sport and its incorporation into local culture: British influence was strong and wide-ranging and extended over a long period of time. The country's le-

gal and political systems, its education system, its dominant religion, and its language all derive from Britain. Cricket had been known in Barbados for more than a hundred years before other, rival British sports were introduced. Today it is played by all sections of society and is as much a part of life in Barbados as sugar, rum, and molasses. With more than a thousand cricket teams in only 166 square miles, cricket is so dominant in relation to other sports that instead of status being attached to different sports, it depends on which cricket club you belong to. All ethnic groups—and each social class within them—have their own clubs, and people gravitate toward the "appropriate" club almost automatically (Stoddart, "Cricket, Social Formation, and Continuity," 17).

85. Chirot, *Social Change in the Twentieth Century,* 18–54.

86. Stein, "Case of Soccer," 64–65.

87. Wildt, *Daten zur Sportgeschichte,* vol. 3, 226, 248–51; Deustua Carvallo et al., "Soccer and Social Change," pt. 1, 19–21; Stein, "Case of Soccer," 64–65.

88. Jürgens, "Beitrag zur Geschichte," 34–36; Deustua Carvallo et al., "Soccer and Social Change," pt. 1, 21–24, 68; Stein, "Case of Soccer."

89. Qtd. in Deustua Carvallo et al., "Soccer and Social Change," pt. 1, 22. See also Jürgens, "Beitrag zur Geschichte."

90. Wildt, *Daten zur Sportgeschichte,* vol. 3, 240–42; Überhorst, "Leibesübungen im Gesellschaft Wandel," 21. Guttmann, *Games and Empires,* 58–59. The first Argentine soccer clubs were founded in large ocean ports, such as Rosario, Blanca, La Plata, and Buenos Aires (Noguera, "Soccer in Argentina," 147).

91. Wildt, *Daten zur Sportgeschichte,* vol. 3, 240–61; Allison, "Association Football and the Urban Ehtos," 218; Levine, "Sport and Society," 233; Jürgens, "Beitrag zur Geschichte," 44; Wagner, "Sport in Revolutionary Societies," 117.

92. Wildt, *Daten zur Sportgeschichte,* vol. 3, 250–53; Jürgens, "Beitrag zur Geschichte," 36.

93. Allison, "Association Football and the Urban Ethos," 219. Ironically, in 1910 a tour of the English Corinthians prompted a painter, a tailor, and a number of factory and railroad workers to set up a club of the same name in Sao Paulo (Lever, *Soccer Madness,* 40–41).

94. Levine, "Sport and Society," 236–37; Jürgens, "Beitrag zur Geschichte," 63; Noguera, "Soccer in Argentina," 147–49.

95. In Uruguay, too, a cricket club and a rowing club in Montevideo abandoned a thirteen-year-old tradition of playing soccer in 1894, when it became popular among a wide section of society (Deustua Carvallo et al., "Soccer and Social Change," pt. 2, 68; see also Jürgens, "Beitrag zur Geschichte," 45).

96. Levine, "Sport as Dramaturgy," 138.

97. Wagner, "Sport Participation in Latin America," 33; "Sports," 139; and "Sport in Revolutionary Societies," 127–30.

98. See Joseph, *Forging the Regional Pastime,* 33; Wagner, "Sports," 139; and "Sport in Revolutionary Societies," 118; Noguera, "Soccer in Argentina"; Shirts, "Socrates, Corinthians, and Questions of Democracy and Citizenship"; Stein, "Case of Soccer"; Klein, *Sugarball,* 16; Guttmann, *Games and Empires,* 80–82.

99. Joseph, *Forging the Regional Pastime.*

100. Krämer-Mandeau, *Sport und Körpererziehung auf Cuba,* 57.

101. Beezley "Introduction," 1, "Rise of Baseball in Mexico," 3–8, and "Bicycle, Modernization, and Mexico," 25; see also Joseph, *Forging the Regional Pastime,* 30–40.

102. Klein, *Sugarball,* 107.

103. See ibid.

104. Johnson, *History of YMCA Physical Education,* 166–73, 249. See also Wildt, *Daten zur Sportgeschichte,* vol. 3, 234; Überhorst, "Leibesübungen im Gesellschaft Wandel," 22; Krämer-Mandeau, *Sport und Körpererziehung auf Cuba,* 26–30.

105. Chirot, *Social Change in the Twentieth Century;* Barraclough, *Introduction to Contemporary History,* 61–62.

106. Rummelt, *Sport im Kolonialismus,* 17–18.

107. Heussler qtd. in Mangan, *Games Ethic and Imperialism,* 112.

108. Rummelt, *Sport im Kolonialismus,* 207, 260–63.

109. Chirot, *Social Change in the Twentieth Century;* Rummelt, *Sport im Kolonialismus,* 263; Mazrui, "Africa's Triple Heritage," 219.

110. Clignet and Stark, "Modernization and the Game of Soccer," 82; Chirot, *Social Change in the Twentieth Century,* 37–44; Uwechue, "Nation Building and Sport in Africa," 540; Godia, "Sport in Kenya," 269–70. See also Mazrui, "Africa's Triple Heritage," 219.

111. Rummelt, *Sport im Kolonialismus,* 163, 179.

112. Mazrui "Africa's Triple Heritage," 219; Wagner, *Sport in Asia and Africa,* 185–281; Monsellier, "Histoire des activités physique traditionales," 368; Opuku Awuku, "Historical and Social Background of Sports in Ghana," 480–87.

113. Clayton, *Sport and African Soldiers,* 119, 131–32.

114. See for example Eichberg, *Leistung,* 146–55; Lema, "Sport in Zaïre," 230; Ojeme, "Sport in Nigeria," 259; Godia, "Sport in Kenya," 271–76.

115. Corlett and Mokowathi, "Sport in Botswana."

116. See for example Clignet and Stark, "Modernization and the Game of Soccer," 85; Uwechue, "Nation Building and Sport in Africa," 540; Stoddart, "Sport, Cultural Imperialism, and Colonial Response"; Wagner, ed., *Sport in Asia and Africa;* Godia, "Sport in Kenya."

117. Kramer, "Sport en staatsvorming in Afrika," 42; Eichberg, *Leistung,* 148; Onifade, "Historical Development of Amateur Sports"; Rummelt, *Sport im Kolonialismus,* 185–87; Clayton, *Sport and African Soldiers,* 117–25.

118. This was striking, given that the percentage of the population of the participating countries that was attending school or college at the time was only 0.11 percent. Academic institutions had the best facilities and good competitive matches (Maksimenko and Barushimana, "Attitude toward Sports Activity"; Kramer, "Sport en staatsvorming in Afrika," 65).

119. Jimu Tembo, "Historical Development of Sports in Malawi," 492.

120. Clayton, *Sport and African Soldiers,* 120–29.

121. Lema, "Sport in Zaïre," 230 and 240; Sfeir, "Sport in Egypt," 190; Opuku Awuku, "Historical and Social Background of Sports in Ghana," 483; Jimu Tembo, "Historical Development of Sports in Malawi," 495.

122. See Douglas, "Sport in Malaysia," 167.

123. See De Swaan, *Perron Nederland,* 12.

Chapter 6: Competition between the Lines

1. See Mills, *Sociological Imagination.*

2. Johan Goudsblom has called this the "one-way mirror" effect; see "Vanachter de doorkijkspiegel" in Goudsblom, *Taal en sociale werkelijkheid,* 69–88.

3. Mart Smeets in *Trouw,* April 11, 1991.

4. Van Bottenburg, "Als 'n man met een baard op 'n bokkewagen," 10.

5. See Becker, *Outsiders.*

6. Holt, ed., *Sport and the Working Class,* 1–2.

7. See Elias, *Het civilisatieproces,* vol. 1, 270.

8. See Bourdieu, "Program for a Sociology of Sport"; De Swaan, *Perron Nederland,* 72.

9. See De Swaan, *Perron Nederland,* 94.

10. Mulling, "Sport in South Korea," 93.

11. Mommaas, "Mondialisering en culturele identiteit."

12. Wallis and Malm, "Patterns of Change"; Mommaas, "Mondialisering en culturele identiteit."

13. De Swaan, *Perron Nederland,* 12.

14. De Swaan, *Widening Circles of Identification;* Lever, *Soccer Madness,* 120 and 145–47; Levine, "Sport and Society," 236.

Bibliography

Memorial Volumes

Amsterdamsche Football Club, 1895–1945
De Bult, 1904–79
De Duinwijcker, 1948–73
Dutch Hockey and Bandy Federation (NHBB), 1898–1938
Haarlem Football Club, 1879–1919, 1879–1979
Hague Soccer Federation (HVV), 1883–1908, 1883–1933
Hercules, 1882–1932
Hilversum Mixed Hockey Club, 1904–79
HLC, 1908–83
HOC-Gazellen Combinatie, 1904–81
Hockey Sport (Royal Netherlands Hockey Federation, 1898–1938), 8 October 1938
Kampong, 1902–52
Lawn tennis, special issue to commemorate the fiftieth anniversary of the Royal Nether-
 lands Lawn Tennis Federation, 1899–1949
Leimonias, 1888–1988
Netherlands Cricket Federation (NCB), 1883–1933
Netherlands Volleyball Federation (NeVoBo), 1947–72
Red and White (Rood en Wit), 1881–1931
Rijtersbeek, 1926–76
Royal Netherlands Hockey Federation (KNHB), 1898–1988
Sparta, 1888–1948, 1888–1988

Records

Clearing House, Records, Council of Europe, Ravenstein Gallery 4–27, Brussels.

Published Sources and Theses

Adelman, Melvin Leonard. *A Sporting Time: New York City and the Rise of Modern Athletics, 1820–70.* Urbana: University of Illinois Press, 1986.

Adriani Engels. *Honderd jaar sport.* Amsterdam: Strengholt, 1960.

Allison, Lincoln. "Association Football and the Urban Ethos." *Stanford Journal of International Studies* 13 (1978): 203–28.

Arbena, Joseph L., ed. *Sport and Society in Latin America: Diffusion, Dependency, and the Rise of Mass Culture.* New York: Greenwood Press, 1988.

Arlott, John, ed. *Oxford Companion to Sports and Games.* Oxford: Oxford University Press, 1975.

Arz, Helmut. "Situationsanalyse des Fussballsports in den USA im Vorfeld der Fussball-Weltmeisterschaft 1994 mit einer Vergleichenden Darstellung der Strukturen im deutschen Fussball." Undergraduate thesis, German Sport University, Cologne, 1989.

Australian Sports Commission. *Annual Report, 1984–1985.* Canberra: Australian Government Publishing Service, 1985.

Bailey, Peter. *Leisure and Class in Victorian England: Rational Recreation and the Contest for Control, 1830–1885.* London: Methuen, 1987.

Baker, William J. *Sports in the Western World.* 1982. Urbana: University of Illinois Press, 1988.

Bale, John. "The Adoption of Football in Europe: An Historical-Geographical Perspective." *Canadian Journal of History of Sport and Physical Education* 9.2 (1980): 56–66.

———. "International Sports History as Innovation Diffusion." *Canadian Journal of History of Sport and Physical Education* 15.1 (1984): 38–63.

———. *Sport and Place: A Geography of Sport in England, Scotland, and Wales.* London: C. Hurst and Co., 1982

———. *Sports Geography.* London: E. and F. N. Spon, 1989.

Barraclough, G. *An Introduction to Contemporary History.* Harmondsworth, U.K.: Penguin Books, 1986.

Baudet, Henri. *Een vertrouwde wereld: 100 jaar innovatie in Nederland.* Amsterdam: Bert Bakker, 1986.

Becker, Howard. *Outsiders: Studies in the Sociology of Deviance.* New York: Free Press, 1963.

Beeltje, A. *Opties met betrekking tot de sportbeoefening van Turken en Marokkanen in Haarlem.* Amsterdam: Free University, 1983.

Beezley, William H. "Bicycle, Modernization, and Mexico." In *Sport and Society in Latin America: Diffusion, Dependency, and the Rise of Mass Culture.* Ed. Joseph L. Arbena. New York: Greenwood Press, 1988. 15–29.

———. "Introduction." *Studies in Latin American Popular Culture* 4 (1985): 1–2.

———. "The Rise of Baseball in Mexico and the First Valenzuela." *Studies in Latin American Popular Culture* 4 (1985): 3–13.

Beran, Janice A. "Physical Education and Sport in the Philippines." In *Sport in Asia and Africa.* Ed. Eric A. Wagner. New York: Greenwood Press, 1989. 147–64.

Bergeson, Albert, ed. *Studies of the Modern World System.* New York: Academic Press, 1980.

Bernett, Hajo. "Drei athletische 'Meetings' im Jahre 1882: Eine exemplarische Rekonstruktion der Wettkämpfe des Hamburger Sport-Clubs." In *Vom Verein zum Verband: Die*

Gründerzeit des Sports in Deutschland. Ed. Hans Georg John. Clausthal-Zellerfeld: Deutsche Vereinigung für Sportwissenschaft, 1986.

Betts, John R. *America's Sporting Heritage, 1850–1950.* Reading, Mass.: Addison-Wesley, 1974.

Bingham, Woodbridge, Hilary Conroy, and Frank W. Iklé, eds. *A History of Asia.* Boston: Allyn and Bacon, 1974.

Birley, Derek. "Bonaparte and the Squire: Chauvinism, Virility, and Sport in the Period of the French Wars." In *Pleasure, Profit, Proselytism: British Culture and Sport at Home and Abroad, 1700–1914.* Ed. James A. Mangan. London: Frank Cass, 1988. 21–41.

Blecking, Diethelm. *Die Slawische Sokolbewegung: Beiträge zur Geschichte von Sport und Nationalismus in Osteuropa.* Dortmund: Johannes Hoffman, 1991.

Bloom, Alan. *The Skaters of the Fens.* Cambridge: W. Heffer and Sons, 1958.

Blumer, Herbert. *Symbolic Interactionism: Perspective and Method.* Englewood Cliffs, N.J.: Prentice Hall, 1969.

Bocobo-Olivar, Celia. *History of Physical Education in the Philippines.* Quezon City: University of Philippines Press, 1972.

Boogman, J. C., et al. *Geschiedenis van het moderne Nederland: Politieke, economische, en sociale ontwikkelingen.* Houten: De Haan, 1988.

Bosma, Jules. *Voordat het gras verdwenen is: De geschiedenis van het handbal in Nederland.* Zaltbommel: Nederlands Handbal Verbond, 1986.

Bourdieu, Pierre. *Choses dites.* Paris: Éditions de Minuit, 1987.

———. *Distinction: A Social Critique of the Judgement of Taste.* Cambridge, Mass.: Harvard University Press, 1984.

———. "Program for a Sociology of Sport." *Sociology of Sport Journal* 5 (1988): 153–61.

Bowen, Rowland. *Cricket: A History of Its Growth and Development throughout the World.* London: Eyre and Spottiswoode, 1970.

Brahim Errahmani, A. "Le sport juvenile en Algerie face aux institutions." In *Sports et Sociétés Contemporaines.* Paris: Institut National du Sport et de L'éducation Physique, 1967.

Brailsford, Dennis. "1787: An Eighteenth-Century Sporting Year." *Research Quarterly for Exercise and Sport* 55.3 (1984): 217–30.

Brandel, Christian. *Volleyball-Weltgeschichte.* Munich: Copress Verlag, 1988.

Briggs, Asa. *The Age of Improvement, 1783–1867.* London: Longman, 1969.

———. *A Social History of England.* London: Weidenfeld and Nicholsen, 1983.

Bromberger, Christian, Alain Hayot, and Jean-Marc Mariottini. "Allez l'O.M.! Forza Juve!" *Terrain* 8 (1987): 8–41.

Brown, Nigel. *Ice-Skating: A History.* London: Nicholas Kaye, 1959.

Buchner, Heide. "Untersuchungen zur Entwicklung des Frauensports in Deutschland von 1880 bis 1914." Undergraduate thesis, German Sport University, Cologne, 1976.

Bundes-Sportorganisation Österreich. *Sport 87/88: Österreichisches Sportjahrbuch.* Vienna: Bohrmann Verlag, 1988.

Burgener, Louis. "Frankreich." In *Geschichte der Leibesübungen,* vol. 5. Ed. Horst Überhorst. Berlin: Bartels and Wernitz, 1976. 161–87.

Burkens, Y. C. "Wielrijden." In *Het boek der sporten.* Ed. J. Feith. Amsterdam: Van Holkema and Warendorf, 1900. 255–60.

Burks, Ardath W. "Japan's Outreach: The Ryugakusei." In *The Modernizers: Overseas Stu-*

dents, Foreign Employees, and Meiji Japan. Ed. Ardath W. Burks. Boulder, Colo.: West-view Press, 1985.

———. "The Role of Education in Modernization." In *The Modernizers: Overseas Students, Foreign Employees, and Meiji Japan.* Ed. Ardath W Burks. Boulder, Colo.: West-view Press, 1985.

Buytendijk, F. J. J. *Het voetballen: Een psychologische studie,* Utrecht: Het Spectrum, 1952.

Cashman, Richard. "Cricket and Colonialism: Colonial Hegemony or Indigenous Subversion?" In *Pleasure, Profit, Proselytism: British Culture and Sport at Home and Abroad, 1700–1914.* Ed. James A. Mangan. London: Frank Cass, 1988. 258–72.

———. *Patrons, Players, and the Crowd: The Phenomenon of Indian Cricket.* New Delhi: Longman Orient, 1980.

———."The Phenomenon of Indian Cricket." In *Sport in History: The Making of Modern Sporting History.* Ed. Richard Cashman and Michael McKernan. St. Lucia: University of Queensland Press, 1979. 180–204.

Centraal Bureau voor de Statistiek. *Sportclubs en sportscholen, 1987.* The Hague: Staatsdrukkerij/uitgeverij, 1989.

———. *Statistiek van de sportbeoefening.* Voorburg: Centraal Bureau voor de Statistiek, 1947.

———. *Statistisch zakboek, 1988.* The Hague: Staatsuitgeverij, 1988.

Centre for Leisure Research. *A Digest of Sports Statistics for the U.K.* London: Sports Council, 1986.

Chandler, Joan M. *Television and National Sport.* Urbana: University of Illinois Press, 1988.

Ch'en, Jerome. *China and the West: Society and Culture, 1815–1937.* London: Hutchinson, 1979.

Chirot, Daniel. *Social Change in the Twentieth Century.* New York: Harcourt Brace Jovanovich, 1977.

Claeys, Urbain. *Sport in European Society: A Transnational Survey into Participation and Motivation.* Strasbourg: Council of Europe, Committee for the Development of Sport, 1982.

Clayton, Anthony. "Sport and African Soldiers: The Military Diffusion of Western Sport throughout Sub-Saharan Africa." In *Sport in Africa: Essays in Social History.* Ed. William J. Baker and James A. Mangan. New York: Holmes and Meier, 1987. 114–37.

Clerici, G. *The Ultimate Tennis Book: 500 Years of the Sport.* Chicago: Follett, 1975.

Clignet, R., and M. Stark. "Modernization and the Game of Soccer in Cameroun." *International Review of Sport Sociology* 9.3–4 (1974): 81–98.

Comitato Olympico Nazionale Italiano. *La Practica Sportiva in Europa.* Strasbourg: Council of Europe, 1990.

Corlett, J. T., and M. M. Mokgwathi. "Sport in Botswana." In *Sport in Asia and Africa.* Ed. Eric A. Wagner. New York: Greenwood Press, 1989. 215–28.

Cushman, Grant. "Trends in Sports in New Zealand." In *Trends in Sports: A Multinational Perspective.* Ed. Teus J. Kamphorst and Kenneth Roberts. Culemborg: Giordano Bruno, 1989. 133–57.

Dahles, Heidi. *Lokale helden, mondiale aspiraties: Verschuivende integratieniveaus in de sportwereld.* Tilburg: University of Brabant, 1992.

Daly, John A. "A New Brittania in the Antipodes: Sport, Class, and Community in Colonial South Australia." In *Pleasure, Profit, Proselytism: British Culture and Sport at Home and Abroad, 1700–1914.* Ed. James A. Mangan. London: Frank Cass, 1988. 163–74.

Dansk Idraets-Forbund. *DIFs Medlemsopgorelse.* Brondby: Dansk Idraets-Forbund, 1990.

Davidson, James. "Social Differentiation and Sports Participation: The Case of Golf." *Journal of Sport Behavior* 2.4 (1979): 171–210.

De Graaff, Bob. "De epistemologische revolutie: Mentaal-culturele voorwaarden voor industrialisering." In *De trage revolutie: Over de wording van industriële samenlevingen.* Ed. Hans Righart. Meppel: Boom, 1991. 429–49.

———. "De vlucht naar voren: Politiek-economische voorwaarden voor industrialisering." In *De trage revolutie: Over de wording van industriële samenlevingen.* Ed. Hans Righart. Meppel: Boom, 1991. 374–97.

———. "Inleiding." In *De trage revolutie: Over de wording van industriële samenlevingen.* Ed. Hans Righart. Meppel: Boom, 1991. 357–73.

Del Court tot Krimpen, A. A. "Golf." In *Het boek der sporten.* Ed. J. Feith. Amsterdam: Van Holkema and Warendorf, 1900. 113–25.

De Regt, Ali. *Arbeidersgezinnen en beschavingsarbeid: Ontwikkelingen in Nederland, 1870– 1940.* Meppel: Boom, 1984.

De Swaan, Abram. *De Olympische hoogte: Over Amsterdam en de Spelen van 1992.* Amsterdam: Meulenhoff, 1985.

———. *Perron Nederland.* Amsterdam: Bert Bakker, 1991.

———. *Widening Circles of Identification: Emotional Concerns in Sociogenetic Perspective.* Amsterdam: Amsterdam School of Social Science Research, 1993.

Deustua Carvallo, José, Steve Stein, and Susan C. Stokes. "Soccer and Social Change in Early Twentieth-Century Peru" (parts 1 and 2). *Studies in Latin American Popular Culture* 3 (1984): 17–27 and 5 (1986): 68–77.

Deutsche Gesellschaft für Freizeit. *Freizeit, Sport, Bewegung: Stand und Tendenzen in der Bundesrepublik Deutschland.* Erkrath: DGF, 1987.

Deutscher, Irwin. *What We Say/What We Do: Sentiments and Acts.* Glenview, Ill.: Scott, Foresman, 1973.

Deutsche Sportbund. *Bestandserhebung.* Frankfurt: DSB, 1971–91.

———. *Mitgliederzahl Spitzenverbände.* Frankfurt: DSB, 1992–98.

De Vries, K. L. "Het aanbod van sportaccommodaties." In *Is er nog speelruimte? Enige visies op gemeentelijk accommodatiebeleid bij het 25-jarig bestaan van het adviesorgaan voor sportaccommodaties van de Vereniging van Nederlandse Gemeenten.* Ed. W. de Heer. The Hague: Vereniging van Nederlandse Gemeenten, 1981. 53–67.

De Vries, Marion, and Hans Righart. "Van achterblijver tot koploper: Sociaal-economische voorwaarden voor industrialisering." In *De trage revolutie: Over de wording van industriële samenlevingen.* Ed. Hans Righart. Meppel: Boom, 1991. 180–206.

Diem, Carl. *Weltgeschichte der Sports und der Leibeserziehung.* Stuttgart: Cotta, 1960.

Diem, Liselotte. "Federal Republic of Germany." In *The World Today in Health, Physical Education, and Recreation.* Ed. John E. Nixon and C. Lynn Verdien. Englewood Cliffs, N.J.: Prentice Hall, 1968. 124–50.

Dixon, J. G. "Prussia, Politics, and Physical Education." In *Landmarks in the History of Physical Education.* Ed. P. C. McIntosh, J. G. Dixon, A. D. Munrow, and R. F. Willes. London: Routledge, 1981. 112–55.

Dodd, Christopher. "Rowing." In *Sport in Britain: A Social History.* Ed. Tony Mason. Cambridge: Cambridge University Press, 1989. 276–307.

Dona, Hans. *Sport en socialisme: De geschiedenis van de Nederlandse Arbeiderssportbond, 1926–1941.* Amsterdam: Van Gennep, 1981.

Douglas, Stephen A. "Sport in Malaysia." In *Sport in Asia and Africa.* Ed. Eric A. Wagner. New York: Greenwood Press, 1989. 165–82.

Dunning, Eric. *Sport Matters: Sociological Studies of Sport, Violence, and Civilizations.* London: Routledge, 1999.

Dunning, Eric, and Kenneth Sheard. *Barbarians, Gentlemen, and Players: A Sociological Study of the Development of Rugby Football.* Oxford: Martin Robertson, 1979.

Durkheim, Emile. *Le suicide: Étude de sociologie.* Paris: Alcan, 1897.

Eichberg, Henning. *Leistung, Spannung, und Geschwindigkeit.* Stuttgart: Klett-Clotta, 1978.

Elias, Norbert. *Die höfische Gesellschaft: Untersuchungen zur Soziologie des Königstums und der hösischen Aristokratie.* Darmstadt: Luchterhand, 1969.

———. "The Genesis of Sport as a Sociological Problem." In *The Sociology of Sport: A Selection of Readings.* Ed. Eric Dunning. London: Frank Cass and Co., 1971. 88–115.

———. *Het civilisatieproces: Sociogenetische en psychogenetische onderzoekingen.* Utrecht: Het Spectrum, 1982.

Elias, Norbert, and Eric Dunning. *Quest for Excitement: Sport and Leisure in the Civilizing Process.* Oxford: Basil Blackwell, 1986.

Elias, Norbert, and John L. Scotson. *The Established and the Outsiders.* London: Frank Cass and Co., 1965.

Essink, Hein. *Elseviers judo-boek.* Amsterdam: Elsevier, 1969.

Eziakor, Ikechukwu G., and Livinus O. Nwali. "Trends in Sports in Nigeria." In *Trends in Sports: A Multinational Perspective.* Ed. Teus J. Kamphorst and Kenneth Roberts. Culemborg: Giordano Bruno, 1989. 357–82.

Falla, Jack. *NCAA—The Voice of College Sports: A Diamond Anniversary History, 1906–1981.* Mission, Kans.: National Collegiate Athletic Association, 1981.

Fallers, Lloyd A. "A Note on the 'Trickle Effect.'" *Public Opinion Quarterly* 18 (1954): 314–21.

Featherstone, Mike. "Lifestyle and Consumer Culture." *Theory, Culture, and Society* 4 (1987): 55–70.

Feith, C. "Cricket." In *Het boek der sporten.* Ed. J. Feith. Amsterdam: Van Holkema and Warendorf, 1900. 31–41.

Finnish Society for Research in Sports and Physical Education. *Sport and Physical Education in Finland.* Helsinki: Government Printing Centre, 1987.

Fisek, Kurthan. "The Genesis of Sports Administration in Turkey." In *Geschichte der Leibesübungen,* vol. 6. Ed. Horst Überhorst. Berlin: Bartels and Wernitz, 1989. 625–44.

Förster, Hans-Dieter. "Der Einfluss Englischen Sports auf die Leibesübungen in Deutschland im 19. Jahrhundert." Undergraduate thesis, German Sport University, Cologne, 1974.

Friederich, Horst. *Ping-Pong: Das Tischtennisspiel um die Jahrhundertwende.* Bonn: n.p., 1989.

———. "Untersuchungen zu den wichtigsten Entwicklungsphasen in Tischtennis." Undergraduate thesis, German Sport University, Cologne, 1988.

Fukutake, Tadashi. *The Japanese Social Structure: Its Evolution in the Modern Century.* Tokyo: University of Tokyo Press, 1986.

Gerschenkron, A. *Economic Backwardness in Historical Perspective: A Book of Essays.* Cambridge: Cambridge University Press, 1962.

Giddens, Anthony. *The Nation-State and Violence.* Cambridge: Polity Press, 1985.

Gillmeister, Heiner. *Kulturgeschichte des Tennis.* Munich: Wilhelm Fink Verlag, 1990.

Godia, George. "Sport in Kenya." In *Sport in Asia and Africa.* Ed. Eric A. Wagner. New York: Greenwood Press, 1989. 267–81.

Goodger, B. C., and F. M. Goodger. "Judo in the Light of Theory and Sociological Research." *International Review of Sport Sociology* 2.12 (1977): 5–34.

Gorter, Simon. *Letterkundige studiën.* Amsterdam: Van Kampen, 1891.

Goudsblom, Johan. *De sociologie van Norbert Elias.* Amsterdam: Meulenhof, 1987.

———. *Taal en sociale werkelijkheid: Sociologische stukken.* Amsterdam: Meulenhoff, 1988.

Gruneau, Richard S. *Class, Sports, and Social Development.* Amherst: University of Massachusetts Press, 1983.

Guttmann, Allen. *From Ritual to Record: The Nature of Modern Sports.* New York: Columbia University Press, 1978.

———. *Games and Empires: Modern Sports and Cultural Imperialism.* New York: Columbia University Press, 1994.

———. "'Our Former Colonial Masters': The Diffusion of Sports and the Question of Cultural Imperialism." *Stadion* 14.1 (1988): 49–64.

———. *Sports Spectators.* New York: Columbia University Press, 1986.

———. *A Whole New Ball Game: An Interpretation of American Sports.* Chapel Hill: University of North Carolina Press, 1988.

———. *Women's Sports: A History.* New York: Columbia University Press, 1991.

Halladay, Eric. *Rowing in England: A Social History.* Manchester: Manchester University Press, 1990.

Halldén, Olle. "Schweden." In *Geschichte der Leibesübungen,* vol. 5. Ed. Horst Überhorst. Berlin: Bartels and Wernitz, 1976. 25–39.

Hannerz, Ulf. "The World in Creolization." *Africa* 57.4 (1987): 546–59.

Hansen, Svend O., ed. *Sport in Denmark.* Copenhagen: Det Danske Selskab, 1978.

Haralampiev, Dimiter. *Physical Culture and Sport in Bulgaria.* Sofia: Sofia Press, 1982.

Harinck, T. *De ontleende kracht Chakuriki.* Amsterdam: Dojo Chakuriki, 1980.

Hart, M., and S. Birrell. *Sport in the Sociocultural Process.* Dubuque, Iowa: William C. Brown, 1972.

Hensen, Siegmund. "Die Entwicklung des Basketballs der Männer in der Bundesrepublik Deutschland." Undergraduate thesis, German Sport University, Cologne, 1988.

HFC'er. Extra issue on the hundredth anniversary of the birth of Pim Mulier. Haarlem, 1965.

Hill, Jeffrey. "League Cricket in the North and Midlands, 1900–1940." In *Sport and the Working Class in Modern Britain.* Ed. Richard Holt. Manchester: Manchester University Press, 1990.

Hobsbawm, Eric. *Industry and Empire: An Economic History of Britain since 1750.* London, 1968.

Holland Rose, J., A. P. Newton, and E. A. Benians. *The Cambridge History of the British Empire.* Cambridge: Cambridge University Press, 1933.

Holt, Richard. *Sport and Society in Modern France.* London: Macmillan, 1981.

————. *Sport and the British: A Modern History.* Oxford: Oxford University Press, 1989.

————, ed. *Sport and the Working Class in Modern Britain.* Manchester: Manchester University Press, 1990.

Hoolt, J. *De sportdeelname van etnische groeperingen, Amsterdam: Bestuursinformatie.* Amsterdam: Municipality of Amsterdam, Research and Statistics Department, 1987.

Hopkins, Terence K., and Immanuel Wallerstein. *World-System Analysis, Theory, and Methodology.* London: Sage, 1982.

Horry, John. *The History of Squash Rackets.* Brighton: A. C. M. Webb, 1979.

Human Sciences Research Council. *Sport in the RSA, 1982.* Pretoria: Blitsköpie, 1982.

Hyam, Ronald. *Britain's Imperial Century, 1818–1914: A Study of Empire and Expansion.* London: Batsford, 1976.

Idorn, John. "History." In *Sport in Denmark.* Copenhagen: Det Danske Selskab, 1978. 9–105.

Inglis, K. S. "Imperial Cricket: Test Matches between Australia and England, 1877–1900." In *Sport in History: The Making of Modern Sporting History.* Ed. Richard Cashman and Michael McKernan. St. Lucia: University of Queensland Press, 1979. 148–79.

International Olympic Committee. *Olympic Charter.* Geneva: IOC, 1990.

International Tennis Federation. *The 75 Years of the International Tennis Federation, 1913–1988.* London: ITF, 1988.

Inter/View. *Inter/View Sport Scanner.* Amsterdam: Inter/View, 1986.

————. *Summo Scanner en doelgroeponderzoek, een onderzoek onder Nederlanders van 13 jaar of ouder.* Amsterdam: Inter/View, 1988–89.

ISI/CONI. *Challenges Ahead for Improving Sports Statistics.* ISI Sports Statistics Committee, 50th session, Beijing, 1995. Italy: CONI, 1996.

Jandacek, L. "The Sokol Movement in Czechoslovakia" (1932). In *Sport and International Relations.* Ed. Benjamin Lowe, David B. Kanin, and Andrew Strenk. Champaign, Ill.: Stipes, 1978. 56–67.

Jansen, Harry. "De sterke en flexibele staat: Politiek-institutionele voorwaarden voor industrialisering." In *De trage revolutie: Over de wording van industriële samenlevingen.* Ed. Hans Righart. Meppel: Boom, 1991. 39–70.

Jimu Tembo, Mark. "The Historical Development of Sports in Malawi." In *Geschichte der Leibesübungen,* vol. 6. Ed. Horst Überhorst. Berlin: Bartels and Wernitz, 1989.

Johnson, Elmer L. *The History of YMCA Physical Education.* Chicago: Association Press, 1979.

Joll, James. *Europe since 1870: An International History.* Harmondsworth, U.K.: Penguin Books, 1990.

Jolles, H. M., ed. *Verenigingsleven in Nederland: Bijdragen tot de sociologie van het verenigingsverschijnsel.* Zeist: De Haan and Van Loghum Slaterus, 1963.

Joseph, Gilbert M. "Forging the Regional Pastime: Baseball and Class in Yucatán." In *Sport and Society in Latin America: Diffusion, Dependency, and the Rise of Mass Culture.* Ed. Joseph L. Arbena. New York: Greenwood Press, 1988. 29–61.

Joseph, P. M. "India." In *The World Today in Health, Physical Education, and Recreation.* Ed. John E. Nixon and C. Lynn Verdien. Englewood Cliffs, N.J.: Prentice Hall, 1968. 247–64.

Jürgens, Claus. "Beitrag zur Geschichte des Fussballs in Chile." Undergraduate thesis, German Sport University, Cologne, 1983.

Kalma, J. J. *Kaatsen in Friesland: Het spel met de kleine bal door de eeuwen heen.* Franeker: Wever, 1972.

Kammeijer, Jules. "Hockey." In *Sportslieden schrijven over hun sport.* Ed. D. H. Schmüll. Amsterdam: Jacob van Campen, 1946. 50–91.

Kamphorst, Teus J., and Kenneth Roberts, eds. *Trends in Sports: A Multinational Perspective.* Culemborg: Giordano Bruno, 1989.

Kemp, Tom. *Industrialization in Nineteenth-Century Europe.* London: Longman, 1985.

King, Helen. "The Sexual Politics of Sport: An Australian Perspective." In *Sport in History: The Making of Modern Sporting History.* Ed. Richard Cashman and Michael McKernan. St Lucia: University of Queensland Press, 1979. 68–85.

Kirsch, George B. *The Creation of American Team Sports: Baseball and Cricket, 1838–72.* Urbana: University of Illinois Press, 1989.

Klein, Alan. *Sugarball: The American Game, the Dominican Dream.* New Haven, Conn.: Yale University Press, 1991.

Kleine, Jan, Hedma Bijlsma, and Karel Verbeek. *Niet over een nacht ijs: Geschiedschrijving van de schaatssport in Nederland ter gelegenheid van het honderjarig bestaan van de Koninklijke Nederlandsche Schaatsenrijders Bond.* Haarlem: De Vrieseborch/KNSB, 1982.

Kloeren, Maria. *Sport und Rekord: Kultursoziologische Untersuchungen zum England des sechzehnten bis achtzehnten Jahrhunderts.* Leipzig: Von Bernhard Tauchnitz, 1935.

Knippenberg, H., and B. de Pater. *De eenwording van Nederland: Schaalvergroting en integratie sinds 1800.* Nijmegen: SUN, 1988.

Knuttgen, Howard G. *Sport in China.* Champaign, Ill.: Human Kinetics, 1990.

Kok, Ch. F. "Schermen." In *Het boek der sporten.* Ed. J. Feith. Amsterdam: Van Holkema and Warendorf, 1900. 160–68.

Kolatch, Jonathan. *Sports, Politics, and Ideology in China.* New York: Jonathan David, 1972.

Kramer, Daan. "Sport en staatsvorming in Afrika." Undergraduate thesis, Sociology Institute, University of Amsterdam, 1980.

Krämer-Mandeau, Wolf. *Sport und Körpererziehung auf Cuba: Von der Sportutopie eines Entwicklunglandes zum Sportmodell Lateinamerikas?* Cologne: Pahl-Ruggenstein, 1988.

Lagendijk, Eric. "De zwarte band van etnische minderheden: Over kleur, macht en kracht van lichaamscultuur." *Vrije Tijd en Samenleving* 9.2 (1991): 45–62.

———. "Lichaamscultuur in beweging: Sociologische analyse van de ontwikkeling en institutionalisering van bodybuilding en fitness." Undergraduate thesis, Free University, Amsterdam, 1988.

Landes, David. *The Unbound Prometheus.* Cambridge: Cambridge University Press, 1969.

Leck, Neville. *South African Sport.* Cape Town: MacDonald South Africa, 1977.

Leeflang, Thomas. *Budo.* Amsterdam: De Lage Landen, 1973.

———. *Zen in actie.* Amsterdam: De Arbeiderspers, 1975.

Lema, Bangela. "Sport in Zaire." In *Sport in Asia and Africa.* Ed. Eric A. Wagner. New York: Greenwood Press, 1989. 229–47.

Lenk, H. *Leistungssport: Ideologie oder Mythos?* Stuttgart: Kohlhammer, 1974.

Lever, Janet. *Soccer Madness.* Chicago: University of Chicago Press, 1983.

Levine, Robert M. "Sport and Society: The Case of Brazilian Futebol." *Luso-Brazilian Review* 17.2 (1980): 233–52.

———. "Sport as Dramaturgy for Society: A Concluding Chapter." In *Sport and Society in Latin America: Diffusion, Dependency, and the Rise of Mass Culture.* Ed. Joseph L. Arbena. New York: Greenwood Press, 1988. 137–46.

Lewis, Robert M. "Cricket and the Beginnings of Organized Baseball in New York City." *International Journal of the History of Sport* 4.3 (1987): 315–32.

Lowerson, John. "Golf." In *Sport in Britain: A Social History.* Ed. Tony Mason. Cambridge: Cambridge University Press, 1989. 187–214.

Lüschen, Günther. "The Interdependence of Sport and Culture." *International Review of Sport Sociology* 2.1 (1967): 27–41.

———. "Social Stratification and Mobility among Young German Sportsman." In *The Sociology of Sport: A Selection of Readings.* Ed. Eric Dunning. London: Frank Cass, 1971. 237–58.

MacAloon, John J. *This Great Symbol: Pierre de Coubertin and the Origins of the Modern Olympic Games.* Chicago: University of Chicago Press, 1981.

Maguire, Joseph. *Global Sport: Identities, Societies, Civilizations.* Cambridge: Polity Press, 1999.

———. "More Than a Sporting Touchdown: The Making of American Football in England, 1982–1990." *Sociology of Sport Journal* 7 (1990): 213–37.

Maksimenko, A., and A. Barushimana. "Attitude toward Sport Activity of Top-Class Athletes of Central Africa." *International Review of Sport Sociology* 13 (1978): 37–50.

Mandell, Richard. *Sport: A Cultural History.* New York: Columbia University Press, 1984.

Manders, T., and J. Kropman. *Sportbeoefening, drempels en stimulansen.* Nijmegen: Institute of Applied Sociology, 1982.

———. *Sportbeoefening en zijn organisatiegraad.* Nijmegen: Institute of Applied Sociology, 1974.

———. *Sportdeelname: Wat weten we ervan?* Nijmegen: Institute of Applied Sociology, 1979.

———. *Sport, ontwikkeling en kosten.* Nijmegen: Institute of Applied Sociology, 1987.

Mangan, James A. *Athleticism in the Victorian and Edwardian Public School.* Cambridge: Cambridge University Press, 1981.

———. *The Games Ethic and Imperialism: Aspects of the Diffusion of an Ideal.* Harmondsworth, U.K.: Viking, 1986.

Markovits, A. S. "The Other 'American Exceptionalism': Why Is There No Soccer in the United States?" *International Journal of the History of Sport* 7.2 (1990): 230–64.

Maso, Benjo. *Het zweet der goden: Legende van de wielersport.* Amsterdam: De Arbeiderspers, 1990.

Mason, Tony. *Associaton Football and English Society, 1863–1915.* Brighton: Harvester Press, 1980.

Mazrui, Ali A. "Africa's Triple Heritage of Play: Reflections on the Gender Gap." In *Sport in Africa: Essays in Social History.* Ed. William J. Baker and James A. Mangan. New York: Holmes and Meier, 1987. 217–28.

McCrone, Kathleen E. *Sport and the Physical Emancipation of English Women, 1870–1914.* London: Routledge, 1988.

McKay, Jim, and Toby Miller. "From Old Boys to Men and Women of the Corporation: The Americanization and Commodification of Australian Sport." *Sociology of Sport Journal* 8 (1991): 86–94.

McPherson, Barry D. "Sport Consumption and the Economics of Consumerism." In *Sport and Social Order: Contributions to the Sociology of Sport.* Ed. Donald W. Ball and John V. Loy. Reading, Mass.: Addison-Wesley, 1975. 239–75.

Meijs, Ton. "Over neutralen en katholieken: Opkomst en ontwikkeling van de georganiseerde voetbalsport in Tilburg, 1896–1940." Undergraduate thesis, University of Utrecht, 1988.

Mennell, Stephen. *All Manners of Food.* 1985. Urbana: University of Illinois Press, 1996.

Merton, Robert K. *Social Theory and Social Practice.* New York: Free Press, 1968.

Meserole, Mike, ed. *The 1991 Information Please Sports Almanac.* Boston: Houghton Mifflin, 1991.

Metcalfe, Alan. "Organized Sport and Social Stratification in Montreal, 1840–1901." In *Canadian Sport: Sociological Perspectives.* Ed. Richard S. Gruneau and John G. Albinson. Ontario: Addison-Wesley, 1976. 77–102.

Miermans, C. *Voetbal in Nederland.* Assen: Van Gorcum, 1955.

Mills, C. Wright. *The Sociological Imagination.* New York: Oxford University Press, 1959.

Minoru, Ishizuki. "Overseas Study by Japanese in the Early Meiji Period." In *The Modernizers: Overseas Students, Foreign Employees, and Meiji Japan.* Ed. Ardath W. Burks. Boulder, Colo.: Westview Press, 1985. 161–86.

Miroy, Nevill. *The History of Hockey.* Staines: Lifetime, 1986.

Mitchell, David. *Alles over vechtsporten.* Utrecht: Kosmos, 1990.

Mommaas, Hans. "Mondialisering en culturele identiteit." *Vrije Tijd en Samenleving* 9.3–4 (1991): 11–41.

Monsellier, Alain. "Histoire des activités physicales traditionelles et des sports modernes au Sénégal." In *Geschichte der Leibesübungen,* vol. 6. Ed. Horst Überhorst. Berlin: Bartels and Wernitz, 1989. 359–72.

Montagu, Ian. "Sports Pastimes in China." *United Asia* 8.2 (1956): 150–52.

Morrow, Don. "The Historical Development of Sport in Canada." In *Geschichte der Leibesübungen,* vol. 6. Ed. Horst Überhorst. Berlin: Bartels and Wernitz, 1989. 37–66.

Mulier, W. J. H. *Athletiek en voetbal.* Haarlem: De Weduwe Loosjes, 1894.

———. "De oprichting van de Haarlemsche Football Club en de oertijd van het bruine monster." *De HFC'er* Extra Issue (1965): 10–15.

Muller, P. N. "Anglomanie." *De Gids* 3 (1889): 263–77.

Mulling, Craig. "Sport in South Korea: Ssirum, the YMCA, and the Olympic Games." In *Sport in Asia and Africa.* Ed. Eric A. Wagner. New York: Greenwood Press, 1989. 83–99.

Naismith, James B. *Basketball's Origins: Creative Problem Solving in the Guilded Age.* Rev. ed. of *Basketball: Its Origins and Development* (1941). Cambridge: Bear Publications, 1976.

Nandy, Ashis. *The Tao of Cricket: On Games of Destiny and the Destiny of Games.* Calcutta: Penguin Books, 1989.

National Collegiate Athletic Association. *The Sports and Recreational Programs of the Nation's Universities and Colleges, 1956–87.* Mission, Kans.: National Collegiate Athletic Association, 1987.

National Federation of State High School Associations. *1989 Sports Participation Survey.* N.p., 1989.

Nederlandse Golf Federatie. *Behoefte-onderzoek Golfsport Nederland.* De Gans: Nederlandse Golf Federatie, 1988.

———. *Nota ontwikkeling golfsport in Nederland.* De Meern: Nederlandse Golf Federatie, 1986.

Nederlandse IJshockey Bond. *IJshockey!* Zoetermeer: Nederlandse IJshockey Bond, 1984.

Nederlandse Sport Federatie. *Cijfers van het georganiseerde sportleven in Nederland.* The Hague: Nederlandse Sport Federatie, 1963.

———. *Ledentallen van de bij de NSF aangesloten organisaties.* The Hague: Nederlandse Sport Federatie, 1963–88.

Netherlands Olympic Committee * Netherlands Sports Federations. *Ledentallen.* Arnhem: NOC*NSF, 1993–99.

Noguera, Alberto. "Soccer in Argentina: A Lecture." *Journal of Sport History* 13.2 (1986): 147–52.

Nordlund, Anders. "Scandanavia (Iceland, Norway, Denmark, Sweden, Finland," In *The World Today in Health, Physical Education, and Recreation.* Ed. John E. Nixon and C. Lynn Verdien. Englewood Cliffs, N.J.: Prentice Hall, 1968. 190–219.

Ojeme, E. O. "Sport in Nigeria." In *Sport in Asia and Africa.* Ed. Eric A. Wagner. New York: Greenwood Press, 1989. 249–66.

Onifade, Ademola. "Historical Development of Amateur Sports and Their Administrative Agencies in Nigeria, 19th–20th Century." *Canadian Journal of History of Sport and Physical Education* 16.2 (1985): 33–43.

Opuku Awaku, Emmanuel. "Historical and Social Background of Sports in Ghana." In *Geschichte der Leibesübungen,* vol. 6. Ed. Horst Überhorst. Berlin: Bartels and Wernitz, 1989. 480–87.

Page, Geoffrey. *Hear the Boat Sing: The History of the Thames Rowing Club and Tidaway Rowing.* London: Kingswood Press, 1991.

Park, Roberta J. "Sport, Gender, and Society in a Transatlantic Victorian Perspective." *British Journal of Sports History* 2.1 (1985): 5–28.

Park, Robert E., Ernest W. Burgess, and Roderick D. McKenzie, eds. *The City.* Chicago: University of Chicago Press, 1967.

Peppard, Victor E. "The Beginnings of Russian Soccer." *Stadion* 8–9 (1983): 151–68.

Pietersen, Lieuwe. *Sociologie van de sport: Afspiegeling en reactie.* Utrecht: Het Spectrum, 1961.

Pieth, Fritz. *Sport in der Schweiz.* Olten: Walter Verlag, 1979.

Piñeyrúa, Darwin. "Geschichtliche Entwicklung und heutige Struktur des Uruguayanischen Leichtathletikverbandes." Undergraduate thesis, German Sport University, Cologne, 1975–76.

Polednik, Heinz. *Sport und Spiel auf dem Eis.* Wels: Welsermühl, 1979.

Pope, Rex, ed. *Atlas of British Social and Economic History since 1700.* London: Routledge, 1989.

Porter, A. N. *Atlas of British Overseas Expansion.* London: Routledge, 1991.

Rader, Benjamin. *American Sports.* Englewood Cliffs, N.J.: Prentice Hall, 1983.

Redmond, Gerald. *Sport and Ethnic Groups in Canada.* Calgary: University of Calgary Press, 1980.

Reid, Howard, and Michael Croucher. *De Oosterse krijgskunst: De paradox van de martial arts.* Haarlem: Rostrum, 1984.

Renson, R. "Sport voor allen: Nieuwe perspectieven in tekst en context." *Sport* 26.102 (1983): 139–46.

Riesman, D., and R. Denney. "Football in America: A Study in Culture Diffusion." In *The Sociology of Sport: A Selection of Readings.* Ed. Eric Dunning. London: Frank Cass, 1971. 152–70.

Riordan, James. *Soviet Sport: Background to the Olympics.* Oxford: Basil Blackwell, 1980.

————. *Sport in Soviet Society: Development of Sport and Physical Education in Russia and the USSR.* Cambridge: Cambridge University Press, 1977.

Rizak, Gene. "Sport in the People's Republic of China." In *Sport in Asia and Africa.* Ed. Eric A. Wagner. New York: Greenwood Press, 1989. 101–19.

Roden, Donald. "Baseball and the Quest for National Dignity in Meiji Japan." *American Historical Review* 85 (1980): 511–34.

Romein, Jan M. *De eeuw van Azië: Opkomst, ontwikkeling en overwinning van het modern-Aziatisch nationalisme.* Leiden: Brill, 1956.

Rummelt, Peter. *Sport im Kolonialismus—Kolonialismus im Sport.* Cologne: Pahl-Ruggenstein, 1986.

Rupnik, Jacques. *Het andere Europa.* Utrecht: Stichting Teleac, 1990.

Saeki, Toshio. "Sport in Japan." In *Sport in Asia and Africa.* Ed. Eric A. Wagner. New York: Greenwood Press, 1989. 51–82.

Sagers, Frans. "Kaatsen, Kegelen, Kolven, Beugelen." In *Het boek der sporten.* Ed. J. Feith. Amsterdam: Van Holkema and Warendorf, 1900. 52–72.

Sandblad, Henrik. "Sport and Ideas: Aspects of the Rise of the Modern Sports Movement—An English Summary of Olympia och Valhalla." *International Journal of the History of Sports* 5.1 (1988): 120–30.

Sansom, G. B. *The Western World and Japan: A Study in the Interaction of European and Asiatic Cultures.* New York: Alfred A. Knopf, 1968.

Schlagenhauf, Karl. *Strukturelemente und Verhaltensdeterminanten im organisierten Freizeitbereich.* Vol. 1 of *Sportvereine in der Bundesrepublik Deutschland.* Schondorf: Verlag Karl Hofmann, 1977.

Schöffler, Herbert. *England das Land des Sportes.* 1935. Münster: Lit-Verlag, 1986.

Seehase, Gerhard, ed. *Der Verein: Standort, Außgabe, Funktion in Sport und Gesellschaft.* Stuttgart: Verlag Karl Hofmann, 1967.

Seymour, Harold. *Baseball: The Early Years.* New York: Oxford University Press, 1960.

Sfeir, Leila. "Sport in Egypt: Cultural Reflection and Contradiction of a Society." In *Sport in Asia and Africa.* Ed. Eric A. Wagner. New York: Greenwood Press, 1989. 185–214.

Sheard, Kenneth Gordon. *Boxing in the Civilizing Process.* Cambridge: Anglia Polytechnic, 1992.

Shirts, Matthew. "Sócrates, Corinthians, and Questions of Democracy and Citizenship." In *Sport and Society in Latin America: Diffusion, Dependency, and the Rise of Mass Culture.* Ed. Joseph L. Arbena. New York: Greenwood Press, 1988. 97–112.

Sieniarski, Stefan. *Sport in Polen.* Warsaw: Verlag Interpress, 1972.

Sleap, M., and P. Duffy. "Factors Affecting Active Participation in Sport by the Working Class." *International Review of Sport Sociology* 17.1 (1982): 5–22.

Smith, Jacqueline. "Sports Involvement in Dunedin Sociological Correlates." Research Papers in Physical Education, no. 3. Dunedin: University of Otago, 1979.

Snow, Edgar. *Red Star over China.* New York: Grove Press, 1961.

Sodusta, Jesucita L. "The Historical Development of Sport in the Philippines." In *Geschichte der Leibesübungen,* vol. 6. Ed. Horst Überhorst. Berlin: Bartels and Wernitz, 1989. 721–34.

Spaans, Eric. "Sociale geschiedenis van de georganiseerde sport in Nederland tot 1920." Undergraduate thesis, University of Utrecht, 1988.

Speak, M. A. "Social Stratification and Participation in Sport in Mid-Victorian England with Particular Reference to Lancaster, 1840–1870." In *Pleasure, Profit, Proselytism: British Culture and Sport at Home and Abroad, 1700–1914.* Ed. James A. Mangan. London: Frank Cass, 1988. 42–66.

Spel en Sport. *Jaarbericht 1987.* Amsterdam: Stichting Spel en Sport, 1987.

Sport Information Bulletin, nos. 1–53. Brussels: Clearing House, 1985–2000.

Stein, Steve. "The Case of Soccer in Early-Twentieth-Century Lima." In *Sport and Society in Latin America: Diffusion, Dependency, and the Rise of Mass Culture.* Ed. Joseph L. Arbena. New York: Greenwood Press, 1988. 63–84.

Steinegger, Hugo. *Sport '78: Handbuch des Schweizer Sports.* Derendingen: Habegger Verlag, 1978.

Stene, Fridtjov. "Norwegen." In *Geschichte der Leibesübungen,* vol. 5. Ed. Horst Überhorst. Berlin: Bartels and Wernitz, 1976. 65–83.

Stoddart, Brian. "Cricket, Social Formation, and Cultural Continuity in Barbados: A Preliminary Ethnohistory." *Journal of Sport History* 14.3 (1987): 317–40.

———. "Sport, Cultural Imperialism, and Colonial Response in the British Empire." *Comparative Studies in Society and History* 30 (1988): 649–73.

Stokvis, Ruud. "Continuities in the Theory of the Differential Popularization of Sports: The Relation between the Numbers of 'Organized' and 'Unorganized' Participants in Different Sports." Paper delivered at the World Congress of Sociology, Madrid, 1991.

———. "De nieuwe sportmoraal." *De Telegraaf,* 1 February 1992.

———. "De populariteit van sporten." *Amsterdams Sociologisch Tijdschrift* 15.4 (1989): 673–96.

———. *De sportwereld: Een sociologische inleiding.* Alphen a/d Rijn/Brussels: Samson, 1989.

———. "The International and National Expansion of Sports." In *Sport in Asia and Africa.* Ed. Eric A. Wagner. New York: Greenwood Press, 1989. 13–24.

———. "Sports and Civilization: Is Violence the Central Problem." In *Sport and Leisure in the Civilizing Process: Critique and Counter-Critique.* Ed. Eric Dunning and Chris Rojek. Houndsmille, U.K.: Macmillan Academic and Professional, 1992. 121–36.

———. *Strijd over sport: Organisatorische en ideologische ontwikkelingen.* Deventer: Van Loghum Slaterus, 1979.

Stokvis, Ruud, and Rob Minnee. "De Olympische Spelen van 1992 en de sportbeoefening in Nederland." *Spel en Sport* 3 (1986): 2–5.

Stone, Norman. *Europe Transformed, 1878–1919.* Glasgow: Fontana, 1983.

Strohmeyer, Hannes. "Österreich." In *Geschichte der Leibesübungen,* vol. 5. Ed. Horst Überhorst. Berlin: Bartels and Wernitz, 1976. 285–310.

Suaud, Charles. "Espace des sports, espace social, et effets d'age: La diffusion du tennis, du squash, et du golf dans l'agglomération nantaise." *Actes de la Recherche en Sciences Sociales* 79 (1989): 2–20.

Szymiczek, Otto. "Griechenland." In *Geschichte der Leibesübungen,* vol. 5. Ed. Horst Überhorst. Berlin: Bartels and Wernitz, 1976. 369–78.

Tadashi, Kaneko. "Contributions of David Murray to the Modernization of School Administration in Japan." In *The Modernizers: Overseas Students, Foreign Employees, and Meiji Japan.* Ed. Ardath W. Burks. Boulder, Colo.: Westview Press, 1985. 301–22.

Taks, Marijke. *Sociale gelaagdheid in de sport: Een kwestie van geld of habitus?* Leuven: Catholic University of Leuven, 1994.

Telegraaf Tijdschriften Groep. *De sportmarkt in ogenschouw.* Amsterdam: Telegraaf Tijdschriften Groep, 1990.

Ter Gouw, Jan. *De volksvermaken.* Amsterdam: Vrienden van het Amsterdamse Boek, 1871.

TERP. *Een verkennend onderzoek naar sportscholen in Nederland.* Amersfoort: TERP, 1984.

Thoutenhoofd, Rien. *Taekwondo: Theorie en praktijk.* Rijswijk: Elmar, 1987.

Tsukuda, Tetsuji. "Die Entwicklung des Sports in Japan nach dem Zweiten Weltkrieg: Hintergrund und Analyse anhand eines Vergleichs mit dem Deutschen Beispiel." Undergraduate thesis, German Sport University, Cologne, 1985.

Turner, Ian. "The Emergence of 'Aussie Rules.'" In *Sport in History: The Making of Modern Sporting History.* Ed. Richard Cashman and Michael McKernan. St. Lucia: University of Queensland Press, 1979. 258–71.

Tutherly, William. *The World at Play: A Program of Practical Athletics for the Millions.* N.p.: Eastern Athletics Association, 1920.

Tyrrell, Ian. "The Emergence of Modern American Baseball c. 1850–80." In *Sport in History: The Making of Modern Sporting History.* Ed. Richard Cashman and Michael McKernan. St. Lucia: University of Queensland Press, 1979. 205–26.

Überhorst, Horst. *Frisch, Frei, Stark, und Treu: Die Arbeitersportbewegung in Deutschland, 1893–1933.* Düsseldorf: Droste Verlag, 1973.

———. "Leibesübungen im gesellschaftlichen Wandel: Auf dem Wege zum Weltsport?" In *Geschichte der Leibesübungen,* vol. 6. Ed. Horst Überhorst. Berlin: Bartels and Wernitz, 1989. 7–30.

Ultee, Wouter, Wil Arts, and Henk Flap. *Sociologie: Vragen, uitspraken, bevindingen.* Groningen: Wolters-Noordhoff, 1992.

Uwechue, Raph C. "Nation Building and Sport in Africa." In *Sport and International Relations.* Ed. Benjamin Lowe, David B. Kanin, and Andrew Strenk. Champaign, Ill.: Stipes, 1978. 538–50.

Van Bottenburg, Maarten. "Als 'n man met een baard op 'n bokkewagen: Het problematische imago van korfbal." In *Tweede Jaarboek Onderzoeksschool Sociale wetenschap Amsterdam.* Ed. J.-W. Gerritsen and H. Sonneveld. Amsterdam: Thesis Publishers, 1992. 9–25.

———. "Het bruine monster en de 'king of sports': De uiteenlopende populariteit van voetbal en cricket in Nederland, 1870–1930." *Amsterdams Sociologisch Tijdschrift* 9.2 (1992): 3–35.

——. "Individualisering en de populariteitsontwikkeling van georganiseerde sporten." *Spel en Sport* 3 (1992): 17–23.

——. "Individualisering en teambinding: Boeten teamsporten aan populariteit in ten gevolge van de individualisering?" Paper delivered at the Dutch Sociological and Anthropological Association Social Science Seminar, Amsterdam, 28–29 April 1992.

Van Buttingha Wichers, J. *Schaatsrijden.* The Hague: Cremer, 1888.

Van Dalen, Deobold B., and Bruce L. Bennett. *A World History of Physical Education: Cultural, Philosophical, Comparative.* Englewood Cliffs, N.J.: Prentice Hall, 1971.

Van de Brug, H. *Voetbalvandalisme.* Haarlem: de Vrieseborch, 1986.

Van den Heuvel, M. *Sport in de Sovjetunie.* Haarlem: De Vrieseborch, 1978.

Van der Molen, G. J. *Levend volksleven: Een eigentijdse volkskunde van Nederland.* Assen: Van Gorcum, 1961.

Van der Zee, Jelle, and Jan Boerop. *Holland Hockeyland.* Amsterdam: Meulenhoff, 1981.

Van de Wouw, M. T. "Realiteit en utopie bij het tot stand brengen van accommodaties." In *Is er nog speelruimte? Enige visies op gemeentelijk accommodatiebeleid bij het 25-jarig bestaan van het Adviesorgaan voor sportaccommodaties van de Vereniging van Nederlandse Gemeenten.* W. de Heer et al. The Hague: Vereniging van Nederlandse Gemeenten, 1981. 85–92.

Van Galen, W., and J. Diederiks. *Sportblessures breed uitgemeten: Een onderzoek naar aantal, aard en achtergronden van sportblessures in de loop van één jaar.* Haarlem: De Vrieseborch, 1990.

Van Laer, G. W. A. *Gedenkboek van den Koninlijken Nederlandschen Schaatsenrijdersbond bij het vijftigjarig bestaan 1882–1932.* Amsterdam: Ellerman, Harms, and Co., 1932.

Van Maanen, E. P., and G. J. Venekamp. *Sporters in cijfers: Ledentalontwikkeling van NSF-organisaties, 1963–1989.* Arnhem: Netherlands Sports Federation, 1991.

Van Nieuwenhuizen, Maurice. *Jiu Jitsu en judo: De feillooze verdedigingssport voor lichaam en geest.* Utrecht: Bruna, 1941.

Vanreusel, Bart, Marijke Taks, and Roland Renson. "Is golfspelen een dure manier van biljarten? De sociale gelaagdheid van de sportbeoefening in Vlaanderen in 1969, 1979, 1989." Paper delivered at the Catholic University of Leuven, "Working Class Culture and Lifestyle" Seminar, 1992.

Varekamp, Inge. "De verandering van de samenstelling van de beroepsbevolking in Nederland tussen 1920 en 1979: De opkomst van een nieuwe klasse." Undergraduate thesis, University of Amsterdam, 1982.

Venekamp, G. J., and M. Wolters. *Sporters in cijfers 1978–1994: Ledentalontwikkeling van NOC*NSF-lidorganisatie.* Arnhem: Netherlands Olympic Committee/Netherlands Sports Federation, 1996.

Verhaegen, Maurice. "Belgien." In *Geschichte der Leibesübungen,* vol. 5. Ed. Horst Überhorst. Berlin: Bartels and Wernitz, 1976. 122–50.

Verrips, Jojada. *En boven de polder de hemel: Een antropologische studie van een Nederlands dorp, 1850–1971.* Groningen: Wolters-Noordhoff, 1978.

Wagner, Eric A. "Sport in Asia and Africa: Americanization or Mondialization?" *Sociology of Sport Journal* 7 (1990): 299–402.

——. "Sport in Revolutionary Societies: Cuba and Nicaragua." In *Sport and Society in*

Latin America: Diffusion, Dependency, and the Rise of Mass Culture. Ed. Joseph L. Arbena. New York: Greenwood Press, 1988. 113–36.

———. "Sport Participation in Latin America." *International Review of Sport Sociology* 17.2 (1982): 29–39.

———. "Sports." In *Handbook of Latin American Popular Culture.* Ed. Harold E. Hinds and Charles M. Tatum. Westport, Conn.: Greenwood Press, 1985. 135–50.

———, ed. *Sport in Asia and Africa.* New York: Greenwood Press, 1989.

Walker, Helen. "Lawn Tennis." In *Sport in Britain: A Social History.* Ed. Tony Mason. Cambridge: Cambridge University Press, 1989. 245–75.

Wallerstein, Immanuel. *The Modern World System.* Vol. 1: *Capitalist Agriculture and the Origins of the European World-Economy in the Sixteenth Century.* New York: Academic Press, 1974.

———. *The Modern World System.* Vol. 3: *The Second Era of Great Expansion of the Capitalist World-Economy, 1730–1840s.* New York: Academic Press, 1989.

Wallis, Roger, and Krister Malm. "Patterns of Change." In *On Record: Rock, Pop, and the Written Word.* Ed. Simon Frith and Andrew Goodwin. London: Routledge, 1990. 160–80.

Walvin, James. *The People's Game: A Social History of British Football.* London: Allen Lane, 1975.

Waser, Anne Marie. "Le marché des partenaires: Etude de trois clubs de tennis." *Actes de la Recherche en Sciences Sociales* 80 (1989): 2–21.

Weber, Eugen. "Gymnastics and Sports in Fin-de Siècle France: Opium of the Classes?" *American Historical Review* 76 (1971): 70–98.

———. *Peasants into Frenchmen: The Modernization of Rural France, 1870–1914.* Stanford, Calif.: Stanford University Press, 1976.

———. "Pierre de Coubertin and the Introduction of Organized Sport in France." *Journal of Contemporary History* 5.2 (1970): 3–26.

Weber, Max. *Wirtschaft und Gesellschaft: Grundriss der verstehenden Soziologie.* 1922. Tübingen: Mohr, 1985.

Whiting, R. *The Chrysanthemum and the Bat: Baseball Samurai Style.* New York: Avon Books, 1977.

Widdershoven, B. "De stagnerende groei van de Koninklijke Nederlandse Roeibond." Undergraduate thesis, University of Amsterdam, 1983.

Wildt, Kl. C. *Daten zur Sportgeschichte,* vol. 2. Schorndorf bei Stuttgart: K. Hofmann, 1972.

———. *Daten zur Sportgeschichte,* vol. 3. Schorndorf bei Stuttgart: K. Hofmann, 1977.

———. *Daten zur Sportgeschichte,* vol. 4. Schorndorf bei Stuttgart: K. Hofmann, 1980.

Willcox, Isabel. *Acrobats and Ping-Pong.* New York: Dodd, Mead, 1981.

Williams, Gareth. "Rugby Union." In *Sport in Britain: A Social History.* Ed. Tony Mason. Cambridge: Cambridge University Press, 1989. 308–43.

Willink, Bastiaan. *Burgerlijk sciëntisme en wetenschappelijk toponderzoek: Sociale grondslagen van nationale bloeiperioden in de negentiende eeuwse bètawetenschappen.* Rotterdam: Erasmus University, 1988.

Wilterdink, Nico. *De vermogensverhoudingen in Nederland: Recente ontwikkelingen.* Amsterdam: University of Amsterdam, 1991.

————. *Vermogensverhoudingen in Nederland: Ontwikkelingen sinds de negentiende eeuw.*
Amsterdam: De Arbeiderspers, 1984.

Wirth, Fritz. "Wo Manager umsonst arbeiten: Der Verein und das Statussymbol." In *Der Verein: Standort, Außgabe, Funktion in Sport und Gesellschaft.* Ed. Gerhard Seehase. Stuttgart: Verlag Karl Hofmann, 1967. 58–72.

Wouters, Cas. *Van minnen en sterven: Informalisering van omgangsvormen rond seks en dood.* Amsterdam: Bert Bakker, 1990.

Zhou Yuan, ed. *China's Contemporary Sports.* N.p.: Press Commission of the Chinese Olympic Comittee, n.d.

Zijderveld, A. C. *De culturele factor: Een cultuursociologische wegwijzer.* The Hague: VUGA, 1983.

Index

MAARTEN VAN BOTTENBURG is managing director of Diopter-Janssens and Van Bottenburg B.V., a social research company specializing in sports policy. He earned a doctorate in social sciences from the University of Amsterdam in 1994 and has published several books and reports on top-level sports, ultimate fighting, quality control in sports, the history of sports in the Netherlands, and other topics. He has also published jubilee volumes of the Dutch Foundation of Labour, the Dutch National Insurance Institute, and the Dutch Medical Insurance Institute.

BEVERLEY JACKSON specializes in translating doctoral dissertations in history, art history, and sociology from Dutch into English. She also works as a translator for the Dutch Ministry of Foreign Affairs, The Hague.

Sport and Society

Red Grange and the Rise of Modern Football   *John M. Carroll*
Golf and the American Country Club   *Richard J. Moss*
Extra Innings: Writing on Baseball   *Richard Peterson*
Global Games   *Maarten Van Bottenburg*

REPRINT EDITIONS

The Nazi Olympics   *Richard D. Mandell*
Sports in the Western World (2d ed.)   *William J. Baker*

Composed in 10.5/13 Minion
by Jim Proefrock
at the University of Illinois Press
Manufactured by Thomson-Shore, Inc.

University of Illinois Press
1325 South Oak Street
Champaign, IL 61820-6903
www.press.uillinois.edu

D0201100